MW00824939

יַד הַגֵּר

# LESSONS FROM
# TARGUM
# ONKELOS

Bereishis - Shemos

MOSAICA PRESS

The Rubin and Ostrovsky Edition

יַד הַגֵּר

# LESSONS FROM
# TARGUM
# ONKELOS

## Bereishis - Shemos

RABBI YEHOSHUA DOVID PORTOWICZ

**Mosaica Press**, with its team of acclaimed editors and designers, is attracting some of the most compelling thinkers and teachers in the Jewish community today. Our books are impacting and engaging readers from around the world.

Published by Mosaica Press, Inc.
www.mosaicapress.com
info@mosaicapress.com

*Note: Although tremendous effort has been invested in thoroughly reviewing the material presented in this sefer, there is always a chance of error. If any errors are found, please be in contact, at www.kollelklal.org. Tizku l'mitzvos.*

In loving memory of our parents

## R' Arye Leib Rubin

and

## Rabbi and Mrs. Jack Ostrovsky

who dedicated their lives to Torah and Yiddishkeit.

And wishing our dear mother

## Mrs. Baila Rubin שתחי׳

many more happy and healthy years to come.
May their children, grandchildren, great-grandchildren, and
great-great-grandchildren continue to emulate their ways, bringing
them much *Yiddishe nachas* and creating a true *kiddush HaShem*.

### לזכרון עולם בהיכל ה'

לעילוי נשמת

הורינו היקרים

אבינו הרב **יעקב** ז"ל בן ר' **יצחק אליעזר** ז"ל

נלב"ע כ"ו חשון תשע"ג

אמנו האשה הצדקנית

מרת **מלכה** בת **נחשון** ע"ה

נלב"ע י"ב תמוז תש"ע

### אסטרובסקי

אבינו הר"ר **אריה לייב** ז"ל בן ר' **אברהם רובין** ז"ל

נלב"ע ל' ניסן תשע"ג

.ת.נ.צ.ב.ה.

SHABSI AND LEAH RUBIN

לכבוד בני היקר אהובי כנפשי הרב ר' יהושע דוד הכהן נ"י ויזרח

הנה ידועים דברי הספורנו בסוף פרשת ויצא על מאמר הכתוב "ויברך אתהם" שברכת האב אשר היא על בניו בכל נפשו בלי ספק ראוי שתחול יותר בסגולת צלם אלוקים המברך כאמרו (ביצחק אבינו ע"ה) "בעבור תברכך נפשי" (בראשית כ"ז, ד').

ומה גדולה היא השמחה אשר עמדי בבואי לברך אותך מעומקא דלבא לרגל שמחת הגילוי לאור עולם את אותם חידושי תורה על פירוש האונקלוס, עליהם יגעת ואותם מצאת ב"ה כמלוא חפניך.

אודה ה' בכל לבב שזכינו לבן יקר דכוותיה שליט"א, יקר שביקרים: השוקד על דלתי התורה והיראה, בעל מדות תרומיות, אהוב ונחמד, אשר רוח המקום ורוח הבריות נוחים ממנו.

ויהי רצון שלא תמוש התורה מפינו, ומפי זרעינו, ומפי זרע זרעינו מעתה ועד עולם, ותזכה להוסיף בלימוד התורה הק' מתוך יגיעה רבה והתמדה גדולה ותזכה לשקוד תמיד באהלה של תורה מתוך שלוות הנפש והרחבת הדעת, ותזכה להוסיף ולחדש בהבנת התורה ולהפיצם ביני רבנן ותלמידיהון אשר יהנו מאורם, אכי"ר.

ואסיים בשבח והודאה להש"ת שנתת שמחה בלבי ובלב אמך מנב"ת תליט"א, ומזכה לראות רוב נחת ממך ומזוגתך שתחי' ומכל בני ביתך שיחיו לאוי"ט. אביך אוהבך בלו"נ,

חיים שלמה הכהן פארטאוויטש

בס"ד

**שמואל קמנצקי**
Rabbi S. Kamenetsky

2018 Upland Way
Philadelphia, PA 19131

Home: 215-473-2798
Study: 215-473-1212

בס"ד כ"ב טבת תשפ"ג

למע"כ הרה"ג ר' יהושע דוד פארטאוויטש שליט"א,

הגליונות מספרו יד הגר הגיעוני, בו הוא מבאר ומפרש בלע"ז כונת התרגום אונקלוס, וראיתי בספרו עבודה רבה ומלאכה גדולה והוא ודאי פרי עמל ויגיעה עצומה, ובודאי רבים יהנו ממלאכתו.

ברכתי שיזכה כב' להמנות ממזכי הרבים ויהיה בהצלחה גדולה.

בברכה מלונ"ח,

בס"ד

**חיים אלעזר ווייס**

רב אב"ד לכל מקהלות האשכנזים

ביתר עילית

---

יום ו' מקץ לסדר ושמחה
דנר החנוכה תש"פ

הן ראיתי את חבור ספרו של ידי"ד
מחברו קרוב ונין הרב הגאון ר' יהושע
פנחס פורטגאנג שליט"א רב
זכרון אה"י ליו"ר, והוא חידוד לבאר
ופי' את דברי התהלים אונקלוס
ויוסף ויוסף מרגשותיו ומחשבותיו
לגלות פנינים יקרים אשר מונח בתוך
דברי התהלים לאם ונוסף והעמיק
והרחיב הדרה מקילי, ומשמי' דא לכ'
שורת העיונים ולחצות החבורות
ואוסיף חיזוק להתהלים
ברכתי שיזכה שורה דלו עדריו
הבא מדורא לרוב ונאמנים לבדה ה' ויצפה
להפיץ מעיינותיו חוצה
הכותב לכבוד התורה
חיים אלעזר ווייס

הרב חיים אלעזר ווייס
ביתר עילית
רב ואב"ד למקהלות האשכנזים

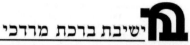
בס"ד

אלול תשפ"ב

ידידי היקר הרה"ג ר' יהושע דוד פארטאוויטש ראש כולל, כולל לזכרון אריה
לייב, מחשובי בוגרי ישיבתנו, עמל ויגע יגיעה גדולה וארוכה לבאר דברי
התרגום אונקלוס בביאורים ועיונים בהרחבה ובהעמקה, וכן בדברי הראשונים
והאחרונים העוסקים בדברי התרגום או חולקים עליו. והכל בטוב טעם ודעת
ובאופן השוה לכל נפש, בהציעו בכל פרשה מפרשיות השבוע שאילות ועיונים
שאפשר וראוי לדון בהם ולהבין, וביאר הדברים מתוך התרגום ודקדוקי דבריו
והמפרשים הנ"ל. והכל בחכמה ובתבונה בס"ד. ובזה בע"ה יזכה המחבר
שליט"א לייקר ולחבב לימוד התרגום שכבר מפורש חובת לימוד שנים מקרא
ואחד תרגום מהגמ' וש"ו"ע וכן מבואר בראשונים ובפוסקים גודל ענין ויחוד
התרגום, וכן גם הרחיב בזה המחבר בהקדמתו. ובעבודה הנפלאה הזאת שהיא
גם מלאכה וגם חכמה זוכה הרה"ג ר' יהושע לפתוח פתח לספר חתום בפני
הרבה אנשים, ולהאיר עיניים להכיר קצת מעוצם עמקותו של התרגום,
והגלויים הנפלאים שנמצאים בדקדוקי דבריו. דבר גדול מאד עושה המחבר
שליט"א בכל זה ובודאי תועלת גדולה ונשגבה בס"ד. תפילתי שימלא ד'
משאלות לבו הטהור בהוציאו ספר זה לאור וכן בכל מפעלותיו להרבצת
התורה, ויזכה להפיץ כל מעיינותיו חוצה ולהגדיל תורה ולהאדירה.

בכבוד ובידידות,

יעקב פרידמן

רח' קעניג 13, ביתר עילית 90500 טל: 02-580-3871 פקס: 02-580-3870
מס' עמותה 580266674

**Rabbi Avraham Y. Elbaz**
Rav , Tzameret HaBira, French Hill
R"M in Yeshivat Aish HaTorah, Rova HaYehudi
Jerusalem, Israel

ב"ה, יום ... לחודש ... שנה ...

הסכמה

...

It is with honour and a privilege to be asked to give a הסכמה to the new Sefer "Yad HaBaz" written by my esteemed cousin Harav Hagoan R' Yehoshua David שליט"א Rosh Kollel

שוכט פרכך אות ריב צבל

Undoubtedly this sefer will enhance both the awareness and level of appreciation of תורה שבכתב while simultaneously strengthing the often forgotten obligation of שנים מקרא ואחד תרגום

The author aside from being an outstanding עמל invested considerable effort in clarifying and uncovering the hidden secrets in Onkelos's commentary. The reader will be amazed at the insights that are right now in front of him.

May this Sefer be an everlasting זכות for the author and his family as well as serve as a medium to enrich the level of עבודת הבורא.

בברכת התורה, ולומדיה רבה,

הק' אברהם יצחק אלבז

# Table of Contents

## Sefer Bereishis

# Sefer Shemos

# Acknowledgments

"הודו לה' כי טוב כי לעולם חסדו." I express my gratitude to Hashem for assisting me with tremendous kindness, and I thank Him for everything He has done and continues to do for me and my entire family.

This project was initiated thanks to a philanthropist in LA whom I met on a fundraising trip for Kollel Klal. He told me, "I say *sh'nayim mikra*, but not *echad targum*." He explained that the reason is because he does not understand what it means. I decided to take the opportunity to help people understand and appreciate Onkelos by pointing out many additions and changes from the literal meaning, by way of a *d'var Torah*, and bring out *yesodos*. I also thank my first cousin, Reb Moshe Rubin, from Sh'or Yoshuv Yeshiva, who advised me to open www.kollelklal.org and send weekly parashah thoughts in appreciation of sponsors for Kollel Klal. A handful of *divrei Torah* on Onkelos were sent out over the years, which started this project.

I thank my parents, *shlita*, for raising me and my siblings in a *bayis* with *chashivus haTorah*, *simchas ha'chaim*, *haarachah* for Gedolim, *shalom*, *chessed, yashrus*, and *tz'nius*. It was a big *chizuk* to see our father learning and reviewing *daf yomi* every single day, *chok v'lo yaavor*, making *siyumim*, and going to *shiurim* by Gedolei Yisrael. There was a constant display of excitement and appreciation for Torah. These qualities of *shimush* are deeply rooted and engraved in our hearts. Also, we are grateful for our father's fifth *Shulchan Aruch*, the one of practical common sense. We are also thankful for their continuous support and encouragement. There is no end to the appreciation we owe, and we hope, *b'ezras* Hashem, that we can reach equally great heights all the way to the Avos Hakedoshim. May Hashem grant Totty and Mommy *arichus yomim v'shanim, nachas, gezunt*, and *parnassah b'revach*.

I thank my in-laws, *shlita*, for being *moser nefesh* to raise their children in Seattle, Washington and send them off to Bais Yaakov Denver to grant them the appropriate *chinuch*, despite the difficulties. Also, we appreciate their continuous support and encouragement. I especially thank Abba for reviewing many *pesukim*, *nuscha'os*, and the Onkelos translation in the caption of each *d'var Torah*. May Hashem grant Abba and Imma *arichus yomim v'shanim, nachas, gezunt*, and *parnassah b'revach*.

*Yasher koach* to my Rosh Yeshiva, Rav Yaakov Friedman, and the Rebbetzin, *shlita*, for over two decades of tutelage, *shadchanus*, advice, and for hosting Kollel Klal. It is a special berachah and *zechus* to be in the vicinity of an *adam gadol* with tremendous *anavah* and *gadlus*.

*Yasher koach* to my previous Rosh Yeshiva, Rav Aharon Schechter, *shlita*, for the inspiration that was impressed upon me and internalized through his meticulous *sh'nayim mikra v'echad Targum*. I was *zocheh* to eat the third *seudah* on Shabbos in the Rosh Yeshiva's house during my four years of *beis midrash* in Yeshiva Rabbeinu Chaim Berlin, during which he continued to review the parashah thoroughly. On *Parashas Bereishis*, the Rosh Yeshiva pointed out that Rashi explains the word "*mi'kedem*" as "from the east," whereas Onkelos translates differently—"from an early time," adding the *Maharal* in his *Gur Aryeh*.

A special *yasher koach* to the *menahel* of Chaim Berlin's Mesivta, Rav Chaim Segal, *zt"l*, who inspired me to appreciate and enjoy learning Torah. He had a tremendous love for Torah, *simchas ha'chaim*, and *she'ifah* for *aliyah* which he shared with his *talmidim*. He cared for every single *talmid* personally, raised them up, and was *mechanech* in a unique way that left an everlasting impression on myself and many others. Also, *yasher koach* to each of my *rebbeim* in Chaim Berlin who exemplified *chashivus haTorah* and *she'ifah* for *aliyah*.

I thank Rabbi Perkal, *shlita*, and my good friends, Rabbi Chaim Koehler and Rabbi Elchonon Sosne, for discussing, clarifying, and reviewing these *divrei Torah*. Also, I thank my good friend Rabbi Pesach Borek, who lent me the *sefer Nefesh HaGer*, which was frequently used throughout the project. I also thank Mr. David Braid for buying me a laptop, which enabled me to do this project.

I'd like to express my deep appreciation to the heads of Mosaica Press, Rabbi Yaacov Haber and Rabbi Doron Kornbluth, for accepting my manuscript and for turning it into a beautiful *sefer*. I thank Mrs. S. Gross for overseeing the project from beginning to end; to the graphics department for the attractive design; and to the members of the editorial department, whose meticulous work and excellent recommendations greatly enhanced the manuscript. It was a pleasure to publish this set with Mosaica Press. May Hashem continue to help you bring out *kevod Shamayim* and be fruitful in all your efforts.

I thank my *eishes chayil* and entire family for their extra effort of holding off and removing many responsibilities to enable me to have the time and *yishuv ha'daas* to learn Torah, finish *Shas*, allow me to complete this project, and much more. What a tremendous *zechus* we have together to provide Klal Yisrael with useful *seforim* that will enhance their weekly *echad Targum* learning to a whole different level of appreciation! May Hashem grant my entire family *gezunt* and *hatzlachah*, and may we merit the *zechus* of one who says *sh'nayim mikra v'echad Targum:* "מאריכין לו ימיו ושנותיו."

# Introduction

## WHAT IS THE PURPOSE AND BENEFIT OF THIS SEFER?

It is common for people to say *echad Targum* quickly, which makes it difficult to notice Onkelos's changes or additions to the literal meaning. Even when one does notice something different, most people will not invest the time it deserves to search through various *mefarshim* to understand it properly. Usually, Onkelos is left undeciphered and unresolved. People don't realize what they are missing—his one-word changes or additions may hint to an entire Chazal! Using a few select examples in each parashah that exemplify Onkelos's nuances, this *sefer* raises questions, brings the relevant words of the *pasuk* with Onkelos's translation and explanation, and adds a lesson to derive from Onkelos or the subject.

Our hope and berachah is that this *sefer*, being one of its kind, will enhance appreciation for Onkelos's translation, shed light on his nuances, and encourage more attention to his insights.

## SOURCES

The main *mefarshim* used to explain Onkelos are *Rashi*, *Ramban*, *Rabbeinu Bachya*, *Nesinah LaGer*, *Nefesh HaGer*, *Hakesav V'Hakabbalah*, and *Me'at Tzari*, in addition to Gemaros and Midrashim.

## THE UNIQUENESS OF TARGUM ONKELOS

*Rashi*[1] and *Tosafos* both say it was given at Sinai.

---

קדושין מט.    1

The *Rambam*[2] writes that Onkelos was an expert in *lashon Ivris* and Aramaic, and he proves ideas based on Onkelos's meticulous and exact translation. The *Rambam* describes Onkelos's thoughts as "great wonders which he received from the *chachamim* of Yisrael."

The *Ibn Ezra*[3] writes that the Aramaic translation of Torah is *emes* and Onkelos explained to us all the hidden secrets. He may choose to translate based on other Midrashim, with which one is not familiar, to teach new thoughts. He adds, "Know that he knew the roots of things better than you."

The *Ramban*[4] quotes *Rashi* in one place who explains, "כתרגומו," as "Onkelos translates." He comments, "How good would it have been for *Rashi* to explain what the correct *nusach* is, as there are a several *nuscha'os* about it!" After a debate with the *Moreh Nevuchim* regarding Onkelos's meticulous translation, the *Ramban*[5] says certain topics are things known in Kabbalah, and Onkelos's secrets are for special people, and the wise will understand. The *Chasam Sofer*[6] brings in the name of the *Ramban* that Onkelos's Kabbalah and translation of holy *sheimos* and *middos* of Hashem was done with great wisdom. No other person is comparable to him in the teaching of these ideas.

The *Tur*[7] says that *Targum Onkelos* was written with *ruach hakodesh*.

The *Maharsha*[8] quotes the *Re'em*, who wonders, "Why does Onkelos translate a certain way? The *Beraisa* says differently; I don't know where he found this logic!" The *Maharsha* responds that one cannot ask a question on Onkelos; he is a Tanna and can argue on a *Beraisa*!

The *Nesinah LaGer* describes Onkelos as "*eloki*," first in *maalah*, the convert *tzaddik* who teaches fundamental belief in Hashem. There are also

---

| | |
|---|---|
| מו"נ ח"א פכ"ז וח"ב פל"ג | 2 |
| הקדמה | 3 |
| שמות י, י | 4 |
| בראשית מו, א | 5 |
| שו"ת ח"ו סי' עו (פו) | 6 |
| או"ח סי' קמה, ג | 7 |
| סנהדרין סה: | 8 |

laws and concepts derived from Onkelos's translation in the Gemara, Midrash, Rishonim, and Acharonim.

The *Nefesh HaGer* says Onkelos is not simply a translation from *lashon hakodesh* to Aramaic. His small changes or additions hint to Midrashim, clarify the intent of the verse, and voice his opinion when the topic is of debate. With the change or addition of just one word, he hints to an entire Chazal and reveals hidden secrets of the Torah by connecting *Torah She'bichsav* with *Torah She'baal Peh*.

The *Avnei Nezer* showed a section of *Targum Onkelos* to Rav Forshlager and commented, "One could derive the entire concept of logic from a certain understanding of the *Targum*."

The Kotzker Rebbe told the *Avnei Nezer*, "If a person is committed to learning *Targum* with great effort, he will find within it many deep messages."

## ONKELOS MI'SINAI

The Gemara[9] teaches, "ויקראו בספר תורת אלקים—And they read in the *Sefer Torah* of G-d;" this refers to the *lashon Ivri* of the Torah's *pesukim*. "מפורש—explained" refers to *Targum Onkelos*, which explains the *pe-sukim*.[10] After the first Beis Hamikdash was destroyed, there was a need to translate the Torah into a language that people understood, so Ezra translated the Torah into Aramaic. Later, Rabbi Eliezer and Rabbi Yehoshua, Onkelos's *rebbeim*, taught him the *Targum*, and he revived it after it was forgotten. The *Nesinah LaGer* points out that sometimes Onkelos translates differently from his *rebbeim*. He proves this from a *Yerushalmi*:[11] "Onkelos received his translation from Sinai and said it over before his *rebbeim*. They praised him, saying that it is a nice language." So we see that it didn't all originate from them.

9  מגילה ג. ונדרים לז:
10  ר"ן ופ' הרא"ש נדרים שם
11  קידושין א, ה

The Rishonim[12] say that *Targum Onkelos* originated from Sinai. The *Aruch Hashulchan*[13] explains that since Targum is close to *lashon hakodesh*, it too is holy, and its explanation was given at Sinai. Simply, this means that at the same time the Torah was given, Targum was also given. Therefore, it preceded all other explanations. The *Levush*[14] says that Targum's explanation merited to be used because it was given at Sinai, for example, "יגר שהדותא" and the like. This can be explained that Targum was given together with the Torah and is in the Torah itself, which makes it *kadosh* and elevated over all other explanations. *Tosafos*[15] says that other languages may not be used to translate; only Targum, because it explains what can't be learned from the *Ivris*. In many places, we find that Rav Yosef said, "If not for the Targum of this *pasuk*, I wouldn't know what it is saying."[16]

## WHY DON'T WE ALSO HAVE A METARGEM IN ARAMAIC?

The *Chasam Sofer* writes that from the time of Moshe until Ezra, people only spoke in *lashon hakodesh*, which was the language that they understood. During Ezra's time, after the languages got mixed up in Bavel and people did not understand *lashon hakodesh*, he kept the *lashon hakodesh* and set up a translator during *k'rias haTorah*. He chose Targum because it was universally accepted that it was from Sinai, as *halachah l'Moshe miSinai*. Throughout[17] the times of the Tannaim, people spoke in Aramaic and everyone understood Onkelos, so it was used to translate the Torah reading. Since nowadays we do not speak Aramaic and most people do not understand Onkelos, there is no benefit to translate into Aramaic, so it was stopped. This seems to be difficult: Chazal say that once there is an enactment, even if the reason does not apply, it still

---

12 רש"י ותוס' קדושין מט.

13 סי' רפה, יב

14 שם ב

15 ברכות ח.-:

16 ע' מעדני יו"ט על הרא"ש בגמ' ברכות פ"א ס"ק ז

17 מגילה כג:-כד. וטוש"ע או"ח סי' קמה, א וג

remains and one needs to keep it; if so, how could Ezra's enactment be stopped? The *Chasam Sofer* says that *Tosafos*[18] answers this question. The Gemara says, "We only *lein* ten *pesukim* for the haftarah in a place where there is a translator." This implies that originally, it was not accepted to translate in all places. Therefore, nowadays, when we don't understand Aramaic, we can rely on this to not have a translator.

## WHY DON'T WE EXPLAIN IN ANOTHER LANGUAGE THAT PEOPLE UNDERSTAND?

The *Chasam Sofer*[19] says that we cannot derive from the above to translate into a language that people understand, since Targum is unique as it was said with *ruach hakodesh*. Rav Moshe Feinstein[20] adds that no rabbi should translate or explain *pesukim* with *Rashi*, *Ramban*, Rabbeinu Bachya, or other *mefarshim* during *k'rias haTorah*—even between *aliyos*—since there are different opinions as to how to explain and there might be an argument. Chazal instituted *k'rias haTorah* to be like *kabbalas haTorah*, which needs to be unanimously accepted. Onkelos is a Tanna, with a tradition from Sinai, and is *Toras emes*. The *Chasam Sofer* says that it is not possible to explain 100 percent correctly if it was not transmitted by Moshe Rabbeinu from Hashem. True, a person could explain with an explanation in whatever language that he wants, but to read before a *tzibbur*, if he won't be explaining the truth, it will be "*dover shekarim lo yikon*."

## IS SH'NAYIM MIKRA V'ECHAD TARGUM A NICE THING OR AN OBLIGATION?

The Gemara[21] teaches that one should always say the *mikra* twice and the Targum once, and such a person will merit length of days and

---

18  כג:
19  ג
20  או"ח ח"ד סי' מ אות כא
21  ברכות שם

years. The *Shulchan Aruch*[22] *paskens* in the name of the *Rambam* that
although one hears the entire Torah with the *tzibbur*, he is obligated
to say *mikra* twice and the Targum once. Rav Wosner[23] infers from the
*Rambam*'s changing the wording of the Gemara, saying "obligated,"
that one should not think it is only a nice thing to do, rather it is an
obligation *mi'd'Rabbanan*. It follows that one should train his children
to say *sh'nayim mikra v'echad Targum* to fulfill *mitzvas chinuch*. Rav
Shlomo Zalman Auerbach[24] says that a minor should be trained to say
*sh'nayim mikra v'echad Targum* when he reaches the age of *chinuch* even
if he won't understand everything.[25] Rav Wosner wonders whether we
should force a person who doesn't want to fulfill this mitzvah as we find
by other *mitzvos aseh mi'd'Rabbanan* according to many opinions. Rav
Moshe Feinstein[26] says that even people who are on the level of Rabbi
Shimon bar Yochai and his friends are obligated to say *sh'nayim mikra
v'echad Targum*. No one is exempt because he learns other things; it is
included in the mitzvah of learning *Torah She'bichsav*.

## ARE WE YOTZEI ECHAD TARGUM
## WITHOUT THINKING ABOUT ITS MEANING?

The Chafetz Chaim[27] teaches that the purpose of *sh'nayim mikra v'echad
Targum* is to understand the *mikra*. As long as learning *sh'nayim mikra*
gets a person to think and clarify the parashah, then he accomplishes
his objective. However, if he does not understand what he learns, it
is not considered learning at all. Nowadays, people are not familiar
with Aramaic and therefore do not understand Targum; they are not
*yotzei* by just saying the words. On the other hand, Rav Shlomo Zalman

22  או"ח סי' רפה, א
23  שו"ת שבט הלוי ח סי' מו
24  הליכות שלמה תפלה פ' יב, לז
25  שם דבר הלכה ס"ק מח
26  אג"מ או"ח ח"ה סי' יז
27  לקוטי אמרים פ"ה

Auerbach[28] says that according to halachah, even if one doesn't understand Aramaic well and is not meticulous while reading it, he is still *yotzei*. However, it is definitely fitting for one to strive to understand the Targum well. The *Vilna Gaon*[29] teaches that one needs to be very meticulous with Targum Onkelos's explanation on each *pasuk* and not just recite it without paying attention.

## WHY SAY MIKRA TWICE AND TARGUM ONCE?

- The *Elyah Rabbah*[30] records from the *Sheyarei K'nesses Hagedolah* that the three readings correspond to the Torah which was given three times: at Sinai, at the *Ohel Moed*, and *Mishneh Torah*.[31] The *Mateh Moshe* explains further that the two rounds of *mikra* correspond to Sinai and the *Ohel Moed*. The third round, relating to *Mishneh Torah* where it states that the Torah was given "*ba'er heiteiv*—explained well," corresponds to Targum, which explains the *mikra*.
- The *Divrei Chamudos*[32] teaches that the two rounds of *mikra* correspond to the two readers: the *baal korei* and the *sheliach tzibbur*, as the *Yerushalmi* writes that there needs to be a *baal korei* and another person standing at the *bimah*. The single round of Targum corresponds to the *metargem*, translator, who would translate the *mikra* into a language which people understood.
- The *Aruch Hashulchan*[33] quotes from the Midrash that for every topic that Hashem taught to Moshe, He first reviewed it twice in His heart, and afterwards transmitted it to Moshe (*ki'veyachol*). Therefore, we should do the same: two rounds of *mikra* and one round of Targum.

28 דבר הלכה ס"ק מח
29 ספר הליקוטים מעשה רב החדש סי' טו
30 או"ח שם ב ובעה"ש שם ב
31 ע' גמ' סוטה לו:
32 ברכות פ"א ס"ק מא בשם אבן העזר להראב"ן ועה"ש שם
33 שם ד

## GENERAL RULES OF ONKELOS[34]

- As much as possible, he distances any descriptions of physicality or human traits from Hashem.
- When Hashem and people are put together, he differentiates between them.
- For the honor of *tzaddikim* and Yisrael, he translates in a nice way rather than use a literal disgraceful translation.
- Often, he adds one word to hint to a comment of Chazal, or to resolve a contradiction, or to fill in what is missing from a short *pasuk*.
- Often, he changes or adds to the literal meaning to explain the intent, and he translates a parable according to its intent.
- Often, he translates one root (e.g., קח) with different translations (סב, דבר) as per the intent.
- Often, he translates a question, as implied by a prefix 'ה, as its intended factual statement.
- He adds a 'ל, to, in order to clarify a comparison: this is like that or this is to that.
- When there are double *leshonos*, he changes one so as not to be repetitive.
- Sometimes, he translates what is unclear from elsewhere which is clear.
- He may translate with a few meanings, or with both the literal translation and the intent, or as a כלומר which explains what he means.
- Often, he translates a singular word as if it were plural (and, sometimes, vice-versa).
- He may change a noun to a verb, or from a verb in present tense to other tenses, or to an active verb.
- He is consistent in tenses and gender. If a translation is changed, he will change the other associated words to maintain consistency.

- Often, he translates the names of places or things with the way they are commonly known by people, for example, "Ararat" as "קרדו" (Kurdistan/Kurd).
- Sometimes, he combines two words as one (e.g., כי אם, אלהין)
- Often, he translates by switching the order, as is common by numbers; he puts the bigger number first, as people speak.
- Sometimes, he does not translate into Aramaic, but rather leaves it as it is or borrows *lashon hakodesh* to translate.
- He may translate several words with the same Aramaic *lashon*.
- He does not always translate את or the prefix 'ה as "the" at the beginning of a word, and sometimes he adds a 'ה.
- Sometimes, he translates without a כוי, "my," or adds a כוי, "his," to put emphasis on the subject.
- He excludes explanations and opinions of the Tzedukim and others.

This *sefer* will specify many examples of these rules throughout the *divrei Torah*.

- Square brackets [ ] represent the literal translation of Onkelos in proper English.
- Round parentheses ( ) represent another *girsa* or explanation.
- In general, we brought sources for our own quotes, not for sources that *mefarshim* quote.
- "My Rosh Yeshiva" refers to Rav Yaakov Friedman of Birchas Mordechai.
- "My previous Rosh Yeshiva" refers to Rav Aharon Shechter of Chaim Berlin.
- "*Avi Mori*" refers to Rabbi Chaim Portowicz.
- "*Mori Chami*" refers to Rabbi Chaim Tatel.
- "Rav Chaim Shmuelevitz" is from *Sichos Mussar*.
- "Rabbi Hartman" is on footnotes of *Gur Aryeh, Maharal*.

# SEFER BEREISHIS

# Parashah Dedications

BEREISHIS–The Gutwirth family
*L'iluy nishmas* Basheva Pesil ben R' Asher Yechiel Hakohen

---

NOACH–Yitzchok and Chaya Rubin
In honor of Reb Shia Portowicz, *shlita*
Continue to go *me'chayil el chayil*!

---

LECH LECHA–Anonymous, Rechov Zvill, Beitar Illit
לזכות של התורם ומשפחתו וכל יוצאי חלציו

---

VAYEIRA–The Fishelis family
לזכר נשמת הרב אברהם שלמה בן הרב יצחק זצ"ל פישעליס

---

CHAYEI SARAH–Moshe and Chava Rubin
In honor of Rabbi Shia Portowicz's *mesirus nefesh*
to support the *kollel* in both *ruchniyus* and *gashmiyus*

---

TOLDOS–Aharon and Ariella Mikail
For the *hatzlachah* and *berachah* of my dear *eishes chayil*, Ariella Rachel,
whose birthday parashah is *Parashas Toldos*

---

VAYEITZEI–The Glanz family
*L'iluy nishmas* Tziporah Rachel bas Aryeh, *a"h*

---

VAYISHLACH–Donny and Tamar Miller
In memory of our brother-in-law, Marc Katz, *a"h*
אלחנן משה רפאל בן יהודה ליב הכהן ע"ה

VAYEISHEV–Chaim and Leah Tatel
לע"נ יוסף בן יעקב יחיאל גולדמן ז"ל
לע"נ שרה בת דוד הלוי גולדמן ע"ה

---

MIKEITZ–The Kohanchi family
In merit of Mr. Kohanchi, *z"l*

---

VAYIGASH–The Mehler family and friends
לעילוי נשמת יהודית ברכה בת נחמיה ע"ה

---

VAYECHI–Chaim and Leah Tatel
לע"נ
מיכל חנא בן אליהו אביגדור הכהן טייטל ז"ל
זעלדא פייגל (טייטל) בת שמואל ע"ה

---

*Lichvod* my dear cousins

# Avi and Chaya Shaindel

A big *yasher ko'ach* for assisting with the publishing of *Yad HaGer*,
in addition to your continuous *chassadim tovim* and *nedivas lev*.
May Hashem grant you and your entire family *gezunt*,
*nachas, parnasah b'revach*, and the *zechus* of one who reviews
*sh'nayim mikra v'echad Targum*, מאריכין לו ימיו ושנותיו!

# Bereishis

## WHAT WAS UNIQUE ABOUT THE CREATION OF ADAM?

וַיִּפַּח בְּאַפָּיו נִשְׁמַת חַיִּים וַיְהִי הָאָדָם לְנֶפֶשׁ חַיָּה (ב, ז)

וּנְפַח בְּאַפּוֹהִי נִשְׁמְתָא דְּחַיֵּי וַהֲוַת בְּאָדָם לְרוּחַ מְמַלְלָא

*And He blew into his nostrils a breath of life,*
*and it was in Adam to be a spirit that speaks.*

The *pasuk* states, "ויפח באפיו נשמת חיים ויהי האדם לנפש חיה—And He blew into his nostrils a breath of life and the person became a living soul." The *Nefesh Hachaim*[1] explains that this teaches that a person is the *nefesh* of the entire creation and universe. The world is directly connected to and affected by the acts of people. A person is comparable to the motor of a car. If the motor has power and energy, it will enable the car to drive; if it doesn't, the car won't move at all. So too, if a person fulfills the Torah and mitzvos, he provides power and energy to the world, but if he doesn't, he destroys it.

*Rashi* explains that although the *pasuk* also calls animals "*nefesh chayah*," the creation of man was unique. Adam has the most life of all since he has knowledge and the ability to talk. Onkelos translates "ויפח באפיו נשמת חיים ויהי האדם לנפש חיה" as, "And He blew into his nostrils a breath of life, and it was in Adam to be a spirit that speaks." (Onkelos translates אדם for Adam HaRishon, אנש for person, גבר for man [*Nefesh HaGer*].) The word "*va'yehi*" is masculine, which Onkelos generally translates as "*va'havah*" and follows the words after it, which would mean, "and Adam became a live being." Here, however, he translates it as "*va'havas*," in feminine, which refers to the *neshamah* mentioned previously, "and it—the *ne-shamah* [feminine]—was blown into the Adam." The *Ramban* explains that it seems that there were two stages of Adam's creation. First, he was created with a *nefesh chayah*, similar to all animals which are alive and move. We find this concept in the Gemara:[2] Rava created a person with the *Sefer Yetzirah* and sent him to Rav Zeira. Rav Zeira spoke with him and he did not respond. He said, "You were created by one of my colleagues; return to your dirt." This person had no ability to speak and was only able to move around as an animal. The *Maharsha* explains that Rava was unable to create a being with speech, which comes from the strength of the *neshamah*. The form did not contain a *neshamah*; it had only a *ruach* of life, just like animals. The *Ramban* says that afterwards, as a second stage of his creation, Hashem blew into Adam a *neshamah* which implanted within him knowledge and the ability to speak.

The berachah of *Asher Yatzar* ends with *"rofei chol basar u'mafli la'asos."* The *Rama*[3] explains that Hashem performs a *pele*, a wondrous thing, by guarding the *neshamah* inside a person, and He ties together the *neshamah*—a spiritual entity—with the body—a physical object—by healing all flesh and not being sick. This enables a person to be healthy, allowing his *neshamah* to fulfill its responsibilities. Rav Hutner[4] explains that the berachah of *Asher Yatzar* mentions the hollows and cavities of the physical body that, if opened or closed, would end a person's life. For this reason, the berachah ends with *"rofei chol basar*—Who heals all flesh." The *Darkei Moshe*[5] explains the final phrase, *"u'mafli la'asos,"* that the reason is because the berachah of *Asher Yatzar* is also connected to *Elokai Neshamah*. Rav Hutner teaches that parallel to the berachah of *Asher Yatzar*, which is about the *nefesh* of the physical body, there is another berachah, *Elokai Neshamah*, which corresponds to the *nefesh Elokis*, the G-dly *nefesh*. The words *"u'mafli la'asos"* bridge these two berachos which mix the spiritual *nefesh Elokis* together with the natural,

---

2   :סנהדרין סה

3   או"ח סי' ו, א

4   פחד יצחק שבועות מאמר מג אות ט-י

5   ב

physical *nefesh*. When Adam was created, Hashem blew into the physical *nefesh* a *nefesh Elokis*. The *pasuk* describes this as, "ויפח באפיו נשמת חיים ויהי האדם לנפש חיה," which Onkelos translates as, "And He blew into his nostrils a breath of life, and it—the *neshamah*—was blown into Adam to be a spirit which speaks." This reflects that through the combination of these two *nefashos*, Hashem introduced and enabled the ability to speak. Rav Hutner[6] says that since the main strength of speech was created through this wondrous combination, therefore, the Torah uses the *lashon* "פלא" by speaking, as in "איש...כי יפליא." Also, this is why the *Rambam* calls the volume in the *Yad Hachazakah* about speech, such as the laws of oaths, vows, *nezirus*, *arachin*, and *charamim*, "הפלאה."

There are four categories in creation: *domem*, inanimate objects, such as stones and metals; *tzomei'ach*, that which grows, such as plants and trees; *chai*, living beings that are alive and move, such as animals and birds; *medaber*, those who speak, people. What is unique about the ability to speak, and why do only people have this ability?

The Gemara[7] teaches that a person is created to toil in learning with his mouth, to say over *divrei Torah*. The *Maharsha* explains that speaking words of Torah is the purpose of a person's creation as a *medaber*. This defines the uniqueness that people have over animals.

May Hashem help us use our speech for *divrei Torah* in order to elevate ourselves and the entire creation!

## WHAT IS OUR AVODAH AFTER EATING FROM THE EITZ HADAAS?

### וְעֵץ הַדַּעַת טוֹב וָרָע (ב, ט)

וְאִילָן דְּאָכְלֵי פֵּירוֹהִי חָכְמִין בֵּין טָב לְבִישׁ

*And a tree, which one who eats its fruits becomes wise to differentiate between good and bad.*

---

6 אות יב
7 סנהדרין צט:

וּמֵעֵץ הַדַּעַת טוֹב וָרָע לֹא תֹאכַל מִמֶּנּוּ
כִּי בְּיוֹם אֲכָלְךָ מִמֶּנּוּ מוֹת תָּמוּת (ב, יז)

וּמֵאִילָן דְּאָכְלֵי פֵּירוֹהִי חַכְמִין בֵּין טָב לְבִישׁ לָא תֵּיכוֹל
מִנֵּיהּ אֲרֵי בְּיוֹמָא דְּתֵיכוֹל מִנֵּיהּ מְמָת תָּמוּת

*And from the tree, which one who eats its fruits becomes wise to
differentiate between good and bad, do not eat from it, because
on the day that you will eat from it, you will, indeed, die.*

כִּי בְּיוֹם אֲכָלְכֶם מִמֶּנּוּ וְנִפְקְחוּ עֵינֵיכֶם
וִהְיִיתֶם כֵּאלֹהִים יֹדְעֵי טוֹב וָרָע (ג, ה)

אֲרֵי בְּיוֹמָא דְּתֵיכְלוּן מִנֵּהּ יִתְפַּתְּחָן עֵינֵיכוֹן וּתְהוֹן כְּרַבְרְבִין חַכְמִין בֵּין טָב לְבִישׁ

*For on the day that you will eat from it your eyes will
be opened up and you will be like leaders, who are
wise to differentiate between good and bad.*

הֵן הָאָדָם הָיָה כְּאַחַד מִמֶּנּוּ לָדַעַת טוֹב וָרָע (ג, כב)

הָא אָדָם הֲוָה יְחִידַאי בְּעָלְמָא מִנֵּהּ לְמִדַּע טָב וּבִישׁ

*Behold, Adam was alone in the world, on
his own to know good and bad.*

The *pasuk* states that inside the garden, along with the *Eitz
Hachaim*, there was the "*Eitz Ha'daas tov va'ra*," which Onkelos translates as "and
a tree, which one who eats its fruits becomes wise to differentiate between good and bad." Hashem commanded Adam, "ומעץ הדעת טוב ורע לא
תאכל ממנו כי ביום אכלך ממנו מות תמות—From all the trees of the garden
you may eat," which Onkelos translates as, "And from the tree, which
one who eats its fruits becomes wise to differentiate between good and
bad, do not eat from it, because on the day that you will eat from it,
you will, indeed, die." The snake tried convincing Chavah to eat from it
by saying, "כי ביום אכלכם ממנו ונפקחו עיניכם והייתם כאלהים ידעי טוב ורע," which
Onkelos translates as "for on the day that you will eat from it your eyes
will be opened up and you will be like leaders, who are wise to differentiate between good and bad." The *Hakesav V'Hakabbalah* explains that

the word "אלהים" reflects strength and ability. This is as the *Rambam*[8] teaches: Onkelos translates כאלהים as "like leaders," great people who are able to judge between good and bad. We see that the uniqueness of the *Eitz Hadaas* was that it makes one wise to differentiate between good and bad.

The *Ramban*[9] explains that the word "*daas*" refers to interest and choice, as the Gemara writes, "לא שנו אלא שדעתו לחזור—We only say this when he intends to return." Also, the Torah states "ידעתיך בשם—I chose you by name." Originally, there was no hatred or love; rather, things were set up to function with honesty, not to change their routine. The fruits of this tree were unique; they were able to produce interest and desire in something for those who ate it, for good or bad.

After the sin of eating from the *Eitz Hadaas*, Hashem said, "הן האדם היה כאחד ממנו לדעת טוב ורע." *Rashi* explains "*k'achad mi'menu*" as a comparison: Hashem said, "Adam is unique in the world below just like I am alone in the world above. What is his uniqueness? To know good and bad." Onkelos translates differently: "Behold, Adam was alone in the world, on his own to know good and bad." The *Nefesh HaGer* says that Onkelos changed it in order to distance any physicality from Hashem, so as not to compare a person to Him. He translates "כאחד" as "יחיד—alone," without the 'כ; Adam is alone in the world below, and "from him [מִנֵּה]," on his own, he is able to differentiate between good and bad. Unlike *Rashi*, the word "*mi'menu*" is not together with "*k'achad*," but, rather, it follows "*la'daas tov va'ra*," meaning that Adam on his own is able to know good and bad. What is the understanding of "on his own to know good and bad"?

The *Rambam*[10] explains that the human species is unique in the world and no other species is similar to him. With a person's own knowledge and thought, he knows about good and bad and is able to do whatever he wants; no one can hold him back. If a person wants to do good and

---

8    מו"נ ח"א פ"ב ע"ע בחזקוני

9    פסוק ט

10   שמונה פרקים הפ' השמיני והל' תשובה ה, א

be a *tzaddik*, he can, and if he wants to do bad and be a *rasha*, he can. Therefore, a person must train himself to perform good deeds, develop proper attributes, and distance himself from evil.

Rav Hutner[11] explains in the name of the *Kadmonim* that originally, bad was outside of Adam's being, not inside. Just as a dog barks and causes one to move, so too, the *yetzer hara* was only able to overpower a person from the outside. After eating from the *Eitz Hadaas*, the snake caused an *el zar* and *el neichar*, a mighty foreign ruler vis-à-vis Hashem, similar to a god, to be put inside Adam. The *Chachmei Emes* say that this came from the *zuhamah*, filth, which the snake put into Chavah, thereby causing the bad to enter the body. It created a mixture of good and bad intertwined inside people, all the way into the roots of their souls. From then on, our *avodah* has been to overcome the evil that is "mixed inside of us."

The *Ruach Chaim*[12] says that before Adam sinned, the food that he ate was all good; there was no mixture of good and bad. This is hinted to in the Gemara which states that angels roasted meat which descended from the heavens for Adam Harishon in Gan Eden. The *Ruach Chaim* explains that this meat was spiritual and was special like the *mahn* that descended from heaven and was fully good. Just as the *mahn* was absorbed in the body and there were no excretions, so too, Adam's food, which was *ruchani*, was absorbed in the body and there were no excretions. Once he sinned, the *Eitz Hadaas* caused food to become mixed with good and bad together. The *ruchniyus* sustains the soul, the *gashmiyus* turns into blood and sustains the body, and the bad goes out in excretions.

Adam was punished with "וקוץ ודרדר תצמיח לך ואכלת את עשב השדה"—And painful thorns and large grown thorns will sprout for you and you will eat the grass of the field." The ground was also cursed to grow things mixed with good and bad together. Rav Hutner explains that this mixture of good and bad in the crops, where one needs to remove the

---

11   מאמרי פ"י סוכות מאמר כה אות י; מאמר צו אות ה; פ"י יו"כ מאמר יז אות ד ויג; מאמר לז אות ה-ז

12   אבות ג, גוה, ה

bad, parallels the mixture of good and bad inside a person where he will need to remove the bad. Adam was also punished with "בְּזֵעַת אַפֶּיךָ תֹּאכַל לֶחֶם—With the sweat of your brow you will eat bread." Sweat is the bad that separates from the body, also demonstrating that a person should remove the bad from within himself.

May Hashem help us separate the bad from within ourselves and only choose good!

## WHAT IS THE SNAKE'S BATTLE WITH PEOPLE?

### הוּא יְשׁוּפְךָ רֹאשׁ וְאַתָּה תְּשׁוּפֶנּוּ עָקֵב (ג, טו)

הוּא יְהֵי דְּכִיר מָא דַּעֲבַדְתְּ לֵיהּ מִלְּקַדְמִין וְאַתְּ תְּהֵי נָטַר לֵיהּ לְסוֹפָא

*He [the person] will remember that which you [the snake] did to him at an earlier time, and you [the snake] will guard him [the person] in the end.*

The *pasuk* states that Hashem cursed the snake, "הוא ישופך ראש ואתה תשופנו עקב." *Rashi* explains: "He [the person] will crush you [the snake] at the head, and you [the snake] will not have stature against him. Rather, you will bite him on his heel, and even from there, you will kill him by injecting poison into him, which will spread throughout his entire body." The *Sifsei Chachamim*[13] adds that *Rashi* explains "and you will not have stature" since *v'atah teshufenu akeiv* is part of the curse to the snake; it will not be able to stand up against a person to battle head to head. *Rashi* explains the curse as a physical battle between the snake and the person.

The *Nefesh HaGer* asks: Hashem cursed Adam with death and toiling, Chavah with childrearing and labor, and the snake with going on its stomach and eating dirt. How do the words "going on its stomach" fit as part of the curse? Also, why does it matter where a person will kill the snake or where the snake will kill the person; either way, each will die?

Additionally, all wild animals who meet a person will harm or kill him, so what is unique about the snake?

The *Nefesh HaGer* answers that the words, "הוא ישופך ראש ואתה תשופנו עקב," are a *mashal*, which Onkelos translates with the *nimshal*. "He [the person] will remember that which you [the snake] did to him at an earlier time, and you [the snake] will guard him [the person] in the end." *Rosh* means a head, which reflects an earlier time, just as the head is the beginning of the body. *Akeiv* means a heel, which reflects the end, just as the heel is the end of the body. With this we can understand as follows: A person should continuously remember the snake, the *yetzer hara*, and what it caused Adam at an earlier time [the head]. The snake convinced Adam to eat from the *Eitz Hadaas* and caused him to transgress the mitzvah of Hashem, which brought death to Adam and his descendants, along with the need to toil. We have to try to stay away from the snake, but the snake will pursue a person by presenting challenges until the end [the heel] of the person's life and not allow him to rest. A person should learn from this *pasuk* to stand firm and strong to triumph over the challenges that confront him. Onkelos translates this *pasuk* not as a curse, but as *mussar* about a spiritual battle between a person's *yetzer hara* and *yetzer tov*. Thus, the battle between man and the snake is essentially the lifelong struggle of man with his *yetzer hara*.

The Gemara[14] teaches that it states, "צופה רשע לצדיק ומבקש להמיתו—The *rasha* looks for the *tzaddik* and seeks to kill him." This refers to a person's *yetzer*, which continuously seeks to overpower him and convince him to sin. The following *pasuk* states, "אלקים לא יעזבנו בידו—G-d will not leave him in his hand." The Gemara explains that if not for Hashem helping a person, he would be lured by the evil inclination. The *Maharsha* adds that although everything is in the hands of Heaven aside from *yiras Shamayim*, if a person wants and tries to do good, Hashem will help him be successful to withstand any challenge.

---

May Hashem help us remember the outcome of the snake's persuasion, to be aware of the *yetzer hara* constantly challenging us, and to be firm to follow the *yetzer tov*!

## IS KAYIN'S NAME BECAUSE OF AN ACQUISITION "WITH HASHEM" OR "FOR HASHEM"?

### וַתַּהַר וַתֵּלֶד אֶת קַיִן וַתֹּאמֶר קָנִיתִי אִישׁ אֶת ה' (ה, א)

וְעַדִּיאַת וִילֵידַת יָת קַיִן וַאֲמַרַת קְנֵיתִי גַּבְרָא (מִן) קֳדָם יְיָ

*And she conceived and gave birth to Kayin, and she said, "I acquired a man (from) before Hashem."*

The *pasuk* states, "ותהר ותלד את קין—And she conceived and gave birth to Kayin." Onkelos translates "ותהר" as "ועדיאת." The *Nefesh HaGer* explains that this is from the word "עדא—remove," as Onkelos translates[15] "ויסר" as "ואעדי—and he removed." This reflects the cessation and removal of the *niddah* cycle which happens when a woman conceives and becomes pregnant.

The *pasuk* continues, "and she said, 'קניתי איש את ה'—I acquired איש את ה'.'" What does this latter phrase mean? *Rashi* explains: "'When Hashem created me and my husband, He alone created us; however, with this child, we are partners.' She called his name 'Kayin,' hinting that she acquired him with Hashem, as they were partners in this new creation." *Rashi* explains "את ה'" as "together with Hashem." The *Sifsei Chachamim*[16] adds, quoting the Gemara, that there are three partners in the creation of a person: Hashem, the father, and the mother. *Avi Mori* told me a story[17] about parents of a *bachur* in Rav Moshe Feinstein's yeshiva who wanted him to go to college. Rav Moshe told them that he should remain in yeshiva and continue learning. They claimed that since there are three

---

15 ל, לה
16 פ
17 Written at http://www.torchweb.org/torah_detail.php?id=205

partners in the child, the Ribbono Shel Olam and the two parents, they have the majority, two out of three. Rav Moshe immediately responded, "The Ribbono Shel Olam has the majority, not you. Let us think of the partnership in your son as nine shares. Hashem has three-ninths, and you and your wife have three-ninths each. Hashem is a part of each of you as well, so you can speak for only two-thirds of your own selves; the other third belongs to Hashem. Therefore, three-ninths of your son, Hashem's share, votes for him to remain in yeshiva. The one-third of both you and your wife, the part which is Hashem's, also wants him to stay. If you add it all together, five-ninths of the relevant parties are in favor of staying in yeshiva and only four-ninths are against. So, the Ribbono Shel Olam has the majority in the child, not the parents!"

Onkelos translates "קניתי איש את ה'" differently: "I acquired a man from before Hashem." The *Ramban* explains that she said, "This son shall be for me as a *kinyan laHashem*, an acquisition for the sake of Hashem. When we will die, he will remain, and he will stand in our place to continue to serve Hashem, his Creator." "*Es*" can mean "to" or "for," as it states, "*V'her'ah es haKohen*—And he will show it to the Kohen." The *Ramban* has the text "קדם ה'—before Hashem," while others have "מן קדם ה'," which means "from before"—because of Hashem.

The following *pasuk* states that she bore another child, Hevel. The *Ramban* says that here, it does not mention a reason for why he was called Hevel. He explains the *lashon* "*hevel*" hints to nothingness; every acquisition of man in this world is for naught. Rav Dessler[18] explains that *hevel havalim* refers to interest in *Olam Hazeh*. No matter how much one attains, it won't suffice; he will not be satisfied and will yearn for more. A person cannot acquire something physical, for example possessions, to become one with his body and certainly not one with his soul. Physical things are outside and separate from him. Also, money is called "*kinyan*—acquisitions" as a borrowed term for things which one owns and can use. Only *ruchniyus* achievements become part of a person, and no one can take such things away. Similarly, the *Beis Halevi*[19] explains that wealth does not make a person into a better person; he just has a bigger safe or a heavier purse. *Ruchniyus*, however, is an intrinsic attribute; the person becomes elevated and more important. The *Ramban* says that Chavah did not want to express the reason for Hevel, so she didn't mention it explicitly, although this was the true reason for his name. The names of Kayin and Hevel reflect a contrast of what acquisitions in the world are for and their relevance. Chavah taught that having a child who will serve Hashem and be dedicated to Him has true meaning, whereas acquisitions of the world are false and insignificant.

May Hashem help us dedicate our *avodah* to Him and recognize that materialism is insignificant!

## DID HASHEM "TURN TO" OR "ACCEPT" THE MINCHAH?

### וַיָּבֵא קַיִן מִפְּרִי הָאֲדָמָה מִנְחָה לַה' (ה, ג)

וְאַיְתִי קַיִן מֵאִבָּא דְאַרְעָא קָרְבָּנָא (תִּקְרוּבְתָּא) קֳדָם יְיָ

*And Kayin brought from the growth of the land*
*a korban (a present) before Hashem.*

### וַיִּשַׁע ה' אֶל הֶבֶל וְאֶל מִנְחָתוֹ (ה, ד)

וַהֲוַת רַעֲוָא מִן קֳדָם יְיָ בְּהֶבֶל וּבְקוּרְבָּנֵיה

*And there was favor from before Hashem with Hevel and his korban.*

### וְאֶל קַיִן וְאֶל מִנְחָתוֹ לֹא שָׁעָה וַיִּחַר לְקַיִן מְאֹד וַיִּפְּלוּ פָּנָיו (ה, ה)

וּבְקַיִן וּבְקֻרְבָּנֵיה לָא הֲוַת רַעֲוָא וּתְקֵיף לְקַיִן לַחֲדָא וְאִתְכְּבִישׁוּ אַפּוֹהִי

*And with Kayin and with his korban there was not*
*favor, and Kayin strengthened [became distressed]*
*very much and he pressed down [buried] his face.*

# לָמָה חָרָה לָךְ וְלָמָּה נָפְלוּ פָנֶיךָ (ה, ו)

## לְמָא תְקֵיף לָךְ וּלְמָא אִתְכְּבִישׁוּ אַפָּךְ

*Why have you strengthened [become distressed], and*
*why has your face been pressed down [buried]?*

The *pasuk* states, "ויבא קין מפרי האדמה מנחה לה'," which Onkelos translates as, "And Kayin brought from the growth of the land a *korban* before Hashem." Onkelos does not translate[20] "מנחה" as "מנחתא," which refers to a flour-offering, but rather as "קרבנא," a *korban*. The reason is because here, the *lashon* "*minchah*" is used for both things which grow from the ground and also sheep. Therefore, Onkelos translates the word as "*korban*," which includes both. *Rashi* specifies that it was from the worst things; some say in Aggadah that it was flax.

The following *pesukim* state: "וישע ה' אל הבל ואל מנחתו ואל קין ואל מנחתו לא שעה." *Rashi* explains "...וישע ה'" and "ואל...לא שעה" as "and Hashem turned to Hevel...and He did not turn to Kayin...." The *Sifsei Chachamim*[21] says that *Rashi* is bothered: how was it known that Hashem turned toward Hevel and not toward Kayin? *Rashi* answers by explaining that a fire descended and consumed Hevel's *minchah*. Onkelos translates "וישע" and "שעה" differently: "'And there was favor' from before Hashem with Hevel and his *korban*, and with Kayin and with his *korban* 'there was not favor.'" The *Hakesav V'Hakabbalah* adds that Onkelos translates "וישע" and "שעה" as it states in *Tehillim*, "ואשעה בחקיך תמיד—And I will constantly have enjoyment and pleasure." Hashem favored Hevel's *korban*, not Kayin's. The *Nefesh HaGer* explains that Onkelos does not translate "שעה" as "turn," since he is careful to distance any physicality from Hashem.

The *pasuk* ends, "ויחר לקין מאד ויפלו פניו," which Onkelos translates as, "And Kayin strengthened [became distressed] very much and he pressed down his face." Hashem asked Kayin, "למה חרה לך ולמה נפלו פניך," which Onkelos translates as, "Why have you strengthened [become distressed] and why has your face been pressed down?" Onkelos translates "*va'yiplu*

---

*panav"* and *"naflu panecha"* as pressing down the face. The *Nefesh HaGer* explains that out of embarrassment, Kayin pressed down his face to cover himself. The *Ramban* brings in the name of the *Ibn Ezra* that Hashem hinted with the word *"s'eis"* that *"s'eis panecha—*your face can be raised up," which parallels *"naflu panecha—*your face falling down." When a person is embarrassed, he buries his face, and when a person is honored, it is as though he raises up his face.

May we serve Hashem properly and merit His turning and accepting our *avodah*!

## WHAT WAS HASHEM'S MESSAGE AND ADVICE TO KAYIN?

הֲלוֹא אִם תֵּיטִיב שְׂאֵת וְאִם לֹא תֵיטִיב לַפֶּתַח חַטָּאת
רֹבֵץ וְאֵלֶיךָ תְּשׁוּקָתוֹ וְאַתָּה תִּמְשָׁל בּוֹ (ה, ז)

הֲלָא אִם תּוֹטֵיב עוֹבְדָךְ יִשְׁתְּבֵק לָךְ וְאִם לָא תּוֹטֵיב עוֹבְדָךְ לְיוֹם דִּינָא חֶטְאָךְ
נְטִיר עָתִיד (וּדְעָתִיד) לְאִתְפְּרָעָא מִנָּךְ אִם לָא תְתוּב וְאִם תְּתוּב יִשְׁתְּבֵק לָךְ

*Is it not so, if you improve your deeds, it [your sin] will*
*leave you [you will be forgiven], and if you do not improve*
*your deeds, your sin will be guarded [kept] in the future*
*until the day of judgment to be punished from you [when*
*retribution will be taken from you] if you don't repent. If*
*you repent, it [your sin] (the yetzer hara) will leave you.*

Hashem said, "הֲלוֹא אִם תֵּיטִיב שְׂאֵת וְאִם לֹא תֵיטִיב לַפֶּתַח חַטָּאת רֹבֵץ," which Onkelos translates as, "Is it not so, if you improve your deeds, it [your sin] will leave you [you will be forgiven], and if you do not improve your deeds, your sin will be guarded [kept] in the future until the day of judgment to be punished from you [when retribution will be taken from you]." Onkelos translates *"im teitiv s'eis"* as, "if you improve your deeds, it—your sin—will leave you [yisht'veik]." The *Nesinah LaGer* explains that the word *"s'eis"* means forgiveness of sin. The *Nefesh HaGer* adds that this is as the *Ramban* explains that Onkelos translates *"nosei—*carry [shaveik]" as "to leave," which refers to forgiveness, getting rid of the sin and its punishment. Hashem tells Kayin, "If you improve your deeds, you will be forgiven." Onkelos translates, "ואם לא תיטיב לפתח חטאת רבץ," as "and if you do not improve your deeds, your sin will be guarded—kept in the future—until the day of judgment to be punished when retribution will be taken from you." *Rashi* explains that *"la'pesach chatas roveitz"* means, "your sin will guard the entrance to your burial plot." The *Nesinah LaGer* adds that the sin will be crouching like a lion by the road, ready to pounce and cause punishment.

The *pasuk* continues, "ואליך תשוקתו ואתה תמשל בו—And its desire will be toward you, yet you can rule over it." *Rashi* explains that the *yetzer hara* will constantly desire to cause you to stumble, yet if you want to overpower it you will be able to do so. Onkelos translates differently: "in the future…retribution will be taken from you if you don't repent. If you repent, it [your sin and punishment] will leave you."

The *Nefesh HaGer* says that Hashem told Kayin three things:

- *Im teitiv, s'eis* (אם תוטב עובדך ישתבק לך)—If you improve your actions, you will be forgiven; there is the possibility of repentance. This is as the Gemara teaches that *teshuvah* was one of the seven things created before the world.
- *V'im lo seitiv la'pesach chatas roveitz* (ואם לא תוטב עובדך ליום דינא חטאך נטיר)—If you do not improve your deeds, your sin will be kept until the day of judgment. Know that when a person dies, there will be a judgment of his actions.
- *V'eilecha teshukaso* (עתיד לאתפרעא מנך אם לא תתוב)—In the future, after the day of judgment, there is reward to be accredited and punishment to be carried out, according to a person's actions.

Onkelos translates *"V'atah timshol bo"* as, "And if you repent, it will leave you—ואם תתוב ישתבק לך." What does this add beyond what he already translated, "If you improve your deeds, it—your sin—will be forgiven"? The *Nefesh HaGer* answers that here, Hashem is giving worthwhile advice not to invite the *yetzer hara* into one's heart. Rather, hurry to repent and eject the evil that mocks and belittles the good. The Gemara describes that sin starts off slender as a spider web, but in the end is comparable to a thick wagon rope, as it states, "הוי מושכי העון בחבלי השוא

וכעבות העגלה חטאה—Woe, one who extends sin with thin, fine ropes, and as thick ropes of the wagon is his sin." It starts off thin and flimsy and ends up thick and heavy. The Gemara writes that the *yetzer hara* starts off as one who passes by, then he becomes a guest who enters inside the home, and finally, he becomes a master, a host. At the beginning, it will still be easy to turn him away and return from sin; you will be able to rule over him. If you don't rebuff him, though, he will rule over you. This is as Rabbi Yitzchak said: If you will say it is not within your ability to conquer the *yetzer hara*, Hashem will respond that I wrote in the Torah, "ואליך תשוקתו ואתה תמשל בו."

May Hashem help us guard ourselves from the *yetzer hara* and return with *teshuvah*!

## WHAT WERE KAYIN'S SINS?

קוֹל דְּמֵי אָחִיךָ צֹעֲקִים אֵלַי מִן הָאֲדָמָה (ה, י)

קָל דַּם זַרְעֲיָן דַּעֲתִידִין לְמִפַּק מִן אֲחוּךְ קָבְלָן קֳדָמַי מִן אַרְעָא

*The blood of offspring, which, in the future, will go out of [be born from] your brother, is screaming before Me from the land.*

גָּדוֹל עֲוֹנִי מִנְּשֹׂוא (ה, יג)

סַגִּי חוֹבִי מִלְמִשְׁבַּק

*My sin is too severe from being forgiven [too great to bear].*

וּמִפָּנֶיךָ אֶסָּתֵר (ה, יד)

וּמִן קֳדָמָךְ לֵית אֶפְשָׁר לְאִטַּמָּרָא

*And from You it is impossible to hide.*

The *pasuk* states, "Hashem said to Kayin, קוֹל דמי אחיך צועקים אלי מן האדמה—The voice of your brother's bloods is screaming to Me from the ground." For what did Hashem rebuke Kayin? *Rashi* explains that the word *d'mei*, bloods, is plural, which indicates: "Not only did you kill Hevel, but you also killed his future descendants." Or, "You smashed Hevel in

many places since you did not know where his soul would leave the body."
Hashem rebuked Kayin for killing Hevel and his future descendants.
Onkelos, however, translates as, "The blood of offspring, which, in the
future, will go out of [be born from] your brother, is screaming before Me
from the land." Why does Onkelos only translate about killing Hevel's descendants, and not about killing "*achicha*, your brother," Hevel himself?

The *Nefesh HaGer* answers that Kayin transgressed two sins: one, he
killed Hevel, and two, he denied Hashem. Hashem asked Kayin, "Where
is Hevel, your brother?" He responded, "Am I the guardian of my
brother?" as though he didn't know what happened to him and that
he shouldn't be blamed for something that he had nothing to do with.
Hashem rebukes Kayin, "I even know about what you did to Hevel's
future descendants who do not yet exist—you caused their blood to
scream out. I certainly know what has happened now that you have
killed Hevel." Onkelos does not need to mention the blood of Hevel
explicitly because it is automatically understood.

After Kayin sinned, he confessed. The *Nefesh HaGer* explains that the
*pesukim* state Kayin's confession in two ways, corresponding to the two
sins. Kayin said, "*Gadol avoni mi'neso*," which *Rashi* explains as a question: "You carry the world above and the world below, and You can't
carry my sin?" Onkelos translates differently: "My sin is too severe
from being forgiven [too great to bear]," portraying it as a factual statement, meaning, "I did such a terrible sin that there seems no atonement for it." With these words, Kayin confessed and repented for the
sin of killing. Kayin also said, "*U'mi'panecha esaser*—And from before
You, shall I hide?" Meaning, "Where shall I go to be safe from anyone
finding me and killing me? There is no place for me to go to escape."
Onkelos translates differently: "And from You, it is impossible to hide,"
again portraying a factual statement: "There is no place for me to go
hide from You." Here Kayin confessed to the sin of denying Hashem.
He sinned by saying to Hashem, "Am I the guardian of my brother?"
as though Hashem didn't know what happened, and he repented by
saying, "Hashem exists in the entire world, and there is absolutely no
place for me to hide from Him."

The *Rambam*[22] says that we don't say *Hallel* on Rosh Hashanah and Yom Kippur because they are days of *avodah*, when one should humble himself and instill fear of Hashem in order to fear Him and run and flee to Him. One cannot escape from being punished for sin, as Hashem fills the entire world. Rather, one's only recourse is to escape by running to Hashem and doing *teshuvah*. Hashem waits and anticipates the *teshuvah* of those who sin, as it states,[23] "כִּי לֹא אֶחְפֹּץ בְּמוֹת הַמֵּת." Rav Chaim Friedlander explains that even when a person is described as dead, Hashem anticipates his *teshuvah*. Out of Hashem's mercy and kindness, He will forgive if one confesses and repents.

May we remember that Hashem is aware of everything that we do and accepts everyone who repents!

## DOES "HUCHAL" MEAN "TO START" OR "TO PROFANE"?

### אָז הוּחַל לִקְרֹא בְּשֵׁם ה' (ה, כו)

בְּכֵין בְּיוֹמוֹהִי חָלוּ בְּנֵי אֲנָשָׁא מִלְּצַלָּאָה (לְצַלָּאָה) בִּשְׁמָא דה'

*Then, in his days, people of mankind profaned from [stopped]
davening (started to daven) in the name of Hashem.*

The *pasuk* states, "And Shem also had born a son, and he called his name Enosh, then, "הוחל לקרא בשם ה'." What does "הוחל" mean? And what did they call out? The *Ibn Ezra* explains that "הוחל" is related to "התחלה—to start." The *Rashbam* says that they started to daven because of the new afflictions that they had. The *Seforno* quotes *Rabboseinu* that at that time, they started to worship idolatry and they needed to disprove it. Therefore, the *tzaddikim* of the generation started to speak publicly about Hashem in order to pronounce His name and teach people about Him. It was necessary to eradicate the opinions of idolatry.

---

22  פהמ"ש ר"ה פ"ד

23  יחזקאל יח, לב

Onkelos translates differently: "In his days, people of mankind profaned from—stopped—davening [*mi'l'tzalaah*] in the name of Hashem." The *Nefesh HaGer* says that Onkelos does not translate "הוחל" as "שריאו—they started," as he translates[24] "החל," but as "חלו—they profaned," which, as *Rashi* explains, is from the same root as חולין. Similarly, Onkelos translates "זר" as "חילוני—one who is profaned." *Rashi* explains that they profaned by calling names of people and idols in the name of Hashem to make them into idolatry and present them as gods. The *Abarbanel* says that the root of their mistake was that they thought that since Hashem is so lofty, it is not honorable for Him to pay attention to the lowly creations that are in the world, so He gave such tasks over to others. The *Hakesav V'Hakabbalah* adds that in place of davening to Hashem, they called out to the constellations. They thought that humans are too lowly to ask Him for anything; instead, they turned toward an intermediary. They didn't deny Hashem's existence, rather they felt it was more appropriate to ask those who serve before Him, rather than going directly to Him. Onkelos adds, "*B'yomohi*, in his days," to point out that during the days of Enosh, they profaned the name of Hashem by calling names of people and idols after Him.

Others have a different text: "חלו...לצלאה—started to daven." The *Biur Onkelos* says that this version must explain "חלו" as "start," like in *lashon hakodesh*. Since idolatry was being influenced, they needed to fight against it, so they started to daven.

The Gemara[25] teaches that whoever guards Shabbos according to its laws, even if he worships idolatry as did the *Dor Enosh*, he will be forgiven, as it states, "אשרי אנוש יעשה זאת...כל שמר שבת מחללו." Don't read "מחללו—from profaning it," but, rather, read "מחול לו—he is forgiven." *Rashi* explains that the generation of Enosh was the first to start worshipping idolatry, as it states, "אז הוחל לקרא בשם ה'."

The *Rambam* says that Enosh himself worshiped idolatry by mistake. He thought to himself: Hashem put the stars and constellations in

---

ו, א    24
שבת קיח:    25

the heavens to lead the world, and He gave them honor and authority. Therefore, they are fitting for praise, thanks, and honor. They started to build chambers, offer *korbanos*, and bow to them in order to come close to Hashem. Later, they claimed that Hashem wants humans to worship them.

The *Tur*[26] quotes the Gemara differently: "Even if he worships idolatry like Enosh, keeping Shabbos properly can yield forgiveness." The *Perishah*[27] explains that the Gemara compares guarding Shabbos to Enosh: if one worships idolatry by mistake, as the *Rambam* explained that Enosh himself did, by thinking that it is an extension of Hashem's honor, and he guards Shabbos according to its laws, he will be forgiven. The *Beis Yosef* says that the reason he'll be forgiven is because Shabbos is equal to all the mitzvos. It demonstrates *hashgachah*, the renewal of the world, and that Torah is from *Shamayim*. Since he guards Shabbos, he definitely does not worship idolatry because he believes in it; therefore, there is hope and anticipation to be forgiven by repenting, whereas one who worships idolatry, thinking and believing that there is something to it, is far away from returning by repenting.

May Hashem help us remain faithful to serve and daven to Him alone!

## WAS CHANOCH TAKEN AWAY ALIVE, AND WHY?

וַיִּתְהַלֵּךְ חֲנוֹךְ אֶת הָאֱלֹקִים וְאֵינֶנּוּ כִּי לָקַח אֹתוֹ אֱלֹקִים (ה, כד)

וְהַלֵּיךְ חֲנוֹךְ בְּדַחֲלְתָּא דַה' וְלֵיתוֹהִי אֲרֵי אֲמִית[28] (וְאִיתוֹהִי אֲרֵי לָא אֲמִית) יָתֵיה ה'

*And Chanoch went in the fear of Hashem, and he was not existing [stopped living] since Hashem caused (and he was existing, since Hashem did not cause) him to die.*

---

26  או"ח סי' רמב

27  ד

28  רמב"ן גרס בפרקי הצלחה ארי אמית יתה ה' ותוס' ביבמות טז: גרס ארי המית יתה ה'

The *pasuk* states, "ויתהלך חנוך את האלקים ואיננו כי לקח אותו אלקים"—And Chanoch went with G-d and he was not, since G-d took him." Both halves of the verse are puzzling; what do they mean? Onkelos answers these questions by translating, "And Chanoch went in the fear of Hashem, and he was not existing [stopped living], since Hashem caused him to die." Chanoch went with Hashem by fearing Him, and he stopped living because Hashem took him away by causing him to die. The *Sifsei Chachamim*[29] says that *Rashi* is bothered: Chanoch, who went with Hashem, was a *tzaddik*, so why did Hashem cause him to die? *Rashi* answers that indeed, he was a *tzaddik*; however, he was liable to be easily persuaded by the *reshaim* of the generation to do bad. Therefore, Hashem hurried to remove him before his allotted time to die. Also, for this reason it states "*v'einenu*—and he wasn't," meaning that he wasn't in the world to complete his years. Although he did not fill up his complete years, Hashem took him away for his benefit, so that he should remain a *tzaddik*.

Chazal say that Chanoch was a shoemaker, and with each stitch he would sew, he designated his entire intent to Hashem. Rav Dessler[30] explains in the name of Rav Yisrael Salanter that he focused on making good, strong stitches in order to produce proper shoes, so that whoever wore them could benefit. He followed Hashem's *middah* of helping and benefiting others, attaching himself to Hashem's ways.

Rabbeinu Bachya and the *Chizkuni* quote Onkelos differently: "ואיתוהי ארי לא אמית יתיה ה'—And he was existing, since Hashem did not cause him to die." The *Yein Hatov* references *Targum Yonasan* to explain, who translates, "Chanoch served in honesty before Hashem, and behold, he was not with the dwellers of the land, since he fainted and ascended to the Heavens with a saying from before [because of] Hashem, and he was called Matat-ron the *safra rabba*." We find the words "*safra rabba*" in Onkelos describing Moshe Rabbeinu as well.[31] The *Maharsha*[32]

| | |
|---|---|
| ח | 29 |
| מכתב מאליהו א קונטרוס החסד פ"ג וע' מדרש תלפיות ערך חנוך | 30 |
| דברים לג, כא | 31 |
| סוטה יג: | 32 |

explains that Moshe was the "great scribe," as he wrote the Torah, or he was the "great counter," as he counted Yisrael several times. Thus, Chanoch was either a great scribe or counter. Rabbeinu Bachya explains that Chanoch's body and name were changed. His flesh transformed into a torch of fire and his name became Matat-ron. This process was a great elevation and reward for him, with nothing else comparable to it. Similarly, Onkelos understands that since Chanoch feared Hashem, He took him up to the Heavens alive, as was done with Eliyahu.

Rabbeinu Bachya says we only find the attribute of "going with Hashem" by *tzaddikim*, such as Chanoch, Noach, and Avraham. All of them were able to understand how the sun functions and recognize its great strength, which reflects Hashem's rulership, that He is master of all. The *pasuk* states that Chanoch lived exactly 365 years, the number of days in the solar year. He was a *tzaddik* and was able to understand the greatness of the sun, recognizing that there is an elevated cause for everything. All the constellations extend from the *ohr Elyon*. This is hinted at when the Torah describes Chanoch's days as *"va'yehi"* rather than *"va'yihiyu,"* as used for the previous generations. The word *"va'yehi"* hints to *"yehi ohr...va'yehi ohr*—there shall be light...and there was light."

Rabbeinu Bachya says that Onkelos hints to Gan Eden and the afterlife of a soul which continuously exists. This world is temporary, and there will be a future world which will last forever.

May we firmly fear Hashem and merit endless years!

# Noach

## DID NOACH DESERVE TO BE SAVED FROM THE MABUL?

אֵלֶּה תּוֹלְדֹת נֹחַ נֹחַ אִישׁ צַדִּיק תָּמִים הָיָה
בְּדֹרֹתָיו אֶת הָאֱלֹקִים הִתְהַלֶּךְ נֹחַ (ו, ט)

אִלֵּין תּוֹלְדָת נֹחַ נֹחַ גְּבַר זַכַּאי שְׁלִים הֲוָה בְּדָרוֹהִי בְּדַחְלְתָא דַיְיָ הַלֵּיךְ נֹחַ

*These are the products of Noach; Noach, a man who is innocent and complete in his generations. Noach walked in the fear of Hashem.*

The *pasuk* states, "אלה תולדות נח נח איש צדיק תמים." *Rashi* explains the placement of the words נח איש צדיק, that since the Torah mentions Noach, it talks about his praise. *Rashi* brings another explanation: this teaches that the main products of the *tzaddik* are his good deeds. Both explanations of *Rashi* understand that the *pasuk* is describing how special Noach and his good deeds were.

Onkelos translates the word "tzaddik" as "zakai, innocent." The *Ramban* explains that "zakai" means innocent from punishment. This is as it states, "והצדיקו את הצדיק והרשיעו את הרשע—And they will make the *tzaddik* innocent and make the *rasha* liable." The Brisker Rav[1] adds that this refers to when there are more merits than sins by a person or the world; the merits will tip the scale, resulting in a judgment for good. Or, vice versa, if the entire world has more liability than merit, the *tzaddik's* minute sins will join everyone else's sins, and he, too, will be punished with them. The Torah also describes Noach as "*tamim*," which Onkelos translates as "*shelim*—complete": Noach was complete in his righteousness. The Brisker Rav teaches that this adds that one who is a complete

---

1   חי' מרן הגרי"ז הלוי החדשות על תנ"ך ואגדה

*tzaddik* won't be judged with everyone else for bad, since he is totally separate from them. According to this, the first *pasuk* of the parashah teaches a more pertinent detail to the story that follows: Noach was innocent, complete, and worthy of being saved from the judgment of the *Dor HaMabul*!

This is hinted to in the *Hoshanos* of Hoshana Rabbah, in which we find, "למען תמים בדורותיו הנמלט ברוב צדקותיו מוצל משטף בבא מבול מים"—Because of Noach, who was complete in his generation, who escaped with his many merits, who was saved from the torrent, with the coming of the *Mabul* water." We see that Noach indeed deserved to be saved through his merits.

The Brisker Rav points out that the last *pasuk* in *Parashas Bereishis* states, "ונח מצא חן בעיני ה'"—And Noach found grace in the eyes of Hashem." Onkelos translates, "ונח אשכח רחמין קדם ה'"—And Noach found mercy before Hashem." (When Onkelos translates the *reish* of רחם with a *patach*, it means "mercy/grace," whereas with a *sheva*, it means "love."[2]) This implies, as the Gemara[3] teaches, that there was also a decree against Noach, but he found grace in the eyes of Hashem; Noach was not deserving of being saved as a result of his own merit. Rabbi Moshe Sheinerman[4] answered this with the *Seforno*: Noach himself was fitting to be saved since he was a complete *tzaddik*. However, since he didn't teach others to follow Hashem, he was unable to save others—the rest of his family, who were not described as complete *tzaddikim*. His family needed grace from Hashem to be saved. Alternatively, as the *Ramban* explains, Noach found grace, or mercy, despite everyone else that Hashem found to be acting in a disappointing way. The rest of the *pasuk* explains why he was good before Hashem: he was a *tzaddik tamim*.

The *pasuk* ends, "את האלוקים התהלך נח"—Noach walked with Hashem," meaning, he fulfilled the will of Hashem. By Avraham, however,

---

2  מעט צרי
3  סנהדרין קח.
4  אהל משה

a different language is used:[5] *"his'haleich le'fanai*—walk before Me," and[6] *"asher his'halachti le'fanav*—that which I walked before Him." Why does it state by Noach that he walked *with* Hashem, whereas by Avraham it states that he walked *before* Hashem?

*Rashi* answers that Noach needed a support to assist him, so Hashem walked with him to help direct him on the proper path. However, Avraham strengthened himself and went on his own without any assistance. The *Sifsei Chachamim*[7] explains that Avraham went among *reshaim* and rebuked them to change their ways and to serve Hashem. Since Avraham was a complete *tzaddik*, he was not afraid that he might learn from their bad ways, and therefore he did not need assistance; he walked before Hashem. However, Noach separated from people so as not to learn from their ways; since he was not such a great *tzaddik*, he went with Hashem alone, not with people.

Onkelos translates *"es haElokim"* differently: "Noach walked in the fear of Hashem." My good friend Rabbi Elchonon Sosne explained that he went in the way that was preferred by Hashem. Or, Onkelos can be explained as the *Ramban*: on his own, Noach feared Hashem alone and was constantly attached to Him. He was not persuaded by magic, sorcery, or anything else. The *Ramban* suggests that Noach received a prophecy that taught him the way which Hashem chose and that is how he went.

The *Nefesh HaGer* points out that regarding Avraham it states, *"His'haleich le'fanai,"* which Onkelos translates as "and serve before Me [*p'lach kadamai*]," and it states, *"Asher his'halachti le'fanav,"* which Onkelos translates as "that I served before Him [*di ph'lachis kadamohi*]." He does not translate, as he does by Noach, "went in the fear of Hashem." The *Nefesh HaGer* explains that Avraham was describing his own actions, so Onkelos translates, "that I served before Him." Also, Hashem commanded Avraham to serve him, so Onkelos translates as

---

יי א,   5

כו, מ   6

ד   7

"serve before Me." Regarding Noach, where the *pasuk* praises him about his greatness, he translates that "he went in the fear of Hashem."

Noach was in a *dor* in which everyone was corrupt, yet he remained a *yerei Shamayim*, so he deserved to be saved. This is comparable to what *Avi Mori* said in the name of Rav Avigdor Miller: there may be many people walking in Times Square, but if one person is thinking about Hashem, Hashem shines a spotlight on that person and shows affection to him, making him unique and different from everyone else.

We are in a world with challenges to our *neshamos* and our bodies. May we learn from Noach to fear Hashem and nothing else, and may we merit protection!

## WHICH BEINGS CORRUPTED THEIR WAYS, AND HOW?

### כִּי הִשְׁחִית כָּל בָּשָׂר אֶת דַּרְכּוֹ עַל הָאָרֶץ (ו, יב)

אֲרֵי חַבִּילוּ כָּל בִּסְרָא אֲנָשׁ יָת אוֹרְחֵיהּ עַל אַרְעָא

*Since all the flesh of people wounded [corrupted] its way on the land.*

### קֵץ כָּל בָּשָׂר בָּא לְפָנַי...וְהִנְנִי מַשְׁחִיתָם אֶת הָאָרֶץ (ו, יג)

קִצָּא דְּכָל בִּסְרָא עָאל לְקֳדָמַי...וְהָאֲנָא מְחַבֵּילְהוֹן עִם אַרְעָא

*The end of all flesh entered before Me...and behold,*
*I will wound [destroy] them with the land.*

### לְשַׁחֵת כָּל בָּשָׂר אֲשֶׁר בּוֹ רוּחַ חַיִּים (ו, יז)

לְחַבָּלָא כָּל בִּסְרָא דְּבֵיהּ רוּחָא דְחַיֵּי

*To wound [destroy] all flesh that has in it a spirit of life.*

The *pasuk* states, "כִּי הִשְׁחִית כל בשר את דרכו על הארץ—Since all flesh corrupted its way on the land." *Rashi* explains that "*kal basar*—all flesh" includes animals, wild animals, and birds who were mating with other species, and they were not staying within their own species. The last *pasuk* of *Parashas Bereishis* states, "אמחה...מאדם עד בהמה," which *Rashi* explains as well that the animals also corrupted their ways. Since both people and animals corrupted their ways, there was a decree to destroy the animals as well.

Onkelos translates *"kal basar"* as "all the flesh of people." The *Nefesh HaGer* explains Onkelos with the *Ramban*: it is as though it states *"kal adam—all man,"* as *basar* reflects *adam*. This implies that only people sinned, unlike *Rashi*. The *Me'at Tzari* teaches that Onkelos translates "השחית כל בשר את דרכו" as "all the flesh of people wounded [corrupted] its way [חבילו...ארחיה]," like it states by Onan,[8] "ושחת ארצה לבלתי נתן זרע לאחיו," which Onkelos translates as "and he would ruin his way [ומחבל אורחיה] so as not to cause offspring to exist for his brother," which refers to *"shich-vas zera l'vatalah—the laying of seed for naught."* Apparently, the *Dor HaMabul* was guilty of the same sin. This accords with the Gemara[9] that teaches that one who holds onto his male organ and urinates is as though he brought a *Mabul* to the world. *Rashi* explains that this was the *aveirah* which the *Dor HaMabul* transgressed, as it states, "כי השחית כל בשר."

Later, it states, "קץ כל בשר בא לפני...והנני משחיתם את הארץ," which Onkelos translates as, "The end of all flesh entered before Me...and behold I will wound [destroy] them with the land." He translates *"es"* as *"im—with,"* unlike *Rashi's* first explanation that it means "destroy them *from* the land." The *Me'at Tzari* explains Onkelos with Menachem ben Saruk: the word את is short for "אתו, with him." The *Nefesh HaGer* says that Onkelos, who translates *"with* the land," hints to *Rashi's* second explanation that the three *tefachim* which a plow digs into the ground became dissolved and obliterated. My *rebbi*, Rabbi Yissachar Landau, explained that this is because this area is connected to the actions of man, therefore, it too, was destroyed. Here, Onkelos translates the words *"kal basar"* literally, as "all flesh"; there was a decree against man, animals, birds, and the entire creation to be destroyed. Also, Onkelos translates "לשחת כל בשר אשר בו רוח חיים" as "to wound [destroy] all flesh which has in it a spirit of life." Why should the entire creation be destroyed because people acted corruptly?

---

8   לח,ט

9   נדה יג.

The *Re'em* answers in the name of *Rashi*[10] that since the entire world was created for man, once he is destroyed, for what purpose is the existence of the rest of creation?! The *Ohr Hatargum* says that in truth, only people are liable for punishment, not animals. Still, the animals were destroyed because the people, who were corrupt, were destroyed. There is no reason for animals to exist without people. The *Nefesh HaGer*[11] answers differently: The Gemara teaches that people took different species of animals and actively mismatched them, animals among other animals and among people. People instigated a sinful drive by mismatching them, causing them to ruin their ways. Man was the source of corruption, as it states, "Since all the flesh of people[12] corrupted its ways," but animals, birds, and the entire creation also became corrupt. Or, as the *Beis Halevi* explains, the actions which people do even among themselves affect and influence the nature of the world to do the same. Rabbi Moshe Sheinerman suggested a contemporary example of this: There are seagulls off the cost of California that mate improperly. This is because the local human residents act immorally, affecting them.[13] By Noach's generation, originally, only people acted with immorality and were corrupt. However, by doing so, they polluted the animals, birds, and the rest of creation, causing them to acquire a drive to sin.

From bad, we can derive good. Just as our actions affect the world for bad, even more so can they affect it for good. Rav Yisrael Salanter and the Chafetz Chaim taught that when a person learns Torah in one place, he is causing people far away not to assimilate. The Torah will influence them to become inspired to want to return to *Yiddishkeit* and fulfill Hashem's mitzvos.

May we recognize our importance in that the entire world was created for people. Our actions can influence everyone and everything accordingly!

---

10  ז,ו

11  ומהרש"א ומהר"ל

12  רמב"ן לעיל

13  N. Y. Times Nov. 23 1977

## WHAT DOES "B'ETZEM" REFLECT?

# בְּעֶצֶם הַיּוֹם הַזֶּה בָּא נֹחַ (ז, יג)

בִּכְרַן יוֹמָא הָדֵין עָאל נוֹחַ

*With the power of that day, Noach entered.*

The *pasuk* states, "בעצם היום הזה בא נח." What is the significance of the word "*b'etzem*"? *Rashi* explains that the people of Noach's generation claimed, "If we will see Noach and his family trying to enter the *teivah*, we won't let them go in, and even more, we will take hatchets and axes and break down the *teivah*." Hashem said, "I will bring them into the *teivah* in front of everyone, and we will see who will be correct." "*B'etzem*" refers to when the sun is at the top of the sky, during midday, when everyone can see. They will see Noach and his family entering the *teivah*, and they will not be able to stop them. *Rashi*[14] notes that Onkelos translates "*b'etzem*" as "*bichran*" (בכרן) and explains that it means "the appearance and brightness" of the day. The *Ramban*[15] brings another *girsa*: "*bikran*" (בקרן), which he explains means "with the power and strength" of that day. The *Ramban* says that the letters 'כ and 'ק are interchangeable. The word *keren* (קרן) means horn, which is the place of an animal's strength. Animals use their horns to fight off others and catch their prey. Similarly, this day had unique power and strength that in only one day, Noach's family and hundreds of thousands of animals, birds, and insects entered the *teivah*. Although naturally it should have taken days for everyone to enter the *teivah*, Hashem decreed for them all to go in on that day and performed a miracle that it should happen.

When B'nei Yisrael left of Mitzrayim, it states,[16] "בעצם היום הזה הוציא ה' את בני ישראל מארץ מצרים." *Rashi*[17] explains that the Egyptians said, "If we see that B'nei Yisrael are trying to leave Mitzrayim, we will not allow them

---

14  מנחות ה:
15  ויקרא כג, כח
16  שמות יב, נא
17  דברים לב, מח

to, and even more, we will take swords and weaponry and kill them."
Hashem said, "I will take them out at midday; whoever has power to
protest, come and protest." Onkelos translates differently: "Hashem
took out B'nei Yisrael from the land of Mitzrayim with the power [בכרן]
of that day."

The *Ramban* explains that it means that in such a short time, all
600,000 men, plus the women and children, plus all their belongings,
came together at Ramses to leave Mitzrayim. Naturally, it would have
taken days to organize such a multitude; however, Hashem decreed for
B'nei Yisrael to leave Mitzrayim on that day, and performed a miracle
to make it happen.

At the end of *Parashas Haazinu*,[18] Hashem commanded Moshe to go up
to Har Ha'avrim, Har Nevo, *"b'etzem ha'yom ha'zeh,"* and there Moshe
would die and be buried. B'nei Yisrael said, "If we sense that Moshe will
die, we won't let him. A person who took us out of Mitzrayim, split the
sea, brought down *mahn* and *slav*, brought up a wellspring, and gave
us the Torah—we will not let him." Hashem said, "I will bring him in
at midday..." Onkelos translates differently: "Ascend to Har Nevo with
the power [בכרן] of that day." This day had unique power and strength
that in one day Moshe said the *shirah*, wrote it down, taught it to B'nei
Yisrael, said *Parashas V'zos Haberachah*, and ascended to the top of the
mountain. In just one day, Hashem miraculously made Moshe able to
accomplish many things that would take an ordinary person many days
to accomplish.

The same way that on certain days, Hashem decrees for miracles to
occur, so too, Hashem decrees for each person, on each day, his situation and attitude.

The *Sefer Hayashar*[19] writes that there is a phenomenon called *yemei
ahavah* and *yemei sinah*—days of love and days of hatred. Some days,
a person has an easy time serving Hashem, such as when one wakes
up rested and happy. He anticipates the accomplishments of that day

18   שם מח-נ
19   השער הששי

and has a feeling of love and closeness to Hashem. On such days, he is meant to put in effort and grab the opportunity to reach high levels of *avodas Hashem* and cherish it. Other days, a person wakes up tired and grumpy, angry and upset. Then, his *avodah* is to be extra careful with how he deals with people, and if he does so successfully, he is victorious with his challenge.

The same is true with challenges in learning. Sometimes, a person sits down to learn and everything is understood. His challenge is to make use of the opportunity, cherish it, and accomplish as much as he can. Yet, other times, he sees clouds and darkness, and hasn't the faintest idea of what is going on. His challenge is not to give up and put in as much effort to understand as best as he can. My Rosh Yeshiva said that one will notice in his reviewing that he will understand the *sugyos* which were originally difficult better than the *sugyos* which were smooth the first time, because of the extra effort he put in.

May we recognize Hashem's daily decrees and be victorious over our daily challenges!

## DOES "SHERETZ" MEAN "SOMETHING LOW AS A CREEPY-CRAWLY," "WHICH MOVES," OR "BORN"?

### וְכֹל אֲשֶׁר רֹמֵשׂ עַל הָאֲדָמָה (ו, ח)

וְכֹל דְּרָחֵישׁ עַל אַרְעָא

*And all that moves on the land.*

### וְשָׁרְצוּ בָאָרֶץ (ח, יז)

וְיִתְיַלְּדוּן בְּאַרְעָא

*And they shall cause to be born in the land.*

### שִׁרְצוּ בָאָרֶץ וּרְבוּ בָהּ (ט, ז)

אִתְיַלָּדוּ בְּאַרְעָא וּסְגוֹ בֵּיהּ

*Cause to have been born in the land and increase in it.*

# כֹּל צִפּוֹר כָּל כָּנָף (ז, יד)

כֹּל צְפַר כָּל דְּפָרַח

*Every bird, all that flies.*

In *Parashas Bereishis*, the *pasuk* states:[20] "Hashem said, ישרצו המים שרץ נפש חיה ועוף יעופף על הארץ." What does *yishretzu* and *sheretz* mean? *Rashi* explains that a *sheretz* is anything which is alive and is not high above the ground, something low, short-footed, which[21] is seen as crawling and moving. For example, by birds: flies, hornets,[22] gnats, and grasshoppers. By *shekatzim*: ants, beetles, and worms. By animals: a weasel, mouse, *chomet*, and the like, and so too, by fish. The *pasuk* means, "The water shall create short [low] creatures which seem as crawling and moving, and birds."

The *Ramban*[23] is bothered by the following: after Noach came out of the *teivah*, Hashem said, "שרצו בארץ ורבו בה." How does "low creeping creatures and crawlers" refer to people? Onkelos does not have this difficulty, since he translates "ישרצו המים שרץ..." differently: "The water shall move which moves [create moving creatures] who have the soul of life and the birds shall fly over the land [ירחשון מיא רחש נפשא חיתא ועופא יפרח על ארעא]." He translates ישרצו...שרץ as "shall move which moves [ירחשון...רחש]," just as he translates "*ha'romeses*" as "that moves [*d'rachasha*]." The *Ramban* explains that Onkelos translates "*sheritzah*" as movement, since *sheratzim* continuously move around. The word "*sheretz*" is comprised of two words, "*she'hu ratz*—that it runs," since they continuously move around. They are also called "*remes*" since they are "*romeis*," they move around on the land. The Mishnah[24] teaches that "*marcheshes*" is "deep frying," and its actions are "*rochshim*." The *Bartenura* explains that *rochesh* is as it states "*romeis al ha'aretz*," which

---

20  כ,א
21  ויקרא יא, י
22  שם כ
23  כ,א
24  מנחות ה, ח

Onkelos translates as "*d'racheish*—that moves." The oil moves around inside the frying pan.

In *Parashas Shemini*, it states:[25] "וכל השרץ השרץ על הארץ שקץ הוא לא יאכל," which Onkelos translates as, "And all which move that moves [*richsha d'racheish*] on the land, it is detestable, it shall not be eaten." The word "*ha'sheretz*" is a noun, which he translates as *richsha*, which move, and the word "*ha'shoretz*" is a verb, which he translates as "*d'racheish*—that moves."

The *Ramban* says that when it states "*sheretz ha'of*" by birds, it refers to flying creatures with four feet, such as flies and gnats. These flying creatures have their feet, with which they move around, close to the ground, as *sheratzim*. Whereas birds which only have two feet are called in *Parashas Bereishis*, "*of kanaf*—winged bird" since their main movement is with their wings, to fly. Onkelos hints to this by translating[26] "*sheretz ha'of*" as "which moves [*richsha*] of the bird," which refers to flying creatures with four feet. Whereas "ואת כל עוף כנף" regarding birds with two feet, he translates[27] as "and every bird that flies [וית כל עופא דפרח]," since the main movement of birds with two feet is by flying, unlike *Parashas Va'eschanan*,[28] where he translates "*tzippor kanaf*" as "*tzippor gapa*—winged bird." In this parashah, it mentions that all the animals and birds entered the *teivah*, and it states, "כל צפור כל כנף." *Rashi* explains that this is one point, a bird of any type of wing, which includes grasshoppers, also entered into the *teivah*. Here again, Onkelos translates differently: "every bird, all that flies."

In *Parashas Va'eira*, it states,[29] "*V'sharatz ha'ye'or tzfarde'im*," which Onkelos translates as "and the river shall raise[30] frogs [וירבי נהרא ערדעניא]." The *Lechem V'Simlah* says that Onkelos does not translate "*v'yasgi*—and increase," or with "*rachash*—crawlers," rather "*vi'rabei*," which means

---

25   ויקרא יא, מא

26   ויקרא יא, כ

27   א, כא

28   דברים ה, יז

29   שמות ז, כח

30   Or "make great"

"raise." By the creation of *sheratzim*, Onkelos translates "*yirchashun*," which reflects a new creation of crawlers, whereas by the *makkah* of the frogs, they will be nurtured and be brought out from the river.

When Noach left the *teivah*, it states, "*V'shartzu va'aretz*," which Onkelos translates as "and they shall cause to be born [*v'yisyaldun*] in the land." And it states, "שרצו בארץ ורבו בה," which Onkelos translates as "cause to have been born [*isyaladu*] in the land and increase in it." The *Ramban* explains that the word "*sheretz*" by people is a borrowed term from crawlers. Also, in *Parashas Shemos*, it states,[31] "ובני ישראל פרו וישרצו," here, too, the *lashon sheretz* is used by people. *Rashi* explains that "*va'yishretzu*" teaches that they gave birth to six babies in one pregnancy. The *Sifsei Chachamim*[32] explains in the name of the *Yalkut* that they reproduced like the *sheretz* mouse, which has the largest amount of reproduction of all eight *sheratzim*:[33] it can have up to six babies at once. Onkelos translates differently: "And B'nei Yisrael became many, and they caused to be born [*v'isyaladu*]." Here, too, he translates "*va'yishretzu*" caus-atively: "and they caused to be born many children." Why does Onkelos not translate here and in *Parashas Shemos* with "*rachash*—to move," as elsewhere?

The *Nefesh HaGer* answers that "*sheretz*" means "movers," as he translates by animals, flying creatures, fish, and insects. However, in this parashah and in *Parashas Shemos*, the *pasuk* speaks about people. Onkelos translates "cause to have been born" in an honorable way for their children. Children are not comparable to other living beings in the world. They are elevated and unique, and their reproduction is signifi-cant. Therefore, Onkelos changes the *lashon* used for the reproduction of people from that of the *lashon* used for the reproduction of animals, flying creatures, fish, and insects.

May we recognize the uniqueness of people's reproduction over all other beings!

---

31  שמות א, ז

32  ח

33  ע' נה"ג בשם מדרש י"א ו' וי"א י"ב וי"א ס' כמו העקרב

# WHY WAS CHAM PUNISHED, WHAT DID SHEM MERIT MORE THAN YEFES, AND WHY?

## וַיַּרְא חָם...וַיַּגֵּד לִשְׁנֵי אֶחָיו בַּחוּץ (ט, כב)

וַחֲזָא חָם...וְחַוִּי לִתְרֵין אֲחוֹהִי בְּשׁוּקָא

*And Cham…saw…and he told his two brothers in the marketplace.*

## וַיִּקַּח שֵׁם וָיֶפֶת אֶת הַשִּׂמְלָה (ט, כג)

וּנְסִיב שֵׁם וָיֶפֶת יָת כְּסוּתָא

*And Shem and Yefes took the garment.*

The *pasuk* states that Noach drank wine, became intoxicated, and was uncovered in the tent. Cham saw and told his two brothers outside. Onkelos translates the word *"ba'chutz"* as "in the marketplace." The *Ramban*[34] explains that Onkelos means that he publicly told his brothers about their father so as to make fun of him.

It states, "וַיִּקַּח שֵׁם וַיֶפֶת אֶת הַשִּׂמְלָה...וַיֵּלְכוּ אֲחוֹרַנִּית וַיְכַסּוּ אֵת עֶרְוַת אֲבִיהֶם"—And Shem and Yefes took the garment…and they walked backwards, and they covered the *ervah* of their father." Onkelos translates *"va'yikach"* in singular as the literal meaning. *Rashi* points out that singular form teaches that Shem strengthened himself for the mitzvah more than Yefes, therefore, Hashem rewarded him with a garment of tzitzis, whereas Yefes was rewarded with burial.

How does the reward of Shem and Yefes correspond *middah k'neged middah* to their righteous act? And how does the reward for Shem reflect his alacrity to do the mitzvah?

The *Re'em* explains that both Shem and Yefes covered their father with a garment, and therefore they received the reward of also being covered with a garment. Since he was first, Shem received the mitzvah of tzitzis, which the *Maharal* adds is an honor to the body and *neshamah*. Yefes, however, received clothing for the dead to be buried in, which the *Maharal* adds is an honor to the body alone. Cham, who did not cover his father, rather disgraced his body and soul, was punished that his future descendants would be left uncovered, a disgrace to both the body and soul. I heard in the name of Rav Shach that by quickly doing the mitzvah, Shem infused the mitzvah of covering his father with life, and therefore he received a reward with the living, whereas Yefes, who was slower to accomplish the mitzvah, received the reward of being buried, as dead people are stationary.

*Rashi* explains that Shem merited the mitzvah of tzitzis because he covered his father. However, the Gemara[35] teaches that because Avraham said to the king of Sedom that he wouldn't take anything from him "אם מחוט ועד שרוך נעל—If from a thread until a shoelace," he merited the mitzvah of a thread of *techeiles* and straps of tefillin. The reference to *techeiles* seemingly includes the mitzvah of tzitzis; if so, how are we to understand this?

The *Maharal* answers that Shem and Avraham joined together to merit the mitzvah of tzitzis. The *Re'em* answers that there are two independent parts to the mitzvah of tzitzis: the white strings and the string of *techeiles*. Shem merited the *tallis* with white strings, and Avraham merited the *techeiles*. Why was Avraham specifically rewarded with the *techeiles*? The Gemara teaches that *techeiles* reminds us of Hashem, as it is a greenish-blue color which reflects the sea, which, in turn, reflects the heavens, which, in turn, reflects the throne of Hashem. So too, Avraham said, "I will not achieve richness from the king of Sedom, but, rather, from Hashem, to Whom everything belongs." Since the *techeiles* reminds us of Hashem, Who is in control of everything, Avraham merited this mitzvah.

*Bereishis Rabbah*[36] comments on the words about tzitzis, *"pesil techeiles,"* that Onkelos translates as *"chuta dis'chilsa*—a thread of *techeiles,"* hinting to the *chut* of *techeiles* that Avraham mentioned to the king of Sedom.

May Hashem help us be alert and ready to fulfill His Torah and mitzvos with alacrity and life!

---

# Lech Lecha

## WHAT DO WE HAVE BECAUSE OF TZADDIKIM?

### וְנִבְרְכוּ בְךָ כֹּל מִשְׁפְּחֹת הָאֲדָמָה (יב, ג)

וְיִתְבָּרְכוּן בְּדִילָךְ כֹּל זַרְעֲיַת אַרְעָא

*All the offspring of the land will be blessed because of you.*

The *pasuk* states, "ונברכו בך כל משפחות האדמה," which *Rashi* explains to mean that a person will say to his son, "You shall be like Avraham." Onkelos translates differently: "All the offspring of the land will be blessed because of you." Similarly, it states[1] about Avraham and Yitzchak, "והתברכו בזרעך כל גויי הארץ," which Onkelos translates as, "And all the nations of the land will be blessed because of your children [ויתברכון בדיל בנך כל עממי ארעא]." And it states about Yaakov,[2] "ונברכו בך כל משפחות האדמה ובזרעך," which Onkelos translates as, "And all the offspring of the land will be blessed because of you and because of your sons [ויתברכון בדילך כל זרעית ארעא ובדיל בנך]." The *Nesinah LaGer* explains with *Bereishis Rabbah*[3] that rain and dew fall in the merit of the Avos. In this way, the whole world benefits from their righteousness. The *Eitz Yosef* adds that the Midrash brings rain and dew as examples, but, in truth, all blessing will come in the merit of the Avos. The *Bereishis Rabbah*[4] brings that the *tzaddikim* bring the Shechinah down into the world. The *D'rashos HaRan*[5] says that a *tzaddik* is like a pipe, a conduit, through which Hashem showers an abundance of good on the world.

---

1. כב, יח: כו, ד
2. כח, יד
3. פ' לט, יב
4. פ' יט, ז
5. הדרוש השמיני

The Gemara[6] brings different examples which reflect the merit of *tzaddikim*. When Rabbi Elyashiv died, robbers dug seventy tunnels in Neharde'a to steal. *Rashi* explains that while Rabbi Elyashiv was alive, robbers did not come to steal and people were protected in his merit. Only after he died, when his merit left and there was no more protection, did the robbers come to steal. When Rabbi Mesharshia died, the palm trees became loaded with thorns. While Rabbi Mesharshia was alive, his merit protected the palm trees from growing thorns. When Rabbi Avahu died, the pillars of Keisari dripped tears. The *Maharsha* explains that the *tzaddikim* are the pillars which hold up the world. When they die, the world is missing its pillars and it is fitting to cry, as with Rabbi Avahu. When Rabbi Yosi died, the gutters of Tzippori flowed with blood. The *Maharsha* explains that while he was alive, in his merit, there were pipes of mercy which flowed from above, and when he died, it changed to flow blood, reflecting *middas ha'din* being brought into the world. When Rabbi Yaakov died, stars were seen during the day. The *Maharsha* explains that stars are in the sky during the day as well, however, when the sun shines, it lights up the sky, so we cannot see the stars. On the day that Rabbi Yaakov died, the day darkened earlier so that the stars were able to be seen in the sky like at night.

The Gemara[7] teaches that after Hordus killed all the *Chachamim*, leaving only Bava ben Buta, whom he blinded, he wanted to do *teshuvah*. Hordus asked Bava ben Buta for advice, and he answered that since Hordus extinguished the light of the world and blinded the light of the world, he should be involved in rebuilding the Beis Hamikdash, which generates light for the world and is called "the desire of your eyes." This indicates that *tzaddikim* are considered the light and the eyes of the generation. Their Torah shines into the world and their eyes reflect advice for the generation.

---

6    מו"ק כה:

7    ב"ב ג:-ה.

The Gemara[8] writes that an *apikores* is one who says, "How do the rabbis help us? They read *pesukim* for themselves and they learn for themselves." *Rashi* explains that the people who say this do not know that the world continuously exists because of *tzaddikim*. The Gemara says that this is worse than just *apikorsus*; it is "*megaleh panim baTorah*— denying that which is written in Tanach." He denies that which is written, "אם לא בריתי יומם ולילה חקות שמים וארץ לא שמתי—If not for My covenant of learning My Torah by day and night, I would not have set up the heavens and earth." *Rashi* explains that *tzaddikim* benefit the heaven and earth and enable their existence. The Gemara adds that they also deny that which states, "ונשאתי לכל המקום בעבורם." Avraham davened to Hashem to save the cities of Sedom and Amorah on behalf of the *tzaddikim* who potentially resided there. We see that *tzaddikim* help us tremendously.

May we recognize the enormous benefit of our *tzaddikim*, and may we be blessed in their merit!

## WHAT IS CONSIDERED "MAKING A SOUL"?

### וַיִּקַּח אַבְרָם...וְאֶת הַנֶּפֶשׁ אֲשֶׁר עָשׂוּ בְחָרָן (יב, ה)

וּדְבַר אַבְרָם...וְיָת נַפְשָׁתָא דְּשַׁעְבִּידוּ לְאוֹרַיְתָא בְּחָרָן

*And Avram led...and the souls that they*
*subjugated to the Torah in Charan.*

The *pasuk* states, "And Avram led Sarai his wife, and Lot his nephew, and all the possessions that they acquired, ואת הנפש אשר עשו בחרן—and the souls that they made in Charan." *Rashi* first explains that "*asu*" refers to acquisitions. Here, it refers to the people that they bought, which were slaves and maidservants.

The *Bereishis Rabbah*[9] asks: if the entire world would gather together to create just one gnat, they would be unable to insert a *neshamah* into it. What, then, is the meaning of "and the souls that they made"?

*Rashi* explains that Avraham and Sarah reached out to inspire many people and bring them underneath the wings of the Shechinah, close to Hashem. They influenced people with their *chessed* and taught people about the world's Creator, Hashem, bringing the awareness of Hashem to many people. Avraham converted the men and Sarah converted the women, as it states "*asu*," in the plural form, "they made." Since Avraham and Sarah caused people to leave idolatry, recognize the truth, and believe in Hashem, the Torah presents it is as though they made these people and created them anew—"*ha'nefesh asher asu.*"

Onkelos translates "ואת הנפש אשר עשו" as "and the souls that they subjugated to the Torah." These people are considered created anew because they were taught Torah. This is as the Gemara[10] teaches: Reish Lakish said: Anyone who teaches the son of his friend Torah is as though he made him, as it states, "ואת הנפש אשר עשו." *Rashi* says this is derived from Onkelos, who translates, "that they subjugated to the Torah." The Torah treats one who taught another Torah as if he made him.

The Gemara[11] teaches in the name of the *Tanna D'bei Eliyahu* that the total amount of the years of the world is six thousand: two thousand years of emptiness, two thousand years of Torah, and two thousand years are the days of Mashiach. When Avraham Avinu was fifty-two years old, the two thousand years of Torah started, as it states, "ואת הנפש אשר עשו בחרן," which Onkelos translates as "that they subjugated to the Torah."

Why, indeed, does the *pasuk* consider the teaching of Torah as creating someone anew? The *Maharsha* explains that before a person acquires the knowledge of Torah, he is no different from an animal. This is hinted to in the *pasuk*, "ומותר האדם מן הבהמה אין"—The superiority of a person

---

9    פ' לט, יד

10    סנהדרין צט:

11    ע"ז ט. ורש"י

over an animal is nothing." By learning Torah, which is the purpose of the creation of mankind, one separates himself from the animals and transforms himself into becoming a "person." Avraham and Sarah taught people the knowledge of Hashem, thereby elevating them from being in the group of animals, to being in the group of people.

May we inspire and influence others with the awareness of Hashem and teach His Torah to create new *nefashos*!

## IS "HARIMOSI YADI EL HASHEM" AN "OATH" OR "DAVENING"?

הֲרִמֹתִי יָדִי אֶל ה' קֵל עֶלְיוֹן קֹנֵה שָׁמַיִם וָאָרֶץ (יד, כב)

אֲרֵימִית יְדַי (יְדִי) בִּצְלוֹ קֳדָם יְיָ קֵל עִלָּאָה דְּקִנְיָנֵיהּ שְׁמַיָּא וְאַרְעָא

*I have raised my hands (hand) in prayer before Hashem, Keil, the most elevated, that to Him is the acquisitions of the heavens and the earth [Owner of the heavens and the earth].*

After Avraham won the battle against the kings, the king of Sedom said to Avraham, "תֶּן לִי הַנֶּפֶשׁ וְהָרְכֻשׁ קַח לָךְ—Give me the people, and take for yourself the possessions." Avraham responded, "הֲרִמֹתִי יָדִי אֶל ה' קֵל עֶלְיוֹן קֹנֵה שָׁמַיִם וָאָרֶץ." *Rashi* explains that "*harimosi yadi*" means, "I shall lift up my hand in affirmation of an oath to Hashem, *Keil Elyon*, who acquires the heavens and the earth by making it." The word "*harimosi*" is in present tense. Avraham swore to the king of Sedom by lifting up his hand and said, "אִם מִחוּט וְעַד שְׂרוֹךְ נַעַל וְאִם אֶקַּח מִכֹּל אֲשֶׁר לָךְ וְלֹא תֹאמַר אֲנִי הֶעֱשַׁרְתִּי אֶת אַבְרָם—If from a thread until a shoelace, if I will take from anything belonging to you, and you shall not say, 'I made Avram rich.'" The *Ramban* brings support for this from the *Sifri*, who says that we find by all *tzaddikim* that they make an oath against their inclination so as not to do something wrong. The oath binds them to keep restricted to the will of Hashem.

The *Hakesav V'Hakabbalah* asks: Were the possessions so important in the eyes of Avraham that he needed to swear to strengthen himself in order to hold back from taking them? Is this not an oath in vain for someone as great as Avraham? My good friend Rabbi Elchonon Sosne answered with an idea from Rav Moshe Feinstein:[12] although it is obvious that stealing is *assur*, one may forget, since he doesn't pay attention to the concept, as it is assumed that he will be careful. However, *tzaddikim* will not rely on their righteousness, and instead they will continuously pay attention so as not to transgress a sin. So too, Avraham swore to cause himself to remember continuously that he is also bound by an oath, and in this way, he will always be reminded not to take what isn't meant for him to have.

Onkelos translates the *pasuk* differently: "I have raised up my hands with davening before Hashem, *Keil*, the most elevated, that to Him is the acquisitions of the heavens and the earth [Owner of the heavens and the earth]." Onkelos translates "ידי" as "*y'dai*—hands," plural, not as the literal singular translation, since it used to be common for a person to daven by raising up both of his hands to Hashem. Others are *gores* "*y'di*—hand," singular, as it is in the *pasuk*. Onkelos translates "*harimosi*, I have raised up," in the past tense. Avraham said, "There was an earlier time when I already raised up my hands to Hashem with davening." Onkelos understands that Avraham did not need to swear in order to hold himself back from taking anything from the king of Sedom. When did Avraham raise up his hands to daven to Hashem, and what was the purpose of doing so?

The *Nefesh HaGer* explains that Avraham said, "I davened to Hashem before going to battle against the four kings to save Lot. I said to Hashem, 'I accepted responsibility to save Lot, and I have aroused mercy to rescue him. My entire intent in going to war is to save him and there is no personal benefit. I know that it is completely in Your hands to be able to accomplish this mission, to make me victorious against the mighty four kings; please save me.'" Therefore, after Avraham was victorious, he said to the king of Sedom, "I will not take any booty from you, just as I davened to Hashem." The *Ramban* adds that Avraham said, "I davened to Hashem, and my palms were spread out toward the Heavens,

---

whether I will take something from you"—meaning, so Hashem shall do to me if I will take anything. The *Me'at Tzari* explains this to mean that Avraham said, "If I were to take anything from you, bad would befall me, so I am definitely not taking anything."

The Gemara[13] teaches from Rabbi Yochanan that Avraham Avinu was punished that his children were subjected to Mitzrayim for 210 years because he stopped people from entering beneath the wings of the Shechinah. *Rashi* explains that he should have converted the captives and influenced them to come close to Hashem. Instead, Avraham returned them to the king of Sedom. The *Maharsha* adds that although the king of Sedom asked for the people, Avraham should have refused. He acquired the captives from *hefker,* and they belonged to him, so he should have kept them. Although Avraham did not want to take anything from the king of Sedom, he should have taken the captives and brought them close to Hashem. We see from here that one who is in a position to help others come close to Hashem is responsible to do so and will be held accountable.

## HOW IS THE SHEMESH A SHAMASH?

### וַיְהִי הַשֶּׁמֶשׁ לָבוֹא (טו, יב)

וַהֲוָה שִׁמְשָׁא לְמֵיעַל

*And the sun was entering [setting].*

### וַיְהִי הַשֶּׁמֶשׁ בָּאָה (טו, יז)

וַהֲוָה שִׁמְשָׁא עָאלַת

*And the sun had entered [set].*

The *pasuk* states, "Va'yehi ha'shemesh la'vo," which Onkelos translates as "And the sun was entering [setting]." A bit later, it states, "Va'yehi

---

*ha'shemesh ba'ah*," which Onkelos translates as "And the sun had entered [set]." The *Meshech Chochmah* says that until this parashah, the sun was called the "*maor ha'gadol*—the great luminary." When Avraham came to the land of Charan, he learned that the sun was made by Hashem and functions by serving Him, so he called it "*shemesh*," similar to "*shamash*, servant." The sun must exist and function by fulfilling its role because of its creator, as it constantly rises in the east and sets in the west, and it serves to do exactly as commanded. The sun is only a שמש, a servant, to serve its creator. From this point on, it is called שמש, like a *shamash* in *shul*, meaning, an attendant who serves its master. Avraham called the sun שמש, which is, in Aramaic, "ישמשונה," as it states in the Aramaic of Navi Daniel. In *lashon hakodesh*, however, a servant is called *meshareis*, and his service is called *sheirus*.

Chazal teach that Avraham looked into the world and recognized that there is a master planner behind everything. The *Chovos Halevavos*[14] illustrates with a *mashal*: an oil painter takes a few different colors and pours them onto a canvas; will they form legible writing or a nice-looking picture? Hashem created the entire world and set each part in its proper place, making it beautiful. Rav Elchonon Wasserman adds,[15] How could a person in his right mind think that the world which was created with such infinite wisdom, which is so intricate, came into being on its own? Avraham was the first to see the world and recognize Hashem through the creation, understanding that everything exists to serve Him.

In *Parashas Ki Savo*, it states that if we don't listen to Hashem, then He will rebuke and punish with "*cheres*." Rabbeinu Bachya[16] says this means "with the sun." Hashem will frighten them with the *makkah* of the sun, which will cause sunstroke or dryness. He says that the sun has three different names: "*shemesh*," "*chamah*," and "*cheres*." The word "שמש" means a servant who serves its master. Because of the attribute of the servant, it will reflect and pronounce the attribute of its master.

---

14   שער היחוד פ"ו
15   קובץ מאמרים מאמר על אמונה ה
16   דברים כח, כז

"חמה" means "חמימות—heat," as the sun provides warmth. And "חרס" indicates that since it was created to shine on the land, it dries up the dirt to make it into "חרס—pottery and earthenware."

In *Parashas Nitzavim*, it states,[17] "I am bringing to you witnesses, the heavens and the earth, life and death I put before you, the *berachah* and the *kelalah*, and you shall choose life." *Rashi* explains that Hashem said to B'nei Yisrael, "Look at the heavens and the earth that I created לשמש, to serve you. Have they changed their character? Did the sun ever not rise in the east and shine for the whole world? Look at the earth; have you ever planted and it did not grow? Or has it produced barley instead of wheat? Just as these don't change, although they don't get reward or punishment, you who get reward and punishment should certainly not change your ways." This reflects that the sun is called "שמש" because Hashem created it to serve us. The *Bamidbar Rabbah*[18] writes that the sun shines light for the world, causes rain to descend, and causes fruits to grow. The *Eitz Yosef* explains that the heat of the sun causes mist to rise from the ground and become clouds, from which comes rain, yielding fruit, which are ripened by the sun. The sun serves Hashem by shining, and it serves us by providing light and growth for the world.

In *Kiddush Levanah* we say, "ששים ושמחים לעשות רצון קונם—The luminaries are joyous and happy to fulfill the will of their Creator." So too, in *Keil Adon* we say, "עושים באימה רצון קונם—With fear the luminaries fulfill the will of their Creator." The *Meshech Chochmah*[19] explains that since the luminaries recognize Hashem with complete clarity, they automatically must fulfill His will.

My Rosh Yeshiva asked: How can we learn this lesson from the heavens and the earth about how we should behave? The heavens and earth are inanimate; they don't have a *yetzer tov* or *yetzer hara* to convince them to do good or bad, while we do. How then can we learn from them not

17   שם ל, יט

18   פ' יב, ד

19   הקדמה לספר שמות

to change our ways? He answered based on the *Tanya*[20] that every Yid has a *neshamah tehorah* that should naturally cause a person to do good, as we say every day in davening, "*Elokai, neshamah...tehorah hi.*" Also, in *Shir Hashirim* it states,[21] "Do not look at me that I am dark, because the sun caused it." *Rashi* explains, "Do not look at me in a disgraceful way, because the darkness, which is a euphemism for sin, was not from birth, but rather from the sun. This darkness can easily become light again by going into the shade (i.e., by staying out of the sun)." *Rashi* explains further, "The people who were around me convinced and persuaded me to do bad." Also, in *Koheles* it states,[22] "אשר עשה האלקים את האדם ישר והמה בקשו חשבונות רבים—G-d made the person straight, and they sought many ideas"; we made ourselves crooked. We see that every Yid is naturally born pure and clean; it is the *yetzer hara* and our surroundings which affect us and cause us to do bad. Just as the heavens and earth, which are inanimate, don't change their character, so too, a Yid has the potential to be as a *domem*, inanimate, and keep to the Torah and mitzvos without being affected by others.

May we take the lesson from the heavens and earth to return to our good nature and constantly serve Hashem!

## DOES "NASATI" MEAN "I HAVE GIVEN" OR "I WILL GIVE"?

### לְזַרְעֲךָ נָתַתִּי אֶת הָאָרֶץ הַזֹּאת (טו, יח)

לִבְנָךְ יְהַבִית יָת אַרְעָא הָדָא

*This land I have given to your children.*

### וְגַם נָתַתִּי מִמֶּנָּה לְךָ בֵּן (יז, טז)

וְאַף אֶתֵּין מִנַּהּ לָךְ בַּר

*And I will also give you a son from her.*

---

20 ע' לקוטי אמרים פ' יח

21 א, ו

22 ז, כט

When Hashem made a covenant with Avraham, the *pasuk* states that He promised, "לזרעך נתתי את הארץ הזאת," which Onkelos translates as, "This land I have given [*yehavis*] to your children," in past tense. The *Nefesh HaGer* quotes from *Bereishis Rabbah*:[23] Rabbi Shmuel bar Nachman said, "The saying of Hashem is also an action, as it states, "*L'zaracha nasati*—To your descendants I have given this land." It does not state "*etein*—I will give," but, rather, "*nasati*—I gave." Similarly, *Rashi* explains that once Hashem says that He will give, it is as though it was done.

In *Parashas Chayei Sarah*, Avraham spoke to Ephron to convince him to sell *Me'aras Ha'machpeilah*, and he said,[24] "*Nasati kesef ha'sadeh*." Onkelos translates this as, "I *will give* the silver, the value of the field [אתן כספא דמי חקלא]," in future tense. Why does Onkelos translate "*nasati*" by Hashem giving the land to Avraham as "I have given," in past tense, whereas by Avraham giving the money to Ephron, he translates as "I will give," in future tense? Rabbeinu Bachya answers that regarding human beings, a person does not finalize a deal until he actually gives the money. Even if the money is in his hand, available and ready to do the transaction, he might retract. Therefore, Onkelos translates regarding Avraham that he "will give" it to Ephron. In regards to Hashem, once He commits to do something, it is as though it has already been done, since there is no retracting and it will indeed happen. For this reason, Onkelos translates regarding Hashem giving the land to Avraham, "I have given."

In *Parashas Balak*, it states,[25] "לא איש קל ויכזב ובן אדם ויתנחם ההוא אמר ולא יעשה ודבר ולא יקימנה," which Onkelos translates as, "The saying of people is not like the saying of Hashem; people say things and are deceitful. Also, His actions are not like the actions of people; they decree to do, but they retract and rethink and don't do, whereas He says and does, and His entire saying exists [לא כמלי בני אנשא מימר אלקא בני אנשא אמרין ומכדבין ואף לא כעובדי בני בסרא דאנון גזרין למעבד תיבין ומתמלכין הוא אמר ועבד וכל מימריה מתקים]." Similarly, in *Baruch She'amar* we say, "ברוך אומר ועושה ברוך."

---

23  פ' מה, כב

24  כג, יג

25  במדבר כג, יט

גוזר ומקיים—Blessed is He who says and does; guarantees and fulfills His guarantee." Hashem is in complete control of everything; therefore, He can guarantee something and it is considered done. People, however, say things, but then change their mind and don't keep to what they said.

Later in this parashah, Hashem tells Avraham about having a child: "וגם נתתי ממנה לך בן," which Onkelos translates as, "And I will also give [*etein*] you a son from her." The *Nefesh HaGer* asks: when it comes to giving the land to Avraham, Onkelos translates "*nasati*" as "I have given [*ye'havis*]," in past tense, yet when Hashem blesses Avraham that He will give him a son, he translates it as "I will give [*etein*]," in future tense. Why the difference? In both *pesukim* Hashem promises to give something, so they should be presented in the same way!

The *Nefesh HaGer* answers that there is a difference between giving land and giving a son. Land currently exists in the world; therefore, once Hashem promised to give the land, it is fitting to say that it is as though He already gave it, even before it was actually taken. However, when Hashem blessed Avraham to have a son, the son did not exist, as Hashem had not yet given him, rather He promised to give him.

We find that the giving of Eretz Yisrael is considered ours, as the *Yerushalmi*[26] teaches. The Torah does not state, "*L'zaracha etein*—To your offspring I will give," but "*l'zaracha nasati*—To your offspring I have given." There is a *d'Oraysa* obligation to take *challah* from dough made of Eretz Yisrael's grain. Before B'nei Yisrael arrived, non-Jews were dwelling in the land of Eretz Yisrael, and there was no need to separate *challah* on their dough. When B'nei Yisrael entered, however, there was immediately a mitzvah to separate *challah*. This demonstrates that even when the non-Jews lived in the land, the grain carried the potential to be considered Jewish grain. Once Hashem promised the land and said, "I gave this land," it became the land of Yisrael.

May we learn from Hashem to fulfill what we say!

26 חלה ב, אור"ש

## WHAT IS THE MIDDAH OF ZERIZUS?

### וַיָּרֶק אֶת חֲנִיכָיו (יד, יד)

וְזָרֵיז יָת עוּלֵימוֹהִי

*And he armed*[27] *his young lads.*

### בְּעֶצֶם הַיּוֹם הַזֶּה נִמּוֹל אַבְרָהָם וְיִשְׁמָעֵאל בְּנוֹ (יז, כו)

בִּכְרַן יוֹמָא הָדֵין אִתְגְּזַר אַבְרָהָם וְיִשְׁמָעֵאל בְּרֵיה

*With the power of that day Avraham was*
*circumcised and Yishmael his son.*

The *pasuk* states, "בעצם היום הזה נימול אברהם וישמעאל בנו." *Rashi* explains
that the word "*b'etzem*" teaches that on the day that Avraham completed
his ninety-ninth year and Yishmael completed his thirteenth year, they
were circumcised. Onkelos translates the word "*b'etzem*" as "*bichran*" or
"*bikran*," meaning, "with the power of that day." The *Ramban*[28] explains
that the 'כ and 'ק are interchangeable. "*Keren*" means "a horn," which
reflects the strength of an animal, as animals fight with their horns.
The word "*b'etzem*" teaches that this day had unique strength and
power. Hashem performed a miracle that on this day; in such a short
time, 320 people were circumcised. This means that each person, young
or old, was circumcised in about two and a half minutes! The *Ramban*
understands differently: "*B'etzem*" teaches that on the day itself that
Avraham was commanded, he, Yishmael, and his 318 servants were
all circumcised. This reflects Avraham's *yiras Hashem*, along with his
entire household; they were all *zerizin makdimin l'mitzvos*—quick to
perform mitzvos.

It states, "ויקח אברהם את ישמעאל בנו ואת כל ילידי ביתו ואת כל מקנת כספו...וימל"—
And Avraham took Yishmael, his son, and all the children born of his
house and all those purchased with his money...and he circumcised."
The following *pasuk* states that Avraham was circumcised. The *Ramban*

---

27   מעט צרי מרש"י

28   ויקרא כג, כח

explains that the *pesukim* reflect an order: first Avraham circumcised Yishmael and his entire household, and afterwards he was circumcised.

The Gemara[29] teaches that the entire day is fitting to do *milah*, but the earlier, the better, as we know: *zerizin makdimin l'mitzvos*. We derive this from Avraham himself, as it states in *Parashas Vayeira*: "*Va'yashkeim Avraham ba'boker*—And Avraham arose early in the morning." Why, then, didn't Avraham have himself circumcised first, before his entire household?

The *Ramban* answers that had Avraham done his circumcision first, he would have been sick and in danger because of his age, and he would not have been able to be involved with taking care of the others' circumcisions. Avraham was *nizdareiz* and first circumcised his household, or he prepared many *mohalim* for them, and he oversaw those *milos*, and afterwards, he had himself circumcised. The *middah* of *zerizus* does not only mean being the first to perform a mitzvah but also being ready and prepared to fulfill mitzvos. Therefore, he first circumcised everyone else and only afterwards himself.

When Avraham heard about Lot being captured, the Torah states: "*Va'yarek es chanichav*," which Onkelos translates as "*v'zareiz*—and he armed his young lads" to go to battle. Onkelos translates "*o'chi*" as "hurried/rushed," "*b'fri'ah*" as "with haste," and "*mav'in*" or "*b'v'hilu*" as "with quickness/swiftly." Here, though, Onkelos translates as "*v'zareiz*," which is exactly how he translates "*va'yachgor*," and similar to how he translates "*neichaletz chushim*," as "*nizdarez mav'in*." *Rashi* explains that this means "we shall quickly arm ourselves" to give power to battle. We see that "*zareiz*" reflects being ready and prepared to do and accomplish. Similarly, the Gemara[30] writes that a *zahir* is one who is careful not to touch bread without washing his hands, while a *zariz* is one who washes his hands to eat. *Rashi* explains that a *zahir* knows to be careful at the time of the situation not to transgress anything. A *zariz* sees the future and fixes himself so as not to come to any possible issue. One

---

29    פסחים ד.
30    חולין קז:

who washes prepares himself and is ready to eat without having to be careful about touching the bread. So too, Avraham prepared his young lads for battle by arming them with weaponry.

In *Parashas Vayeira*,[31] the Torah states: "ויקח את המאכלת לשחוט את בנו—And he took the knife to slaughter his son." The Gemara[32] brings a proof from Avraham, who took a knife to slaughter his son, that a knife first needs to be detached from the ground in order to use it for slaughtering. The Gemara disproves this by suggesting that Avraham was a *zariz*, and he prepared a knife in case he wouldn't have a way to slaughter Yitzchak. Here, too, we see that a *zariz* is one who is prepared and ready to fulfill mitzvos. Avraham is our role model for *zerizus*; he did his utmost to fulfill all of Hashem's mitzvos.

May we learn from Avraham Avinu to always be prepared and ready to perform all of Hashem's mitzvos!

---

31   כב, י

32   חולין טז.

# Vayeira

## WHICH LAUGHING WAS OK AND WHICH WAS NOT?

וַתִּצְחַק שָׂרָה בְּקִרְבָּהּ לֵאמֹר אַחֲרֵי בְלֹתִי הָיְתָה לִּי עֶדְנָה (יח, יב)

וְחַיְּיכַת שָׂרָה בִּמְעַהָא לְמֵימַר בָּתַר דְּסֵיבִית תְּהֵי לִי עוּלֵימוּ

*And Sarah mocked about her stomach saying, "After becoming old, shall I have youth?"*

לָמָּה זֶּה צָחֲקָה שָׂרָה (יח, יג)

לְמָא דְּנַן חַיְּיכַת שָׂרָה

*What is this before us [why is it] that Sarah mocks?*

וַתְּכַחֵשׁ שָׂרָה לֵאמֹר לֹא צָחַקְתִּי...וַיֹּאמֶר לֹא כִּי צָחָקְתְּ (יח, טו)

וְכַדֵּיבַת שָׂרָה לְמֵימַר לָא חַיֵּיכִית...וַאֲמַר לָא בְּרַם חַיֵּיכְתְּ

*And Sarah denied, saying, "I did not mock...," and he said, "No, in truth you mocked."*

כִּמְצַחֵק (יט, יד)

כִּמְחַיֵּיךְ

*As mocking.*

וַתֹּאמֶר שָׂרָה צְחֹק עָשָׂה לִי אֱלֹקִים כָּל הַשֹּׁמֵעַ יִצְחַק לִי (כא, ו)

וַאֲמַרַת שָׂרָה חֶדְוָא עֲבַד לִי יְיָ כָּל דְּשָׁמַע יֶחְדֵּי לִי

*And Sarah said, "Hashem has made for me joy; all who will hear will rejoice for me."*

מְצַחֵק (כא, ט)

מְחַיֵּיךְ

*Mocking.*

The *pasuk* states, "ותצחק שרה בקרבה לאמר אחרי בלתי היתה לי עדנה"—And Sarah laughed about her stomach, saying, 'After my body has become wrinkled, will I become smooth again?'" Hashem said to Avraham, "למה זה צחקה שרה—Why is this that Sarah laughs?" Sarah denied and said, "*Lo tzachakti*—I did not laugh," and Avraham replied, "*lo ki tzachakt*—No, rather you did laugh." In *Parashas Lech Lecha*, Hashem told Avraham that he will have a son, and it states,[1] "ויפל אברהם על פניו ויצחק—And Avraham fell on his face, and he laughed." Both *pesukim* state that Avraham and Sarah laughed; the *Ohr Hachaim Hakadosh* asks: Why does Hashem only rebuke Sarah, and not Avraham?

The *Ohr Hachaim Hakadosh* says that *Rashi* quotes Onkelos, who answers this question by translating *"tz'chok"* by Avraham and Sarah differently. By Avraham, *Onkelos* translates *"va'yitzchak"* as "and he rejoiced [*va'chdi*]," whereas by Sarah, he translates *"va'titzchak"* as "and she mocked [*v'chayeichas*]." The *Ramban* explains that sometimes *"tz'chok*—laughter" reflects laughing out of happiness, while other times, it reflects laughing to make fun of something or someone. Avraham believed the news and laughed out of happiness, while Sarah laughed from disbelief and made light of it.

There are other places in this parashah where Onkelos specifies in his translation if the word *"tz'chok"* refers to rejoicing or to mocking. After Yitzchak was born, it states, "ותאמר שרה צחק עשה לי אלקים כל השומע יצחק לי," which *Onkelos* translates as, "And Sarah said, 'Hashem has made for me joy [*chedvah*]; all who will hear will rejoice for me [*yichdei*].'" Here, *"tz'chok"* is used for happiness and rejoicing.

When Lot tried convincing his sons-in-law to leave Sedom, it states, "ויהי כמצחק בעיני חתניו," which Onkelos translates as "and it was as mockery [*"k'm'chayeich"*] in the eyes of his sons-in-law." Also, when Sarah saw Yishmael doing improper things, she described it as *"m'tzacheik,"* which Onkelos translates as "mocking [*m'chayech*]."

When Hashem told Avraham that he would give birth to a son, Avraham believed that it would happen and awaited the good news. In *Parashas Lech Lecha*, it states[2] that Avraham said in his heart, "הלבן מאה שנה יולד ואם שרה הבת תשעים שנה תלד." Simply, this means that Avraham was uncertain and wondered, is it possible that a hundred-year-old man and a ninety-year-old woman will be able to have a child? The *Ramban* explains, according to Onkelos's translation, Avraham rejoiced about the good news and believed it would, indeed, come true. Avraham thought to himself, "Will it not be an unbelievably wondrous miracle for a hundred-year-old man and a ninety-year-old woman to give birth?" Sarah, on the other hand, did not believe, as it states, "ותצחק שרה בקרבה לאמר אחרי בלתי היתה לי עדנה," which Onkelos translates as, "And Sarah mocked about her stomach, saying, 'After becoming old, shall I have youth?'" Hashem rebuked Sarah, saying, "למה זה צחקה שרה," which Onkelos translates as, "What is this before us [why is it] that Sarah mocks?" "ותכחש שרה לאמר לא צחקתי," which Onkelos translates as, "And Sarah denied, saying, 'I did not mock.'" Avraham then said, "*Lo ki tzachakt*—No, in truth, you did mock." Therefore, Hashem rebuked Sarah for mocking since she did not believe, unlike Avraham who believed and anticipated the berachah.

May we laugh out of happiness and belief, and may Hashem fulfill the words "אז ימלא שחוק פינו"!

## WHAT DID AVRAHAM DO FOR SEDOM AND WHY?

### וְאַבְרָהָם עוֹדֶנּוּ עֹמֵד לִפְנֵי ה' (יח, כב)

וְאַבְרָהָם עַד כְּעַן מְשַׁמֵּישׁ בִּצְלוֹ קֳדָם יְיָ

*Avraham was, until now, [still] serving by davening before Hashem.*

## הַאַף תִּסְפֶּה צַדִּיק עִם רָשָׁע (יח, כג)

הֲבִרְגַז תְּשֵׁיצֵי זַכָּאָה עִם חַיָּבָא

*Will Your anger convince You to destroy the innocent with the guilty?*

## וַיַּשְׁכֵּם אַבְרָהָם בַּבֹּקֶר אֶל הַמָּקוֹם אֲשֶׁר עָמַד שָׁם אֶת פְּנֵי ה' (יט, כז)

וְאַקְדֵּים אַבְרָהָם בְּצַפְרָא לְאַתְרָא דְּשַׁמֵּישׁ תַּמָּן בִּצְלוֹ קֳדָם יְיָ

*And Avraham arose early in the morning to the place where he served there by davening before Hashem.*

The Gemara[3] teaches that anyone who makes himself a *makom kavu'a*, a permanent place to daven, the G-d of Avraham will be at his assistance...as it states, "ויישכם אברהם בבקר אל המקום אשר שם עמד את פני ה'"— And Avraham arose early in the morning to the place where he stood before Hashem." The word *"amidah"* refers to davening, as it states, *"Va'yaamod Pinchas va'yefalel*—And Pinchas stood and davened." Similarly, Onkelos translates this *pasuk* as, "And Avraham arose early in the morning to the place where he served there by davening before Hashem." To what davening does the *pasuk* about Avraham refer? And where do we find that Avraham always davened in the same place?

The Torah states, "And the men," referring to the angels, "turned from there and they went to Sedom, ואברהם עודנו עומד לפני ה'—and Avraham was still standing before Hashem." Onkelos translates differently: "Avraham was, until now, [still] serving by davening before Hashem." The *Ramban* explains that once Hashem told Avraham about the possibility of destroying Sedom, he immediately started davening to save them. The angels left to go to Sedom, and Avraham understood that his davening had not been accepted, yet he still continued to daven.

The *Seforno* adds that even after the angels reached Sedom, Avraham did not lose hope; rather, he continued to daven, seeking mercy and searching for a merit to save them. This is as Chazal say: "Even if a sharp sword is placed upon a person's neck, he should not hold back from davening." It states, "*Va'yigash Avraham*—Avraham then came close" and davened, "הַאַף תִּסְפֶּה צַדִּיק עִם רָשָׁע." *Rashi* explains the word "*af*" as "*gam*—also": "Will you also destroy a *tzaddik* with a *rasha*?" Onkelos translates the word "*af*" as "*kaas*—anger:" "Will Your anger convince You to destroy the innocent with the guilty?" All of this shows that Avraham davened as much as he could to save Sedom.

Regarding the next morning, it states, "אֶל הַמָּקוֹם אֲשֶׁר עָמַד שָׁם אֶת פְּנֵי ה'," which Onkelos translates as, "And Avraham arose early in the morning to the place where he served by davening before Hashem" to save Sedom. This shows that Avraham continued davening in the same place as the day before, even though Hashem did not accept his *tefillah*.

Why do we find specifically by Avraham the *inyan* of davening more than by anyone else in the Torah? Avraham recognized Hashem as the Creator of the world, completely believed in Hashem, and taught everyone about Him. Avraham understood that Hashem, Who creates a difficult situation, can certainly enable it to be resolved. Therefore, we find Avraham continuously davening to Hashem. Alternatively, Avraham, who epitomized *chessed*, did *chessed* by davening for people.

May we learn from Avraham Avinu to daven to Hashem in a *makom kavu'a* and do the *chessed* of davening for other people!

## WHAT DOES "BA'ASHER HU SHAM" MEAN?

### בַּאֲשֶׁר הוּא שָׁם (כא, יז)

בַּאֲתַר דְּהוּא תַּמָּן

*In the place which he is there [where he is].*

The *pesukim* mention that Avraham sent Hagar and Yishmael away. Yishmael was sick; he quickly finished up the water and needed more. They davened, and an angel called out, "Don't worry, because Hashem listened to the voice of the lad '*ba'asher hu sham*,' and Hashem opened her eyes and she saw a well of water." Onkelos translates the words "*ba'asher hu sham"* as "in the place which he is there [where he is]." The *Me'at Tzari* explains in the name of the *Ramban* that Hashem let Hagar know that she would not have to move from there to go to a spring or well. Rather, in the same place that they were at, they would be able to quench their thirst immediately. Hashem performed a miracle to save Yishmael.

The *Bereishis Rabbah*[4] teaches on the words, "ויפקח אלקים את עיניה ותרא באר מים—And G-d opened her eyes and she saw a well of water": Rabbi Binyamin says, from here we see that everyone is in the category of a blind person, until Hashem opens up his eyes and he can see the good. Hashem allowed Hagar to open her eyes and in that exact spot see the wellspring before her to be able to fill up water and drink. Hashem allowed her to see the good; the well was right before her.

My good friend Rabbi Elchonon Sosne explained in the name of the *Sefas Emes* that everything that a person needs exists right before him; he only needs to open his eyes to see it, as it states, *"Gal einai v'abitah*—Open my eyes and I will see." A person is created with the *tzelem* of G-d, and every limb is connected to the *tzelem*. Our physicality and sin cover and darken the connection, making us unable to see the good before us. Hashem gave us 613 mitzvos to refine our body in order for the *nefesh* to be revealed in the body. Just as sins darken the shine, so too mitzvos lighten the shine, as it states, "מצות ה' ברה מאירת עינים," and *"ner mitzvah."* They enable us to see the good before us.

*Rashi* explains *"ba'asher hu sham"* differently: "How he is now." He will be judged according to the actions which he has done now, presently, and not according to what he will do in the future. The angels wanted to prosecute, and they said, "Ribbono Shel Olam, for one whose descendants will kill Your children with thirst, will you bring up a well?!" This is referring to when Nevuchadnetzar exiled Klal Yisrael and they were brought next to the Arabs. Yisrael said to their captors, "I beg of you to bring us next to the children of our uncle, Yishmael, and they will have pity on us." B'nei Yishmael came out toward Klal Yisrael with salty meat and fish and flasks of air, instead of water. Klal Yisrael thought the flasks were full of water and when they brought them to their mouths, the air went inside their bodies and they died.

Hashem answered the angels, "What is Yishmael now, a *tzaddik* or a *rasha*?" They replied, "A *tzaddik*." Hashem said to them, "I judge *ba'asher hu sham*, according to his actions now."

*Rashi* specifies those "who will kill Your children *with thirst*" and not just "will kill," emphasizing the question: will You bring up a well to quench *his thirst*, if in the future his descendants will kill us with thirst?! *Avi Mori* added a similar idea from a Gemara[5] which tells about Nechunia, who dug pits for the Jewish People that traveled to the Beis Hamikdash for the *Shalosh Regalim*. One day, his daughter fell into a deep pit. They notified Rabbi Chanina ben Dosa. After an hour passed, he said, "All is well." After the second hour passed, he repeated, "All is well." After the third hour passed, he proclaimed, "She has come up." He explained, "I know this because something for which a *tzaddik* put in extra effort will not cause harm to his descendants."

We see that Hashem saves according to the type of *mesirus nefesh* that one has, and Hashem punishes according to the type of *aveirah* that one does. Regarding Yishmael, if not for *ba'asher hu sham*, how he was at the time, Hashem would not have provided water to quench his thirst, for his descendants would sin through thirst.

May we merit to see Hashem's good before us, and may we notice that Hashem's punishment and protection is according to our sin and *mesirus nefesh*!

## WHAT IS THE MEANING OF "MORIAH"?

וְלֶךְ לְךָ אֶל אֶרֶץ הַמֹּרִיָּה (כב, ב)

וְאִיזֵיל לָךְ לַאֲרַע פֻּלְחָנָא

*And go for yourself to the land of the service.*

## וַיִּקְרָא אַבְרָהָם שֵׁם הַמָּקוֹם הַהוּא ה' יִרְאֶה
## אֲשֶׁר יֵאָמֵר הַיּוֹם בְּהַר ה' יֵרָאֶה (כב, יד)

וּפְלַח וְצַלִּי אַבְרָהָם תַּמָּן בְּאַתְרָא הַהוּא אֲמַר קֳדָם יְיָ הָכָא יְהוֹן פָּלְחִין
דָּרַיָּא בְּכֵן יִתְאֲמַר (כ)בְּיוֹמָא הָדֵין בְּטוּרָא הָדֵין אַבְרָהָם קֳדָם יְיָ פְּלַח

*And Avraham served [did avodah] and davened there in that*
*place; he said before Hashem, "Here the generations will*
*serve [do avodah]," then will be said, "On (as) this day, on this*
*mountain, Avraham served [did avodah] before Hashem."*

The *pasuk* states that Hashem told Avraham, "קח נא את בנך את יחידך אשר אהבת את יצחק ולך לך אל ארץ המוריה—Take your son, your only one, the one whom you love, Yitzchak, and go to *Eretz HaMoriah*." What place is *Eretz HaMoriah*, and why is it called "Moriah"? *Rashi* explains that Moriah is Yerushalayim, as it states, "To build the Beis Hashem in Yerushalayim, on *Har HaMoriah*."

*Rashi* writes that Onkelos translates Moriah as "*pulchana—avodah* or service," a land of *avodah*. *Rashi* explains that this refers to the *avodah* of *Ketores*, as one of its eleven herbs was called *mor*. The *Nesinah LaGer* explains that "Moriah" is from the word *mor*. This is as it states in *Shir Hashirim*: "אלך לי אל הר המור," which refers to the mountain of the Beis Hamikdash. The *Ramban* adds that the land was going to be called Moriah in the future, or it was already called Moriah, because of the incense *mor* which will be offered. The *Ramban* is bothered by the following: Onkelos's translation of "*pulchana*," which means "*avodah*—service," does not reflect *mor*. If Onkelos meant the offering of *Ketores*, he should have translated it as *Ketores busmin*, *Ketores* incense, as he translates for the *avodah* of *Ketores*. Also, there were eleven herbs which were needed to make the *Ketores*; why would Moriah specifically be called after *mor*, and not after any other herb? The *Ramban* therefore explains differently: Onkelos translates "Moriah" from the word "*mora*—fear," hinting to the performance of the *avodah* in the Beis Hamikdash. Moriah is the place where people will serve Hashem and fear Him.

Later in the parashah, it states, "ויבן שם אברהם את המזבח—And Avraham built the *mizbeiach* there." The *Ramban* quotes from *Pirkei D'Rabi*

*Eliezer*: Hashem showed Avraham Avinu with His "finger" the *mizbeiach* on which he was meant to offer Yitzchak as a sacrifice. It was the same *mizbeiach* on which Adam Harishon had offered *korbanos*, as well as Kayin and Hevel, and Noach and his sons. This is as it states, "*es ha'miz-beiach*—the *mizbeiach*," not "*mizbeiach*—a *mizbeiach*." The *Ramban* explains that Hashem directed Avraham to go to the place where *avodah* had already been performed.

In *Tehillim*, it states,[6] "*Nora Elokim mi'mikdashecha*." The *Metzudos Dovid* explains that because of the honor of Hashem which rested in the Mikdash, indicated by the miracles that He performed there, people will come to *yiras Hashem*. In *Parashas Re'eh*, regarding *maaser sheini*, the Torah states:[7] "למען תלמד ליראה את ה' אלקיך כל הימים"—In order to learn to fear Hashem, your G-d, all the days." *Tosafos*[8] explains that *maaser sheini* is great since it brought a person to Torah learning. A person would stand in Yerushalayim to eat his *maaser sheini*, and he would see all of the people involved in *avodas Hashem*. He, too, would be directed to have *yiras Shamayim* and learn Torah. The *Mabit* adds that when the Beis Hamikdash existed and the Shechinah rested among Klal Yisrael, it was well-known that *hashgachas Hashem* was publicly revealed and recognized by everyone. There were miracles constantly happening for the nation, in addition to the ten miracles in the Beis Hamikdash, and there were too many to list. People were aware of Hashem and afraid of Him.

After Avraham brought the ram in place of Yitzchak, the Torah states: "ויקרא אברהם שם המקום ההוא ה' יראה אשר יאמר היום בהר ה' יראה," which Onkelos translates as, "And Avraham served [did *avodah*] and davened there in that place; he said before Hashem, 'Here, the generations will serve [do *avodah*].' Then it will be said, 'On this day, on this mountain, Avraham served [did *avodah*] before Hashem.'" The *Nefesh HaGer* explains that "*asher yei'amer ha'yom*" refers to what future generations will say about the past: "We will perform *avodah* on this mountain, just as Avraham did *avodah* before Hashem on this mountain." Additionally, this hints

---

6    סח, לו

7    דברים יה, כג

8    ב"ב כא.

that Har HaMoriah refers to the *avodah* of both Avraham and the future generations. *Rashi* explains "*asher yei'amer ha'yom*" differently: "All the future generations will say that on this mountain Hashem will be seen by His nation in the future."

The *Bereishis Rabbah*[9] teaches that Shem, also known as Malkitzedek, called that place "*shalem*—complete," while Avraham Avinu called it "*yireh*—fear." Hashem joined the two names together and called the place "Yerushalayim." Similarly, Onkelos translates[10] "*Melech Shalem*" as "*Malka di'Rushelem*—king of Yerushalayim." We see that the Har HaMoriah was a place where *avodah* was performed and brought a person to "*mora*—fear of Hashem."

May Hashem rebuild the Beis Hamikdash and bring back the *avodah* together with *yiras Shamayim*!

## WHAT DOES "AYIL ACHAR" AND "TACHAS B'NO" MEAN? WHAT DOES IT MEAN THAT HASHEM CONSTANTLY REMEMBERS?

וַיִּשָּׂא אַבְרָהָם אֶת עֵינָיו וַיַּרְא וְהִנֵּה אַיִל אַחַר נֶאֱחַז בַּסְּבַךְ בְּקַרְנָיו
וַיֵּלֶךְ אַבְרָהָם וַיִּקַּח אֶת הָאַיִל וַיַּעֲלֵהוּ לְעֹלָה תַּחַת בְּנוֹ (כב, יג)

וּזְקַף אַבְרָהָם יָת עֵינוֹהִי בָּתַר אִלֵּין וַחֲזָא וְהָא דִכְרָא אֲחִיד בְּאִילָנָא
בְּקַרְנוֹהִי וַאֲזַל אַבְרָהָם וּנְסֵיב יָת דִּכְרָא וְאַסְקֵיהּ לַעֲלָתָא חֲלָף בְּרֵיהּ

*And Avraham stood up [lifted up] his eyes after this, and he
saw, that behold, a ram was held, caught in the tree with
its horns, and Avraham went and he took the ram, and he
brought it up for a burnt-sacrifice in exchange for his son.*

Hashem commands Avraham to bring up Yitzchak for a burnt-sacrifice. After Avraham takes the knife to slaughter Yitzchak, an angel says to Avraham, "Do not slaughter the lad." The following *pasuk* states, "וישא

9  פ׳ נו, י
10  בראשית יד, יח

אברהם את עיניו וירא והנה איל אחר נאחז בסבך בקרניו—"And Avraham lifted up his eyes and he saw, and behold, another ram was caught in the bush by its horns." The *Bereishis Rabbah*[11] asks: "*Ayil achar*" means "*another ram*"; what other ram did he see? There was only the one stated in the *pasuk*! The *Nefesh HaGer* explains that Onkelos answers this question by translating the word *achar* before the word *va'yar*, as though it states, "וישא אברהם את עיניו אחר וירא והנה איל נאחז בסבך בקרניו—And Avraham lifted up his eyes after this, and he saw, that behold, a ram was caught in the tree by its horns." *Rashi* explains that this implies that he saw the ram after the words of the angel who told Avraham not to slaughter Yitzchak.

The *pasuk* ends, "And Avraham went and he took the ram and he brought it up for a burnt-sacrifice *tachas b'no*," which Onkelos translates as "in exchange for his son." *Rashi* explains that this teaches that by each *avodah* that Avraham did, he davened that it should be considered as though he was doing it to his own son, Yitzchak. Avraham davened, "Let it be as though my son is being slaughtered, his blood is being sprinkled, and his flesh is being skinned, burned, and made into ash." Although Avraham was told not to slaughter his son, he did everything in his power to sacrifice a *korban* in his place. The Brisker Rav[12] adds that therefore, it is considered as though Yitzchak was slaughtered and burned through the *avodah* of the ram with ash piled up on the *mizbeiach*. For this reason, the Gemara[13] says that when they searched for the place of the *mizbeiach*, they saw the ash of Yitzchak and recognized that this was meant to be the place of the *mizbeiach*.

In *Parashas Bechukosai* it states,[14] "וזכרתי את בריתי יעקוב ואף את בריתי יצחק ואף את בריתי אברהם אזכר," which Onkelos translates as, "And I am remembering My covenant that was with Yaakov, and also My covenant that was with Yitzchak, and also My covenant that was with Avraham I am remembering [ודכירנא ית קימי דעם יעקב ואף ית קימי דעם יצחק ואף ית קימי דעם אברהם אנא דכיר]." Onkelos translates the words "*v'zacharti*" and "*ezkor*"

11    פ' נו, ט

12    חי' מרן הגרי"ז הלוי החדשות על תנ"ך ואגדה

13    זבחים סב.

14    ויקרא כו, מב

in the present tense, unlike the words of the *pasuk* which are written in future tense. Why does Onkelos change to the present tense? The *Pas'shegen* answers that there is no forgetting by Hashem; everything is revealed before Him. Therefore, Onkelos translates Hashem's remembering with present tense. So too, the *Eichah Rabbah*[15] teaches that B'nei Yisrael says before Hashem, "Forgetting is found by us, however, forgetting is not found by You; therefore, remember."

*Rashi* is bothered: Why does the Torah state the *lashon* of *zechirah* by Avraham and Yaakov, but not by Yitzchak? *Rashi* answers that the ash of Yitzchak is constantly seen by Hashem since it is piled up on the *mizbeiach*. Therefore, *zechirah* is not necessary, as one does not need to remember something that is in front of him.

The *Maharal* explains that Yitzchak was willing to give up his life completely for the sake of Hashem. He was totally *mevatel* himself to Hashem and connected to Him without any separations. We know that Hashem exists forever and does not forget anything, He constantly remembers everything. Therefore, Yitzchak, who gave himself up for Hashem, became one with Hashem, and is always together with Hashem before Him.

May Hashem constantly remember and favor Klal Yisrael!

# Chayei Sarah

## WAS ME'ARAS HA'MACHPEILAH ACTUALLY WORTH FOUR HUNDRED SELA'IM OF SILVER?

אֲדֹנִי שְׁמָעֵנִי אֶרֶץ אַרְבַּע מֵאֹת שֶׁקֶל
כֶּסֶף בֵּינִי וּבֵינְךָ מַה הִוא (כג, טו)

רִבּוֹנִי קַבֵּיל מִנִּי אֲרַע שָׁוְיָא אַרְבַּע מְאָה סִלְעִין דִּכְסַף בֵּינָא וּבֵינָךְ מָא הִיא

*My master, accept from [listen to] me, what is a [piece of] land worth four hundred sela'im of silver between me and between you?*

וַיִּשְׁמַע אַבְרָהָם אֶל עֶפְרוֹן וַיִּשְׁקֹל אַבְרָהָם
לְעֶפְרֹן...אַרְבַּע מֵאוֹת שֶׁקֶל כֶּסֶף עֹבֵר לַסֹּחֵר (כג, טז)

וְקַבֵּיל אַבְרָהָם מִן עֶפְרוֹן וּתְקַל אַבְרָהָם לְעֶפְרוֹן...אַרְבַּע
מְאָה סִלְעִין דִּכְסַף מִתְקַבַּל סְחוֹרָה בְּכָל מְדִינָה

*And Avraham accepted Ephron's request, and Avraham weighed for Ephron...four hundred sela'im of silver which is accepted wares [currency] in every country.*

In this parashah, Avraham purchases the *Me'aras Ha'machpeilah* for four hundred silver *shekalim*. Was Avraham cheated, or was this the amount that it was worth?

The *pasuk* states, "אדני שמעני ארץ ארבע מאות שקל כסף ביני ובינך מה היא," which Onkelos translates as, "My master, accept from [listen to] me, what is a [piece of] land worth four hundred *sela'im* of silver between me and between you?" The *Ramban*[1] says that the Torah's *shekel* coin is Chazal's

---

*sela* coin. The *Ramban* explains that Onkelos understands that *Me'aras Ha'machpeilah* was actually worth four hundred *sela'im* of silver. It was common for there to be a set price for land in each place according to the size of the land.

The *Vilna Gaon*[2] explains how the *Me'aras Ha'machpeilah* was worth exactly four hundred silver *shekalim*. A *beis saasayim* is two *se'ah*, like the courtyard of the *Mishkan*, which was one hundred cubits by fifty cubits. When you split the total into cubits, each being one cubit by one cubit, it will equal five thousand square cubits (100 x 50). A *beis kor*, which is fifteen *beis saasayims*, will have seventy-five thousand square cubits (15 x 5,000). Eight *korim* will have six hundred thousand square cubits (8 x 75,000).

The Gemara teaches that just as the Torah was given at Sinai among six hundred thousand people, so too, when a *neshamah* is taken away, along with its learning, six hundred thousand people are needed at the funeral. Therefore, Sarah's eulogy needed to have an area big enough to contain space for six hundred thousand people. The Gemara teaches that a person sits in a one-cubit space. If so, six hundred thousand people would need a space of eight *kor* in order to fit.

What is the price for an area of six hundred thousand square cubits? The Gemara writes that one who sanctifies a *beis kor* can redeem it for fifty silver *shekalim*. Eight *korim* multiplied by fifty *shekalim* per *kor* equals four hundred silver *shekalim* (8 x 50). This shows that the *Me'aras Ha'machpeilah* was an area of 600,000 square cubits which was purchased for exactly four hundred silver *shekalim*, just as Onkelos translates!

The *Ramban* quotes from *Rabboseinu* that Ephron set an overly expensive price according to his interest. Out of Avraham's generosity, he accepted. The Gemara[3] gleans from here that *tzaddikim* say a little and do a lot. Similarly, Avraham said to his guests in the beginning of *Parashas Vayeira*, "*V'ekchah phas lechem*—And I will take a piece of

---

bread," yet it states, "*V'el ha'bakar ratz Avraham*—And Avraham ran to the cattle." Originally, Avraham said he would give a piece of bread, yet he actually gave them meat. The *Maharsha* explains that if one offers to do a lot, a guest may feel uncomfortable to cause the host to prepare so much and he may decline coming. Therefore, it is more appropriate for the host to offer to do something small, which will make the guest feel comfortable to come. Once the guest joins, the host can give more, as much as he wants to honor the guests.

The Gemara adds that we find the opposite by *reshaim*: they say a lot and do not even do a little. Thus, Ephron originally said, "ארץ ארבע מאת שקל כסף ביני ובינך מה היא—A land worth four hundred silver *shekalim* between me and you, what is it?" *Rashi* explains, between the two of us, who love each other as ourselves, what is it considered at all? Rather, forget the sale and bury your dead. The *Maharal* explains that this meant, take it without a sale at all, for free. There's no need for any money to be paid at all. In the end, though, the *pasuk* states, "וישמע אברהם אל עפרון וישקל אברהם לעפרון את הכסף...ארבע מאות שקל כסף עובר לסוחר," which Onkelos translates as, "And Avraham accepted Ephron's request, and Avraham weighed for Ephron...four hundred *sela'im* of silver which is accepted wares [currency] in every country." Ephron did not accept standard *shekalim*; he only accepted from Avraham the big *shekalim* which are usable all over.

The *Sifsei Chachamim*[4] says that throughout the entire parashah, עפרון is spelled with a 'ו. Here, though, it is spelled "לעפרן," without a 'ו. *Rashi* explains that this is because he said a lot and he did not do even a little. First, Ephron promised to give the land for free, and then he asked for four hundred *shekalim*, and finally, he only accepted the best-quality coins. The *Maharal* explains that the word "לעפרון" is written *chaser*, "לעפרן," because he was so exact and stingy, demonstrating an *ayin ra*. And in fact, the *gematria* of "עפרן" is "עין רע"!

May we learn from *tzaddikim* to say a little and do a lot!

## WHAT WAS ELIEZER'S METHOD
## OF FINDING RIVKAH, AND WHY?

---

### הַקְרֵה נָא לְפָנַי הַיּוֹם (כה, יב)

זַמֵּין כְּעַן קֳדָמַי יוֹמָא דֵין

*Prepare now before me on this day.*

### אֹתָהּ הֹכַחְתָּ לְעַבְדְּךָ לְיִצְחָק (כה, יד)

יָתַהּ זַמֵּינְתָּא לְעַבְדָּךְ לְיִצְחָק

*She is the one You have prepared for Your servant Yitzchak.*

### הִוא הָאִשָּׁה אֲשֶׁר הֹכִיחַ ה' לְבֶן אֲדֹנִי (כה, מד)

הִיא אִתְּתָא דְּזַמֵּין יְיָ לְבַר רִבּוֹנִי

*She is the woman Hashem prepared for my master's son.*

The *pasuk* states that Eliezer davened to Hashem to be successful with finding a *shidduch* for Yitzchak. He said, "הקרה נא לפני היום—Let it happen before me today." Onkelos translates the word "*hakreh*" with the *lashon* "*hazmanah*": "Prepare now before me on this day," meaning, let the *shidduch* be ready and let me immediately find the maiden who is meant to be the bride. Eliezer asks to find a maiden who will give him and his camels to drink and says, "אותה הוכחת לעבדך ליצחק." *Rashi* explains that a woman who does *chessed* is the one who is fitting to marry Yitzchak. Here, too, Onkelos translates the word "*hochachta*" as "*hazmanah*": "She is the one You have prepared for Your servant Yitzchak." Also, when Eliezer tells over the story to Lavan, he said, "היא האשה אשר הוכיח ה' לבן אדני," which *Rashi* explains as, "She is the woman whom Hashem has proven and is known to be the right one." Once again, Onkelos translates "*hochiach*" as "*hazmanah*": "She is the woman Hashem prepared for my master's son."

In *Parashas Ki Seitzei*, describing the mitzvah of *shiluach ha'ken*, the Torah states, "כי יקרא קן צפור לפניך בדרך." There, Onkelos translates "*yikarei*" as "when you will chance upon [תערע] a nest of a bird before you on the road." He does not translate "*yikarei*" as "*hazmanah*" as he does in our parashah. The *Nefesh HaGer* explains like *Rashi*: this suggests that the word *"yikarei,* to chance upon" excludes a nest which is *me-zuman,* prepared. Onkelos translates each place according to its intent. Alternatively, he differentiates between יקרא with an 'א, which means "to chance upon," and with a 'ה, which means "to prepare" or "make ready."

What does Onkelos mean to hint at with the *lashon* of *hazmanah?* This can be explained as the *Seforno* quotes from the Gemara: "A *bas kol* goes out forty days before a child is created and announces: this girl is for this boy." Rivkah had already been prepared for the *shidduch.*

The *Nefesh HaGer* explains differently: *hazmanah* reflects *hashgachas Hashem.* Hashem is the one who prepared the *shidduch.* Eliezer noticed and felt the *hashgachas Hashem* leading him and directing him with his mission from the beginning until the end: his trip was quickened as he had *kefitzas ha'derech;* even before he finished davening, Rivkah appeared to give him and the camels to drink, the water in the well came up to Rivkah, and she was from the correct family!

My good friend Rabbi Elchonon Sosne said in the name of Rav Hirsch that the words הקרא, call, and הקרה, chance upon, are two different types of calling. The calling with an 'א is a known call, loud and clear, whereas the calling with a 'ה is a quiet, hidden call of Hashem. *Avi Mori* added that the letters of "מקרה—by chance" spells "רק מה—only from Hashem." Both the clear and hidden callings are from Hashem.

The *Hakesav V'Hakabbalah* quotes from the *Rama* that Eliezer was worried that the family of the maiden would refuse to send her. Therefore, he davened for a specific way to find the maiden so that there would be *hashgachas Hashem* throughout the entire search. This way, he felt that the family of the bride would be more likely to agree to send her without an argument. The Brisker Rav[5] adds that Eliezer asked for everything to happen *"ha'yom*—on this one day," which necessitated unusual success from Hashem. This is indeed what happened; the exact way that Eliezer davened to find the *shidduch* was how Hashem made it happen! There is no greater way of knowing that this is the true match than by seeing the clear-cut *hashgachas Hashem!*

The *Chazon Ish* says that people were able to see *hashgachas Hashem* by Gedolim up until his generation. There were non-Jews who would push Rav Moshe from Pinsk to walk through their fields because everyone knew that wherever he walked was blessed. The city of Minsk had dangerous dogs who injured anyone who passed by them. The entire city knew that when the Gadol from Minsk passed them, though, they would run away. The *Chazon Ish* recounted that when he was in Minsk at the time of the war, he did not have a passport. The punishment for being caught without a passport was to be shot immediately. He heard that the soldiers were coming to search the city, so he fled—but instead of running away from the enemy, he ran toward them! Faced with no other choice, he passed between the soldiers, who stood in rows facing each other. Not one said a word or did anything to him. He said that he felt secure because he had just finished writing his *sefer* on *hilchos eiruvin*. The *Chazon Ish* concluded, "Whoever wants to notice *hashgachas Hashem* will notice."

Even in our days, we can personally notice *hashgachas Hashem*. The Gemara[6] teaches that when a person pulls the wrong coin out of his pocket, that counts as *yissurim* from Hashem. We can deduce that when one puts his hand in his pocket and finds what he was looking for, Hashem is helping him. Nothing happens by chance, so we should take nothing for granted. Any good is a reflection of Hashem's assistance and kindness.

May we constantly notice *hashgachas Hashem* in our everyday lives!

## WHY DIDN'T ELIEZER AND THE CAMELS ENTER LAVAN'S HOUSE?

### הֲיֵשׁ בֵּית אָבִיךְ מָקוֹם לָנוּ לָלִין (כה, כג)

הָאִית בֵּית אֲבוּיִיךְ אֲתַר כָּשַׁר לָנָא לְמִבָּת

*Is there a kosher [appropriate] place to lodge by your father's house?*

## גַּם מָקוֹם לָלוּן (כה, כה)

אַף אֲתַר כָּשַׁר לִמְבָּת

*Also, a kosher [appropriate] place to lodge.*

## וְאָנֹכִי פִּנִּיתִי הַבַּיִת וּמָקוֹם לַגְּמַלִּים (כה, לא)

וַאֲנָא פַנֵּיתִי בֵּיתָא וַאֲתַר כָּשַׁר לְגַמְלַיָּא

*And I cleared out the house and a kosher
[appropriate] place for the camels.*

The *pasuk* states that Eliezer asked Rivkah, "היש בית אביך מקום לנו ללין—Is
there a place to sleep overnight in your father's house?" She responded,
"גם מקום לנו ללון," which *Rashi* explains means that there is also place to
sleep overnight for many nights. When Lavan hears about Eliezer's visit,
he says, "Why shall you stand outside? ואנכי פניתי הבית ומקום לגמלים." The
*Seforno* explains that Lavan cleared out his house to make space for both
Eliezer and his servants, and for the camels. Onkelos translates the word
*makom* as "a kosher place," which simply means a place fitting for lodging; there was space and proper conditions to sleep overnight.

The *Avos D'Rabi Nosson*[7] records that just as the early *tzaddikim* were
pious, so too, their animals were pious. The camels of Avraham Avinu
did not enter into the house of idolatry, as it states "ואנכי פניתי הבית ומקום
לגמלים—And I cleared out the house and place for the camels." The
*Maharal* explains that Lavan's words "That I cleared out the house," are
extraneous, as Rivkah had already said that there was place to sleep.
Lavan adds that not only is the place physically available, but it is also
clear of the *tumah* from idolatry. The *pasuk* continues, "*u'makom la'ge-
malim*," teaching that the camels did not enter into the house of Lavan
until all the idolatry was gotten rid of. Avraham's camels would not enter
into a place of *tumah* so as not to be together with detestable things and
become affected by them. *Avi Mori* explained that Onkelos, who translates the word "*makom*" as "a kosher place," is hinting to this *Avos D'Rabi*

*Nosson*: it was a kosher place which did not have any idols remaining in the house.

The *Avos D'Rabi Nosson* then tells a story with the donkey of Rabbi Chanina ben Dosa.[8] Robbers stole his donkey and tied it up in their courtyard. They placed before it wheat and barley to eat and water to drink, yet the donkey did not eat or drink. This was because the donkey would not eat from the robbers' untithed or stolen food. They said, "Why should we leave the donkey to die and cause the courtyard to smell?" So they opened the door and let the donkey out. The donkey left and walked until it reached the house of Rabbi Chanina, where it made noise. The son of Rabbi Chanina heard the donkey making noise and said to his father, "It sounds like the noise of our animal." Rabbi Chanina said, "Open up the door for the donkey, for it will soon die of starvation." His son opened up the door and placed before the donkey wheat, barley, and water, and it ate and drank. Rabbi Chanina knew that his donkey would not eat any prohibited food.

May we learn from Eliezer and from Avraham Avinu's camels to distance ourselves from *tumah* and *issur*, which will enable ourselves to retain our level of *kedushah*!

## WHEN WERE BOTH ELIEZER AND YITZCHAK ANSWERED?

### וְיִצְחָק בָּא מִבּוֹא בְּאֵר לַחַי רֹאִי (כה, סב)

וְיִצְחָק עָאל בְּמֵיתוֹהִי (מִמֵּיתוֹהִי רמב"ן) מִבֵּירָא דְמַלְאַךְ קַיָּמָא אִתְחֲזֵי עֲלַהּ

*And Yitzchak entered with (from) his coming, from*
*the well that an existing angel was seen upon it.*

### וַיֵּצֵא יִצְחָק לָשׂוּחַ בַּשָּׂדֶה לִפְנוֹת עָרֶב (כה, סג)

וּנְפַק יִצְחָק לְצַלָּאָה בְּחַקְלָא לְמִפְנֵי רַמְשָׁא

*And Yitzchak went out to daven in the field*
*to the turn of [toward] evening.*

The *pasuk* states, "ויצחק בא מבוא באר לחי רואי." *Rashi* explains that Yitzchak went to bring Hagar for Avraham, his father, to marry her. Onkelos translates differently: "And Yitzchak entered with his coming, from the well that an existing angel was seen upon it." He translates *"mi'bo"* as "with his coming [*b'meisohi*]," in present tense. The *Ramban* has the text "from his coming [*mi'meisohi*]," in present tense. What does this mean? The *Ramban* explains that Yitzchak would continuously go back and forth to daven in the place where Hager saw an angel in Be'er Sheva by the *eshel Avraham*. Since an angel was seen there, it was a special place which was fitting for davening. Now, Yitzchak was returning from there, and he found Eliezer and Rivkah. Yitzchak came from the city where the well was to another city which was on the way back home. The *Seforno* and *Hakesav V'Hakabbalah* add that even before Yitzchak davened to Hashem to find his bride, he was answered: Rivkah was found and was being brought to him. It was a fulfillment of the *pasuk*: "טרם יקראו ואני אענה—Before they will call out, I will answer."

The *pasuk* which follows states, "And Yitzchak went out *la'suach ba'sa-deh*," which the *Rashbam* explains as relating to *"v'chol siach ha'sadeh—* and all the saplings of the field." In other words, Yitzchak went to plant trees and inspect the area. Onkelos translates *"la'suach ba'sadeh"* differently: "to daven in the field." As *Rashi* explains, *"la'suach"* denotes davening, as it states, *"Yishpoch sicho—*To say his request," referring to davening. The *Nesinah LaGer* quotes from the Gemara that from here Chazal derive that Yitzchak instituted the prayer of *Minchah*. The *Seforno* explains that Yitzchak went to the field to daven to Hashem so as not to be disrupted by passersby, although he already davened in Be'er Lachai Roi.

First, Yitzchak davened in Be'er Lachai Roi and afterwards he went to the field to daven again for a *shidduch*. Even before he davened, he was already answered. We see that just as Rivkah was found immediately through Eliezer's davening, so too, Yitzchak found Rivkah when he went out to the field to daven.

May we daven to Hashem for all our needs and trust in Him to help us!

## WHEN DID YITZCHAK RECOGNIZE THAT
## RIVKAH WAS FITTING TO MARRY?

וַיְבִאֶהָ יִצְחָק הָאֹהֱלָה שָׂרָה אִמּוֹ וַיִּקַּח אֶת
רִבְקָה וַתְּהִי לוֹ לְאִשָּׁה וַיֶּאֱהָבֶהָ (כה, סז)

וְאַעֵלַהּ יִצְחָק לְמַשְׁכְּנָא וַחֲזָא וְהָא תַּקְנִין עוֹבָדָהָא כְּעוֹבָדֵי שָׂרָה
אִמֵּיהּ וּנְסֵיב יָת רִבְקָה וַהֲוָת לֵיהּ לְאִתּוּ וְרִיחֲמַהּ

*And Yitzchak brought her into the tent, and he saw, behold, her*
*ways were like the ways of his mother, Sarah, and he married*
*Rivkah, and she was to him for a wife, and he loved her.*

When Eliezer returned from Charan, it states, "ויספר העבד ליצחק את כל
הדברים אשר עשה—And the servant told Yitzchak all the things which
he did." *Rashi* explains that Eliezer told Yitzchak about all the miracles
that had happened: the time that it took to reach Lavan's house was
shortened, and he got there unusually quickly; before he even finished
davening, Rivkah appeared at the well with a pitcher on her shoulder;
etc. The entire sequence of events occurred exactly as he had davened
for it to be, and he found Rivkah in just one day. This was as Avraham
had said, "הוא ישלח מלאכו לפניך—He shall send His angel before you."
There was clear *hashgachas Hashem* from the beginning until the end.

The following *pasuk* states, "ויבאה יצחק האהלה שרה אמו—And Yitzchak
brought her into the tent of Sarah, his mother." Onkelos translates
these words as, "And Yitzchak brought her into the tent, and he saw,
behold, her ways were like the ways of his mother, Sarah." How were
Rivkah's ways similar to that of Sarah's ways?

The *Nesinah LaGer* explains in *Rashi*'s name that when Sarah was alive,
the cloud of the Shechinah rested over the tent, berachah was found in
the bread, and the candle was lit from Friday to Friday. When Rivkah
entered the tent, these miracles returned. The *Nefesh HaGer* suggests
another explanation from the *Bereishis Rabbah*:[9] when Sarah was alive,

the doors were open with abundance to help people; after she died, the abundance stopped. When Rivkah entered the tent, she was also able to help others the same way. Alternatively, Rivkah would knead and separate *challah* with purity, just as Sarah did. The *Hakesav V'Hakabbalah* adds that "*ohel*" also means light. There were many lights of *kedushah* which left when Sarah died; when Rivkah entered, they returned.

It states, "ויקח את רבקה ותהי לו לאשה ויאהבה—And he married Rivkah and she was to him for a wife, and he loved her." The *Ramban* explains that the Torah mentions Yitzchak's love for Rivkah after he noticed that Rivkah's good deeds were similar to Sarah's to highlight that he loved her because of her righteousness and good deeds. Yitzchak did not marry Rivkah because of how she looked or for other reasons. This is as Onkelos translates, "And he saw, behold, her ways were like the ways of his mother, Sarah." Because he saw that she was similar to Sarah, his mother, therefore he loved her. She was indeed fitting to marry and continue on the legacy of the family.

The Brisker Rav[10] infers from Onkelos's translation that after Eliezer recounted all the miracles that occurred, Yitzchak did not yet take Rivkah for a wife. Only after Yitzchak saw that her actions were similar to that of his mother did he marry her. The Brisker Rav says that this reflects that although throughout the entire story Eliezer and Yitzchak saw clear-cut *hashgachas Hashem* and miracles, these were insufficient. Yitzchak needed to recognize her good actions and deeds in order to know that she was the one who was fit to marry.

Rav Sternbuch adds that Eliezer recognized the miracles that happened, yet he still tested Rivkah to make sure that she was a *baalas chessed*. So too, Yitzchak was only ready to marry Rivkah when he saw that she had good deeds like Sarah, as Onkelos translates. From here, we see that one needs to clarify, even beyond miracles, if a woman is a true *baalas chessed*.

---

10    חי' מרן הגרי"ז הלוי החדשות על תנ"ך ואגדה

At the end of *Parashas Vayeira*, it states, "ויגד לאברהם לאמר הנה ילדה מלכה גם היא בנים לנחור אחיך...ובתואל ילד את רבקה—And it was told to Avraham saying, 'Behold, Milkah gave birth to Nachor, your brother...and Besuel gave birth to Rivkah.'" *Rashi* explains that after Avraham returned from Har HaMoriah, he thought, 'Had my son been slaughtered, he would have left this world without children. I should have married him off to the daughters of Aner, Eshkol, and Mamrei.' Hashem then told him that Yitzchak's mate, Rivkah, had been born. Why did Avraham send Eliezer to find a *shidduch* when he already knew who the maiden was? I heard the following answer: although it was told to Avraham, he did not rely on a miracle to find a *shidduch*. Yitzchak, as well, followed in his father's footsteps by not relying on a miracle, and he made sure that Rivkah was similar to Sarah, his mother.

May we seek *shidduchim* with people who are righteous and have good deeds!

# Toldos

## WHAT DOES "VA'YETAR" AND "VA'YEI'ASER" MEAN, AND WHY IS IT USED HERE?

וַיֶּעְתַּר יִצְחָק לַה' לְנֹכַח אִשְׁתּוֹ כִּי עֲקָרָה הִוא וַיֵּעָתֶר לוֹ ה' (כה, כא)

וְצַלִּי יִצְחָק קֳדָם יְיָ לָקֳבֵיל אִתְּתֵיהּ אֲרֵי עֲקָרָא הִיא וְקַבֵּיל צְלוֹתֵיהּ יְיָ

*And Yitzchak davened opposite his wife, since she was*
*barren, and Hashem accepted his davening.*

The *pasuk* states, "ויעתר יצחק לה' לנכח אשתו כי עקרה היא ויעתר לו ה'." *Rashi* explains that the word "*atar*" is from "*va'asar anan ha'ketores*—and a cloud of smoke increased"; both Yitzchak and Rivkah increased, urged, and appeased Hashem by davening to Him to have children. The Gemara[1] teaches that both Yitzchak and Rivkah were unable to have children naturally. The *Maharsha* explains that this is derived from the words "*l'nochach ishto*—opposite his wife," meaning that they both equally needed extra davening, since they were both unable to have children. The words, "*va'yei'aser lo*," mean, "and Hashem accepted his increase, urging, and appeasing by davening." The *Nefesh HaGer* says that Rashi does not explain "*atar*" as davening because the *Devarim Rabbah*[2] does not list "*atar*" as one of the ten *leshonos* used for davening.

Onkelos translates "*va'yetar*" and "*va'yei'aser*" as davening. The *Nefesh HaGer* explains that this is as the *Sifrei*[3] teaches that there are ten

---

יבמות סד.  1
פ' ב, א  2
דברים ג, כג  3

*leshonos* of davening, one of which is *"atar,"* as it states by Yitzchak, *"Va'yetar."* What does *"atar"* mean, and how does it reflect davening?

The Gemara[4] asks: Why is the davening of *tzaddikim* compared to an *atar*, a pitchfork? Just as a pitchfork turns over grain in the granary from place to place, so too a *tzaddik* changes the will of Hashem from the *middah* of anger to the *middah* of mercy. *Rashi* says[5] that we see that *"atar"* means to turn over and change. The *Maharsha* explains that the granary is a place where grain is trampled on, loosened, and then thrown up into the wind to separate the chaff. The light straw, which is the bad part, is separated by being blown away, and the heavier kernels, which are the good part, fall back down and remain. So too, the davening of a *tzaddik* changes the *middah* of Hashem from being harsh and angry, for bad, to the *middah* of being merciful, for good. Onkelos explains that davening has the strength and power to influence the *shefa* to switch from a place of anger to a place of mercy, and to increase *shefa* from Hashem.

The *Maharsha*[6] points out that this lesson is specifically taught by Yitzchak and not by the other Avos, Avraham or Yaakov. This is because it states by Yitzchak, *"Pachad Yitzchak*—The Fear of Yitzchak,"* which teaches that Yitzchak had a unique connection to Hashem through *middas ha'din.* Although Yitzchak and Rivkah were both barren, Yitzchak was able to change the *middah* of *din* to the *middah* of *rachamim* through davening.

The *Maharal*[7] explains that *tzaddikim* are able to completely change a *middah* of Hashem from one end to the other, from being harsh and angry to being merciful, because their davening reaches to the level of complete mercy. They humble themselves before Hashem, recognizing that He is completely in charge of everything and is the cause of all causes. Whereas when an ordinary person davens, he will not change the *middah* of Hashem from one extreme to the other, although Hashem will still answer his request.

| | |
|---|---|
| 4 | סוכה יד. |
| 5 | תענית כ. פשט ראשון |
| 6 | יבמות שם |
| 7 | ח' אגדות |

The Gemara teaches that Hashem made Avraham and Yitzchak barren because Hashem cherished their davening. The *Maharal* explains that *tefillah* is about attaching oneself to Hashem. Hashem wanted the Avos to turn to the Source of all, to connect to Him and request their needs from Him. *Tzaddikim* humble themselves before Hashem and daven to Him, bringing themselves close to the Source of everything. With this, they are able to receive complete mercy from Hashem.

May Hashem answer each of our *tefillos* and bring *yeshuos* and *refuos* to Klal Yisrael!

## WHAT IS THE MEANING OF "אִישׁ יֹדֵעַ צַיִד אִישׁ שָׂדֶה" AND "אִישׁ תָּם יֹשֵׁב אֹהָלִים," AND WHY DID YITZCHAK LOVE EISAV?

### וַיְהִי עֵשָׂו אִישׁ יֹדֵעַ צַיִד אִישׁ שָׂדֶה וְיַעֲקֹב אִישׁ תָּם יֹשֵׁב אֹהָלִים (כה, כז)

וַהֲוָה עֵשָׂו גְּבַר נַחְשִׁירְכָן (נְחַשׁ יִרְכָן) (נַחְשִׁידְכָן) גְּבַר נָפֵיק חֲקַל
(לְחַקְלָא) וְיַעֲקֹב גְּבַר שְׁלִים מְשַׁמֵּישׁ בֵּית אֻלְפָנָא

*And Eisav was a man, a snake at his thigh (would rest and
be idle), a man who would go out to the field, and Yaakov
was a complete man who served in the house of learning.*

### כִּי צַיִד בְּפִיו (כה, כח)

אֲרֵי מִצֵּידֵיהּ הֲוָה אָכֵיל

*Since he would eat from his trapping.*

The *pasuk* describes Eisav as "אִישׁ יודע ציד איש שדה—A man who knows trapping, a man of the field." *Rashi* explains that "*ish yodei'a tzayid—* a man who knows trapping" refers to Eisav fooling Yitzchak by making him think that he was meticulous about fulfilling mitzvos. He would ask, "How does one tithe salt and straw?" *Rashi* explains that "*ish sadeh—*a man of the field" refers to an idle person who trapped wild animals and birds with his bow and arrow. The *pasuk* hints to two types of trapping: one with Eisav's mouth and the other in the field.

Onkelos translates "*ish yodei'a tzayid*" as "a man who was *nachshirchan*."
The *Nesinah LaGer* quotes from Rabbeinu Tam that this word is comprised of two words: "*nach*—to rest," and "*sherach*—idle." Eisav lazed
around, avoiding work. The *Nesinah LaGer* explains differently that it
is comprised of "*nachash*—snake" and "*yirchan*—of the thigh." Since
he was a hunter, Eisav had a snake on his thigh to help him trap. The
*Nesinah LaGer* notes that the Aruch has the text "*nachshidchan*," which
is comprised of "*nach*—to rest," and "*shidchan*—to cease." Eisav was
idle and didn't work, as a ruler who rests and indulges with hunting
food to eat. (It's interesting to note that the *Ran*[8] explains "*meshadchin
es ha'tinokos*—to be *meshadeich* the young girls," as *menuchah*, for when
the woman finds her mate, she is calm. *Avi Mori* added that when one
gets engaged, it is called *shidduch*, which means cease and tranquil, as
the two sides come to an agreement and things are settled.) Onkelos
translates "*ish sadeh*" as "a man who would go out to the field." The
*Nefesh HaGer* explains that Eisav did not work the field by sowing and
harvesting, rather he enjoyed rest, loved idleness, refrained from doing
work, and went out to trap.

The *pasuk* describes Yaakov as "איש תם יושב אהלים." *Rashi* explains that
Yaakov was not sharp with trickery; as his heart was, so was his mouth,
similar to a *tam*, a simpleton, unlike Eisav, who was a trickster. Yaakov
sat and learned in the tents of Shem and Ever. Onkelos translates "*ish
tam*" differently: "a complete man [*shelim*]." Rabbeinu Bachya[9] explains
that "*shelim*—being complete" hints to "*shalom*—peace," as Yaakov
chose the *middah* of *shalom*. Eisav, who hunted and killed, was the exact
opposite. Onkelos translates "*yoshev ohalim*" as "who served in the house
of learning." The *Nefesh HaGer* says that "the house of learning" refers
to learning in the tents of Shem and Ever, as *Rashi* explains. Although
"*ohalim*—tents" is plural, as *Rashi* explains, Onkelos translates as "in the
house of learning [*beis ulfana*]" in the singular, since the Torah means to
emphasize what he did—he learned.

---

8    שבת בדפי הרי"ף ה:
9    ויקרא א, ב

The following *pasuk* states, "And Yitzchak loved Eisav...and Rivkah loved Yaakov." The *pasuk* explains that Yitzchak loved Eisav because "*tzayid b'fiv*." *Rashi* quotes from the Midrash that "trappings were in the mouth of Eisav," meaning that he would trick Yitzchak into thinking that he was meticulous with mitzvos. Yitzchak loved Eisav, thinking that he was an excellent son. Rivkah, on the other hand, knew the truth about Eisav, so she loved Yaakov. Onkelos translates "*ki tzayid b'fiv*" differently: "since he—Yitzchak—would eat from his—Eisav's—trapping." Eisav would trap and bring food for Yitzchak to eat, so he loved him. The *Nefesh HaGer* asks: why should Yitzchak love Eisav because he ate from his trapping and not Yaakov who learned Torah?

The *Nefesh HaGer* answers in the name of the *Seforno* that the *pasuk* means Yitzchak *also* loved Eisav. There is no need to mention explicitly that Yitzchak loved Yaakov, as it is obvious. Since the Torah describes Yaakov as one who learned Torah, it is clear that Yitzchak loved him. Although people knew about Eisav's bad ways, Yitzchak was unaware. He only knew that Eisav was idle and went out to the field to trap and did not learn Torah. However, since he was meticulous about performing mitzvos, he loved him. The *pasuk* proves this by stating, "*ki tzayid b'fiv*": since Yitzchak ate from Eisav's trappings he must have regarded him as an honest and trusted person regarding *kashrus*. Rivkah, however, only loved Yaakov, since she recognized the wickedness of Eisav and knew the truth.

May we learn from Yaakov to be honest and learned, unlike Eisav who tricked, was idle, and went out to the field!

## WHAT DOES "MICHRAH KA'YOM" AND "HISHAV'AH LI KA'YOM" MEAN?

מִכְרָה כַיּוֹם אֶת בְּכֹרָתְךָ (כה, לא)

זַבֵּין כְּיוֹם דִּילְהוֹן (דִּלְהֵין/דְּלְהֵי רמב"ן) יָת בְּכֵירוּתָךְ לִי

*Sell to me your firstborn rights like the day which is clear (as the day when Yitzchak will die—Ramban) (like the day which was to them).*

# הִשָּׁבְעָה לִי כַּיּוֹם (כה, לג)

## קַיֵּים לִי כְּיוֹם דִּילְהוֹן (דִּלְהֵין/דְּלְהִי רמב"ן)

*Swear to me like the day which is clear (as the day when Yitzchak
will die—Ramban) (like the day which was to them).*

The *pasuk* states, "And Yaakov said, 'מכרה כיום את בכורתך לי—sell to me
your firstborn rights *ka'yom*.'" Later on, it states, "*Hishav'ah li ka'yom*—
Swear to me *ka'yom*." What does the word "*ka'yom*" mean and what is
its intent?

*Rashi* writes that Onkelos translates "*ka'yom*" as "*k'yom di'l'hon*—like
the day which is clear." Yaakov said to Eisav, "Sell to me your firstborn
rights, like the day which is clear" and "swear to me like the day which
is clear," meaning it should be a clear and complete sale. The *Nesinah
LaGer* says that *Rashi* understands Onkelos as saying that "*di'l'hon*"
means "*asher la'hem*—which was to them." The day which was to them
refers to light and brightness in the field, which is clear, whereas in
the house, it is dark because of the walls. Yaakov wanted the sale to be
complete without any option of denial.

The *Nefesh HaGer* says that it is unclear how *Rashi's* explanation fits in the
word "*di'l'hon*," or "*di l'hon*" as two words. The *Ramban* quotes Rashi's text
as "*dil'hein*," which means "to which" or "to where." He says that the more
precise text is "*d'l'hi*—to which," meaning, which day will the sale of the
firstborn rights come out to be? When it will actually take effect? Only
after a father dies does a son inherit the firstborn rights. So too, Yaakov
said, "Sell to me your firstborn rights and swear to me about them that
I shall purchase and acquire them when our father, Yitzchak, will die."
The *Ramban* suggests that Onkelos understands the word "*ka'yom—like
the day*," as "*ba'yom—on the day*," as we find that a כ can mean a ב.

The *Nefesh HaGer* teaches another explanation in Onkelos based on
the *Tanna D'bei Eliyahu*:[10] "*k'yom d'l'hon*" means "like the day which was
to them." This reflects an earlier time, when Yaakov and Eisav were

---

together in the stomach of their mother, Rivkah. Yaakov said to Eisav, "We are two brothers to our father, and there are two worlds before us: *Olam Hazeh* and *Olam Haba*. *Olam Hazeh* has eating, drinking, business, marriage, and having children, whereas *Olam Haba* does not have these things. If you want take *Olam Hazeh*, I will take *Olam Haba*. This is as it states, "Yaakov said to Eisav, מכרה כיום את בכורתך לי—Sell to me your firstborn rights of *Olam Hazeh*, just as the day that we were in the stomach.'" At that time, Eisav took his portion in *Olam Hazeh* and Yaakov took his portion in *Olam Haba*.

The *Nefesh HaGer* says that although the firstborn rights in this world are connected to *Olam Haba*, as a person who will not have *Olam Haba* is not fitting to do *avodah*, still, the firstborn rights in this world were not yet divided inside Rivkah. At that point, Yaakov had been conceived and created first; thus, he was the firstborn. *Rashi*[11] explains this with a *mashal* of two stones entering a tube. The one which is inserted first leaves second; the one which is inserted second leaves first. So too, Yaakov was conceived and created first, however, he came out second, after Eisav. While inside, there was no need for Yaakov to acquire firstborn rights to *Olam Hazeh*, as inside he was firstborn. He held onto Eisav's heel in order to try and hold back Eisav and preempt his exit, thereby being first by law. Onkelos adds the words "*di l'hon*—which was to them," as a *k'lomar*, explaining the meaning of "*ka'yom*—like the day." Like the day—which day? The previous day, which was when they were together and discussed the worlds. "Which was to them" indicates a day of an earlier time. Yaakov said to Eisav, "Sell to me your firstborn rights and swear to me about the firstborn rights of *Olam Hazeh*, like that day that we had previously discussed in our mother's stomach when we divided *Olam Hazeh* and *Olam Haba*."

The *Tanna D'bei Eliyahu* teaches that when Eisav met Yaakov in *Parashas Vayishlach*, he saw that Yaakov had wives and children, slaves and maidservants, animals, silver, and gold. Eisav asked him, "Did you not say to me that you are taking *Olam Haba* and I am taking *Olam Hazeh*?

Why are you using and benefiting from this world like me?" Yaakov responded, "This is the little bit which Hashem gave to me for what I need in this world."

The Chafetz Chaim taught a *mashal* about *Olam Hazeh*:[12] A person traveled to a faraway country to find a job in order to sustain his family. The place had precious stones and pearls thrown around the streets; they were not worth much in that town since there was so many of them. Instead, the inhabitants of the town prized their expensive, unique food. He stayed there a few years and became wealthy, and he decided to leave. He saw that the food was important in their eyes, so he bought as much food as he could and placed it on his boat to bring back home and sell for a profit. When he reached the entrance of the city, the tax collectors made him open his luggage, and they saw that all the food was spoiled. They commanded him to throw everything into the sea. He used his last handful of coins to hire workers to throw away the boxes, and he was left with nothing. He returned home to his family tremendously embarrassed that after the past few years of being away, he brought back absolutely nothing, and went to sleep depressed. His wife searched through his clothing and noticed a small box of precious stones—useless in the town the husband had been working, but incredibly valuable there—which she took and sold for thousands of gold coins. She decorated the house with nice utensils, linen, and all types of beautiful things. When he woke up, he saw the beautiful house and wondered, "What is this? A moment ago, there was nothing!" His wife told him that she had found a box of precious stones stuck in his luggage and sold it. He then started to cry uncontrollably: he could have brought back so many precious stones, yet instead brought worthless things! What a disgrace; what a wasted opportunity.

So too, *Olam Hazeh* is compared to the fleeting temptations and desires that one has for material things, such as gourmet food, whereas in *Olam Haba*, the only thing with any value will be Torah, mitzvos, and good deeds, which are compared to precious stones and pearls. The

---

main purpose of coming into this world is to pay attention to spiritual growth by learning Torah and doing mitzvos and good deeds. One often forgets this, and instead eats, drinks, clothes himself, and buys a nice apartment in which to live. We are here in a temporary world to collect Torah, mitzvos, and *maasim tovim*, and we should pack our suitcase to bring provisions with us for the everlasting world and eternal life.

May we utilize this world as preparation for the next world by learning Torah and doing mitzvos and *maasim tovim*!

## WAS THERE A POSSIBILITY OF CURSE IF YITZCHAK WOULD HAVE NOTICED IT WAS YAAKOV?

### וַיִּתְרֹצֲצוּ הַבָּנִים בְּקִרְבָּהּ...וַתֵּלֶךְ לִדְרֹשׁ אֶת ה' (כה, כב)

וְדָחֲקִין בְּנַיָּא בִּמְעָהָא...וַאֲזַלַת לְמִתְבַּע אֻלְפָן מִן קֳדָם יְיָ

*And the sons pushed in her stomach...and she went to seek teaching from before Hashem.*

### וְרַב יַעֲבֹד צָעִיר (כה, כג)

וְרַבָּא יִשְׁתַּעְבַּד לִזְעֵירָא

*And the big one will be subjected to the smaller one.*

### עָלַי קִלְלָתְךָ בְּנִי (כו, יג)

עֲלַי אִתְאֲמַר בִּנְבוּאָה דְּלָא יֵיתוֹן לְוָטַיָּא עֲלָךְ בְּרִי

*It was prophetically told to me that no curses will come upon you, my son.*

### וְהָיָה כַּאֲשֶׁר תָּרִיד וּפָרַקְתָּ עֻלּוֹ מֵעַל צַוָּארֶךָ (כו, מ)

וִיהֵי כַּד יַעְבְּרוּן בְּנוֹהִי עַל פִּתְגָמֵי אוֹרָיְתָא וְתַעְדֵּי נִירֵיהּ מֵעַל צַוְרָךְ

*And it will be when they will transgress (pass over) the things of the Torah, you will remove his yoke from upon your neck.*

The *pesukim* state that Rivkah told Yaakov to prepare food to bring to Yitzchak in order to receive Yitzchak's berachos. Yaakov said, "Behold,

Eisav, my brother, is a hairy person, whereas I am a smooth person. Maybe my father will feel me and it will be in his eyes as a mocking, and it will bring upon me curse and not blessing." Rivkah responded, *"alai kilelasecha b'ni."* What does this mean, and how does it allay Yaakov's worry?

The *Seforno* explains that Rivkah said, "If there will be any curses that shall befall you, I accept responsibility for the consequences; you do not have to worry." This is similar to that which Shlomo Hamelech did; he accepted upon himself the curses of Yoav which befell him.

Onkelos translates the words *"alai kilelasecha b'ni"* differently: "It was prophetically told to me that no curses will come upon you, my son." Since Rivkah quoted a prophecy, Yaakov did not need to worry, because nothing bad would occur. The *Hakesav V'Hakabbalah* suggests that *"alai"* means "remove," as it states, "העלו מסביב למשכן קרח—Move away from around the tent of Korach." Rivkah said, "There is no worry in my heart that he will curse you; it is 100 percent clear to me that he will not curse you." Where do we find this prophecy said to Rivkah?

It states toward the beginning of the parashah, "ויתרוצצו הבנים בקרבה...ותלך לדרש את ה'," which Onkelos translates as, "And the sons pushed in her stomach...and she went to seek teaching from before Hashem." The following *pasuk* states that Hashem said to her that there are two nations in her stomach which will split into two individual kingdoms. The *pasuk* ends, *"V'rav yaavod tza'ir,"* which literally means, "And the big one will subject the small one." It is unclear who will be subject to whom; will the big one be subjected to the smaller one, or will the big one subject the smaller one? The *Nefesh HaGer* says that Onkelos translates by adding a 'ל (לזעירא), yielding *"l'tza'ir—to the small one,"* to clarify and emphasize that the big one will be subjected to the smaller one, and not vice versa. The *Rashbam* explains that Rivkah felt secure from the prophecy of *"v'rav yaavod tza'ir,"* which expresses that the older one, Eisav, will be subjected to the younger one, Yaakov. She was confident that no curse would befall Yaakov. The *Hakesav V'Hakabbalah* quotes from Rabbi Shimon bar Yochai that when Yitzchak called Eisav, Yaakov wasn't there. The Shechinah let Rivkah know about it, and she told

Yaakov. For this reason, she went against the interest of her husband and forced Yaakov to go against his father's interest. This was all done to fulfill the prophecy of *"v'rav yaavod tza'ir."*

Is the blessing of *"v'rav yaavod tza'ir"* guaranteed without condition? After Eisav convinces Yitzchak to also bless him, Yitzchak says, "והיה כאשר תריד ופרקת עולו מעל צוארך." Both Onkelos and *Rashi* explain: Yitzchak tells Eisav, "When Yaakov will transgress the Torah, there will be an opening to reclaim the blessings that Yaakov took." So too, the Gemara[13] writes that Eisav will take the opportunity to reign and be king, while Yaakov will fall down. *Rashi* explains that when Eisav is mighty, Yaakov will be weak. *Targum Yonasan ben Uziel* translates in *Shiras Devorah*,[14] "Hashem, Your Torah that You gave to Yisrael, when they transgress it, the nations will rule over them, and when they return to it, they will be mightier over their enemies." We see that although the berachos were told over from Hashem as a prophecy to Rivkah, there is still a crucial clause that we must remember. If we fulfill the Torah, we will retain the berachos; if not, *chas v'shalom*, we will lose them.

May Hashem help us constantly fulfill the Torah and thereby retain the berachos!

## DOES "V'YISHTACHAVU" MEAN "AND THEY WILL BOW DOWN," "BE SUBJECTED," OR "REQUEST"?

יַעַבְדוּךָ עַמִּים וְיִשְׁתַּחֲוּ [וְיִשְׁתַּחֲווּ] לְךָ לְאָמִּים הֱוֵה גְבִיר לְאַחֶיךָ וְיִשְׁתַּחֲווּ לְךָ בְּנֵי אִמֶּךָ (כז, כט)

יִפְלְחוּנָךְ עַמְמִין וְיִשְׁתַּעְבְּדָן לָךְ מַלְכְוָן הֱוֵי רַב לַאֲחָךְ וְיִסְגְּדוּן לָךְ בְּנֵי אִמֶּךְ

*Nations will serve [do labor for] you, and kingdoms will be subjected to you; be a leader to your brothers, and your mother's sons will bow down to you.*

---

13    פסחים מב:

14    שופטים ה, ד

The *pasuk* states, "יעבדוך עמים וישתחוו לך לאמים הוה גביר לאחיך וישתחוו לך בני אמך," which Onkelos translates as, "Nations will serve [do labor for] you, and kingdoms will be subjected to you; be a leader to your brothers, and your mother's sons will bow down to you." "*V'yishtachavu*—and they will bow down" is mentioned twice in this *pasuk*: first about *le'umim*, which Onkelos translates as "kingdoms," and again regarding the sons of Rivkah. The *Nefesh HaGer* says that Onkelos translates "*v'yishtachavu lecha le'umim*" as "and kingdoms will be subjected [*v'yishtaabdan*] to you," which means that they will be subjected by paying head taxes and land taxes. He translates "וישתחוו לך בני אמך" as "and your mother's sons will bow down [*v'yisgedun*] to you." Why doesn't Onkelos also translate the first "*v'yishtachavu*" literally, as "and kings will bow down to you"?

The *Yein Hatov* answers that it is reasonable to say a few people will bow down, like *b'nei imecha*, but not an entire nation. The *Nesinah LaGer* answers differently: Onkelos does not translate "bow down" in deference to the honor of kings, to say this in a nicer way. The *Nefesh HaGer* adds that this is as *Rashi* explains the *pasuk*, "וירדו כל עבדיך אלה אלי והשתחוו לי לאמר צא אתה—And all your servants will descend to me and they will bow down to me, saying, 'Go out.'" Although in the end, Pharaoh himself descended to Moshe and said, "Go out of my nation," Moshe did not say, "וירדת אלי והשתחוית לי—And you will descend to me, and you will bow down to me." Rather, in order to give honor to Pharaoh, he said, "And all your servants will descend to me, and they will bow down"; he did not mention Pharaoh himself. The *Maharsha*[15] points out that we never find in the Torah that Pharaoh actually bowed down to Moshe. He explains that just as it does not state explicitly that the servants bowed down, but it is assumed, so too, Pharaoh must have also bowed down.

Onkelos translates "וירדו...והשתחוו לי לאמר" differently: "And all of your servants will descend next to me and they will request from me, saying [וייחתון כל עבדך אלין לותי ויבעון מני למימר]." The *Nefesh HaGer* explains that

---

this refers to when the Mitzrim said, "We will all die." Why does Onkelos not translate *"v'hishtachavu li"* literally, as "and they will bow down to me"? The *Nefesh HaGer* answers that since it states *"leimor*—saying," following bowing down, it must mean "requesting." The *Nesinah LaGer* adds that we don't find the word "לאמר" following the action of bowing down. The *Nefesh HaGer* offers another explanation: since Moshe said this before Pharaoh, Onkelos does not translate "and they will bow down to me," as it is not respectful to say this to a king.

The *Nesinah LaGer* says that Onkelos, who translates *"v'hishtachavu li"* as "and they will request from me," answers the *Maharsha*'s question— we never find that Pharaoh actually bowed down to Moshe. Onkelos explains that Moshe said that the servants will *request*, in place of Pharaoh, which the Torah explicitly states happened. In truth, Pharaoh himself descended to Moshe and requested for them to leave Mitzrayim.

What message can we take from honoring kings? The Gemara[16] records that Geniva came to Rav Huna and Rav Chisda and said, "Peace be upon you, kings, peace be upon you, kings." They asked him, "From where do you know that the *Rabbanan* are called kings?" He responded, "*Bi melachim yimlochu.*" We have a mitzvah to honor and fear *talmidei chachamim*, who are like kings. Once, I was standing next to a *rosh yeshiva*, and I touched him on the arm, as one does with a friend. He gave me a stare and moved away a bit, but didn't say a word. I felt like jumping out the window. We can't talk to our *rebbeim* as our friends; rather, we must remember that they are like kings whom we need to honor and fear. Once, someone went to talk to Rav Hutner, and the person left with his back to him. Rav Hutner called him back in so that he could walk out properly. Even when one leaves a great person, he has to do so in the appropriate way.

May we learn from the honor of kings to honor and fear our *rebbeim*!

---

16   .גיטין סב

# Vayeitzei

## WHAT WAS THE PLACE WHERE YAAKOV SLEPT, AND HOW WAS IT UNIQUE?

אֵין זֶה כִּי אִם בֵּית אֱלֹקִים וְזֶה שַׁעַר הַשָּׁמָיִם (כח, יז)

לֵית דֵּין אֲתַר הֶדְיוֹט אֱלָהֵין אֲתַר (אַתְרָא) דְּרַעֲוָא בֵּיה מִן קֳדָם יְיָ
וְדֵין תְּרַע קָבֵיל שְׁמַיָּא

*"This is not an ordinary place; rather, it is a place which
has in it favor from before [because of] Hashem, and
this is the gateway opposite the Heavens."*

After Yaakov woke up, he was afraid and said, "אֵין זֶה כִּי אִם בֵּית אלקים וזה
שער השמים—This is not, rather the house of G-d, and this is the gateway
of the Heavens." What is the meaning of "This is not, rather the house
of G-d"? What is it not, and what indeed is it? Onkelos translates "אֵין
אלקים בית אם כי זה" as, "This is not an ordinary place, rather it is a place
which has in it favor from before [because of] Hashem." The *Nefesh
HaGer* says that Onkelos adds this is not an "ordinary place" in order
to clarify what it is not. This is not a regular, ordinary place, rather it is
a special, unique place, as it has in it favor from Hashem.

The *Nefesh HaGer* says that Onkelos does not translate *"beis Elokim"* literally, since it states in *Navi*, "אֵי זֶה בַית אשר תבנו לי—Which house can you
build for Me?" There is no place to which Hashem is confined! Rather,
the *pasuk* means a place where Hashem's favor is found. This is similar
to *Rashi's* explanation: it is a place for people's davening to ascend to
the Heavens. The *Ibn Ezra* adds that any person in need can go there
to daven and it will be heard, since it is a chosen place where Hashem
answers people's prayers.

The *Pirkei D'Rabi Eliezer* writes:[1] this *pasuk* teaches that whoever davens in this place in Yerushalayim is considered to have davened before the *Kisei HaKavod*, Throne of Hashem. The gateway to the Heavens is in that place, and the door is open to listen to people's davening. The *Maharik*[2] says there is no bigger mitzvah than to build a Beis K'nesses in Yerushalayim, the holy city, a place that is prepared for davening to ascend to the Heavens.

In *Kedushah*, we say, "*M'lo chal ha'aretz kevodo*—The entire world is filled with His honor." Yet, we also say "*Ayei mekom kevodo*—Where is the place of His honor?" This seems to be a contradiction; on the one hand, His honor fills the whole world, yet it is not known where His honor is. The *Maharsha*[3] says that indeed, Hashem's honor fills the entire world; however, His Shechinah is revealed in specific, designated places, such as the *Mishkan*, Beis Hamikdash, and in exile. Moreover, there are different levels of *kedushah* depending on the place. Rabbeinu Yonah[4] writes that if a person cannot daven with a *minyan*, he should still daven in a shul because it is a designated and permanent place for davening. The *Shulchan Aruch*[5] *paskens* this, and the *Mishnah Berurah*[6] explains that since it is a place set permanently for *kedushah*, his davening will be answered there, more than in a regular place. We see that the *kedushah* of an ordinary place is not like the *kedushah* of a shul or *beis midrash*, while their *kedushah* is not as great as the Beis Hamikdash. This is because there are different levels of *kedushah* in the world, each in their respective places. Hashem fills the whole world, but there is more *kedushah* in certain places over others. The question of "Where is the place of His honor?" refers to a level of *kedushah* which is beyond the angels' sight and awareness.

| | |
|---|---|
| 1 | לה |
| 2 | שורש ה |
| 3 | מגילה כט. |
| 4 | ברכות בדפי הרי"ף ד. |
| 5 | או"ח סי' צ, ט |
| 6 | ס"ק לג |

In *Parashas Chayei Sarah*, it states,[7] "ויצחק בא מבוא באר לחי ראי," which Onkelos translates as, "And Yitzchak entered with (from) his coming, from the well that an existing angel was seen upon it [ויצחק על במיתוהי מבירא דמלאך קימא אתחזי עלה]." The *Ramban* explains that "*mi'bo*" is something ongoing, his continuous coming. Yitzchak would constantly go to daven in the place where the angel appeared to Hagar, since it was fit for davening. The *Seforno* adds that he specifically went to daven in a place where his maidservant's davening was answered. Similarly, we see that there are different places where it is more fitting to daven.

The *pasuk* ends, "*V'zeh shaar haShamayim*—And this is the gateway of the Heavens." The *Nesinah LaGer* asks: how is it possible for a place on land to be considered the gateway of the Heavens? The *Nesinah LaGer* says that Onkelos answers this by translating "*v'zeh shaar haShamayim*" as "and this is the gateway opposite the Heavens." The *Nefesh HaGer* explains this with *Rashi* in the name of the Midrash: the Beis Hamikdash in the Heavens above is situated exactly opposite the Beis Hamikdash below.

This is as the *Midrash Tanchuma* teaches:[8] our Mikdash below is exactly aligned with Hashem's throne above, as it states, "*Machon l'shivt'cha.*" The *Eitz Yosef* explains that "מכון" is related to "מכוון—aligned." The Mikdash is aligned with Hashem's dwelling place. Also, the *Midrash Tanchuma* teaches[9] that the Yerushalayim above is aligned with the Yerushalayim below. Because of Hashem's great love for the Yerushalayim below, He made another one above. Yaakov slept in the place which is the gateway opposite the Heavens, where people's davening ascends to Hashem.

May Hashem build the Beis Hamikdash, the gateway to the Heavens, and answer our davening!

7    כה, סב

8    פקודי ב

9    שם א

## DID YAAKOV MAKE A VOW OR A PROMISE?

וַיִּדַּר יַעֲקֹב נֶדֶר לֵאמֹר אִם יִהְיֶה אֱלֹקִים עִמָּדִי (כח, כ)

וְקַיֵּים יַעֲקֹב קְיָם לְמֵימַר אִם יְהֵי מֵימְרָא דַיְיָ בְּסַעֲדִי

*And Yaakov swore an oath saying, "If the saying
[word] of Hashem will assist me.*

וְהָאֶבֶן הַזֹּאת אֲשֶׁר שַׂמְתִּי מַצֵּבָה יִהְיֶה בֵּית אֱלֹקִים (כח, כב)

וְאַבְנָא הָדָא דְּשַׁוִּיתִי קָמָא תְּהֵי דְּאֵיהֵי פָּלַח עֲלַהּ קֳדָם יְיָ

*And this stone that I placed as a stand will be
where I will serve upon it before Hashem.*

אֲשֶׁר נָדַרְתָּ לִּי שָׁם נֶדֶר (לא, יג)

דְּקַיֵּימְתָּא קֳדָמַי תַּמָּן קְיָם

*Where you swore an oath before Me.*

When Yaakov goes to Charan to stay with Lavan, the *pasuk* states, "וידר
יעקב נדר לאמר אם יהיה אלקים עמדי—And Yaakov vowed a vow saying, 'If
Hashem will be with me...'" Onkelos translates these words as, "And
Yaakov swore an oath [*v'kayem Yaakov k'yam*], saying, 'If the saying
[word] of Hashem will assist me...'" He translates *"neder"* as *"k'yam,"*
which is a form of *shevuah*—oath. Also, when Yaakov recounts to
Rachel and Leah about what the angel of Hashem said to him, he says,
"אשר נדרת לי שם נדר," which literally means "that you vowed there a vow to
Me." There, too, Onkelos translates, "that you swore there an oath before Me [דקימתא קדמי תמן קים]." We also find this change from Onkelos in
*Parashas Chukas.* The Canaani king of Arad came to fight against Yisrael,
and it states,[10] "וידר ישראל נדר לה' ויאמר אם נתן תתן את העם בידי והחרמתי את
עריהם—And Yisrael vowed a vow before Hashem and said, 'If You will,
indeed, give over this nation into my hand, then I will ban their cities.'"
There, too, Onkelos translates *neder* as an oath: "And Yisrael swore an

oath before Hashem [וקיים ישראל קים קדם ה']." Why does Onkelos change from "vow" to "oath" by both Yaakov and B'nei Yisrael?

The *Nefesh HaGer* and *Nesinah LaGer* answer that Onkelos translates *neder* as a *shevuah* since it states in *Tehillim*: "נשבע לה' נדר לאביר יעקב." This reflects that aside from a vow, Yaakov also made an oath. Also, the *Bereishis Rabbah*[11] teaches that the *pasuk* in *Parashas Chukas* states, "*Va'yidar Yisrael*," in singular, not "*Va'yidru Yisrael*," in plural. This hints to *Yisrael Saba*, Yaakov Avinu, who made both a vow and an oath.

The *Shaarei Aharon* answers differently: The Gemara explains that there is a fundamental difference between an oath and a vow. To take an oath means for the person to obligate himself to do or not do something. An example is when one swears and says, "I will eat something." To take a vow means to restrict something from himself. An example is when one says, "This food is forbidden for me to eat." Yaakov declares, "If Hashem will guard me on this path, and will give me bread to eat and clothes to wear, and return me in peace to my father's house, then, והאבן הזאת אשר שמתי מצבה יהיה בית אלקים." Onkelos translates as, "And this stone that I placed as a stand will be where I will serve upon it before Hashem." Yaakov promised to serve Hashem, which is similar to an oath. Just as with an oath, one obligates himself to do something, so too, Yaakov promised to actively serve Hashem. In this case, Yaakov committed himself to do something; there was no object for a vow to apply to. Therefore, Onkelos does not translate as a vow, but rather, as an oath.

Similarly, in *Parashas Chukas*, Yisrael declared, "If You will, indeed, give over this nation into my hand, I will ban their cities." Onkelos translates "*v'hacharamti*" as "and I will finish off." Yisrael promised to completely destroy their cities, which is similar to an oath, to actively do something, unlike a vow, as there was nothing on which for it to take effect.

Rabbeinu Yonah[12] says that even if a person fulfills his vows, if he pushes them off even by accident, Hashem will punish him. Since it is

---

11    פ' ע, ב
12    שע"ת שער ג, עד

common for people to forget, a person should make sure to remember his vow. Also, it states, "It is better not to vow than to vow and not pay." However, one should make a vow when in a time of affliction, as Yaakov did. Additionally, important people should vow at gatherings, when there is a need to strengthen others who would otherwise not give to contribute tzedakah, so that they too will be inspired to do the same.

The Gemara[13] teaches that Yaakov was punished for the twenty-two years that he was away from his parents and did not fulfill *kibbud av va'eim*. Yaakov worked for fourteen years for Rachel and Leah, six years for the sheep, and traveled for two years, including his time in Beis El where he brought *korbanos* and fulfilled his vow. The *Maharsha* asks: Why was Yaakov punished for the time that he waited in Beis El to bring his *korbanos*? After all, Hashem commanded him, "עלה בית אל...ועשה שם מזבח —Ascend to Beis El...and make a *mizbeiach*." Hashem commanded him to go there and bring *korbanos*! My previous Rosh Yeshiva answered that although Hashem commanded Yaakov to go there, he was also punished for this time because he initially put the responsibility on himself to bring *korbanos*.

May we only make vows we definitely can and will fulfill, and may Hashem help us fulfill our word!

## WHAT WERE THE DUDA'IM, AND WHAT WAS THEIR PURPOSE?

וַיֵּלֶךְ רְאוּבֵן...וַיִּמְצָא דוּדָאִים בַּשָּׂדֶה...תְּנִי
נָא לִי מִדּוּדָאֵי בְּנֵךְ (ל, יד)

וַאֲזַל רְאוּבֵן...וְאַשְׁכַּח יַבְרוּחִין בְּחַקְלָא...הֲבִי כְּעַן לִי מִיַּבְרוּחֵי דִּבְרִיךְ

*And Reuven went...and he found yavruchin in the
field..."Now give me from the yavruchin of your son."*

---

## הַמְעַט קַחְתֵּךְ אֶת אִישִׁי וְלָקַחַת גַּם אֶת דּוּדָאֵי בְּנִי וַתֹּאמֶר רָחֵל לָכֵן יִשְׁכַּב עִמָּךְ הַלַּיְלָה תַּחַת דּוּדָאֵי בְנֵךְ (ל, טו)

הַזְעֵיר דִּדְבַרְתְּ יָת בַּעְלִי וְתִסְּבִין אַף יָת יַבְרוּחֵי דִבְרִי וַאֲמֶרֶת רָחֵל בְּכֵן יִשְׁכּוֹב עִמֵּיךְ בְּלֵילְיָא חֲלָף יַבְרוּחֵי דִּבְרִיךְ

*Is it little [not enough] that you led [took] my husband, and you will
also take the yavruchin of my son? And Rachel said, "With this, he
will lie with you at night, in exchange for the yavruchin of your son."*

## וַיִּזְכֹּר אֱלֹקִים אֶת רָחֵל וַיִּשְׁמַע אֵלֶיהָ אֱלֹקִים וַיִּפְתַּח אֶת רַחְמָהּ (ל, כב)

וְעָאל דֻּכְרָנַהּ דְּרָחֵל קֳדָם יְיָ וְקַבֵּיל צְלוֹתַהּ יְיָ וִיהַב לַהּ עִדּוּי

*And the remembrance of Rachel entered before Hashem, and
Hashem accepted her davening and gave her conception.*

The *pasuk* states, "וילך ראובן...וימצא דודאים בשדה—And Reuven went
during the days of the wheat harvesting, and he found *duda'im*." What
are *duda'im* and what was their purpose?

*Rashi* explains that they are *"sigli,"* a certain type of grass; in the language of Yishmael, it is called ישמי"ן, which the *Targum HaLaaz* says is
jasmine. This is the opinion of Levi in the Gemara.[14] Onkelos translates
*"duda'im"* as *"yavruchin."* The *Nesinah LaGer* says this is Rav's opinion in
the Gemara. The *Ibn Ezra* explains that *"duda'im"* are called *"yavruchin"*
in the language of Yishmael. They have a good smell and are in the shape
of a person, in the form of a head and hands. There are those who say
that they are beneficial for conception; however, it is not known why
this should be so, as their nature is cold. The *Ramban* says that Rachel
wanted them to play with and enjoy their good smell. She was answered
by davening, not through medicines, as it states, "ויזכר אלקים את רחל
וישמע אליה אלקים," which Onkelos translates as, "And the remembrance
of Rachel entered before Hashem, and Hashem accepted her davening
and gave her conception." Reuven brought the branches of *duda'im* or

their fruit, which is similar to an apple and has a good smell. However, he did not bring the root, which is what is in the form of a head and hands. People say that the root is beneficial for conception. If it is true, it is by way of a *segulah*, not naturally, as the *Ramban* did not find anything in any of the books of healing which speak about this.

It states, "And he brought them to Leah his mother, and Rachel said to Leah, 'תני נא לי מדודאי בנך.'" Onkelos translates this as, "Now give me from the *yavruchin* of your son." Leah responds, "המעט קחתך את אישי ולקחת גם את דודאי בני," which Onkelos translates as, "Is it little [not enough] that you led [took] my husband, and you will also take the *yavruchin* of my son?" The *pasuk* mentions two *leshonos* of "kach"; the first is "kachteich," which Onkelos translates as "that you led [di'dvart]," and the second is "v'lakachas," which Onkelos translates as "and you will take [v'sise'vin]." *Rashi*[15] explains that whereas in *lashon hakodesh* the Torah uses the same word for taking both people and inanimate objects, Onkelos differentiates between them. In the context of taking people, he translates "kach" as "devar," since they are "taken" with words, by convincing them to come. In the context of taking inanimate objects, he translates "kach" as "sav." The word "kachteich" refers to taking Yaakov, her husband, so Onkelos translates "di'dvart." The word "v'lakachas" refers to taking the *duda'im*, so Onkelos translates as "v'sise'vin."

Rachel responded, "לכן ישכב עמך הלילה תחת דודאי בנך," which Onkelos translates as, "With this, he will lie with you at night, in exchange for the *yavruchin* of your son." Rav Yerucham asks: why does Leah claim that Rachel is taking away her husband? After all, Yaakov worked for Rachel for seven years and Lavan tricked him into marrying Leah!

Rabbi Moshe Sheinerman[16] answered that Rachel suspected that Lavan would trick Yaakov. Therefore, the entire time she made Leah feel as though she was the wife who was meant for Yaakov. Rachel gave over the *simanim* in such a modest way that Leah did not realize Rachel's kindness. I heard in the name of the Midrash that when Yaakov sent

---

15  מג, טו
16  אהל משה

presents to Rachel, she passed them on to Leah, making Leah think that they were sent directly to her. When Yaakov checked to verify that Leah was indeed Rachel, Rachel responded for Leah and made Yaakov think that she was Rachel so that Yaakov would not catch Lavan and cause Leah tremendous embarrassment. Leah did not realize that she took Yaakov for a husband instead of Rachel! Therefore, Leah said to Rachel, "How come you are taking Yaakov, my husband!"

May we learn from Rachel's extreme sensitivity and kindness to care for others!

## DID HASHEM BLESS LAVAN "BECAUSE OF YAAKOV" OR "WHEN HE CAME"?

### נִחַשְׁתִּי וַיְבָרֲכֵנִי ה' בִּגְלָלֶךָ (ל, כז)

נַסִּיתִי וּבָרְכַנִי יְיָ בְּדִילָךְ

*I tested and Hashem blessed me because of you.*

### וַיְבָרֶךְ ה' אֹתְךָ לְרַגְלִי (ל, ל)

וּבָרֵיךְ יְיָ יָתָךְ בְּדִילִי

*And Hashem blessed you because of me.*

At the end of fourteen years, Yaakov asks permission from Lavan to leave. Lavan responds, "If I have found favor in your eyes, נחשתי ויברכני ה' בגללך—I checked into my charms and recognized that Hashem blessed me because of you." *Rashi* explains that when Yaakov came, Lavan's daughter, Rachel, was shepherding the sheep since he had no sons. No person would send his daughters in place of sons to shepherd sheep. After Yaakov came to Lavan's house, it states "וישמע את דברי בני לבן—And he heard the words of the sons of Lavan," which indicates that now, Lavan indeed had sons. The Gemara[17] brings that immediately when *talmidei chachamim* come, *berachah* comes as well, as it states,

---

"*Va'yevarcheini Hashem biglalecha*—and Hashem blessed me because of you." The *Maharsha* explains that this refers to the few sheep that became many, as it states, "כי מעט אשר היה לך לפני ויפרוץ לרב ויברך ה' אותך לרגלי—Since the little that there was to you before me became numerous, and Hashem blessed you because of my coming."

Onkelos translates "*nichashti*" as "*nasisi*—I tested," meaning by trial, not literally referring to charms. The *Nefesh HaGer* quotes from the *Ramban* and *Ibn Ezra* that in truth, Lavan asked his idols whether his success came through nature or because of Yaakov. Onkelos changes this, as he is especially careful not to associate incantations or magic with Hashem, *chas v'shalom*, as it states "נחשתי ויברכני ה' בגללך."

Yaakov responds to Lavan, "You know that which I worked for you…the little that there was to you before me became numerous, ויברך ה' אותך לרגלי—and Hashem blessed you *l'ragli*." *Rashi* explains the 'ל of לרגלי to mean "nearby"[18]; because of the coming of my feet to you, berachah came to you soon after, as well. Onkelos translates the word "*l'ragli*," which literally means "to my feet," as "*biglali*—because of me." The *Nefesh HaGer* says that this is consistent with the same language that Lavan used when he spoke to Yaakov and said, "*Va'yevarcheini Hashem biglalecha*."

Both Onkelos and *Rashi* understand that Yaakov admits that because of him, berachah came to the house of Lavan. Why, then, does Yaakov respond to Lavan with an indirect *lashon* of "*l'ragli*" and not a clear *lashon* of "*biglali*"—"ויברך ה' אותך בגללי"?

The *Nefesh HaGer* answers in the name of the Ramban that Yaakov responded with "*l'ragli*" to be modest. Although Yaakov knew that all of Lavan's success was due to his own credit, he didn't say that explicitly so as not to take credit. Yaakov placed Lavan's success completely upon Hashem, not on himself.

The *Orchos Tzaddikim* teaches regarding the *middah* of *anavah*, modesty: one who is healthy and well and has *parnassah* should think to himself that Hashem caused it all and he is undeserving. "What am I before Hashem, Who is great, exalted, and everlasting, whereas I am lowly and fleeting? There is no limit to the amount of good deeds I owe Hashem to repay Him for all His kindness."

May we learn from Yaakov Avinu's *anavah* to recognize that all of our berachos are from Hashem and that we are undeserving, and we should do our best to repay Him with our good deeds!

## DID RACHEL STEAL LAVAN'S IDOLS, DID YAAKOV STEAL THE KNOWLEDGE OF LAVAN, AND DID HE FLEE?

וַתִּגְנֹב רָחֵל אֶת הַתְּרָפִים אֲשֶׁר לְאָבִיהָ (לא, יט)

וּנְסֵיבַת (וְכַסִּיאַת) רָחֵל יָת צַלְמָנַיָּא דְּלַאֲבוּהָא

*And Rachel took (concealed) the idols that belonged to her father.*

וַיִּגְנֹב יַעֲקֹב אֶת לֵב לָבָן הָאֲרַמִּי עַל בְּלִי
הִגִּיד לוֹ כִּי בֹרֵחַ הוּא (לא, כ)

וְכַסִּי יַעֲקֹב מִן לָבָן אֲרַמָּאָה עַל דְּלָא חַוִּי לֵיהּ אֲרֵי אָזֵיל הוּא

*And Yaakov concealed his leaving from Lavan the Arami by not telling him that he was going.*

וַיִּבְרַח (לא, כא)

וַאֲזַל (וַעֲרַק)

*And he went (and he fled).*

וַתִּגְנֹב אֶת לְבָבִי (לא, כו) וַתִּגְנֹב אֹתִי (לא, כז)

וְכַסִּיתָא מִנִּי

*And you concealed from me.*

לָמָּה גָנַבְתָּ אֶת אֱלֹהָי (לא, ל)

לְמָא נְסֵיבְתָּא יָת דַּחְלְתִי

*Why did you take [the objects of] my reverence?*

# וְלֹא יָדַע יַעֲקֹב כִּי רָחֵל גְּנָבָתַם (לא, לב)

## וְלָא יָדַע יַעֲקֹב אֲרֵי רָחֵל נְסֵיבַתְנוּן

*And Yaakov did not know that Rachel took them.*

The *pasuk* states, "וַתִּגְנֹב רָחֵל אֶת הַתְּרָפִים אֲשֶׁר לְאָבִיהָ—And Rachel stole the idols that belonged to her father." Onkelos translates *"va'tignov Rachel"* as "and Rachel took [*u'ne'seivas*]." Others have the text *"v'chasias*—and Rachel concealed." Onkelos changes from the literal translation of "stole" to "took" or concealed" Similarly, later, when it states that Lavan said to Yaakov, "לָמָה גָּנַבְתָּ אֶת אֱלֹהָי—Why did you steal my gods," Onkelos translates, "Why did you take [the objects of] my reverence?" The *Nesinah LaGer* explains that "my reverence" refers to the idolatry that he feared. Here too, Onkelos changes from the literal translation of "steal" to "take." Why does Onkelos switch from "stole" to "took" or "concealed," and from "steal" to "take"?

One answer is that Onkelos translates as "taking" because the *pasuk* itself states later on in the parashah, "וְרָחֵל לָקְחָה אֶת הַתְּרָפִים—And Rachel took the idols." The *Nesinah LaGer* explains that *"geneivah"* reflects when one takes something from someone else for himself. Here, Rachel did not take the idols for herself, but to remove idolatry from Lavan's house and stop him from worshiping idolatry. Onkelos translates "and Rachel *took*" or *"concealed"* and "why did you *take*" to teach that Rachel did not take the idols for herself, but to get rid of idolatry.

The *Bereishis Rabbah*[19] teaches that after Yaakov left Lavan's house, Lavan chased after him and said, "לָמָה גָנַבְתָּ אֶת אֱלֹהָי—Why did you steal my gods?" When Yaakov's sons heard this comment, they said to their grandfather, Lavan, "We are embarrassed about what you are saying. At your old age, you are requesting, 'Where is my idolatry to worship?'" The *Matnos Kehunah* explains that the sons said, "If the idol was able to be stolen, it definitely has no importance and is not worth anything at all!" The *Nefesh HaGer* says that from here, we see that Rachel's stealing

---

was with proper intention, to remove idolatry from Lavan. Therefore, Onkelos changes from "*geneivah*" to "*lekichah*."

It states, "ויגנוב יעקב את לב לבן הארמי על בלי הגיד לו כי בורח הוא"—And Yaakov stole the heart of Lavan the Arami on account of his not telling him that he was fleeing." What was the "stealing" which the Torah states Yaakov did? Also, the *pasuk* is difficult to understand: when one flees, he does not tell others that he is fleeing. If so, what does it mean that Yaakov did not tell Lavan that he was fleeing?

Onkelos answers these questions by translating, "And Yaakov concealed his leaving from Lavan…by not telling him that he was going." He translates "*va'yignov*" as "and he concealed," not "and he stole." The *Ibn Ezra* explains that Yaakov only did *geneivas daas*—he "stole Lavan's knowledge" by not telling him that he was leaving, as the main knowledge of a person is in the heart. Similarly, later in the parashah Lavan blames Yaakov for leaving without telling him, and he said, "*va'tignov es levavi*" and "*va'tignov osi*," both of which Onkelos translates as "and you concealed from me." Yaakov wanted to leave, but he knew that Lavan was a trickster and would not allow him. Lavan tricked Yaakov many times when he was working as a shepherd, and he even claimed,[20] "הבנות בנותי והבנים בני והצאן צאני וכל אשר אתה רואה לי הוא—The daughters are mine, and the sons are mine, and the sheep is mine, and everything that you see is mine." Also, he denied attributing success because of Yaakov, although in truth, Yaakov brought blessing to Lavan's house: before Yaakov came, Lavan did not yet have sons, only afterwards, and Yaakov caused Lavan to become very wealthy. Shockingly, Lavan was even ready to physically harm Yaakov for taking away what was the result of Yaakov's own accomplishments. Therefore, Yaakov had complete rights to leave Lavan, and he did not tell Lavan since this would interfere with his decision.

The *Nesinah LaGer* explains that Onkelos translates both "*va'tignov Rachel*—and Rachel took" or "concealed" and "*va'yignov Yaakov*—and Yaakov concealed" for their honor, so as not to imply an improper action.

---

Onkelos translates *"ki vorei'ach hu"* as "that he was *going*," not literally that he was *"fleeing."* Also, he translates the following word, *"va'yivrach,"* as "and he went," not "and he fled." The *Nefesh HaGer* explains that *"berichah"* connotes leaving without permission by escaping secretively or without plans to return, but it does not mean fleeing quickly. He proves this from Lavan, who claimed against Yaakov, *"V'atah haloch halachta*—And now you indeed left," and not *"baroch barachta*—you indeed fled." Yaakov did not run away as a fleeing thief, rather he went calmly. This is as *Bereishis Rabbah*[21] teaches: Rabbi Avahu said, that which Yaakov traveled in three days, Lavan traveled in one day. Lavan was told about Yaakov on the third day of his *berichah*, and Lavan chased after him and reached him in one day. This reflects that Yaakov went calmly, whereas Lavan chased after him quickly. Here, too, Onkelos translates "going" and "went," not "fleeing" and "fled," for the honor of Yaakov.

May we learn from Onkelos to be extra careful with how we perceive another person's actions!

# Vayishlach

## WHY WERE YAAKOV'S MERITS MADE SMALL?

קָטֹנְתִּי מִכֹּל הַחֲסָדִים וּמִכָּל הָאֱמֶת אֲשֶׁר עָשִׂיתָ אֶת עַבְדֶּךָ כִּי
בְמַקְלִי עָבַרְתִּי אֶת הַיַּרְדֵּן הַזֶּה וְעַתָּה הָיִיתִי לִשְׁנֵי מַחֲנוֹת (לב, יא)

זְעֵירָן זָכְוָתִי מִכֹּל חִסְדִּין וּמִכָּל טָבְוָן דַּעֲבַדְתְּ עִם עַבְדָּךְ אֲרֵי יְחִידַאי
עֲבָרִית יָת יַרְדְּנָא הָדֵין וּכְעַן הֲוֵיתִי לְתַרְתֵּין מַשְׁרְיָן

*My merits are little [too few] for all the kindnesses and for all
the good that You did with Your servant, since I passed through
this Yarden alone and now I have become two camps.*

The *pasuk* states, "קטונתי מכל החסדים ומכל האמת אשר עשית את עבדך." The
*Ramban* explains, "My merits are small from deserving the past kindnesses that Hashem has done for me, and I am not fitting for His
kindness in the future." Yaakov expressed to Hashem that he has never
deserved anything that Hashem did for him, and he is undeserving of
any more kindness.

Onkelos translates these words differently: "My merits are little [too
few] for all the kindnesses and for all the good that You did with your
servant." The *Nesinah LaGer* explains that Onkelos translates "*ha'emes*"
as "the good [*tavivan*]" in plural like the previous word, "*ha'chassadim*."
The *Chovos Halevavos*[1] explains that Yaakov was worried that his merits became less because of all the different kindnesses that Hashem
did for him, and therefore he did not deserve any more kindness. This
is as the Gemara brings that a person should never stand in a place of

danger and say a miracle will occur, because maybe a miracle will not occur, and even if a miracle will happen for him, he will lose his merits. So too, Yaakov was worried that although Hashem had promised to save him, maybe he used up his merits with all the kindnesses which Hashem had done for him, and now he might be given over into the hands of Eisav.[2]

The *Ramban* points out that Onkelos generally translates the word "*chassadim*" as "*tivu*—good," and the word "*emes*" as "*keshot*—truth." Here, however, Onkelos translates "*ha'chassadim*" as "*chisdin*—kindnesses" and "*ha'emes*" as "*tavivan*—good." The *Nesinah LaGer* explains that it states, "*U'mi'kal ha'emes*—and from all the truth," which could, *chas v'shalom*, be understood to imply that there are some things which are not true about Hashem. Therefore, Onkelos translates as "for all the good." The *Ramban* explains that Onkelos understands that "the kindnesses" refers to being saved from many difficult situations, while "the good" refers to all the good that he had. This includes having sons and daughters, attaining wealth, acquiring possessions, and receiving honor. Since Hashem did so much for Yaakov, he was worried that his merits had become small.

The *pasuk* ends, "כי במקלי עברתי את הירדן הזה ועתה הייתי לשני מחנות—Since with my staff I passed through this Yarden and now I have become two camps." *Rashi* explains, "When I crossed the Yarden, I only had a staff with me, nothing else, not silver, gold, or cattle, and now I have become two camps." *Rashi* also quotes from the *Midrash Aggadah* that Yaakov put his staff into the Yarden and the Yarden split. Onkelos translates the word "*v'makli*" differently: "alone." The *Nesinah LaGer* explains that Onkelos translates the word "*v'makli*," which literally means "with my staff," as a metaphor which really means "alone." A person with just a staff reflects extreme poverty, with no belongings or company. Onkelos translates "*ki v'makli...*" as "since I passed through this Yarden alone, and now I have become two camps." The *Marpei Lashon* says that here, Yaakov contrasts two stages in his life. At first, he was "*v'makli*," alone by himself

---

with nothing, and now, he has become many, as the *pasuk* ends, "and now I have become two camps," with many people. Yaakov expressed the great kindness and good which Hashem performed for him and also contrasted what he was at the beginning to what he had become.

The *Chovos Halevavos*[3] writes that it is common for people not to appreciate what Hashem does for them. Some reasons are because we take things for granted, we expect them, and we are greedy. We think that we deserve the good bestowed upon us, and we feel that we should have more. In truth, everything that we have is from Hashem, and who says we even deserve that which we have? The *Tiferes Yisrael*[4] says that Hashem continuously causes our existence and He constantly does good for us, undeservingly, as though lending us something and holding onto a collateral to be paid back. He keeps our existence in order to enable us to repay Him for the constant good that we receive from Him. Hashem brought us into the world to serve Him and return all the good which He bestows upon us by fulfilling His Torah and mitzvos to the best of our abilities.

Yaakov, who was so great, was afraid that maybe he had used up his merits; certainly, we should feel undeserving of Hashem's kindness. May we learn from Yaakov Avinu to recognize and appreciate all the kindnesses and good that Hashem does for us and express our appreciation!

## WHAT DOES IT MEAN TO WIPE AWAY SIN?

וַיִּשְׁלַח יַעֲקֹב מַלְאָכִים לְפָנָיו אֶל עֵשָׂו אָחִיו (לב, ד)

וּשְׁלַח יַעֲקֹב אִזְגַּדִּין קֳדָמוֹהִי לְוָת עֵשָׂו אֲחוּהִי

*And Yaakov sent messengers before [ahead of] him next to his brother, Eisav.*

---

3   שער הבחינה בפתיחה

4   אבות ג, טז יכין ס"ק קב

מִנְחָה (לב, יד)

תִּקְרְבְתָּא

*A present [mundane offering].*

כִּי אָמַר אֲכַפְּרָה פָנָיו (לב, כא)

אֲרֵי אֲמַר אֲנִיחֵנֵיה לְרֻגְזֵיה

*Since he said, "I will rest [subside] his anger."*

The parashah starts, "וישלח יעקב מלאכים לפניו אל עשו אחיו—And Yaakov sent *malachim* before him to Eisav, his brother." What are these *malachim*? *Rashi* explains that Yaakov sent angels to Eisav. The *Sifsei Chachamim*[5] adds that these were the same angels who met Yaakov at the end of *Parashas Vayeitzei*. The *Chizkuni* writes that Onkelos translates *malachim* differently, as "messengers [*izgadin*]," unlike in *Parashas Vayeitzei*[6] where Onkelos translates "*malachei*" as "angels [*Malachaya*]." Yaakov sent messengers to Eisav.

The messengers returned to Yaakov and responded, "Eisav is coming with four hundred men," at which point Yaakov became very worried. Yaakov then sent Eisav a "*minchah*" to appease him, which Onkelos translates as "*tikruvta*—an offering." He does not use his standard translation for "*korban*[7] [*korbana*]" or "*minchah*[8] [*minchasa*.]" The *Sefer Hameturgaman*[9] says that Onkelos uses "*tikruvta*" when the *minchah* refers to a mundane offering given as a present, and he uses "*minchasa*" when it refers to a meal-offering brought up and burned on the *Mizbeiach*. Similarly, Onkelos uses the *lashon* "*korban*" when something is offered to Hashem, such as with Hevel. Here, Yaakov sent Eisav many types of animals for a mundane present, so Onkelos translates as "*tikruvta*."

---

| | |
|---|---|
| א | 5 |
| לב, ב | 6 |
| ה, ד | 7 |
| ויקרא ב, א | 8 |
| קרב ומנח | 9 |

Yaakov commands the messengers to say, "Also, behold, Yaakov, your servant, is after us, כי אמר אכפרה פניו." What does this mean? The *Ramban* explains that in addition to Yaakov sending presents, he told the messengers to say, "Behold, Yaakov is following after us" in an honorable way, "and he sent us before him to bring *kofer nafsho*, redemption and atonement of his soul, for the honor of being able to see you with this offering." This is similar to a servant who gives something for his redemption when he requests permission to see the king, hoping that his request will be accepted. Yaakov meant that maybe he will be able to see Eisav's face if Eisav would accept his request and honor him by granting permission to greet Eisav. In *lashon hakodesh*, "כפר" always refers to redemption for atonement, whereas in Aramaic, it means wiping away and removing sin.

Onkelos translates the words *"achaprah fanav"* differently: "I will rest [subside] his anger." *Rashi* in *Parashas Haazinu*[10] explains that Onkelos understands "כפר" to mean "favor" and "appease." In this case, Yaakov meant, "I will cause Eisav's anger regarding my receiving the berachos from Yitzchak to subside by appeasing him with all of these presents." In this parashah, *Rashi* explains that any time *"kapparah"* is next to the word *"avon*—sin," or *"panim*—face," it is an Aramaic usage which means "wipe away" and "remove." In *Sefer Ezra*, receptacles of the Beis Hamikdash are called *"ke'forei zahav"* since the Kohen wiped his hands on their tips to remove blood from his hand. Rav Yosef Dov Halevi Soloveitchik[11] adds that *"kapparah"* refers to cleaning and protecting from punishment because of sin. The *Ramban* says that Onkelos, who translates "I will rest [subside] his anger," understands like *Rashi*. Yaakov said, "I will cause Eisav's anger to be wiped away and removed by appeasing him with all of these presents in order to disregard my actions and not punish me." What does it mean "to wipe away and remove sin and punishment"?

On the words *"V'over al pesha*—And He passes over guilt," the *Tomer Devorah*[12] teaches that Hashem does not forgive a person through

---

10   דברים לב, מג

11   הררי קדם א בעניני המועדים סי' סט, ד

12   פ"א הג'

a messenger, but rather, He Himself forgives. This is as it states, "*Ki imcha ha'selichah*—Since with You is the forgiveness." What is this forgiveness? Hashem Himself rinses away the sin, as it states, "אם רחץ ה' את צואת בנות ציון—If Hashem washes off the excretions of the daughters of Tzion." Also, it states, "וזרקתי עליכם מים טהורים וטהרתם—And I will throw purification waters upon you and you will become cleansed." Rabbeinu Yonah[13] writes that a person who sins is comparable to one who soils his garment, causing the garment to need to be laundered. We soiled our body and soul through our transgressions, and Hashem Himself cleans them. A bit of laundering will remove the repulsive thing on a garment, but it will still be left with a stain. The more and better one washes, the cleaner and whiter it will cause the garment to become. This is as it states, "*Herev kabseini mei'avoni*—Launder me a lot from my sin." According to the amount that one repents in his heart, so will be the amount of cleaning and whitening that he will cause to his soul.

The *Tomer Devorah* adds that a person is supposed to follow in the ways of Hashem and do the same. If someone sinned against you, don't say, "Shall I fix what the other person sinned or corrupted?" Rather, just as we sin against Hashem and He Himself comes to wash away the filth, so too, we ourselves should help the person who sinned against us to become clean and be rid of his sin.

The *Bereishis Rabbah*[14] teaches that Yaakov is called an "*ish chalak*— a smooth person," whereas Eisav is called an "*ish sa'ir*—a hairy person." This is comparable to two people in the granary, one bald and the other with a lot of hair. When the grain is winnowed, the chaff lands on both of their heads. The hairy person will have tangled chaff in his hair, whereas the bald person will be able to wipe it away with a simple swipe. So too, Eisav is dirtied with sin throughout the year with no opportunity to become clean, whereas Yaakov, although dirtied with sin, has Yom Kippur for atonement. My Rosh Yeshiva explained: true, we are affected by our sins and need atonement, but we are not entangled in

---

13   שע"ת שער א, ט

14   פ' סה, טו

our sins; rather, we can wipe them away by repenting, whereas Eisav is caught up and entangled in sin. "כפר" also hints to being able to easily wipe away sins and separate from them.

The *Ramban* says that Onkelos, who explains "כי אמר אכפרה בפניו" as "I will rest [subside] his anger," understands that Yaakov thought this in his heart. The *Ibn Ezra* adds that Moshe Rabbeinu is the one who said these words. Yaakov only thought "*achaprah fanav*" in his heart, but he did not tell the messengers to say that to Eisav. It would be improper for the messengers to tell Eisav that Yaakov had said that he was simply giving the gifts to assuage Eisav's feelings of anger. The *Seforno* explains differently: Yaakov indeed gave over these words to be said by his servants, in order to lessen Eisav's anger by saying over words of humility together with giving the offering.

May Hashem remove our filth, clean and purify us from sin and punishment, and may we separate from sin!

## WHAT WAS YAAKOV'S BATTLE WITH THE MAN ABOUT?

### הַצִּילֵנִי נָא מִיַּד אָחִי מִיַּד עֵשָׂו (לב, יב)

שֵׁיזִבְנִי כְּעַן מִיְדָא דְּאָחִי מִיְדָא דְעֵשָׂו

*Save me now from the hand of my brother,*
*from the hand of Eisav.*

### וַיֵּאָבֵק אִישׁ עִמּוֹ (לב, כה)

וְאִשְׁתַּדַּל גַּבְרָא עִמֵּיהּ

*And a man fought verbally with [convinced] (hugged) him.*

### וַיִּגַּע בְּכַף יְרֵכוֹ וַתֵּקַע כַּף יֶרֶךְ יַעֲקֹב בְּהֵאָבְקוֹ עִמּוֹ (לב, כו)

וּקְרִיב בִּפְתֵי יַרְכֵּיהּ וְזָע פְּתֵי יַרְכָּא דְּיַעֲקֹב בְּאִשְׁתַּדָּלוּתֵיהּ עִמֵּיהּ

*And he came close [touched] in the width of his thigh,*
*and moved the width of the thigh of Yaakov when he*
*fought verbally with [convinced] (hugged) him.*

כִּי רָאִיתִי אֱלֹהִים פָּנִים אֶל פָּנִים וַתִּנָּצֵל נַפְשִׁי (לב, לא)

אֲרֵי חֲזֵיתִי מַלְאֲכָא דַּיְיָ אַפִּין בְּאַפִּין וְאִשְׁתֵּיזַבַת נַפְשִׁי

*Since I saw the angel of Hashem, faces with*
*faces [face to face], and I was saved.*

The *pasuk* states, "*Va'yei'aveik ish imo.*" *Rashi* teaches in the name of Menachem that "*va'yei'aveik*" is from the word "*avak*—dirt." They stirred up dirt with the movements of their feet while they fought. *Rashi* himself explains differently: "*Va'yei'aveik*" is an Aramaic word from the root "*kesher*—tie." When people wrestle with each other and one wants to throw the other down, they become knotted and tied together; one hugs tightly and entangles the other with his arms. Yaakov wrestled with the *sar* of Eisav who came to kill him. This indicates that there was a physical battle.

The *Ramban* writes that Onkelos translates "*Va'yei'aveik ish imo*" differently: "And a man fought verbally [*v'ishtadal*] with him" by convincing and appeasing him.

Also, in the following *pasuk* Onkelos translates the words, "ויגע בכף ירכו ותקע כף ירך יעקב בהאבקו עמו" as, "And he came close [touched] in the width of his thigh and moved the width of the thigh of Yaakov when he fought verbally [*b'ishtadaluseih*] with him" by convincing and appeasing him. The *Ramban* explains that Onkelos translates with the word "*v'ishtadal*," just like he translates "*v'chi yefateh*—when he will convince [*yeshadel*]" by appeasing with hugging and kissing. The word "ויאבק" means "ויחבק," from the root "חבוקה—a hug," as a 'ח is sometimes exchanged for an 'א, or totally dropped. The man came and hugged Yaakov to convince him of something.

The *Ramban* also suggests that "*va'yei'aveik*" means to trick, by attempting different tactics and actions. The man put in effort with tricks for a specific intent to convince Yaakov. Onkelos understands that there was a verbal battle. What does "and a man fought verbally by convincing him" and "when he fought verbally to convince him" mean? And what was the purpose of giving a hug?

The *Nefesh HaGer* explains in the name of the *Bereishis Rabbah*[15] that Yaakov thought that this person was the leader of the robbers, and they struggled by debating with words. The "person" tried to convince Yaakov to join with him as friends and be with him as one nation, but he wasn't able to convince Yaakov. This is as it states, *"Va'yei'aveik ish imo"* which implies that it was a person (*guvra*) who fought with Yaakov. Later in the parashah, Yaakov calls the name of the place Penu'el, explaining: "כי ראיתי אלהים פנים אל פנים ותנצל נפשי," which Onkelos translates as "since I saw the angel of Hashem, faces with faces [face to face], and I was saved." This implies that the man was an angel. The *Nefesh HaGer* explains that at the time that Yaakov met the *ish*, Yaakov did not realize he was an angel; he only realized afterward.

We find the angel's conflict with Yaakov throughout the parashah. Yaakov davened, "הצילני נא מיד אחי מיד עשו," which Onkelos translates, "Save me now from the hand of my brother, from the hand of Eisav." The *Beis Halevi* asks: We know that Yaakov only had one brother. Why did Yaakov mention "from the hand of Eisav"? Shouldn't the words *"mi'yad achi*—from the hand of my brother"* be enough? Also, why did Yaakov mention "from the hand" twice?

The *Beis Halevi* answers that Yaakov knew Eisav had two possible ways of fighting against him. One way was to simply wage war and try to kill him. The other way was to be friendly toward Yaakov, acting peacefully in the hope of influencing Yaakov for the bad. *"Mi'yad Eisav"* reflects Eisav's desire to kill Yaakov, whereas *"mi'yad achi"* reflects Eisav's false "brotherly" love and his desire to negatively influence Yaakov. One may think that the first way is worse than the second because Eisav would try to kill Yaakov, whereas the second way, at least Yaakov wouldn't die, he would just become tainted with bad. However, in reality, the second tactic is even worse than the first, because being influenced for bad can bring a person to deny Hashem, *chas v'shalom*. Yaakov davened to be saved from both possibilities: first, from the hand of *"achi,"* the friendly, brotherly, peaceful tactics which could draw him away from Hashem,

---

which is worse, and second, from the hand of "Eisav," who was coming to kill him.

After Eisav meets Yaakov, he suggests, "Let us travel together." Yaakov responds that it won't be good for the young. Then Eisav wants to send some of his people to accompany Yaakov, but Yaakov declines the offer. Here, too, we see that Eisav wanted to befriend Yaakov and cause him to ruin his ways.

We find these two types of battles by Chanukah and Purim. On Purim, there is an obligation to make a *seudah*, while on Chanukah, there is not. The *Levush*[16] explains that the reason is because on Purim, the decree against the Jewish People was physical: to kill all of B'nei Yisrael. Therefore, Chazal required us to make a *seudah*, in order to praise Hashem through our eating and express our *hakaras hatov* for physically saving us. On Chanukah, however, the danger was different. The *Yevanim* wanted to destroy us spiritually, decreeing against mitzvos such as Shabbos, learning Torah, and *bris milah*, and were happy for us to become friends with them. This was a spiritual battle, with our *neshamah* at stake. Distancing us from Hashem's mitzvos is essentially the same as distancing us from Hashem. The Chashmonaim were called "מכבים," which stands for "מי כמוך באלים ה'"—Who is like You among the mighty, Hashem?" You are in charge of the world, and we are loyal to You, as there is nothing like You. Therefore, on Chanukah, we sing *Hallel* and say *Al Hanissim* in the berachah of *hodaah* to thank and praise Hashem for saving our *neshamos* and not letting us be destroyed spiritually. Because it was a spiritual salvation, we are not obligated in a *seudah*, but rather in expressions of *hallel* and *hodaah*.

May Hashem save us from the physical and spiritual attacks of the non-Jews!

## WHAT IS UNIQUE ABOUT THE THIRD DAY AFTER CIRCUMCISION? WHO WAS TRANQUIL? DID YAAKOV AND HIS SONS FIGHT AGAINST NEIGHBORING CITIES?

וַיְהִי בַיּוֹם הַשְּׁלִישִׁי בִּהְיוֹתָם כֹּאֲבִים...וַיָּבֹאוּ
עַל הָעִיר בֶּטַח וַיַּהַרְגוּ כָּל זָכָר (לה, כה)

וַהֲוָה בְּיוֹמָא תְלִיתָאָה כַד תְּקִיפוּ עֲלֵיהוֹן כֵּיבֵיהוֹן...וְעָאלוּ
עַל קַרְתָּא דְּיָתְבָא לְרָחְצָן וּקְטַלוּ כָּל דְּכוּרָא

*And it was on the third day when their pains strengthened*
*[increased] upon them...and they entered upon the city that*
*was dwelling in tranquility, and they killed every male.*

עֲכַרְתֶּם אֹתִי לְהַבְאִישֵׁנִי בְּיֹשֵׁב הָאָרֶץ בַּכְּנַעֲנִי וּבַפְּרִזִּי וַאֲנִי
מְתֵי מִסְפָּר וְנֶאֶסְפוּ עָלַי וְהִכּוּנִי וְנִשְׁמַדְתִּי אֲנִי וּבֵיתִי (לה, ל)

עֲכַרְתּוּן יָתִי לְמִתַּן דְּבָבוּ בֵּינָא וּבֵין יָתֵיב אַרְעָא בִּכְנַעֲנָאָה וּבִפְרִזָּאָה וַאֲנָא
עַם דְּמִנְיָן וְיִתְכַּנְשׁוּן עֲלַי וְיִמְחוֹנַנִי וְאֶשְׁתֵּיצֵי אֲנָא וֶאֱנַשׁ בֵּיתִי

*You dirtied me to give [place] hatred between me and*
*between the dwellers of the land with the Canaani and*
*with the Prizi, and I am a nation of count [small in number],*
*and they will gather against me, and they will smite me,*
*and I and the people of my house will be destroyed.*

וַיִּסָּעוּ וַיְהִי חִתַּת אֱלֹהִים עַל הֶעָרִים אֲשֶׁר
סְבִיבוֹתֵיהֶם וְלֹא רָדְפוּ אַחֲרֵי בְּנֵי יַעֲקֹב (לה, ה)

וּנְטָלוּ וַהֲוָת דַּחְלָא מִן קֳדָם יְיָ עַל עַמְמַיָּא דִּבְקִרְוֵי סַחְרָנֵיהוֹן וְלָא רְדַפוּ בָּתַר בְּנֵי יַעֲקֹב

*And they traveled, and there was fear from before [because of]*
*Hashem upon the nations that were in the cities surrounding*
*them, and they did not chase after B'nei Yaakov.*

The *pasuk* states, "...ויהי ביום השלישי בהיותם כואבים—And it was on the third day when their pains strengthened upon them, and Shimon and Levi, the two sons of Yaakov, the brothers of Dinah, took, a man his sword." Onkelos translates the words *"bi'hiyosam ko'avim"* as "when their

pains strengthened [כד תקיפו עליהון כיביהון]." They specifically waited for
the third day after circumcision because it was most painful on that day.
This is as the *Hakesav V'Hakabbalah* quotes from *Rashi* that any wound
hurts more on the third day than on the previous days. However, the
*sugya* in *Maseches Shabbos* does not seem this way, but rather, *even* the
third day hurts, and certainly the first day, which is worse. The *Nesinah
LaGer* explains Onkelos like the *Ran*: the third day was most dangerous,
as is the nature of many sick people for whom the third day is the most
serious. The *Chizkuni* explains Onkelos differently: they waited until
the entire city was circumcised, which finished on the third day, and
while the entire city was wounded and in pain, only then did they come.

The *pasuk* continues, "ויבאו על העיר בטח ויהרגו כל זכר." *Rashi* explains that
Shimon and Levi were confident because the people were in pain,
or, as the *Midrash Aggadah* says, because they relied on the merit of
the *zakein*. The *Sifsei Chachamim*[17] says that this refers to Yaakov or
Avraham davening for them. The *Riva* explains that *Rashi* understands
that "*betach*" follows "*va'yavo'u*"; Shimon and Levi were confident to
come fight. Onkelos translates differently: "And they entered upon the
city that was dwelling ["*d'yasva*"] in tranquility and killed every male."
The people in the city were tranquil, as they were dwelling without
fear; "*betach*" follows "*ha'ir*," meaning that the people of the city were
dwelling in tranquility.

After they fought and looted, Yaakov said to Shimon and Levi, "עכרתם אתי
להבאישני ביושב הארץ בכנעני ובפרזי ואני מתי מספר..." which Onkelos translates
as, "You dirtied me to give [place] hatred between me and between the
dwellers of the land with the Canaani and with the Prizi, and I am a nation of count [small in number], and they will gather against me, and
they will smite me, and I and the people of my house will be destroyed."
Onkelos translates "*l'hav'isheini b'yosheiv ha'aretz*" as "to give [place]
hatred [*l'mitan devavu*] between me and between the dwellers of the
land." "*L'hav'isheini*" literally means "to make me have a foul smell." The
*Nefesh HaGer* says that Onkelos translates the *nimshal*: the intent is that

killing the inhabitants of Shechem will cause neighboring cities, who are proper, peaceful people, to hate me, and in return, I will also hate them. A bit later, it states, "ויסעו ויהי חתת אלקים על הערים אשר סביבותיהם ולא רדפו אחרי בני יעקב—And they traveled, and the fear of G-d was upon the cities that were surrounding them and they did not chase after B'nei Yaakov." "The cities that surround them" refer to the Chivi nation. The *Nefesh HaGer* is bothered because this seems that only the Chivi cities which were surrounding them were afraid, whereas other cities, such as those of the Canaani and Prizi, were not afraid. This is difficult because earlier, Yaakov was upset at Shimon and Levi and he said, "להבאישני ביושב הארץ בכנעני ובפרזי...ונאספו עלי והכוני ונשמדתי אני וביתי." This reflects that Yaakov was also worried about the Canaani and Prizi who would come smite and destroy—what happened to them?

The *Nefesh HaGer* says that in order to resolve this difficulty, Onkelos translates "על הערים אשר סביבותיהם" as "upon the nations that were in the cities surrounding them." Onkelos changes three things: He adds "the nations," he translates *"asher"* before *"he'arim,"* and he translates the 'ה of "הערים—of the cities" as "בערים—in the cities." Onkelos's translation of, "and there was fear from before [because of] Hashem upon the nations that were in the cities" reflects that Hashem's fear was not only upon the immediate surrounding cities, such the Chivi, but also upon the Canaani and Prizi nations.

This *pasuk* implies that Hashem placed fear upon the nations and they automatically surrendered without battle. However, in *Parashas Vayechi*, Yaakov said,[18] "ואני נתתי לך שכם אחד על אחיך אשר לקחתי מיד האמורי בחרבי ובקשתי." *Rashi* explains that when Shimon and Levi killed the people of Shechem, all those surrounding Shechem gathered against them to battle. Yaakov girded himself with weaponry to fight. This seems that Yaakov actually fought with the sword and the bow and arrow.

The *Ramban* brings in the name of the *sefer Milchamos B'nei Yaakov*[19] that the neighbors of Shechem fought three battles. Had Yaakov not put on

---

18  מח,כב

19  ספר הישר

weaponry to fight, they would have been in danger. The brothers were mighty, and it seemed as though it was through their own strength that they won. Therefore, the Torah only hints to this battle since the miracle was hidden. They did not all chase after them; suddenly, many people started to fall as sand upon the seashore. Hashem placed fear upon them from what they saw in battle. This is as the Midrash brings that there are three examples where, with just a little effort, there was dreaded fear and B'nei Yisrael were saved. The *Yalkut Me'am Lo'ez* says that immediately, everyone was scared and did not attack the Shevatim; however, later on, they chased after Yaakov. The *Hakesav V'Hakabbalah* answers in the name of the Midrash that they did not chase them until seven years later. Onkelos answers by translating *"b'charbi u'v'kashti"* as "with my davening [*b'tzlosi*] and with my requesting [*u'v'va'usi*]." If so, Yaakov did not actually have to fight!

May Hashem bring the final battle against the nations along with the coming of Mashiach *bi'meheirah bi'yameinu, Amen*!

# Vayeishev

## WHAT WAS YOSEF'S UNIQUENESS AS YAAKOV'S WISE SON?

כִּי בֶן זְקֻנִים הוּא לוֹ (לז, ג)

אֲרֵי בַּר חַכִּים הוּא לֵיהּ

*Since he was the son who was wise to him.*

The *pasuk* mentions that Yaakov loved Yosef more than the brothers, "כִּי בֶן זְקֻנִים הוּא לוֹ," which simply means, "because he was a son born to him in his old age." However, in *Parashas Vayigash*, it states[1] that Binyamin is called, *"v'yeled zekunim katan,"* which Onkelos translates as "and a young son of old age [*u'var seivsin z'eir*]." This seems that Binyamin is called the son born to Yaakov in his old age. Which son was born to Yaakov in his old age? The *Nefesh HaGer* says that Onkelos answers this question by translating regarding Yosef that he was the son who was *wise* to Yaakov, whereas regarding Binyamin, he translates that he was born in Yaakov's old age.

What does Onkelos mean that Yosef was the son who was "wise" to Yaakov? The *Ramban* explains that whatever Yaakov learned from Shem and Ever he gave over to Yosef. Yosef had the understanding of old people, who are wise. Yaakov taught Yosef the deep wellsprings of Torah and found Yosef capable of grasping the secrets as though he was well on in his years, an elder (*zakein*). The *pasuk* states, "*Hu lo*—Yosef was to Yaakov" a wise lad, because Yaakov noticed the quick and deep understanding that Yosef had above his brothers. The *pasuk* teaches

---

that because of his tremendous abilities, Yaakov loved Yosef more than the standard, natural love that Yaakov had for each of his children.

Rav Yaakov Kamenetsky suggests a different explanation. Before Yaakov went to Lavan's house, he learned in the *beis midrash* of Shem[2] and Ever for fourteen years because Yaakov needed to prepare himself for the challenges that he would encounter in exile. Why wasn't the Torah that he learned from Avraham and Yitzchak, the *Avos Hakedoshim*, not enough to prepare him to dwell with Lavan? Rav Kamenetsky explains that Shem and Ever were unique. They were among the wicked people of the *Dor HaMabul* and the *Dor Haflagah*, and they had no one to teach them to stay safe from the *reshaim*. They learned to guard themselves from the challenges of their surroundings. Yaakov specifically went to Shem and Ever to learn this *"Toras HaGalus"* that he too needed, in order to be safe from Lavan and other *reshaim*. There was a *kabbalah* from the *Bris Bein Habesarim* that Avraham's descendants would eventually go into exile. Yaakov felt that Yosef would be the one who would go into exile, thereby needing this specific Torah, so Yaakov taught the *Toras HaGalus* to him. Yaakov did not need to teach the rest of the brothers this area of Torah because Yosef was the one meant to set up and prepare the land of Mitzrayim for the brothers who would come down after him. Because only Yosef knew this Torah, he was called Yaakov's *"ben zekunim."*

May we all learn and become proficient in our own portion of Torah to be a *ben chakim*!

## WERE THE BROTHERS NOT ABLE TO SPEAK WITH YOSEF PEACEFULLY, OR DID THEY NOT WANT TO?

### וְלֹא יָכְלוּ דַּבְּרוֹ לְשָׁלֹם (לז, ד)

וְלָא צָבֵן לְמַלָּלָא עִמֵּיה שְׁלָם

*And they did not want to speak peacefully with him.*

The *pasuk* states, "ולא יכלו דברו לשלום—and they were not able to speak peacefully with him." The *Hakesav V'Hakabbalah* explains that we find two different meanings for the words "לא יכול": "unable" and "unwilling." Sometimes, a person is held back from something because he is missing the ability and strength to do it; he is literally unable to do it, as in *"lo uchal."* We find this when Yosef couldn't stop himself from letting the brothers know who he was. It states, "ולא יכול יוסף להתאפק," which Onkelos translates as "and Yosef was unable to be strong [ולא יכל יוסף לאתחסנא]." The *Ramban* explains that there were many people there who were beseeching Yosef to free Binyamin as they pitied him. Yosef was not able to be strong against all of them. *Rashi* explains differently: Yosef was not able to bear the disgrace that the brothers would experience when he revealed himself to them while the Mitzrim were standing there.

Another meaning of *"lo yachol"* is that one is unable to do something because of *mussar* or mitzvah. For example, it states "כי לא יוכלון המצרים לאכל את העברים לחם," which Onkelos translates as "since the Mitzrim were not able [*yachlin*] to eat bread with the Ivrim." It was not proper morally to sit and eat with the *Ivrim*, although the Mitzrim were physically able to do so. Also, it states, "ולא יכלו לעשות הפסח ביום ההוא—And they were unable [*y'chilu*] to make the Pesach-offering on that day." There were people who were impure and were not fit to perform the mitzvah of bringing the Pesach-offering, though they were physically able to do so. What does *"v'lo yachlu"* mean by the brothers with Yosef?

The *Hakesav V'Hakabbalah* explains that when Yosef would greet the brothers, they were not able to bear him and listen to his words. Although Yosef felt their hatred, he still ran after them to act peacefully and would greet them with *"shalom."* The words *"lo yachlu"* mean unable; it was beyond the brothers' abilities to speak peacefully with Yosef.

Onkelos translates *"lo yachlu"* differently: "And they did not want [*v'lo tzavan*]." The *Hakesav V'Hakabbalah* says that this implies that the brothers did not want to speak peacefully with Yosef, although they were indeed able to do so. He does not translate "not able," but, rather, "did not want" in order to lessen the hatred of the brothers toward Yosef. The reason why the brothers did not speak to Yosef was not because they hated him so much. Rather, as *Rashi* explains, it was so that they shouldn't be dishonest by talking nicely as though they were at peace, while inside they were really distant and far removed.

The *Hakesav V'Hakabbalah* points out that the *pasuk* seems to be degrading the brothers' behavior with Yosef. Also, the *pasuk* testifies that they had bad feelings as they said, "*Lechu v'nahargeihu*—Let us go and kill him." Why, then, does Onkelos translate "*v'lo yachlu*" as "and they did not *want*"?

The *Hakesav V'Hakabbalah* answers that the *pasuk* itself hints to Onkelos's translation as it states, "*dabro*," in one word. It does not state, "*daber imo*—speak with him," as two words, separating the *kinui*, 'ו— him, from the verb. Instead, the 'ו is put together with the verb, "*daber*." He explains that when the *kinui* is together with the verb, it includes everything about the word, whereas when the *kinui* is separated from the word, it reflects something specific. My good friend Rabbi Tzvi Goldberg gave an example in the name of Rabbi Reisman: When Eisav kissed Yaakov, it states, "*Va'yishakeihu*—And he kissed him." *Rashi* teaches in the name of Rabbi Shimon bar Yochai that while it is a law that Eisav hates Yaakov, this specific time was an exception, and Eisav had mercy and kissed Yaakov with his whole heart. Since the *kinui*, וה—him, is together with the word וישק, it reflects a complete expression of a kiss. The *Hakesav V'Hakabbalah* adds an example where the *kinui* is not together with the word, as it states, "*Va'achaltem oso b'chipazon*—And you shall eat it in haste." The word "*oso*—it" is the *kinui*, which reflects that the *Korban Pesach* itself needs to be eaten in haste, not other things.

Had the *pasuk* meant that the brothers could not speak to Yosef at all because of their hatred, it would have stated "*daber imo*" to reflect something specific. They hated Yosef and were unable to talk peacefully with him. Since it states "*dabro*," it must include all of their dealings with him. They did not deceive him by pretending that they were at peace with him. By "making their mouths and hearts the same," they acted in a more appropriate way. Although the brothers felt hatred, they were able to speak peacefully; however, they did not want to do so.

They acted with honesty by being consistent between their feelings and what came out of their mouth.

May Hashem help us be honest by having our words express what we feel in our heart!

## WHY DIDN'T TAMAR SAY, "I CONCEIVED FROM YEHUDAH"?

### לְאִישׁ אֲשֶׁר אֵלֶּה לּוֹ אָנֹכִי הָרָה (לח, כה)

לִגְבַר דְּאִלֵּין דִּילֵיהּ מִנֵּהּ אֲנָא מְעַדְּיָא

*To the man to whom these belong, from him I am pregnant.*

### צָדְקָה מִמֶּנִּי (לח, כו)

זַכָּאָה מִנִּי מְעַדְּיָא

*She is innocent; she is pregnant from me.*

The *pasuk* states that when Tamar was sent out to be burned, she said, "לאיש אשר אלה לו אנכי הרה—To the man to whom these are his, I have conceived." Onkelos generally translates "*lo*—to him," as "ליה," whereas when "*lo*" means "belonging to him," he translates as "דיליה—that belongs to him." Here, Onkelos is *medayek* in translating "*lo*" as דיליה: "to the man to whom these belong, from him I have conceived."

The following *pasuk* states, "And Yehudah recognized, and he said, '*Tzadkah mi'meni.*'" The *Ramban*, *Rashbam*, and *Seforno* explain that as "she is more righteous than me." In this explanation, the words are connected. The literal translation of "*tzadkah mi'meni*" is "she is righteous from me." What does this mean? The *Nefesh HaGer* says that Onkelos answers this by translating "*tzadkah*" as "she is innocent," and "*mi'meni*" as "she is pregnant from me." He translates "*mi'meni—from me*" separate from the word "*tzadkah—she is innocent.*" Similarly, *Rashi* explains "*tzadkah*" as "she is righteous with her words," and "*mi'meni*" as "from me she is expecting," as two points. The *Nefesh HaGer* points out that Onkelos translates both Tamar's comment and Yehudah's response with the same *nusach*. Onkelos translates that Tamar said, "*Mi'menu anochi harah*—from him I am pregnant," and Yehudah responded, "*Tzadkah, mi'meni harah*—she is innocent; she is pregnant from me." *Rashi* quotes *Rabboseinu* who *darshen* another explantion of "*mi'meni*": "a *bas kol* went out and said, '*mi'meni*—from Me went out these things.' Because she was modest in her father-in-law's house, I decreed that kings shall descend from her, from the tribe of Yehudah."

Why did Tamar not say clearly from whom she conceived to save herself from being killed? The Gemara[3] teaches that Tamar did not want to embarrass Yehudah and say, "From you I conceived," rather, she hinted, "to whom these belong." She said, "If he admits on his own, good; if not, burn me and I won't embarrass him." Chazal derived from here that "It is better to be thrown into a burning furnace than to embarrass a person publicly." *Tosafos*[4] says that the word "מוצאת—she was taken out," is spelled "מוצת," missing an א', implying a connection to "ויצת אש בציון—and He lit a fire in Tzion." The fire was already burning (מוצת), and she was sent out to be burned, yet she did not embarrass Yehudah.

*Rabbeinu Yonah*[5] quotes from the Gemara that when someone embarrasses another person, he causes the person's face to turn red and then white, since the blood rushes from his face. This is similar to killing, which causes blood to leave. Also, *Rabboseinu* say that the pain of embarrassment is even more bitter than death. Therefore, it is better for one to be thrown into a fire than embarrass someone, as Tamar was willing to do.

The Gemara[6] writes that there are three cardinal *aveiros* which *pikuach nefesh* does not override: immorality, murder, and idolatry. If someone comes to a person and says, "Worship idolatry or I will kill you," he cannot worship idolatry to save himself. *Tosafos* asks: why don't we count not embarrassing someone in this group? As we see from Tamar, it is better to be killed than to embarrass someone!

3   סוטה י:

4   ב"מ נט. לפי גירסתו

5   שע"ת שער ג, קלט

6   סנהדרין עד.

Some Rishonim are of the opinion that one does not have to give up his life so as not to embarrass someone; Tamar volunteered to do this, but it was not obligated as it is for the three cardinal sins. *Tosafos*[7] disagrees, maintaining that one indeed does need to give up his life so as not to embarrass someone. The reason why it is not part of the list is because it is not explicit in the Torah, whereas the three cardinal sins are explicit in the Torah.

I heard another answer based on Rabbeinu Yonah[8] who writes that even the "light" parts of the three cardinal *aveiros* have a stricter punishment than other severe sins. *Rabboseinu* called this "*avak aveirah.*" The following are examples of *avak aveirah*. A person who is dangerously sick can use any type of medicine to heal himself, except for wood of an *asheirah*, an idolatry tree. If doctors say bring wood of an *asheirah* to be healed, one should rather die and not be healed. Even though deriving pleasure from an *asheirah* tree does not transgress the *aveirah* of worshipping idolatry, it is *avak avodah zarah*, as it strengthens those who worship it, lest they will say that the *asheirah* cured the sick person. An example of *avak giluy arayos* is if one desires to speak or gaze at a married woman or else he will die; we do not indulge his desires to save his life. An example of *avak retzichah* is that one cannot embarrass another to save himself from being killed. In Rabbeinu Yonah's commentary on *Avos*,[9] he says that the three cardinal *aveiros* are "*avos*" and that there are also "*toldos*," related offshoots which have the same laws. Only the three cardinal sins are listed as they are the *avos*, whereas the offshoots are subcategories, *toldos*, and therefore are not mentioned in the list.

May we pay attention to the feelings of others and be careful not to embarrass anyone!

---

7    סוטה שם

8    שע"ת שם קלז-קלט

9    ג, י"א

# WHY DID YOSEF ENTER THE HOUSE OF POTIPHAR'S WIFE, AND WHY DID HE FLEE TO THE MARKETPLACE?

## וַיָּבֹא הַבַּיְתָה לַעֲשׂוֹת מְלַאכְתּוֹ (לט, יא)

וְעָאל לְבֵיתָא לְמִבְדַּק בִּכְתָבֵי חֻשְׁבְּנֵיה

*And he entered the house to check on the writings*
*[receipts] of his calculations [accounts].*

## וַיָּנָס וַיֵּצֵא הַחוּצָה (לט, יב וטו)

וַעֲרַק וּנְפַק לְשׁוּקָא

*And he fled, and he went out to the marketplace.*

## וַיָּנָס הַחוּצָה (לט, יג ויח)

וַעֲרַק לְשׁוּקָא

*And he fled to the marketplace.*

The *pasuk* states, "ויבא הביתה לעשות מלאכתו—And he came to the house to do his work." Onkelos translates *"la'asos melachto"* as "to check on the writings [receipts] of his calculations [accounts]." The *Nesinah LaGer* explains that this is like the opinion in the Gemara that Yosef came to do work. Since it was a holiday of their idolatry, he couldn't do standard heavy work; all he could do was light work, such as to check his calculations. Or, Yosef always only did light work, as he was the one in charge. The servants did the difficult work, and he did the easy and light work.

*Rashi* quotes another opinion: Yosef came to the house to sin with the wife of Potiphar, but the image of his father appeared to him and warned, "If you will sin, you won't be together with your brothers on the stones of the *Eiphod*." *Tosafos*[10] quotes from Rabbi Moshe Hadarshan that this is inferred from the words, "ואין איש מאנשי הבית שם בבית—And there was no man from the people of the house, there in the house." This reflects that a man *not* from the house *was* there—his father, who appeared to

---

him and warned him not to sin. Onkelos does not translate like *Rashi*, since he always translates to preserve honor and grant the benefit of doubt. Furthermore, the *Hakesav V'Hakabbalah* proves Onkelos's opinion: How could it be that Yosef would bring himself into such a tremendous challenge? Rather, he must have entered to complete his work.

The following *pasuk* states that Potiphar's wife grabbed Yosef's garment and tried to make him sin, so he left his garment in her hand, "*va'yanas va'yeitzei ha'chutzah*—and he fled, and he went outside." Onkelos translates "*ha'chutzah*" as "to the marketplace." Also, the following *pasuk* states, "And it was when she saw that he left his garment in her hand, *va'yanas ha'chutzah*, and he fled outside." Again, Onkelos translates "*ha'chutzah*" as "to the marketplace." In general, Onkelos translates[11] "*ha'chutzah*" as "outside [*l'vara*]." Why does he translate it here as "to the marketplace"?

The *Nesinah LaGer* answers that Onkelos translates "*ha'chutzah*" or "*ba'chutz*" as "outside" when it is used in contrast to "inside." The *Nefesh HaGer* adds that had Onkelos translated "*ha'chutzah*" as outside, it would seem that Yosef only ran out of the room or outside of the house. By translating it as "to the marketplace," which was not near the house, it reflects that he fled far away from the place of challenge so as not to sin. The *pasuk* is enhancing Yosef's *zechus* by emphasizing that he fled far away to the marketplace in order to be safe from the challenge of Potiphar's wife.

The *Midrash Tehillim*[12] records that the Yam Suf saw Yosef's coffin before it, and Hashem said, "Flee from before the one who fled, as it states, '*Va'yanas va'yeitzei ha'chutzah*,' so too, the sea shall flee from before him." Rav Chaim Shmuelevitz[13] explains that the main *avodah* of a person is to run away from a place of danger and distance himself from *nisayon*, challenge, as much as possible. One should not put himself in a situation where he has to face a challenge head-on. Although, from time to time, the *yetzer hara* doesn't directly try to cause one to sin, he does not allow

---

11  כה, כט

12  קיה, ג

13  מאמר כא

a person to be distanced from a place of challenge. At least he wants that a person should be near the challenge so that it will be easy for him to sin. For this reason, Yosef did not stay to grab back his garment from Potiphar's wife, so as not to be in the place of challenge for even another second, although by doing so, he allowed the libel that would be raised against him. Therefore, when the sea saw the coffin of Yosef, Hashem said, "Flee from before the one who fled."

After Yosef fled, Potiphar's wife called out to the people of her house and she related what happened, including that he left his garment in her hand, and claimed, "*Va'yanas va'yeitzei ha'chutzah.*" Here, too, Onkelos translates as, "And he fled, and he went out to the marketplace." Why did Potiphar's wife mention that Yosef went to the marketplace? The *Nefesh HaGer* explains that she said this to disgrace Yosef and enhance the libel against him. Similarly, the *Seforno* explains that she claimed to her husband, who didn't know what actually happened, "*Va'yanas ha'chutzah*—and he fled far away," although it states, "*Va'yanas va'yeitzei ha'chutzah*—and he fled, and he went outside." She lied that he fled far away in order to enhance the libel against Yosef, although in reality he only fled from the house, and then went away slowly, as any regular person walks. The *Nefesh HaGer* adds that she claimed that he fled to the marketplace in order to hide by being among other people, as though he didn't know anything had happened at all. This way he would be able to deny any possible claim against him. Despite the possible libel, Yosef fled and went far away to distance himself from being near a place of *nisayon*.

May we distance ourselves from places of *nisayon* and be saved from the *yetzer hara*!

## WAS YOSEF FORCEFULLY THROWN INTO PRISON?

וַיִּקַּח אֲדֹנֵי יוֹסֵף אֹתוֹ וַיִּתְּנֵהוּ אֶל בֵּית הַסֹּהַר (לט, כ)

וּדְבַר רִבּוֹנֵיהּ דְּיוֹסֵף יָתֵהּ וּמַנְּיֵהּ (וִיהַבֵּיהּ) בְּבֵית אֲסִירֵי

*And the master of Yosef led [took] him and appointed (placed) him over (in prison) the prison.*

# וַיִּתֵּן שַׂר בֵּית הַסֹּהַר בְּיַד יוֹסֵף אֵת כָּל הָאֲסִירִם (לט, כב)

וּמַנִּי (וִיהַב) רַב בֵּית אֲסִירֵי בִּידָא דְיוֹסֵף יָת כָּל אֲסִירַיָּא

*And the head of the prison appointed (placed)*
*in the hand of Yosef all the prisoners.*

After the episode with the wife of Potiphar and Yosef, the *pasuk* states, "ויקח אדני יוסף אותו ויתנהו אל בית הסהר," which Onkelos translates as, "And the master [Potiphar] of Yosef led [took] him and appointed him over the prison." Also, it states, "ויתן שר בית הסהר ביד יוסף את כל האסירם," which Onkelos translates as, "And the head of the prison appointed in the hand of Yosef all the prisoners." Why does Onkelos translate "*va'yitnehu*" and "*va'yiten*" as "appointed," and not literally as "gave" or "placed"?

The *Nesinah LaGer* answers that Onkelos hints to the Midrash which states that Potiphar said, "I know that you did nothing wrong; you are clean from libels and are innocent from sin. I have to put you in jail, though, because of what my wife and others claim." Therefore, Potiphar appointed Yosef in charge, giving him authority and honor. Moreover, in general, when the Torah refers to taking people or animals, Onkelos translates as "*devar*—to lead," whereas when people or animals are taken forcefully, against their will, Onkelos translates as "*sav*—to take." For example, regarding *korbanos*, whenever it states[14] "*kach*," "*l'kach*," or "*tikach*," he translates as "*sav*" because animals don't have a choice to go from place to place; they are not led, but rather, taken forcefully. Also, when the brothers threw Yosef into prison, the Torah states,[15] "ויקחהו וישלכו אותו הברה," which Onkelos translates as "*v'nasbuhi*—and they took him and they threw him into the pit." Here, although Potiphar threw Yosef into the pit, Onkelos does not translate "*va'yikach*" as "*v'sav*—and the master...took him," but as "*u'devar*—and the master...led him." This reflects that he was led with words, the regular way of taking a person, not in a forceful way, since Potiphar knew that Yosef was innocent.

---

14    ויקרא ט, ב ושמות כט, א וטו

15    לז, כד

We see from Onkelos's translations of *"va'yikach," "va'yitneihu,"* and *"va'yiten"* that although the wife of Potiphar slandered Yosef, Potiphar knew[16] that he was not to blame. The entire episode occurred because of Potiphar's wife. Very often, we see things and are quick to judge and decide whether they are proper and correct or not. It states,[17] "כי האדם יראה לעינים וה' יראה ללבב—Since a person sees and perceives, however, Hashem sees the heart." We judge based on what we see and think. The Gemara[18] teaches that there is a mitzvah to judge favorably, as it states, *"B'tzedek tishpot amisecha*—With righteousness judge your friend." If one sees an ordinary person doing an act which can be equally judged for good or bad, judge him for good. Or, if one sees a *tzaddik* doing an act which tilts toward bad, even so, judge him favorably. The Gemara[19] brings a few stories about judging favorably and ends, "Just as you judged me favorably, so too, Hashem should judge you favorably." The reward for judging favorably is that Hashem will also judge you favorably.

There is a pressing question: when I see someone doing something, I do not know exactly why he's doing it, therefore, I am required to judge him favorably. However, Hashem has absolutely no doubt regarding a person's motivations and actions; everything is known. If so, what does it mean that Hashem will judge favorably?

The Gemara[20] writes that even if a person has 999 angels prosecuting against him and only one defending him, he will be saved, as it states, "אם יש עליו מלאך מליץ אחד מני אלף להגיד לאדם ישרו ויחננו ויאמר פדעהו מרדת שחת—If there is one out of a thousand angels speaking good, saying the straightness of a person, he will be redeemed and saved from descending to Gehinnom." Rabbi Eliezer says that even if one side of an angel praises a person and 999 sides of that same angel accuse him, he will be saved. The *Maharsha* asks: How is it possible that one action can have 999 sides for bad and one side for merit? Rav Chaim Kanievsky answered that

16  וכן פירש בספר יין הטוב על תרגום יונתן פסוק יד וכ' בס"ק 05

17  שמואל א: טז, ז

18  שבועות ל.

19  שבת קכו:

20  שם לב.

a person's actions can flow from different intentions. We find this in the story with Peninah, who teased Chanah; the Gemara records that Peninah intended her actions for the sake of Hashem. Another example is with a person who works; why does he work? It can be because he loves making money and desires to become wealthy, or because he has a responsibility to support his wife and family, or because he wants to assist those who learn Torah and help the needy, and so on. Rav Kanievsky says that since in each action there are many possible sides for good and for bad, if a person will judge others favorably, Hashem will also focus on the good side of his actions and judge him favorably.

Rav Aryeh Finkel answers differently: the reason why Hashem will judge a person favorably is because it is a *hanhagah*. The way a person acts with his friend is how Hashem will act with him. True, Hashem knows why you did what you did, but He will reflect your behavior with others.

May we judge others favorably and merit to be judged by Hashem favorably!

## DID YOSEF SERVE THE PEOPLE OR DID THEY SERVE HIM? WHERE WAS YOSEF PUT COMPLETELY IN CHARGE?

וְהַמְּדָנִים מָכְרוּ אֹתוֹ אֶל מִצְרָיִם לְפוֹטִיפַר
סְרִיס פַּרְעֹה שַׂר הַטַּבָּחִים (לז, לו)

וּמְדְיָנָאֵי זַבִּינוּ יָתֵיהּ לְמִצְרָיִם לְפוֹטִיפַר רַבָּא דְּפַרְעֹה רַב קָטוֹלַיָּא

*And the Midyanim sold him to Mitzrayim, to Potiphar*
*the minister of Pharaoh, the head executioner.*

וַיְהִי ה' אֶת יוֹסֵף וַיֵּט אֵלָיו חָסֶד וַיִּתֵּן חִנּוֹ
בְּעֵינֵי שַׂר בֵּית הַסֹּהַר (לט, כא)

וַהֲוָה מֵימְרָא דַּיְיָ בְּסַעֲדֵיהּ דְּיוֹסֵף וּנְגַד לֵיהּ חִסְדָּא וִיהַבֵיהּ לְרַחֲמִין בְּעֵינֵי רַב בֵּית אֲסִירֵי

*And the saying [word] of Hashem would assist Yosef,*
*and He extended kindness to him, and He gave him*
*mercy in the eyes of the head of the prison.*

וַיִּתֵּן שַׂר בֵּית הַסֹּהַר בְּיַד יוֹסֵף אֵת כָּל הָאֲסִירִם אֲשֶׁר בְּבֵית
הַסֹּהַר וְאֵת כָּל אֲשֶׁר עֹשִׂים שָׁם הוּא הָיָה עֹשֶׂה (לט, כב)

וּמַנִּי (וִיהַב) רַב בֵּית אֲסִירֵי בִּידָא דְיוֹסֵף יָת כָּל אֲסִירַיָּא דִּבְבֵית
אֲסִירֵי וְיָת כָּל דְּעָבְדִין תַּמָּן מִמֵּימְרֵיהּ הֲוָה מִתְעֲבֵיד

*And the head of the prison appointed (placed) in Yosef's*
*hand all the prisoners of that prison and all that was*
*being done there was done through his saying [word].*

אֵין שַׂר בֵּית הַסֹּהַר רֹאֶה אֶת כָּל מְאוּמָה
בְּיָדוֹ בַּאֲשֶׁר ה' אִתּוֹ (לט, כג)

לֵית רַב בֵּית אֲסִירֵי חָזֵי יָת כָּל סָרְחָן בִּידֵיהּ בְּדִמֵימְרָא דַיְיָ בְּסַעֲדֵיהּ

*The head of the prison did not see any spoilage [flaw] in his*
*hand, because Hashem's saying [word] assisted him.*

After Yosef is placed in prison, it states, "ויהי ה' את יוסף ויט אליו חסד ויתן חנו
בעיני שר בית הסהר," which Onkelos translates as, "And the saying [word] of
Hashem would assist Yosef, and He extended kindness to him, and He
gave him mercy in the eyes of the head of the prison." The *Nefesh HaGer*
says that Onkelos translates *"chino"* as *"l'rachamin*—for mercy," since it
is unclear who gave favor to whom. Onkelos adds a 'ל to emphasize that
it was Yosef who found favor in the eyes of the head of the prison, and
not that the head of the prison found favor in Yosef's eyes.

The following *pasuk* states, "And the head of the prison put all the prisoners in the hand of Yosef, ואת כל אשר עושים שם הוא היה עושה—and all that
was being done there, he would do.'" This implies that Yosef did all that
was needed to be done for the people in prison, as though he was their
servant. Onkelos translates the words *"hu hayah oseh"* differently: "was
done through his saying [word]." The *Sifsei Chachamim*[21] explains that
this reflects that Yosef was in charge and had servants that he would
command to do things for him. Yosef did not do things for others, but

rather, other servants did things for him. Yosef was granted complete authority and responsibility.

The following *pasuk* states, "אין...רואה את כל מאומה בידו באשר ה' אתו," which Onkelos translates as, "The head of the prison did not see any spoilage [flaw] in his hand, because Hashem's saying [word] assisted him." Onkelos generally translates "*meumah*" as "nothing at all [*midaam*]," whereas here, he translates it as "spoilage, flaw [*surchan*]." The *Nefesh HaGer* points out that first it states, "*kal*—everything," and afterwards it states, "*meumah*—nothing." This seems to be a contradiction; did he see everything or nothing, and what does it mean if he saw nothing? Onkelos answers this by translating "*meumah*" as "spoilage," which reflects that Yosef had no fault and was flawless in his actions. We see that the head of prison recognized that Yosef was worthy to be trusted with authority.

Earlier in the parashah, when Yosef was sold, it states, "והמדנים מכרו אותו אל מצרים לפוטיפר סריס פרעה שר הטבחים," which Onkelos translates as, "And the Midyanim sold him to Mitzrayim, to Potiphar the minister of Pharaoh, the head executioner." The *Ramban* explains that "*tabach*" reflects killing people, as it states in *Daniel*, "רב טבחיא די מלכא—the head executioner of the king," and in *Eichah*, "*Tavachta lo chamalta*—You slaughtered [by the destruction of the Beis Hamikdash] and You did not have mercy." Yosef was sold to Potiphar, who was in charge of killing people who were sentenced to death. *Rashi* explains differently: Potiphar slaughtered animals of the king to prepare them to eat. The *Re'em* says that "*tavachta lo chamalta*" is a *mashal*: You slaughtered B'nei Yisrael as the slaughter of animals without having mercy. The *Sifsei Chachamim*[22] explains that "*sar ha'tabachim*" cannot mean "the head executioner" because if Hashem sent sweet-smelling incense for Yosef to be carried in the caravan down to Mitzrayim, for sure Hashem wouldn't send Yosef to kill people, which is even more repulsive! Onkelos understands that although Yosef was appointed over all those who were deserving of being killed, he himself did not kill them. Here, too, we see that Yosef was put in charge, and he had servants to serve him and follow his command.

Hashem assisted Yosef and gave him complete leadership and authority in each situation in which he was placed. May we merit Hashem's assistance and be favored by others!

# Mikeitz

## WHAT CAUSED PHARAOH TO APPOINT
## YOSEF OVER MITZRAYIM?

וּפֹתֵר אֵין אֹתוֹ וַאֲנִי שָׁמַעְתִּי עָלֶיךָ לֵאמֹר
תִּשְׁמַע חֲלוֹם לִפְתֹּר אֹתוֹ (מא, טו)

וּפְשַׁר לֵית לֵיהּ וַאֲנָא שְׁמַעִית עֲלָךְ לְמֵימַר דְּאַתְּ שָׁמַע חֶלְמָא וּמְפַשַּׁר לֵיהּ

*And there is no one to interpret it, and I heard about
you saying that you hear a dream and interpret it.*

בִּלְעָדָי אֱלֹקִים יַעֲנֶה אֶת שְׁלוֹם פַּרְעֹה (מא, טז)

לָא מִן חָכְמְתִי אֱלָהֵין מִן קֳדָם יְיָ יִתְּתַב שְׁלָמָא דְּפַרְעֹה

*It is not from my wisdom, rather from before [because
of] Hashem will Pharaoh's peace be returned.*

הֲנִמְצָא כָזֶה אִישׁ אֲשֶׁר רוּחַ אֱלֹקִים בּוֹ (מא, לח)

הֲנִשְׁכַּח כְּדֵין גְּבַר דְּרוּחַ נְבוּאָה מִן קֳדָם יְיָ בֵּיהּ

*Shall we find as this a man whom the prophecy from
before [because of] Hashem is within him?*

אַתָּה תִּהְיֶה עַל בֵּיתִי וְעַל פִּיךָ יִשַּׁק כָּל עַמִּי (מא, מ)

אַתְּ תְּהֵי מְמַנָּא עַל בֵּיתִי וְעַל מֵימְרָךְ יִתְּזָן כָּל עַמִּי

*You will be appointed over my house, and upon your
saying my entire nation will be sustained.*

The *pesukim* state that Pharaoh searched for someone to interpret his
dreams and Yosef was brought before him. Yosef interpreted the dream
that there would be seven years of plenty and seven years of famine.

Afterwards, Pharaoh says, "אחרי הודיע אלקים אותך את כל זאת אין נבון וחכם
כמוך—After G-d has let you know all of this, there is no one knowledge-
able and wise like you." And Pharaoh says, "אתה תהיה על ביתי ועל פיך ישק
כל עמי," which Onkelos translates as, "You will be appointed over my
house, and upon your saying my entire nation will be sustained." The
*Hakesav V'Hakabbalah* says that this is like the *Ibn Ezra*'s explanation:
"You will be a ruler over my house." The *Hakesav V'Hakabbalah* says that
"*al*" implies elevation and authority.

Pharaoh, the king of Mitzrayim, was a great king with many rulers and
servants. Suddenly, Pharaoh gave rulership over the entire land to a lad,
a servant, an *Ivri*, a people hated by the Mitzrim—and just because he
interpreted Pharaoh's dreams. Rav Chaim Shmuelevitz asks:[1] What did
Pharaoh notice about Yosef, in addition to his interpreting the dreams,
that made Pharaoh choose to appoint him as his second-in-command?
What made Yosef fit to rule?

The Brisker Rav[2] explains that in *Parashas Vayeishev*, when Yosef responded to the butler, he said, "*Ha'lo lEilokim pisronim*," which Onkelos
translates as, "Is the interpretation not from before [because of]
Hashem [הלא מן קדם ה' פשרן]?" Similarly, here too, Yosef responds, "בלעדי
אלקים יענה את שלום פרעה," which Onkelos translates as, "It is not from my
wisdom, but rather, from before [because of] Hashem will Pharaoh's
peace be returned." In both places, Yosef hints that what he was saying was not because of his own wisdom, but a result of prophecy from
Hashem. This is as Pharaoh comments about Yosef, "הנמצא כזה איש אשר
רוח אלקים בו," which Onkelos translates as, "Shall we find as this a man
whom the prophecy from before [because of] Hashem is within him?"
*Rashi* explains, "Even if we were to search for someone like him, will
we be able to find anyone comparable?" The Brisker Rav is bothered:
one doesn't need prophecy to interpret dreams, so what was the need
for Yosef to have prophecy? He answers that Chazal say that Pharaoh
changed his dreams so as to test Yosef, in order to verify that Yosef's
ability came solely from Hashem. Once Pharaoh saw that Yosef was

1   מאמר כב

2   חי' מרן הגרי"ז הלוי החדשות על תנ"ך ואגדה

correct in his interpretation, he realized that the interpretation must have been revealed to him through prophecy. Now, he also knew that Yosef was wise, just as Chazal say, "Hashem only gives prophecy to the wise." Since Pharaoh recognized that Yosef was a prophet, he knew that he was wise and was, indeed, fit to be appointed over Mitzrayim.

The Alter of Kelm offers a different answer: Pharaoh appointed Yosef over the entire Mitzrayim because he noticed Yosef's *yiras Shamayim.* When Yosef was brought to Pharaoh, Pharaoh said, "I dreamed a dream, ופתר אין אותו ואני שמעתי עליך לאמר תשמע חלום לפתר אתו," which Onkelos translates as, "And there is no one to interpret it, and I heard about you saying that you hear a dream and interpret it."

The *Me'at Tzari* explains that the words "תשמע חלום לפתר אתו" imply that Yosef listened to dreams, and he needed to determine whether he would be able to interpret them. Onkelos translates that Yosef hears the dream which he will definitely interpret. Pharaoh put his complete faith in Yosef that he will indeed be able to provide the correct resolution of the dreams.

Yosef responds, "בלעדי אלקים יענה את שלום פרעה," which Onkelos translates as, "It is not from my wisdom, but from before [because of] Hashem will Pharaoh's peace be returned." *Rashi* also explains: "It is not from my wisdom, but rather, Hashem will give me a response for Pharaoh's peace." Although Yosef was told by Pharaoh how great he was, instead of taking an iota of honor and credit for himself as an interpreter of dreams, he admitted that only Hashem interprets dreams. Similarly, Yosef told the head butler and head baker the words *"ha'lo lEilokim pisronim,"* which Onkelos translates as, "Is the interpretation not from before [because of] Hashem?" Here, too, Yosef said, "Although I do not interpret dreams, Hashem does; I will tell you Hashem's interpretation, not my own." The Alter of Kelm says that Pharaoh was surprised about Yosef's unusual fear of Hashem, expressed by belittling himself and admitting that his ability was solely from Hashem. This caused Pharaoh to recognize Yosef as a person who is reliable and trustworthy. Such a person can be given rulership in Mitzrayim, as there is no one comparable to him.

May we fear Hashem, belittle ourselves, and credit all our success to
Him alone!

## HOW DID YOSEF ACT AS A NOCHRI WITH THE BROTHERS?

וַיַּכֵּר הֶם וַיִּתְנַכֵּר אֲלֵיהֶם וַיְדַבֵּר אִתָּם קָשׁוֹת (מב, ז)

וְחַשֵּׁיב מָא דְּמַלֵּיל (דִּימַלֵּיל) עִמְּהוֹן וּמַלֵּיל עִמְּהוֹן קַשְׁיָן

*And he thought about what he had spoken (will speak)
with them, and he spoke with them harshly.*

אֲבָל אֲשֵׁמִים אֲנַחְנוּ עַל אָחִינוּ אֲשֶׁר רָאִינוּ צָרַת
נַפְשׁוֹ בְּהִתְחַנְנוֹ אֵלֵינוּ וְלֹא שָׁמָעְנוּ (מב, כא)

בְּקֻשְׁטָא חַיָּבִין אֲנַחְנָא עַל אֲחוּנָא דַּחֲזֵינָא בְּעָקַת נַפְשֵׁיהּ
כַּד הֲוָה מִתְחַנַּן לָנָא וְלָא קַבֵּילְנָא מִנֵּיהּ

*In truth, we are guilty about our brother, that we
saw the pain of his soul when he would plead to
us, but we did not accept from [listen to] him.*

The *pasuk* states, "And Yosef saw his brothers, ויתנכר אליהם וידבר אתם קשות."
*Rashi* explains that Yosef made believe as though he was a stranger by
speaking to them harshly. The *Ibn Ezra* adds that "ויתנכר" is from the
root "נכרי—stranger." Onkelos translates ויתנכר differently: "and he
thought about what he had spoken with them." The *Nefesh HaGer* has
the text "*d'maleil*," in past tense: Yosef thought about the words which
he had spoken with them when they sold him; he had pleaded to be left
alone, and they did not listen. The *Nesinah LaGer* says that Onkelos
translates ויתנכר אליהם as "and he thought about that which he will speak
[*di'malel*] to them," in future tense. Rav Yaakov Kamenetsky[3] explains
that Onkelos translates "ויתנכר" as "*va'yisnakel*—and he thought by
plotting," like it states by the brothers about Yosef, "*va'yisnaklu*," which

Onkelos translates as "*v'chashivu*—and they thought," meaning that they conspired against him.

The *pasuk* states that the brothers said to each other, "אשר ראינו צרת נפשו בהתחננו אלינו ולא שמענו," which Onkelos translates as "that we saw the pain of his soul when he would plead to us, but we did not accept from [listen to] him." The *Ramban* says that this was even crueler than the selling of Yosef. The brothers confessed and said, "אבל אשמים אנחנו על אחינו..." which Onkelos translates as, "In truth, we are guilty about our brother..." The *Nefesh HaGer* says that the feeling of cruelty from when the brothers didn't accept Yosef's pleas had taken root in his heart. When Yosef saw them for the first time in Mitzrayim, he suddenly remembered the brothers' cruelty, so he spoke harshly with them in order to afflict them. Inwardly, he definitely forgave them immediately for what they had done, so as not to transgress "Do not take revenge, and do not hold a grudge." However, he felt that they needed to repent for Hashem to forgive them and that speaking harshly to them would help cause them to admit their sin and attain forgiveness.

It states, "ויכר יוסף את אחיו והם לא הכרהו"—And Yosef recognized his brothers, but they did not recognize him." *Rashi* quotes from the *Midrash Aggadah* that earlier, when Yosef fell into their hands, they did not "recognize him" enough to act mercifully toward him. However, now when *they* were given over into *Yosef's* hands, he recognized them and had mercy on them. The *Nefesh HaGer* asks: In what way did Yosef express mercy toward them by concealing his identity and speaking harshly to them? On the contrary, he acted as a stranger and made it difficult for them; this is the opposite of having kindness and mercy!

The *Nefesh HaGer* answers that this way of acting, indeed, was kind and merciful, as it was in order to cause them to confess and atone for their sin. True, Yosef immediately forgave them in his heart; however, he also wanted that Hashem should forgive them. Therefore, Yosef made libels against them in order to cause them to repent. The brothers took Yosef's harshness as a sign and reminder, which, indeed, caused them to confess, as they said, "אבל אשמים אנחנו על אחינו"—In truth, we are guilty for what we did to our brother." There is no greater kindness and mercy than Yosef forgiving them and also wanting Hashem to forgive them as well in order to completely uproot their sin. This is included in Onkelos's translation of "And he thought about what he had spoken with them." Yosef thought about their harshness and forgave them, and thought about how to cause them to repent.

May Hashem help us always act with kindness and mercy!

## WHY DIDN'T YOSEF SIT THE BROTHERS NEAR THE MITZRIM?

וַיָּשִׂימוּ לוֹ לְבַדּוֹ...כִּי לֹא יוּכְלוּן הַמִּצְרִים לֶאֱכֹל
אֶת הָעִבְרִים לֶחֶם כִּי תוֹעֵבָה הוּא לְמִצְרִים (מג, לב)

וְשַׁוִּיאוּ לֵיהּ בִּלְחוֹדוֹהִי...אֲרֵי לָא יָכְלִין מִצְרָאֵי לְמֵיכַל עִם עִבְרָאֵי
לַחְמָא אֲרֵי בְּעִירָא דְּמִצְרָאֵי דָּחֲלִין לֵיהּ עִבְרָאֵי אָכְלִין

*And they placed him by himself...since the Mitzrim were
not able to eat bread with the Ivrim, because the Mitzrim
feared [worshipped] the animal that the Ivrim would eat.*

The *pasuk* states, "And they placed him by himself and them by themselves and the Mitzrim who were eating with him by themselves." Why were they sat in this specific way? The *pasuk* explains, "כי לא יוכלון המצרים לאכל את העברים לחם כי תועבה היא למצרים," which Onkelos translates as, "Since the Mitzrim were not able to eat bread with the Ivrim, because the Mitzrim feared [worshipped] the animal that the Ivrim would eat." *Rashi* explains that the Mitzrim hated to eat together with the Ivrim. Also, in *Parashas Va'eira*,[4] it states, "לא נכון לעשות כן כי תועבת מצרים נזבח לה' אלקינו הן נזבח את תועבת מצרים לעיניהם," which Onkelos translates as, "It is not fixed [appropriate] to do so, because the animal that the Mitzrim fear [worship], from it we are taking to slaughter before Hashem our G-d. Behold, we will slaughter the animal that the Mitzrim fear [worship] and they will see [לא תקן למעבד כן ארי בעירא דמצראי דחלין ליה מנה אנחנא נסבין לדבחא קדם ה' אלהנא הא נדבח ית בעירא דמצראי דחלין ליה ואנון יהון חזן]." The

*Nesinah LaGer* says that Onkelos translates *"to'avas Mitzrayim"* as "the Mitzrim feared [*dachalin*]." *"Dachalin"* means *"yirah*—fear," which reflects their idolatry; they were afraid of the gods they worshipped. Yosef placed the Ivrim, who were eating meat, separate from the Mitzrim, who were eating bread, to keep them away from being repulsed by the brothers who were eating their god.

The *Rambam*[5] explains that Onkelos understands that the Mitzrim worshipped the *"mazal taleh*—the lamb constellation," therefore, they forbade people to slaughter the lamb, and shepherds of sheep were repulsive to them. Other groups, such as the Kasdim, worshipped demons, which were similar to goats, and they thought the demons would return in the form of goats. This is as it states, "ולא יזבחו עוד את זבחיהם לשעירים אשר הם זנים אחריהם," which Onkelos translates as, "And they shall not slaughter their slaughter any more to the demons which they are mistaken after them [ולא ידבחון עוד דבחיהון לשדין דאנון טען בתריהון]." He translates *"la'se'irim"* as *"l'sheidin,"* like it states in *Parashas Haazinu*,[6] *"yizbechu l'sheidim*—they slaughtered to demons," just as some groups of non-Jews did. The people of Hodu and most other nations worshipped cattle. In order to erase these false ideals, Hashem commanded to offer these three specific types of animals; oxen, goats, and sheep for *korbanos*. What was assumed to be the most important idol is to be removed from idolatry and is instead used to facilitate closeness to Hashem. In place of worshipping these animals, we are supposed to do the exact opposite and use them for good, to attain forgiveness for our transgressions. The *Ramban*[7] disagrees: the point of *korbanos* can't just be to rid ourselves of the idolatrous practices of the non-Jews. Rather, *korbanos* are meant to enable us to come close to Hashem.

The *Me'at Tzari* points out that Onkelos translates *"to'eiva hee l'Mitzrayim"* by adding the word *"b'ira*—animal," and does not translate as *"ana*—sheep." This seems to fit with the *Zohar's* explanation that the

---

5   מו"נ ח"ג פמ"ו
6   דברים לב, יז
7   ויקרא א, ט

Mitzrim worshipped any living animal. For this reason, it states by *makkas bechoros*, "מבכור אדם ועד בכור בהמה—From the first-born person to the first-born animal." Hashem killed out all different types of first-born animals in Mitzrayim since they were also worshipped.

Here it states, "כי תועבה היא למצרים," which Onkelos translates as "because the Mitzrim feared [*dachalin*] the animal that the Ivrim would eat." However, in *Parashas Vayigash*[8] it states, "כי תועבת מצרים כל רעי צאן," which he translates as "because the Mitzrim distance [*merachakin*] all who shepherd sheep." Why does Onkelos translate "*to'evah*" as "fear," but "*to'avas*" as "distance"?

The *Nesinah LaGer* answers in the name of the *Hakesav V'Hakabbalah* that here, "*to'evah*" refers to the sheep itself as idolatry; therefore, he translates "fear." Whereas in *Parashas Vayigash*, he translates "*to'avas*" as "distance" since it refers to shepherding the sheep. The translation "because the Mitzrim distance all who shepherd sheep" refers to raising up, making great, and sanctifying those who pastured their idolatry. Or, on the contrary, those who shepherded sheep knew that there was nothing special about them to worship. Therefore, they did not treat the sheep with honor, and the Mitzrim distanced the shepherds out of disgrace and embarrassment for themselves.

May we use the types of animals which were originally used to worship idolatry to bring *korbanos* and come close to Hashem!

## DID YOSEF CHARM?

לַאֲשֶׁר עַל בֵּיתוֹ...לָמָה שִׁלַּמְתֶּם רָעָה תַּחַת טוֹבָה (מה, ד)

לְדִמְמַנָּא עַל בֵּיתֵיהּ...לְמָא שַׁלֵּימְתּוּן בִּשְׁתָּא חֲלָף טָבְתָא

*To that whom was appointed over his house...for what reason did you pay back bad in exchange for good?*

## וְהוּא נַחֵשׁ יְנַחֵשׁ בּוֹ (מה, ה)

וְהוּא בַּדְקָא מְבַדֵּיק בֵּיהּ

*And he indeed checks with it.*

## כִּי נַחֵשׁ יְנַחֵשׁ אִישׁ אֲשֶׁר כָּמֹנִי (מה, טו)

אֲרֵי בַדְקָא מְבַדֵּיק גַּבְרָא דִּכְוָתִי

*Since a man as myself indeed checks.*

The *pasuk* states, "And Yosef said *la'asher al beiso*," which Onkelos translates as "to that whom was appointed over his house." He commanded them to chase after the brothers and say, "למה שלמתם רעה תחת טובה," which Onkelos translates as, "For what reason did you pay back bad in exchange for good?" Instead of appreciating what I did for you, you stole the goblet. Then it states, "Did you not know that my master drinks from this goblet," and "והוא נחש ינחש בו," which Onkelos translates as "and he indeed checks with it." The *Nefesh HaGer* explains in the name of *Ibn Ezra* that Yosef said, "I put the goblet before you to test you and check you out, so I looked away until you took it. I tested you with the goblet itself to check and see whether you are honest or not. Why weren't you afraid to steal the goblet?" Why does Onkelos not translate "*nachesh yenachesh*" literally, as "charms," as he translates in other places?

The *Nefesh HaGer* answers that Yosef definitely did not charm, as that is *assur*. Rather, he set up a test before the brothers in order to check whether they were honest. The *Nesinah LaGer* says that Onkelos is careful for the honor of Yosef Hatzaddik, so that people won't say about him that he charmed. The *Nefesh HaGer* adds that it is common for Onkelos to change the literal translation for the honor of *tzaddikim*.

After the brothers return to Yosef, he says to them, "What is this action that you are doing? Do you not know כי נחש ינחש איש אשר כמוני?" *Rashi* explains, "Do you not know that a man as honorable as myself knows to charm and is aware through knowledge, logic, and understanding that you stole the goblet?" The *Sifsei Chachamim*[9] adds that Yosef said to them, although you stole the goblet with which I charm, I don't need it. You should have known that I am indeed aware from my own wisdom, who stole the goblet. Onkelos translates "*nachesh yenachesh*" differently: "Since a man as myself, indeed, checks." Why does Yosef speak to the messenger and brothers with the words "*nachesh yenachesh*" if it is *assur* to charm and he didn't actually charm?

The *Nefesh HaGer* answers that Yosef definitely did not charm, but, rather, he delved into the situation and checked it out, which is certainly permitted. Yosef claimed "*nachesh yenachesh*" to scare the brothers that he is a Mitzri man who knows how to charm, so that they would be afraid of him. This is as *Rashi* teaches: when Yosef sat the brothers around the table in order of their age, he first hit on his goblet and called out, "Reuven, Shimon, Levi...are of one mother," in order of the oldest to the youngest. They were astounded and they thought he knew magic. Yosef specifically placed fear on them in order to make them think he charmed.

Yosef said, "Do you not know כי נחש ינחש איש אשר כמוני, that another man as myself will charm in Mitzrayim?'" Yosef was careful to specifically say "a man like myself charms" and not "*nachesh anachesh*—I myself do charming," so as not to lie at all. The entire land of Mitzrayim was full of witchcraft, as *Rashi* explains that Pharaoh said to Moshe and Aharon, "You are bringing magic into a place which is full of magic!" Still, Yosef himself did not practice witchcraft.

Yosef claimed, "Once you left, the goblet was also lost; now I see that you are thieves. You must have stolen the goblet! There was no one else together by the same table aside from you who ate and drank with me." Yosef's intent was to make a libel, *middah k'neged middah* for what Yosef said, "גנב גנבתי מארץ העברי—I was indeed stolen from the land of the Ivrim." He wanted the brothers to confess and repent in order to receive atonement for what they did, *middah k'neged middah*. And so they did, as they said, "מה נאמר לאדוני מה נדבר ומה נצטדק האלקים מצא את עון עבדיך, what shall we say to out master? What shall we speak and what shall we merit? G-d found sin by your servant."

May we learn from Onkelos to be extra careful with the honor of *tzaddikim*!

# Vayigash

## HOW DID YOSEF USE LASHON HAKODESH TO PROVE THAT HE IS YOSEF?

### כִּי פִי הַמְדַבֵּר אֲלֵיכֶם (מה, יב)

אֲרֵי כְּלִישָׁנְכוֹן אֲנָא מְמַלֵּיל עִמְּכוֹן

*Since as [it is] your language that I am speaking with you.*

When Yosef reveals himself to his brothers, he proves his identity by saying, "כי פי המדבר אליכם—Since it is my mouth that is speaking to you." What does Yosef mean? Onkelos translates as "since as [it is] your language I am speaking with you." The *Ramban* explains that Yosef spoke in *lashon hakodesh*. Yosef said, "Indeed, I am Yosef your brother, since my mouth speaks to you with *lashon hakodesh*."

The *Ramban* asks: the language of Canaan was *lashon hakodesh*, so they all spoke it. How, then, is Yosef proving anything at all? Maybe he was a Canaani! The *Ramban* answers that it is not a clear proof, but rather, Yosef was giving an excuse to appease them; don't worry, it is indeed me. The *Nesinah LaGer* answers differently: Yosef showed the brothers that he knew their usage of words in *lashon hakodesh* and the type of talk which was used uniquely by their family. This is hinted to in Onkelos's translation "*k'li'shanchon*—as your language," meaning how you speak the language, and not "*b'li'shanchon*—with your language."

In *Parashas Vayechi*, Yosef requests to bury his father in Canaan as he had sworn. Pharaoh responds, "Ascend and bury your father as you swore." *Rashi* explains that if not for the oath, Pharaoh would not have let Yosef go. Pharaoh was afraid to tell Yosef to transgress his oath and stay in Egypt, because then Yosef could respond the same about the oath which he had sworn to Pharaoh. Yosef knew all seventy languages plus *lashon hakodesh* while Pharaoh only knew seventy languages, but not *lashon hakodesh*. Pharaoh made Yosef swear that he wouldn't reveal that he knows the language of *lashon hakodesh* and Pharaoh doesn't.

The *Maharal* notes that Pharaoh should have said, "Swear that you won't tell anyone that you are smarter than me." Instead, Pharaoh said, "Swear that you won't reveal that you know more languages than I do." This shows that he was more concerned with Yosef revealing that he knew one more language than he was with Yosef being smarter than him. The *Maharal* explains that the function of a king is to be able to relate to his nation. If he can't talk their language, there is something intrinsically lacking with his rulership. He is not fit or able to rule over everyone. Yosef, who knew all the languages including *lashon hakodesh*, was therefore more fit for rulership than Pharaoh. Therefore, Pharaoh made Yosef swear that he would not reveal Pharaoh's ignorance of *lashon hakodesh*, which reflected that he was not as fit to be king.

The *Maharal* asks: Since Pharaoh was able to learn the other seventy languages, why did he not learn *lashon hakodesh* as well? In addition, since according to the *Ramban*, everyone in Canaan knew *lashon hakodesh*, what was stopping Pharaoh from learning it? The *Maharal* answers that *lashon hakodesh* is a holy language and was given to Hashem's holy nation. Pharaoh and the people of Canaan were able to say the words of *lashon hakodesh*, but they could not understand its holiness and depth.

Based on the *Maharal*, we can answer the original question. Yosef understood the language of *lashon hakodesh* with its holiness and depth, as did Yaakov and the brothers, who were part of the chosen nation. Therefore, when Yosef spoke the holy and deep language of *lashon hakodesh*, the brothers recognized that it was Yosef; it could not have been a Mitzri!

May Hashem return us to Eretz Yisrael together with the holiness and depth of *lashon hakodesh*!

## WHY DID YAAKOV NOT BELIEVE
## THAT YOSEF WAS STILL ALIVE?

וַיָּפָג לִבּוֹ כִּי לֹא הֶאֱמִין לָהֶם (מה, כו)

וַהֲוָאָה מַלְיָא פָּיְגָן עַל לִבֵּיה אֲרֵי לָא הֵימֵין לְהוֹן

*And the words were changing (unsettled/weak/happiness/stopping
or ceasing/piercing) on his heart since he did not believe them.*

וַיְדַבְּרוּ אֵלָיו אֵת כָּל דִּבְרֵי יוֹסֵף אֲשֶׁר דִּבֶּר אֲלֵהֶם וַיַּרְא
אֶת הָעֲגָלוֹת אֲשֶׁר שָׁלַח יוֹסֵף לָשֵׂאת אֹתוֹ (מה, כז)

וּמַלִּילוּ עִמֵּיה יָת כָּל פִּתְגָמֵי יוֹסֵף דְּמַלֵּיל עִמְּהוֹן וַחֲזָא
יָת עֶגְלָתָא דִּשְׁלַח יוֹסֵף לְמִטַּל יָתֵיה

*And they spoke with him all the points of Yosef that he [Yosef] spoke
with them, and he [Yaakov] saw the wagons which Yosef sent.*

After the brothers told Yaakov that Yosef was alive and is the ruler in
Mitzrayim, the *pasuk* states, "ויפג לבו כי לא האמין להם." What does "*va'yafag*"
mean? *Rashi* explains that it means "change," as the Mishnah teaches
"*mefigin taaman*—their taste was changing, getting worse." Yaakov's
heart "changed and went" from believing; it did not turn toward believing that Yosef was still alive. Onkelos translates "*va'yafag*" as "and
the words were *puygun*." The *Maharal* explains this with *Rashi*: "the
words were changing and they were unsettled on his heart." The *Radak*[1]
explains Onkelos differently: "And it was weak and light," meaning the
point did not register and enter. Why couldn't Yaakov believe the good
tidings about Yosef being alive?

The *Sifsei Chachamim*[2] teaches in the name of the *Nachalas Yaakov*
that Yaakov couldn't believe that a strange person who was not from
Mitzrayim would be able to become a ruler over Mitzrayim. Also, he
couldn't believe that a slave would become a ruler, as there was a rule in
Mitzrayim that a slave cannot have authority.

---

1    ורש"י מגילה כה:

2    ל

The *Nefesh HaGer* explains differently: Yosef told the brothers who he was and said, "וישימני לאב לפרעה ולאדון לכל ביתו ומושל בכל ארץ מצרים"—And He made me for a father to Pharaoh, and a master for his household, and a ruler over the entire land of Mitzrayim." However, Yosef told his brothers to specifically say to his father, "שמני אלקים לאדון לכל מצרים רדה אלי"—G-d made me as a master for the entire Mitzrayim, descend to me." Yosef did not want the brothers to mention that he was an *av*, a father, as Yaakov might think that he was a priest. Also, he did not want to mention that he was a master over the household, as Yaakov might think that he ate with them carcasses and *tereifos*, which are *assur*. Lastly, he did not want to mention that he was a ruler, as Yaakov may think that he was busy as a ruler and went away from being like a Yehudi. After the brothers said, "*Od Yosef chai*—Yosef is still alive," they mentioned on their own, "וכי הוא מושל בכל ארץ מצרים"—And he is a ruler in the entire land of Mitzrayim." After hearing this, Yaakov thought to himself, this seems to be a contradiction. If it is true that Yosef became a ruler, he must have lost his *ruchniyus*, and he won't be considered "*od Yosef chai*" as Yosef still being "alive" means existing as an *ish ruchani*. He would have needed to be involved and busy with the entire Mitzrayim and would not have had time to learn and properly serve Hashem. Yaakov did not understand how to resolve this contradiction.

The following *pasuk* states, "וידברו אליו את כל דברי יוסף אשר דבר אליהם וירא את העגלות אשר שלח יוסף," which Onkelos translates as, "And they spoke with him all the points of Yosef that he [Yosef] spoke with them, and he [Yaakov] saw the wagons which Yosef sent." *Rashi* explains that Yosef gave over a sign to the brothers; he told them that he and his father were involved in *eglah arufah*, which was the last topic he had learned with his father before being separated from him. This is as it states, "And he saw the wagons [*agalos*, related to *eglah*] which Yosef sent," instead of, "and he saw the wagons which Pharaoh sent." Yaakov recognized that Yosef remembered the Torah that he had learned; he was still an *ish ruchani*, a person with spirituality. Yaakov did not care about all the honor that Yosef had. Only after he saw the wagons and recognized that Yosef was able to remain an *ish ruchani* was he appeased.

The *Chizkuni* explains Onkelos differently: "And the words were a happiness, a rejoicing on his heart" from excitement and enjoyment. The *Ramban* explains "and the words caused his heart and *neshamah* to stop or cease" from the sudden shock of hearing such amazing news.

The *Nesinah LaGer* has the text "פִיגִין," with a *chirik* under the 'פ and 'ג. The *Nefesh HaGer* brings from Rav Ovadia MiBartenura that a פִיגִין is a knife with blades on both ends. The *Nesinah LaGer* explains that here it refers to a piercing instrument as a knife: "The words were a stabbing on his heart." The *Nefesh HaGer* explains that Yaakov was in pain that Yosef was possibly not the *ish ruchani* he was before he left. Seeing the wagons and understanding the sign appeased him.

May Hashem help us stay firm in our Yiddishkeit as *anashim ruchaniyim* in *galus*!

## WHY DID YAAKOV'S RUACH HAKODESH OR PROPHECY LEAVE HIM AND RETURN TO HIM?

### וַתְּחִי רוּחַ יַעֲקֹב אֲבִיהֶם (מה, כז)

וּשְׁרַת רוּחַ קֻדְשָׁא (נְבוּאָה) עַל יַעֲקֹב אֲבוּהוֹן

*And ruach hakodesh (the spirit of prophecy)*
*rested upon Yaakov, their father.*

### רַב עוֹד יוֹסֵף בְּנִי חָי (מה, כח)

סַגִּי לִי חֶדְוָא עַד כְּעַן יוֹסֵף בְּרִי קַיָּם

*The rejoicing is great (enough) for me; my son,*
*Yosef, until now is existing [still alive].*

The *pasuk* states, "And he saw the wagons that Yosef sent, ותחי רוח יעקב אביהם." Onkelos translates "*va'techi*" as "and *ruach hakodesh* rested upon Yaakov, their father." The *Ramban* has the text, "and the spirit of *prophecy* [*nevuah*] rested upon Yaakov, their father." The *Nesinah LaGer* explains in the name of *Rashi* that from the time that Yosef was sold and he was separated from Yaakov, Hashem's Shechinah left Yaakov. Now, after all those years, it returned. The *Ramban* says that Onkelos translates "a spirit of prophecy" since it is something true which occurred, his prophecy returned. This is implied, as it does not state, "*Vayechi Yaakov avihem*—And Yaakov, their father, lived," but rather, "ותחי רוח יעקב אביהם—And the spirit of Hashem was with their father, Yaakov." The *Sifsei Chachamim*[3] explains that it is inferred from the word "*ruach*," as it states, "ורוח לבשה את עמשי," a reference to *ruach hakodesh*. Why did *ruach hakodesh* or prophecy leave Yaakov while Yosef was sold, and why did it return?

The Gemara[4] teaches that the *pasuk* "ושבחתי אני את השמחה—and I praise the *simchah*" refers to the rejoicing of a mitzvah. The Shechinah does not rest while one is distraught, lazy, joking, or lightheaded; only out of *simchah* of mitzvah. The Gemara derives this from the *pasuk* which states, "ועתה קחו לי מנגן והיה כנגן המנגן ותהי עליו יד ה'—And now, take for me the musical instrument, and it would be when the musical instrument played music, the spirit of Hashem rested on him." *Rashi* explains that Elisha commanded the musical instrument to be played in order to cause the Shechinah to rest on him. The *Maharsha* suggests that the music was meant to remove sorrow and anger which he might have had that would cause the Shechinah to leave, so that he could have prophecy. We see that when a person is distraught or angry, the Shechinah will not rest upon him and he won't be able to prophesize. As long as Yaakov thought Yosef had been killed, he was in mourning, so the Shechinah left him. Now that Yosef was alive, Yaakov rejoiced and the Shechinah and prophecy returned.

In *Parashas Behaalosecha*, it states[5] that a lad told Moshe about Eldad and Meidad who were prophesizing in the camp. Yehoshua said, "My master Moshe, *kela'eim*." *Rashi* explains that Yehoshua was saying, "Place upon them the needs of the *tzibbur* and they will be finished off on their own." *Tosafos*[6] says that Yehoshua's intent to stop them from prophesizing was based on the concept that the Shechinah only rests

---

3  נ
4  שבת ל:
5  במדבר יא, כז-כח
6  סנהדרין יז.

on a person out of happiness, not while distraught, mourning, or as the *Sifsei Chachamim*[7] adds, experiencing disturbances. Since they would be overburdened, disturbed, and upset by their involvement in the needs of the community, the Shechinah would leave them. So too, *Tosafos*[8] writes that Hashem only spoke directly to Moshe after the decree stopped for all the men twenty years and up to die in the desert. While there was mourning for B'nei Yisrael who were dying in the Midbar, the Shechinah did not rest on Moshe, since it was in their merit that Hashem spoke with Moshe, and they were sad.

We find this concept in other areas aside from prophecy. Chazal discuss the size of *tefachim*. In addition to the standard *tefach*, there is also the slightly larger *tefach sochek* and slightly smaller *tefach atzev*.[9] The *Aruch* explains that "*sochek*" means smiling and laughing; when a person is happy, he smiles and laughs and his face widens. Therefore, "*sochek*" refers to a larger *tefach*. The opposite of "*sochek*" is "*atzuv*," which means distraught; when a person is sad, he presses his face tightly together and it becomes smaller. The Gemara[10] teaches that before Rabbah started a discourse, he would open up with a joke, and the Rabbanan would laugh. Once he started teaching, however, they sat with fear. *Rashi* explains that the joke opened up their hearts through their *simchah*. We see that when a person is happy, he is open for things to enter his heart, whereas when a person is sad or angry, he is closed and things won't be able to enter.

The following *pasuk* states, "And Yisrael said, רב עוד יוסף בני חי." The *Biur Onkelos* explains that Onkelos translates as, "The rejoicing is great [*sagi*] for me! My son, Yosef, until now is existing [still alive]." The *Nesinah LaGer* explains differently in the name of the *Rashbam*: "I have enough [*sagi* as *dai*] happiness! My son, Yosef, until now is existing [still alive]." Onkelos adds the word "*chedvah*," which means "joy," to emphasize that Yaakov's happiness returned when he heard that Yosef was still alive.

---

| | |
|---:|---:|
| 7 | ש |
| 8 | ב"ב קכא. |
| 9 | רע"ב מש' עירובין א, א |
| 10 | שבת שם |

Because Yaakov rejoiced, the Shechinah and prophecy that had left him, returned.

May Hashem help us be happy and open so that we may understand and connect to the Torah and the Shechinah!

## WHAT DID YOSEF TELL THE BROTHERS TO SAY TO PHARAOH, AND DID THEY LISTEN?

וְהָאֲנָשִׁים רֹעֵי צֹאן כִּי אַנְשֵׁי מִקְנֶה הָיוּ (מו, לב)

וְגֻבְרַיָּא רָעַן עָנָא אֲרֵי גֻּבְרֵי מָרֵי גֵּיתֵי הֲווֹ

*And the men shepherded sheep, since they were men, masters of flock.*

וַאֲמַרְתֶּם אַנְשֵׁי מִקְנֶה הָיוּ עֲבָדֶיךָ...בַּעֲבוּר תֵּשְׁבוּ
בְּאֶרֶץ גֹּשֶׁן כִּי תוֹעֲבַת מִצְרַיִם כָּל רֹעֵה צֹאן (מו, לד)

וְתֵימְרוּן גֻּבְרֵי מָרֵי גֵּיתֵי הֲווֹ עַבְדָּךְ...בְּדִיל דְּתִתְּבוּן בְּאַרְעָא
דְגֹשֶׁן אֲרֵי מְרַחֲקִין מִצְרָאֵי כָּל רָעֵי עָנָא

*And you shall say, 'Men, masters of flock were your servants...in order that you shall dwell in the land of Goshen because the Mitzrim distance all who shepherd sheep.'"*

The *pasuk* states that Yosef tells his brothers, "I will tell Pharaoh that you have come..., והאנשים רועי צאן כי אנשי מקנה היו," which Onkelos translates as "and the men shepherded sheep, since they were men, masters of flock." Onkelos translates the words *anshei mikneh"* as "men, masters of flock," not literally as "people who had flock." The *Nefesh HaGer* explains this with the *Ramban*: Yosef said he would tell Pharaoh that the brothers were shepherds; however, they did not actually shepherd sheep of other people or even their own. They were wealthy, and had servants and people in their household who shepherded and did the work for them. Yosef specifically wanted to mention this for the honor of the brothers. The *Nefesh HaGer* explains that Yosef's intent was to boost the brothers so that they shouldn't be eligible to work for Pharaoh. They were above the caliber of working, as they had workers to do their jobs. This would cause Pharaoh to let them live in Goshen and not consider taking them as servants.

Yosef then tells the brothers to mention this to Pharaoh, as it states, "And it will be when Pharaoh calls for you, ואמרתם אנשי מקנה היו עבדיך מנעורינו ועד עתה גם אנחנו גם אבותינו בעבור תשבו בארץ גושן," which Onkelos translates as, "And you shall say, 'Men, masters of flock were your servants, from when we were little until now, also us, also our father,' in order that you shall dwell in the land of Goshen." The *pasuk* ends, "כי תועבת מצרים כל רועי צאן," which Onkelos translates as "because the Mitzrim distance all who shepherd sheep." Here, Yosef adds, "Aside from mentioning that you are honorable and don't work, tell Pharaoh that your entire family only knows about pasturing sheep. This will force Pharaoh to allow you to dwell in the land of Goshen, away from the Mitzrim." Because the Mitzrim worship sheep, they distance all who shepherd and keep them separated.

When the brothers came before Pharaoh, they said, "רועה צאן עבדיך גם אנחנו גם אבותינו—Your servants are shepherds of sheep, also us, also our father." "לגור בארץ באנו כי אין מרעה לצאן—We came to dwell in the land, since there is no pasture for the sheep." The *Nefesh HaGer* asks: Why did the brothers not mention "*anshei mikneh*—men, masters of flock," as Yosef had directed them? The *Nefesh HaGer* answers that when the brothers came to Yaakov and told him what they would say to Pharaoh, he vetoed it. Yaakov said, "Do not mention your wealth and your acquisitions before Pharaoh. Do not brag or show off." This is similar to what Yaakov said to the brothers at the beginning of the famine, "*Lamah tisra'u*—Why should you be seen?" *Rashi* explains, "Why should you show off before B'nei Yishmael and B'nei Eisav as though you are satisfied and have food?" Yaakov exemplified *anavah*, humility, and he told the brothers not to mention their special attributes. Instead, they should just tell Pharaoh that their family pastures sheep, needs place to pasture, and wants to dwell in Goshen.

May we learn the *middah* of humility from Yaakov and not boast about our success!

# Vayechi

## WHAT DOES A SWORD HAVE TO DO WITH DAVENING AND AN ARROW WITH REQUESTING?

וַאֲנִי נָתַתִּי לְךָ שְׁכֶם אַחַד עַל אַחֶיךָ אֲשֶׁר לָקַחְתִּי
מִיַּד הָאֱמֹרִי בְּחַרְבִּי וּבְקַשְׁתִּי (מח, כב)

וַאֲנָא יְהָבִית לָךְ חוּלָק חַד יַתִּיר עַל אֲחָךְ דִּנְסֵיבִית מִיְּדָא
דֶּאֱמוֹרָאָה בִּצְלוֹתִי וּבְבָעוּתִי (בְּחַרְבִּי וּבְקַשְׁתִּי)

*And I [Yaakov] have given to you [Yosef] one additional portion
over your brothers which I took from the hand of the Emori with my
davening and with my requesting (with my sword and with my bow).*

The *pasuk* states, "ואני נתתי לך שכם אחד על אחיך אשר לקחתי מיד האמורי בחרבי
ובקשתי." *Rashi* explains that Yaakov said, "I gave you, Yosef, the land of
Shechem for a portion over your brothers, which I took from the hand
of the Emori with my sword and with my bow." The Gemara[1] is bothered because this implies that Yaakov fought with the sword and arrow
and conquered the land, which he then gave to Yosef. However, another
*pasuk* states, "כי לא בקשתי אבטח וחרבי לא תושיעני—I did not believe in my
bow, and my sword did not save me." This reflects that Yaakov did not
fight a battle. How do we reconcile this contradiction?

Onkelos answers this question by translating the word *"b'charbi"* as
*"b'tzlosi*—with my davening," and *"u'v'kashti"* as *"u'v'va'usi*—and with
my requesting," just like the Gemara answers! We see that Yaakov got
the land by davening and requesting it, not by fighting a regular battle.

---

1    ב"ב קכג.

165

What are the two types of davening of *tzlosi* and *ba'usi*? And why is *tzlosi* compared to a sword, and *ba'usi* compared to a bow and arrow? The Brisker Rav[2] explains that a sword and an arrow have different strengths in terms of causing damage. A sword is something which is intrinsically sharp. It can injure even from up close, without much strength behind it, just by touching something. An arrow's strength, on the other hand, is not its sharpness. Rather, it causes damage only when it is shot with much force from a distance.

So too, says the Brisker Rav, there are two types of davening. One type is set and established by Chazal, called *Shemoneh Esreh*, which was fixed by the *Anshei K'nesses Hagedolah*. The other type is personal, when a person davens to Hashem and requests his needs in his own words. The second type, the personal davening, may depend on who the individual is. The Gemara says that if one has a sick person in his house, he should go to a *chacham* to daven for him. Not always does his davening have enough strength to reach Hashem, so he should go to a *chacham* whose davening is stronger and more likely to be accepted by Hashem. Also, the sincerity of the request can make a difference. The Gemara[3] teaches that Rabbi Elazar said that from the day the Beis Hamikdash was destroyed, the gateways of *tefillah* were closed...yet the gateways of tears were not closed. A personal request, which is dependent on the person and his sincerity, is comparable to an arrow, where the amount of damage it will do depends on the strength of the one who shot it. *Shemoneh Esreh*, which is intrinsically powerful, is comparable to the sword, which can damage just by making contact, without much force behind it. Chazal set up a *nusach* from which we daven that Hashem listens to and accepts. Similarly, at the end of every *tefillah*, there is *Kaddish* said with the words, "*Tiskabel tzlosehon u'va'us'hon*—You shall accept their davening and their beseeching." Here, too, both types of davening are mentioned, and we request that both of them should be answered.

---

חי' מרן הגרי"ז הלוי החדשות על תנ"ך ואגדה    2

ב"מ נט.    3

Yaakov said, "I took possession of Shechem with my sword and bow," meaning with the *nusach* of davening set up by Chazal and with my own personal requesting.

May Hashem help us daven *Shemoneh Esreh* and our own personal *tefillos* with more concentration and sincerity and bring *yeshuos*, *refuos*, and *besuros tovos* to ourselves and all of Klal Yisrael!

## WHY WERE SHIMON AND LEVI REBUKED?

שִׁמְעוֹן וְלֵוִי אַחִים כְּלֵי חָמָס מְכֵרֹתֵיהֶם (מט, ה)

שִׁמְעוֹן וְלֵוִי אַחִין גֻּבְרִין גִּבָּרִין בַּאֲרַע תּוֹתָבוּתְהוֹן עֲבַדוּ גְּבוּרָא

*Shimon and Levi are brothers, honorable men, mighty;*
*they acted with might in the land of their dwelling.*

בְּסֹדָם אַל תָּבֹא נַפְשִׁי בִּקְהָלָם אַל תֵּחַד כְּבֹדִי כִּי
בְאַפָּם הָרְגוּ אִישׁ וּבִרְצֹנָם עִקְּרוּ שׁוֹר (מט, ו)

בְּרָזְהוֹן לָא הֲוַת נַפְשִׁי בְּאִתְכַּנּוֹשֵׁיהוֹן (לְמִהָךְ) לָא נְחָתִית מִן יְקָרִי
אֲרֵי בְּרֻגְזְהוֹן קְטַלוּ קְטוֹל וּבִרְעוּתְהוֹן תָּרָעוּ שׁוּר סָנְאָה

*[Yaakov said,] "My soul was not in their secret plot,*
*[and] in their gathering (to go), I did not descend from my*
*honor, since with their anger, they killed a kill, and with*
*their will, they smashed down the wall of the enemy."*

The *pasuk* states, "שמעון ולוי אחים כלי חמס מכרותיהם," which Onkelos translates as, "Shimon and Levi are brothers, honorable men, mighty; they acted with might in the land of their dwelling," which refers to Shechem. The *Ramban* explains that Onkelos translates "*mecheiroseihem*" as "*meguroseihem*—their dwelling place." The *Sifsei Chachamim*[4] adds that the כ' can be exchanged with a ג', since they are from the letters גיכ"ק.

---

4 י

Yaakov continues to rebuke Shimon and Levi saying, "בסדם אל תבוא נפשי בקהלם אל תחד כבודי," which Onkelos translates as, "My soul was not in their secret plot, [and] in their gathering; I did not descend from my honor." Yaakov said that he was not included in their secret plot to kill the people of Shechem, and he did not join them in their attack on the people of Shechem to take revenge for what Shechem the son of Chamor did to Dinah. Yaakov continues, "כי באפם הרגו איש וברצונם עקרו שור," which Onkelos translates as, "since with their anger, they killed a kill, and with their will, they smashed down the wall of the enemy." The *Ramban* says that Onkelos understands "שׁוֹר" as "שׁוּר—a wall." They smashed down the wall which surrounded Shechem in order to take revenge.

Yaakov rebuked them, saying, "ארור אפם כי עז ועברתם כי קשתה אחלקם ביעקב ואפיצם בישראל—Cursed is their anger, since it is strong, and their wrath, since it is hard; I will divide them in Yaakov and I will scatter them in Yisrael." Why was Yaakov angry about what Shimon and Levi did? One reason is stated in *Parashas Vayishlach*. Yaakov said to Shimon and Levi, "*Achartem osi*," which *Rashi* explains means, "You have dirtied my situation." The *pasuk* continues, "להבאישני ביושב הארץ בכנעני ובפריזי," which Onkelos translates as "to give [place] hatred between me and between the dwellers of the land with the Canaani and with the Prizi." Yaakov was disturbed because he was afraid that the Canaanim and the Prizim would come to fight against them.

Here, Onkelos reveals another reason. Yaakov rebuked Shimon and Levi, saying that they acted with might in the land of their dwelling. He was not in their secret plot to kill the inhabitants of Shechem, and he did not join together with them in their battle against Shechem. It was because of their anger that they killed, and with their own interest they smashed down the wall of their enemy, uprooting the entire city of Shechem. The *Ramban* explains that Yaakov was upset at Shimon and Levi for killing an entire city whose residents did nothing wrong. True, Shimon and Levi had the right to kill Shechem, the leader, for abducting Dinah and forcefully taking her. However, they had no right to kill the entire city and take the city's children and wives as captives and their possessions for booty. Their anger and wrath caused them to go overboard beyond what needed to be implemented. The people in Shechem did not sin; they entered a covenant with the sons of Yaakov and circumcised themselves, planning to join together as one nation. There was a chance that the entire city might have turned to Hashem and become part of the household of Avraham. Also, Yaakov was disturbed about a *chillul Hashem*, as people might say that their actions were based on his advice. Despite Shimon and Levi's zealousness for their sister, there is a claim against them for killing the city of Shechem and preventing them from possibly coming close to Hashem.

The *Ramban* explains "*achalkem b'Yaakov*" to mean that Shimon received an inheritance spread throughout Yehudah's territory. "*Va'afitzem b'Yisrael*" means that Levi received *arei miklat*, cities of refuge scattered throughout Yisrael. Yaakov cursed them to be spread out and scattered so that they wouldn't come to secret conspiracies and join together to fight. I'd like to suggest that the curse was *middah k'neged middah*. They made secret conspiracies and joined together to fight; therefore, they were cursed to be separated and scattered.

My good friend Rabbi Chaim Koehler pointed out that Yaakov did not immediately rebuke Shimon and Levi, but waited until the end of his life. This is as *Rashi*[5] explains that Moshe Rabbeinu learned from Yaakov that one should not rebuke until he is close to death. Yaakov did not rebuke Reuven until he was close to dying; he said, "Reuven, my son, I did not rebuke you all these years so that you should not leave me and go attach yourself to Eisav, my brother." Here too, Yaakov did not want to rebuke Shimon and Levi right away for killing the people of Shechem and not allowing them the opportunity to come close to Hashem. Now that he was on his deathbed and his sons were grown up, it was the proper time to deliver the rebuke. He would say all that was needed, and he would not be afraid of the consequences.

May Hashem help us be in control of our feelings and not make decisions out of anger!

---

5     דברים א,ג

# HOW IS DAN COMPARED TO TWO SNAKES?
## AND WHAT TYPES OF WARRIORS DID HE KILL, AND HOW?

דָּן יָדִין עַמּוֹ כְּאַחַד שִׁבְטֵי יִשְׂרָאֵל (מט, טז)

מִדְּבֵית דָּן יִתְבְּחַר וִיקוּם גַּבְרָא בְּיוֹמוֹהִי יִתְפְּרֵיק עַמֵּיהּ
וּבִשְׁנוֹהִי יְנוּחוּן כַּחֲדָא שִׁבְטַיָּא דְיִשְׂרָאֵל

*From the house of Dan will be chosen, and a man will
arise; in his days, his nation will be redeemed, and in his
years, the tribes of Yisrael will rest as one.*

יְהִי דָן נָחָשׁ עֲלֵי דֶרֶךְ שְׁפִיפֹן עֲלֵי אֹרַח הַנֹּשֵׁךְ
עִקְּבֵי סוּס וַיִּפֹּל רֹכְבוֹ אָחוֹר (מט, יז)

יְהֵי גַּבְרָא דְּיִתְבְּחַר וִיקוּם מִדְּבֵית דָּן אֵימָתֵיהּ תִּתְרְמֵי עַל
עַמְמַיָּא וּמַחֲתֵיהּ תִּתַּקַּף בִּפְלִשְׁתָּאֵי כְּחִוֵּי חֻרְמָן יִשְׁרֵי עַל אוֹרְחָא
וּכְפִתְנָא יִכְמוֹן עַל שְׁבִילָא יִקְטַל גִּבָּרֵי מַשִּׁרְיַת פְּלִשְׁתָּאֵי פָּרָשִׁין
עִם רִגְלָאִין יְעַקַּר סוּסָן וּרְתִכִּין וִימַגַּר רָכְבֵיהוֹן לְאַחֲרָא

*It will be the man that will be chosen and will stand up from
the house of Dan—his fear will be lifted up (placed/⁶fall⁷),
on the nations, and his smite will be strong against the
Pelishtim, as chermon snakes he will rest on the road, and
as a python he will wait in hiding on the path. He will
kill the mighty Pelishtim's camps, riders with footmen;
he will uproot horses and chariots, and he will cause
their riders to fall (be smashed/thrown) backwards.*

The *pasuk* states, "דן ידין עמו כאחד שבטי ישראל," which Onkelos translates
as, "From the house of Dan will be chosen, and a man will arise; in his
days, his nation will be redeemed, and in his years, the tribes of Yisrael
will rest as one." The *Nefesh HaGer* explains in the name of the *Ramban*
that this refers to Shimshon. Although he was not a king, he would
punish the Pelishtim and take revenge for Yisrael and save them. Yaakov

---

6  יין הטוב
7  מעט צרי

hints to one specific person from the tribe of Dan, not the entire tribe. The words *"k'achad Shivtei Yisrael"* literally mean, "as one of the tribes of Yisrael." The *Nesinah LaGer* says that Onkelos, however, translates *"k'achad"* on its own, separate from the words *"Shivtei Yisrael"*; thus, it means "as one, the tribes of Yisrael." Yisrael will be together with unity. The *Me'at Tzari* adds that "as one, the tribes of Yisrael" is a result of the first part of the *pasuk*: because Shimshon will take revenge against the Pelishtim, the tribes will rest as one. *Rashi* explains differently: *"k'achad Shivtei Yisrael"* are connected and serve as a continuation of the first part of the *pasuk*: Shimshon will take revenge for all of Yisrael against the Pelishtim.

The following *pasuk* states, "יהי דן נחש עלי דרך שפיפון עלי אורח," which Onkelos translates as, "It will be the man that will be chosen and will stand up from the house of Dan; his fear will be lifted up on the nations, and his smite will be strong against the Pelishtim. As *chermon* snakes he will rest on the road, and as a python he will wait in hiding on the path." The *Nesinah LaGer* explains that Onkelos translates "נחש עלי דרך שפיפון עלי אורח" with both the literal meaning, the *mashal*, and also its *nimshal*. "His fear will be lifted up on the nations, and his smite will be strong against the Pelishtim" is the *nimshal*. "As *chermon* snakes he will rest on the road, and as a python he will wait in hiding on the path" is the *mashal*. The *Nefesh HaGer* explains that here, too, Onkelos translates with an introduction: "It will be the man who will be chosen and will stand up from the house of Dan," referring to Shimshon. "His fear will be lifted up on the nations and his smite will be strong against the Pelishtim" was fulfilled in *Shoftim*, "ויך אותם...מכה רבה—and he smote them...a great smite."

*Rashi* explains that "*nachash*" refers to the *chermon* snake, also called *tzifoni*, which has no cure for its bite. It is called *chermon* since it makes everything "banned," from the word "*cherem*," meaning not functional. The *shefifon* is different type of snake that shrieks and hisses, from the word *nosheif*. The *Nesinah LaGer* explains the *nimshal*: just as a snake places fear, so too Dan will cause fear to the nations, and just as a *shefifon* frightens, so too he will frighten the Pelishtim.

The *pasuk* ends, "הנושך עקבי סוס ויפול רכבו אחור—which bites the heels of the horse and will cause the rider to fall backwards." Onkelos translates differently: "He will kill the mighty Pelishtim's camps, riders with footmen; he will uproot horses and chariots, and he will cause their riders to fall [be smashed/thrown] backwards." The *Nesinah LaGer* explains that the word "*sus*" literally means "a horse," in singular, but Onkelos translates as "horses," in plural, after the intent, many horses. Also, he adds "chariots" to glorify the *lashon*. Here, too, Onkelos translates with both the literal meaning, which is the *mashal*, and with the *nimshal*. "He will kill the mighty Pelishtim's camps, riders with footmen" is the *nimshal*. "He will uproot horses and chariots" is the *mashal*.

The *Nesinah LaGer* explains, "He will kill the mighty Pelishtim's camps" refers to Shimshon, who will take revenge for B'nei Yisrael. The "riders [פרשין]" are soldiers who ride on horses, called פרשים in the Torah.[8] The "footmen [רגלאין]" are soldiers who walk on the ground which are called רגלאין, from רגל, feet. This is similar to the *pasuk* in *Shoftim* that states, "ויך אותם שוק על ירך מכה רבה," which *Targum Yonasan ben Uziel* translates as "פרשין עם רגלאין," just as Onkelos translates here. The *Metzudos Dovid* explains that the riders are compared to the *yarech*, thigh, which is the upper part of the leg, as this part of the leg is used for riding. The footmen are compared to the *shok*, leg, which is the lower part of the leg, as this part of the leg is used for walking. The "riders with footmen" refer to two different types of soldiers. The *Nesinah LaGer* brings a different explanation in *Rashi's* name: a horseback rider leans on his *shok*, lower bone, not on his *yarech*, thigh bone, and the foot is placed in the stirrup, which hangs down from the chariot. According to *Rashi*, "*parashin im rigla'in*" means "riders with their feet holders," which refers to one type of soldier.

The *pasuk* ends, "*Va'yipol rochvo achor*." The *Ramban* explains that when the snake bites the heels of the horse, the horse picks up its head and two front feet, and the rider will fall backwards. Onkelos translates as, "and he will cause their riders to fall [be smashed/thrown] backwards." The *Nesinah LaGer* explains that Onkelos translates *"va'yipol"* as *"v'yapil,"* which is a causative verb.

The *Nefesh HaGer* says that Onkelos translates the comparison of the two snakes, how they attack, how they injure, and their corresponding *nimshal*. The *chermon*, called the copper-snake, is a snake whose copper-colored back shines at a distance. The copper color shines into the eyes of a person who sees it, causing him to run away from it. This snake is brazen and is not afraid of anyone. It lays on the road in public, where people walk, and openly chases after people. Shimshon was the same. In the beginning, he single-handedly and publicly fought against the mighty Pelishtim and was victorious. The Pelishtim were frightened and fled as though fleeing from before this snake. Later, Shimshon was similar to another type of snake, the python. *Tosafos* teaches in the name of the *Yerushalmi* that there is a python which is the size of a hair and is called *"shefifon."* It hides among the paths, since it is afraid to go where people walk, and waits in ambush. When a person passes by riding on a horse, it comes and bites the heel of the horse, and its poison burns the horse's entire foot. The horse quickly collapses, crushing its rider. This describes how Shimshon met his end. The Pelishtim bored out his eyes, and they disgraced and belittled him by displaying him at a celebration for finally overcoming the Jewish resistance. Without warning, he pushed down the pillars of the house, collapsing the house on them. He killed more Pelishtim at that time than he killed when he was alive. It did not even enter their minds that they needed protection from him, just as the rider doesn't realize that he needs to be protected from the tiny *shefifon*.

*Rashi* explains the comparison to the snake's bite differently: the snake will bite the horse, causing the rider to fall back even without being touched by the snake. So too, we find this by Shimshon: he pushed over the pillars of the building and collapsed the roof, killing the people on the roof without Shimshon actually touching them.

May Hashem guard us from our enemies and bring the *geulah sheleimah bi'meheirah bi'yameinu*, Amen!

## WHAT WERE YOSEF'S MERITS FOR HIS PROPHECY TO COME TO FRUITION?

וַתֵּשֶׁב בְּאֵיתָן קַשְׁתּוֹ וַיָּפֹזוּ זְרֹעֵי יָדָיו (מט, כד)

וְתָבַת בְּהוֹן נְבִיּוּתֵיהּ עַל דְּקַיֵּים אוֹרָיְתָא בְּסִתְרָא וְשַׁוִּי בְּתָקְפָּא (תָּקְפָּא) רְחָצָנֵיהּ
בְּכֵן אִתְרְמָא (יִתְרְמָא)[9] דְּהַב עַל דְּרָעוֹהִי אַחֲסֵין מַלְכוּתָא וּתְקוֹף (וּתְקֵיף)

*And his prophecy was returned with them for that which he*
*fulfilled the Torah in private, and he placed his trust in the Strong*
*One, then gold was lifted up[10] (will be lifted up) on his arms, he*
*inherited[11] (held onto)[12] royalty and strength (he became powerful).*

The *pasuk* states, "*Va'teishev b'eisan kashto*," which Onkelos translates as, "And his prophecy was returned with them for that which he fulfilled the Torah in private, and he placed his trust in the Strong One." The *Nefesh HaGer* explains that Onkelos translates "*va'teishev*" as "and his prophecy [*nevi'usei*] was returned [*v'savas*] with them [*b'hon*]." This refers to the dreams that Yosef had about the brothers. The word "*va'teishev*" literally means "and he dwelled," as *Rashi* explains, "and he dwelled with strength." Onkelos, though, translates "*va'teishev*" as "*va'tashav*," which means "and was returned." *Rashi* explains that Onkelos understands it as referring to Yosef's dreams concerning the brothers which were fulfilled. That happened because [*al*] he fulfilled [*d'kayeim*] the Torah [*Oraysa*] in private [*b'sisra*]. *Rashi* explains that Onkelos adds to the *pasuk*,[13] "for that which he fulfilled the Torah in private." This refers to not sinning with the wife of his master, Potiphar, in private, as it states, "ואין איש מאנשי הבית שם בבית—and there was no person from the people of the house there in the house." The Gemara[14] teaches: Rav Chama says, Yosef, who sanctified *Shem Shamayim* in

---

9   רש"י

10   "Placed," *Beurei Onkelos*; "placed down or thrown," *Me'at Tzari*

11   בעל היאר ונל"ג

12   נה"ג

13   ש"ח ע

14   סוטה י:

private, merited to have one letter from Hashem's name added to his name, therefore it states "עדות ביהוסף." The *Maharsha* writes that the words "עדות י-ה" hint that Hashem testified that Yosef did not touch the wife of Potiphar.

Onkelos translates *"b'eisan kashto"* as "and he placed [*v'shavi*] his trust in the Strong One." *Rashi* explains that *"v'shavi"* means "because he placed," with the ו indicating an explanation. *Rashi* explains that *"b'eisan"* refers to Yosef's strength in placing his trust in Hashem, Who is One and Who is strong and dependable. Therefore, he merited the prophecy of the dreams to come true. The *Nesinah LaGer* explains differently: *"b'eisan"* refers to Hashem's strength, which caused the prophecy to happen.

*Rashi* quotes from *Rabboseinu* that *"kashto"* hints at "his arrow," which refers to semen that flows like an arrow and reflects Yosef's inclination with the wife of Potiphar. "ויפזו" means "ויפצו—and they scattered." The *Sifsei Chachamim*[15] adds that a ז can replace a צ. "זרועי" means "זרע—semen," which went out and scattered [*va'yafozu*] from between the fingers of his hands [*zro'ei yadav*]. This is as the Gemara[16] teaches: he stuck his hands in the ground to restrain himself and semen came out from between his fingers. Originally, Yosef was supposed to have twelve tribes, but he lost ten for this "sin" with his ten fingers. The Gemara says, "משם רועה אבן ישראל—From this episode, he merited to shepherd Yisrael." The *Maharsha* explains that since Yosef refrained from being together with the wife of Potifar, he merited to sustain his father and his entire household in Mitzrayim.

Onkelos translates *"va'yafozu zero'ei yadav* as, "Then gold was lifted up on his arms; he inherited royalty and strength [he became powerful]." The *Nefesh HaGer* explains that this refers to the *pasuk* that states, "And Pharaoh removed his ring from upon his hand and placed it on Yosef's hand...and he placed a chain of gold on his neck." The *Ralbag* explains that this refers to the gold placed on Yosef's arms for greatness and

---

rulership. "ויפזו" is from the root "פז—gold." The *Nesinah LaGer* suggests that Onkelos translates *"va'yafozu zero'ei yadav"* with two explanations: first, "then gold was lifted up on his arms," and second, "he inherited royalty and strength." The *Nefesh HaGer* explains *"achsein"* to mean "take hold": "and he took hold of rulership by being given Pharaoh's ring, and he became strong.

The *Nefesh HaGer* says that Onkelos hints that Yosef merited the prophecy of the dreams to be fulfilled because of two reasons: first, for fulfilling the mitzvos of the Torah by not touching the wife of Potiphar, and second, because he put his trust in Hashem. The *Nefesh HaGer* is bothered by the following question: what is the connection between putting trust in Hashem and not sinning? The *Nefesh HaGer* quotes from the *Bereishis Rabbah*[17] that the wife of Potiphar said, "If you don't listen to me, I swear that I will oppress you with other things," and he responded, *"Oseh mishpat la'ashukim*—He performs judgment for those who are oppressed." She threatened, "I will cut off your *parnassah*," and he responded, *"Nosein lechem la'r'eivim*—He gives bread to those who are starving." She continued, "I will tie you up," and he responded, *"Hashem matir assurim*—Hashem unties those who are bound." She said, "I will bend [lower] your height," and he responded, *"Hashem zokef kefufim*—Hashem straightens those who are bent." She tried, "I will blind your eyes," and he responded, *"Hashem pokei'ach ivrim*—Hashem opens the eyes of those who are blind." She put an iron spit underneath his neck so he should gaze at her, and even so, he did not gaze at her. The *Nefesh HaGer* says that this is the greatest possible thing that one could have done; Yosef completely put his trust in Hashem and fulfilled the Torah.

May we learn from Yosef to withstand challenges in private and put our complete trust in Hashem!

## HOW DID YAAKOV PERCEIVE YOSEF'S ROLE OF SUSTAINING MITZRAYIM?

מִידֵי אֲבִיר יַעֲקֹב מִשָּׁם רֹעֶה אֶבֶן יִשְׂרָאֵל (מט, כד)

דָּא הֲוָת לֵיהּ מִן קֳדָם אֵל תַּקִּיפָא דְּיַעֲקֹב דִּבְמֵימְרֵיהּ זָן אֲבָהָן וּבְנִין זַרְעָא דְּיִשְׂרָאֵל

*This was to him from before [because of] Keil, the Strong
One of Yaakov, that with his (His) saying [word], he
sustained fathers and sons, the offspring of Yisrael.*

The *pasuk* states, "מידי אביר יעקב רועה אבן ישראל." The *Nefesh HaGer*
explains that Onkelos translates "*mi'dei avir Yaakov*" as "this was to him
from before [because of] *Keil*, the Strong One of Yaakov." The *Nesinah
LaGer* suggests that Onkelos translates "*da havas lei*" together with
the previous word, "*u'skof*," as "and this strength was to him." Onkelos
translates "משם רועה אבן ישראל" as "that with his saying [word] he sustained fathers and sons, the offspring of Yisrael." Simply, "*d'v'meimreih*"
means that with his—Yosef's—saying, he sustained the rest of the
family. The *Hakesav V'Hakabbalah* explains differently: it refers to
Hashem's saying, since "*mi'sham*" reflects back on "*avir Yaakov*," which,
as the *Ibn Ezra* explains, refers to Hashem. The word "*mi'sham*" is like
"*mi'sheim*—from the *Shem Hashem*—which caused Yosef to be able to
sustain everyone.

The *pasuk* ends, "אבן ישראל." *Rashi* explains "אבן" as "אב ובן—a father and
son." He then quotes Onkelos, who translates "fathers and sons," and
explains that this refers to Yaakov and his sons. "אבן" reflects *malchus*,
kingship; Yosef was the leader over all of Yisrael. The *Nesinah LaGer*
says that *Rashi* explains "אבן ישראל" together: Yosef was the one with the
kingship of Yisrael. The *Me'at Tzari* says that Onkelos, who translates
"fathers" and "sons" in plural, seems to explain "אבן" differently: it refers
to the brothers, the tribes, who were also fathers, plural, and their sons.
The *Nesinah LaGer* says that Onkelos translates "אבן ישראל" separately,
as two ideas: first, fathers and sons [*avahan u'vnin*], and second, the
offspring of Yisrael [*zara d'Yisrael*]. The *Nefesh HaGer* says that this
hints to the *pasuk* which states, "ויכלכל יוסף את אביו ואת אחיו ואת כל בית אביו"

לֶחֶם לְפִי הַטָף—And Yosef sustained his father, and his brothers, and the entire household of his father, bread, according to the child."

The *Nefesh HaGer* says that Onkelos translates as "this was to him from before [because of] *Keil*, the Strong One of Yaakov, that with His saying [word] he sustained fathers and sons…" since Yaakov attributed Yosef's authority and sustenance solely to Hashem. This is hinted at in *Tehillim*, which states, "אַשְׁרֵי שֶׁקֵל יַעֲקֹב בְּעֶזְרוֹ שִׂבְרוֹ עַל ה' אֱלֹקָיו." "שִׂבְרוֹ" is with a *sin* and refers to Yosef hoping and putting trust in Hashem. It also hints to שֶׁבֶר with a *shin*, which refers to the food which Yosef supplied Mitzrayim. "מִשָּׁם רֹעֶה אֶבֶן יִשְׂרָאֵל"—that with His saying [word] he sustained…" refers to what Hashem said to Yaakov in a dream, "*ki lo e'ezavecha.*" *Rashi* explains that one who seeks bread is called "*ne'ezav.*" Yaakov did not want to praise and thank Yosef for the sustenance that he provided, since the Gemara says that there are three keys in the hand of Hashem, one being rain, which refers to *parnassah*. Yaakov looked up to Hashem and said, "You support all of us, and Yosef is only a messenger," as it states, "כִּי לְמִחְיָה שְׁלָחַנִי אֱלֹקִים לִפְנֵיכֶם—Since for sustenance G-d sent me before you," and "וַיִּשְׁלָחֵנִי אֱלֹקִים לִפְנֵיכֶם לְהַחֲיוֹת לָכֶם—And G-d sent me before you to sustain you." Yaakov attributes Yosef's assistance to his simply being a messenger from Hashem to help his family.

May we learn from Yaakov to put our hope solely in Hashem!

## TO WHAT DOES "HA'SACHAS ELOKIM UHNI" REFER?

### וַיֹּאמְרוּ לוּ יִשְׂטְמֵנוּ יוֹסֵף (נ, טו)

וַאֲמָרוּ דִּלְמָא יִטַּר לָנָא דְּבָבוּ יוֹסֵף

*And they said, "Maybe Yosef will guard [keep] hatred against us."*

### אַל תִּירָאוּ כִּי הֲתַחַת אֱלֹקִים אָנִי (נ, יט)

לָא תִדְחֲלוּן אֲרֵי דָּחֲלָא דַּיְיָ אֲנָא

*Do not be afraid, since I am one who fears Hashem.*

After Yaakov died, the brothers said, "*Lu yistemeinu Yosef*," which Onkelos translates as "maybe Yosef will guard [keep] hatred against us," and now he will take revenge for the bad that we did to him. Yosef responds, "אל תיראו כי התחת אלקים אני." *Rashi* explains this as a question: "Do not worry; am I in Hashem's place?" Meaning, can I do anything bad even if I would want to? All of you tried to do bad to me, and Hashem made it so that it was for the good. Certainly, I alone will not be able to do anything bad; therefore, you do not need to worry. The *Nesinah LaGer* says that Onkelos translates the words "*Ha'sachas Elokim uhni*" as a statement: "I am one who fears Hashem;" you do not need to worry, since I fear Hashem. It is common for Onkelos to translate the prefix ה', which hints to a question, as a statement. The *Me'at Tzari* explains in the name of the *Daas Zekeinim MiBaalei HaTosafos* that "הֲתַחַת" is like "וְאַל תֵּחָת—And do not become broken," hinting that Yosef feared Hashem. The *Nefesh HaGer* says that Onkelos does not translate as a question, like *Rashi*, since this would degrade Hashem's honor by *chas v'shalom* equating Hashem with people.

How does Yosef's response, "I am one who fears Hashem," resolve the brothers' fear?

The Gemara[18] teaches that when Rabbi Yochanan ben Zakkai was sick, his students came to visit him; at some point, he started to cry. The students asked, "Why are you crying?" Rabbi Yochanan responded, "If I were to be brought before a king of flesh and blood, I would cry. This is before a human king, who is here today and tomorrow is in the grave, who if he was to get upset at me, it would not be forever, and if he was to kill me, it is not a death forever. Also, I can appease him with words and I can bribe him with money. Now, they are bringing me before Hashem, the King of all Kings who exists forever and His anger is everlasting, and He kills forever. Also, I cannot appease Him with words or bribe Him with money. Certainly, I should cry!"

The students then asked Rabbi Yochanan to bless them. He said, "It should be the will of Hashem that the fear of Hashem shall be upon

---

18    ברכות כח:

you as the fear of a person of flesh and blood." His students asked, "Is that it? Not any more than the fear of a person?" He responded, "If only you are able to achieve that level! When a person is alone and thinks about doing an *aveirah*, he checks that nobody is watching, although he knows that Hashem sees everything. Such a person is more afraid of a person than Hashem, for had a person been there, he would not have sinned. *Halevai*, you should fear Hashem as much as you fear people."

Rabbi Yochanan taught two parallel lessons. First, he taught that he was as afraid of Hashem as one is afraid of a king of flesh and blood. Second, he taught his students to also internalize this lesson: a person should be afraid to do what is improper before Hashem as if a person would see what he was doing.

The same is true with Yosef. He responded to the brothers, "The reason I did not take revenge was not because I was afraid of our father, but because I fear Hashem. I will not transgress *"lo sikom*—do not take revenge" or *"v'lo sitor*—do not keep hatred." There is no difference now that our father is not around; it is the same as when he was around."

Yosef says in *Parashas Mikeitz*,[19] "את האלקים אני ירא—From before [because of] Hashem I fear [מן קדם ה' אנא דחיל]." Here too, Onkelos translates *"Ha'sachas Elokim uhni"* as "I am one who fears Hashem." Simply, Yosef comes to appease the brothers: "Don't worry, I fear Hashem." The *Panim Yafos* says that we derive from these two places that one is permitted to be *mispa'er*, proud, about his *yiras Hashem*. Although a person is supposed to be modest, this is an exception. The Gemara teaches that "everything is in the hands of Hashem—except for *yiras Shamayim*." Since Hashem helps a person accomplish everything else in life, he cannot be so proud about his achievements, for they are not really his. *Yiras Shamayim*, though, the one thing a person accomplishes on his own, is the exception.

May Hashem help us use the models of our *roshei yeshiva*, *rebbeim*, parents, and bosses to maintain an awareness of Hashem and fulfill His mitzvos!

# SEFER
# SHEMOS

# Parashah Dedications

SHEMOS–Donny and Tamar Miller
In memory of our brother-in-law, Marc Katz, *a"h*
אלחנן משה רפאל בן יהודה ליב הכהן ע"ה

---

VA'EIRA–Donny and Tamar Miller
In memory of our brother-in-law, Marc Katz, *a"h*
אלחנן משה רפאל בן יהודה ליב הכהן ע"ה

---

משפחת הול–BO
לזכות של התורם ומשפחתו וכל יוצאי חלציו

---

BESHALACH–Rabbi and Mrs. Chaim Portowicz
לע"נ
אבינו מורינו ורבנו הרה"ג רב יוסף ב"ר אברהם יצחק הכהן פארטאוויטש זצ"ל
ואמנו מורתינו מרת גיטל בת ר' דוב בער ע"ה

---

YISRO–Rabbi and Mrs. Efraim Eisenberg
לע"נ תקוה בת אפרים דוד הי"ו לבית איזנברג

---

MISHPATIM–Sruli Portowicz
לרפו"ש חנה בת ברוריה ורפאל אברהם יצחק בן גיטל

---

TERUMAH–Mr. Epstein
לזכות של התורם ומשפחתו וכל יוצאי חלציו

---

TETZAVEH–The Gross family
לע"נ ישראל מאיר בן משה שמואל ז"ל

נדבה ע"י משפחתם–KI SISA
לע"נ ישראל בן נפתלי ז"ל

---

נדבה ע"י משפחתם–VAYAKHEL
לע"נ זאב בן יהודה ז"ל

---

נדבה ע"י משפחתם–PEKUDEI
לע"נ
אברהם יוסף בן שמשון הלוי ז"ל
יצחק אייזיק בן מאיר ז"ל

# Shemos

## WHAT WERE SAREI MISSIM, AND WHAT WAS THE PURPOSE OF BUILDING STOREHOUSES?

הָבָה נִתְחַכְּמָה לוֹ...וְהָיָה כִּי תִקְרֶאנָה מִלְחָמָה
וְנוֹסַף גַּם הוּא עַל שֹׂנְאֵינוּ וְנִלְחַם בָּנוּ וְעָלָה מִן הָאָרֶץ (א, י)

הֲבוּ נִתְחַכַּם לְהוֹן...וִיהֵי אֲרֵי יְעָרְעִנָּנָא קְרָב וְיִתּוֹסְפוּן אַף
אִנּוּן עַל סָנְאַנָא וִיגִיחוּן בָּנָא קְרָב וְיִסְּקוּן מִן אַרְעָא

*Let us outsmart them...and it will be when a war will occur
and they too, will join with our enemies, and they will wage
war against us, and they will go up from the land.*

וַיָּשִׂימוּ עָלָיו שָׂרֵי מִסִּים לְמַעַן עַנֹּתוֹ בְּסִבְלֹתָם
וַיִּבֶן עָרֵי מִסְכְּנוֹת לְפַרְעֹה (א, יא)

וּמַנִּיאוּ עֲלֵיהוֹן שִׁלְטוֹנִין מַבְאֲשִׁין בְּדִיל לְעַנּוֹאֵיהוֹן
בְּפֻלְחָנְהוֹן וּבְנוֹ קִרְוֵי בֵּית אוֹצָרֵי לְפַרְעֹה

*And they appointed over them evil rulers in order to pain [oppress]
them with their labors, and they built storage cities for Pharaoh.*

The *pasuk* states that Pharaoh tells his nation that the nation of
B'nei Yisrael is more numerous than us. He says, "*Havah nischakmah
lo,*" which Onkelos translates as "let us outsmart them," in plural, as
it refers to the people from the nation of Yisrael. He continues, "והיה כי
תקראנה מלחמה ונוסף גם הוא על שונאינו ונלחם בנו ועלה מן הארץ," which Onkelos
translates as, "And it will be when a war will occur and they [plural,
Yisrael] too, will join with our enemies, and they will wage war against
us, and they [plural, Yisrael] will go up from the land." Because of this
worry, the following *pasuk* states, "וישימו עליו שרי מסים למען ענותו בסבלותם,"

185

which Onkelos translates as "and they appointed over them evil rulers in order to pain [oppress] them with their labors." The *Nefesh HaGer* says that Onkelos generally translates the word[1] "*sarei*" as "leaders [*rabbanei*]," whereas here, he translates it as "rulers [*shiltonin*]." Also, Onkelos translates "*missim*" as "bad-evil [*mav'ashin*]," not literally as "taxes of money." The *Hakesav V'Hakabbalah* suggests that "מסים" is from the root "מאס—repulsive," as the root "מאס" and "מסס" are interchangeable. Out of their repulsive and detestable nature, they acted cruelly to do bad to innocent people. The *Nefesh HaGer* explains that these evil rulers did not take money; rather, they took souls, as it states, "*L'maan anoso*—In order to oppress them." They physically abused them. When *sarim* follow their orders and do as instructed, Onkelos translates as "*rabbanei*—leaders." Whereas when they do not follow their orders, they are called "*shiltonin*—rulers," which are enforcers. Here, the *sarim* did worse than the king commanded; therefore, Onkelos translates as "evil rulers."

Why was Pharaoh afraid that there would be an occurrence of war, and what explains his concern that B'nei Yisrael would join with the enemies of the Mitzrim? In order to stop this, Pharaoh did two things: he appointed evil rulers, and "ויבן ערי מסכנות לפרעה," which Onkelos translates as "and they built storage cities for Pharaoh." How was building storehouses a resolution of their worry that their enemies would attack and B'nei Yisrael would team up with them?

The *Baal Haturim* explains that Pharaoh was afraid that the kings of Canaan might come to fight in order to retrieve the money which Yosef had taken from them during the years of famine. The *Nefesh HaGer* explains that the function of these storehouses was to safeguard that money. Also, the Gemara[2] teaches that with Yosef's wisdom and prophecy, he collected all the gold and silver in Mitzrayim, Canaan, and throughout the entire world! Pharaoh was worried that B'nei Yisrael would claim that everything which their father, Yosef, had collected

---

1   יח, כא

2   פסחים קיט.

belonged to him, and they should inherit it. If so, when Canaan comes, B'nei Yisrael would join with the enemies of Mitzrayim. Therefore, they made B'nei Yisrael build storehouses to guard the money in an area which was not fitting to walk through. It had quicksand, was dangerous to get to, and was well protected.

The *Nefesh HaGer* brings another explanation in the name of the Midrash. Pharaoh's intent in making B'nei Yisrael build storehouses with backbreaking labor was in order to stop them from reproducing. The enforcers would keep them at their labor until late at night and force them to sleep in the fields. They would not allow them to return home to their wives.

May Hashem appoint good leaders to assist us in exile!

## WHAT WERE YOSEF'S DECREES? CAN ONE DO ANYTHING TO STOP HASHEM'S WILL FROM BEING FULFILLED?

וַיָּקָם מֶלֶךְ חָדָשׁ עַל מִצְרָיִם אֲשֶׁר לֹא יָדַע אֶת יוֹסֵף (א, ח)

וְקָם מַלְכָּא חֲדַתָּא עַל מִצְרָיִם דְּלָא מְקַיֵּים גְּזֵירַת יוֹסֵף

*And a new king arose over Mitzrayim who*
*did not fulfill Yosef's decree.*

וְכַאֲשֶׁר יְעַנּוּ אֹתוֹ כֵּן יִרְבֶּה וְכֵן יִפְרֹץ (א, יב)

וּכְמָא דִמְעַנַּן לְהוֹן כֵּן סָגַן וְכֵן תָּקְפִין

*And just as they would pain [oppress] them, so they*
*would increase and so they would be strong.*

וַיְצַו פַּרְעֹה לְכָל עַמּוֹ לֵאמֹר כָּל הַבֵּן
הַיִּלּוֹד הַיְאֹרָה תַּשְׁלִיכֻהוּ (א, כב)

וּפַקֵּיד פַּרְעֹה לְכָל עַמֵּיה לְמֵימַר כָּל בְּרָא דְּיִתְיְלֵיד לִיהוּדָאֵי בְּנַהֲרָא תִּרְמוֹנֵיה

*And Pharaoh commanded to his entire nation saying,*
*"Any boy who will be born to the Jews, throw him into the river."*

The *pasuk* states, "ויקם מלך חדש על מצרים אשר לא ידע את יוסף"—And a new king arose over Mitzrayim who did not know Yosef." *Rashi* writes that some explain that this Pharaoh was a new king who did not know Yosef, while others explain that he was the same king, but he enacted new decrees, treating Yosef with coldness, as though he did not know him. Onkelos translates the words "*asher lo yada*" as "who did not fulfill Yosef's decree." What is this decree which the new king did not fulfill? The *Romzei Rabbeinu Yoel al HaTorah* explains that this refers to Yosef's decree to rest on Shabbos and to perform circumcision. The *Me'at Tzari* explains that this refers to being sharecroppers, instead of becoming slaves. The *Nefesh HaGer* teaches from the Midrash that beneficial rules for the good of Yisrael were written in the laws and customs of Mitzrayim, enacted by Yosef. Originally, Pharaoh did not want to annul them, however, the Mitzrim removed him from the throne for three months. Finally, he accepted and said, "Whatever you want, I will do," and they returned him to the throne. Pharaoh was actually the same king, but introduced new enactments.

The Gemara[3] writes that Pharaoh made three decrees against Yisrael. First, he said, "אם בן הוא והמתן אתו"—If it is a boy, kill him." *Rashi* explains that initially, Pharaoh relied on the midwives and did not appoint guards. Second, when that didn't work, he said, "כל הבן הילוד היארה תשליחוהו"—Any boy who will be born, throw him into the water." *Rashi* explains that "*tashlichuhu*" indicates that he appointed guards to throw the boys into the river. Third, he made the decree apply to the entire nation. *Rashi* explains that the words "*l'chal amo*—to his entire nation" reflect that Pharaoh also decreed on his entire nation that they too, were included in this command. This is as it states, "*Kol ha'ben ha'yilod*—Any boy who will be born," and it does not state, "*Ha'yilod laIvrim*—Who will be born to the Jews." *Rashi* writes: Rabbi Tanchuma taught that the astronomers saw that the savior of Yisrael was going to be born that day and he would be struck by water, but they did not know whether he was from Yisrael or from Mitzrayim. Therefore, Pharaoh decreed on everyone to

---

throw his son into the river until the day that the savior of Yisrael was thrown in and then the astronomers saw that he was struck.[4]

Onkelos translates the words "כל הבן הילוד היארה תשליחוהו" as, "Any boy who will be born to the Jews, throw him into the river." This implies that there was not a decree against Pharaoh's nation to throw their boys into the river. The *Nesinah LaGer* quotes from *Shemos Rabbah*[5] that the Mitzrim did not want to accept the last decree. They had no doubt that a Mitzri would not be the one to save the Jews. The beginning of the *pasuk* states, "ויצו פרעה לכל עמו"—And Pharaoh commanded his entire nation": he told them about the new decree and requested for them to be involved and help him throw the Jews into the water. No proper king would make a decree against his nation which would cause upheaval.

The *Nesinah LaGer* suggests that the Gemara which teaches that Pharaoh made the decree on his nation sides with the opinion that Pharaoh was a new king. He did not yet build a relationship with the nation and did not care about the complaints of the Mitzrim. Therefore, he decreed to kill all the boys, Jewish or not, since this would kill the savior of Yisrael. Onkelos, however, is of the opinion that Pharaoh was an old king who already had a relationship with his nation and cared about what the Mitzrim would say. Therefore, he certainly would not decree for his nation to kill their sons, but rather only the Jewish boys.

Pharaoh's plan was meant to ensure that the savior of Yisrael should not be saved. The saying goes, *"Mensch tracht un G-t lacht—*people plan and G-d laughs." The end result of this decree was that the daughter of Pharaoh was the one who saved Moshe Rabbeinu, and Pharaoh himself raised him. It was through Pharaoh's decree that Basyah bas Pharaoh found and brought Moshe Rabbeinu, the savior of Yisrael, into Pharaoh's own palace! The *Steipler*[6] says that from here we see that all of people's machinations won't change what was decreed in *Shamayim* by

4   רש"י על גמ' הנ"ל
5   פ' א, יח
6   ברכת פרץ

even an iota. Even more, the very action that one does to bring out his own personal desire will be what brings out Hashem's decree! Anything that a person plans will not help him to change, add to, or subtract from that which was decreed on Rosh Hashanah, aside from davening, *teshuvah*, or a *zechus*.

The Gemara[7] records a famous story about Yosef Mokir Shabbos ["Yosef who honored Shabbos"]. A stargazer told a wealthy non-Jew that his neighbor, Yosef, would end up getting all of his possessions. The non-Jew sold all his possessions and bought a precious pearl, which he put on his hat for protection. While he was walking over a bridge, though, the wind blew off his hat—with the stone inside—and it flew into the water, where a fish swallowed it. Later, a fisherman caught the fish and sold it to the well-known Yosef, who would buy fish for Shabbos. He cut open the fish to prepare it to eat and found the precious pearl. He sold the pearl for a lot for money. An elderly person met him and said, "Whoever borrows for Shabbos, in its merit, Hashem will pay it back." Not only did the non-Jew not prevent Yosef from getting his money, but by selling all his possessions and buying a pearl, he actually made it easier for Yosef to get his money!

It states, "וכאשר יענו אתו כן ירבה וכן יפרץ," which Onkelos translates in present tense: "And just as they would pain [oppress] them, so they would increase and so they would be strong." The *Ohr Hachaim Hakadosh* explained that despite their efforts to oppress Yisrael and weaken them, the exact opposite occurred: Hashem gave them the strength needed to survive and increased them. No one can stop Hashem's decree from coming to fruition. Also, *Rashi* quotes from the Midrash that Pharaoh was afraid about the increase of B'nei Yisrael and said, "*Pen yirbeh*—Lest they will become many"; he wanted to eradicate Klal Yisrael. *Ruach hakodesh* responded, "You say, 'Lest they will become many?' I say, 'כן ירבה וכן יפרץ—Indeed, they will become many and strong.'" What the Mitzrim tried to do, Hashem caused the exact opposite to happen.

May we recognize that everything that happens is according to Hashem's *ratzon* and anything that a person does will lead to what Hashem decreed!

## "אֶ-הְיֶה" AND "אֶ-הְיֶה אֲשֶׁר אֶ-הְיֶה" ARE SHEIMOS OF HASHEM AND HOW?

וַיֹּאמֶר אֱלֹקִים אֶל מֹשֶׁה אֶ-הְיֶה אֲשֶׁר אֶ-הְיֶה וַיֹּאמֶר
כֹּה תֹאמַר לִבְנֵי יִשְׂרָאֵל אֶ-הְיֶה שְׁלָחַנִי אֲלֵיכֶם (ג, יד)

וַאֲמַר יְיָ לְמֹשֶׁה אֶ-הְיֶה אֲשֶׁר אֶ-הְיֶה (אֶהֵא עִם מַאן דְּאֶהֵא)
וַאֲמַר כִּדְנָן תֵּימַר לִבְנֵי יִשְׂרָאֵל אֶהְיֶה שַׁלַחַנִי לְוַתְכוֹן

*And Hashem said to Moshe, "*א-היה אשר א-היה
*(I will be with whom that I will be)," and He*
*said, "The following you shall say to B'nei*
*Yisrael,* א-היה *is sending me next to you."'*

The *pasuk* states, "And Moshe said before Hashem, "Behold, I will come next to B'nei Yisrael, and I will say to them, 'The G-d of your fathers sent me to you.' And they will say to me, 'What is His name?' What shall I say to them?" The following *pasuk* states, "ויאמר אלקים אל משה א-היה אשר א-היה—And G-d said to Moshe, 'א-היה אשר א-היה.'" The *pasuk* continues, "ויאמר כה תאמר לבני ישראל א-היה שלחני אליכם—And He said, 'So shall you say to B'nei Yisrael: א-היה is sending me to you.'" *Rashi* explains that Hashem first said, "א-היה אשר א-היה—I will be with them in this suffering just as I will be with them in other subjugations." To which Moshe responded, "What's the need to mention future suffering?" Hashem responded, "אהיה, I am sending to you." Meaning, Hashem said to Moshe, "You said well. Rather, say this: 'I will be with them in this suffering.'" "א-היה" hints to Hashem being together with Yisrael and assisting them.

Onkelos translates א-היה אשר א-היה as the *lashon* of the Torah, א-היה אשר א-היה, rather than translating into Aramaic." The *Nesinah LaGer* says that א-היה is the *shem Hashem,* and therefore Onkelos does not translate it. So too, Rav Yaakov Kamenetsky[8] teaches in the name of the *Gra* that all three היה-א's are *Sheimos* of *Hashem*; additionally, Rav Yaakov points out that the word אשר is also not translated, implying that it too is part of *Hashem's* name. The *Keses Hasofer*[9] records the same idea in the name of the *Noda B'Yehudah*, but disagrees, arguing that it is not a *shem*. Rather, it simply would not have fit for Onkelos to translate as "*Ekyeh* that [די] *Ekyeh*," since a verb would have to follow די, not a noun. Therefore, Onkelos retains the words of the *pasuk*, "*asher*." The *Pilpula Charifta* is also of the opinion that "*asher*" is not *kodesh* and can be erased.

The *Ramban* has the text "אהא עם מאן דאהא—I will be with whom that I will be," which is the translation of these words. He explains that Moshe wanted to know the ways of *Hashem*, to which *Hashem* responded, "I will be known to whom I will be known; no one can reach the depth of this name." The *Hakesav V'Hakabbalah* says that *Hashem* has different "garments" in which He dresses, as if to say, He can be described in different ways. *Hashem* is called "א-היה," which means "I will be": I will do according to My will as fitting for the situation, according to the preparation of those who are accepting and according to the need. Sometimes, "I will be" with the *shem Shakai*, within the rules of nature, and other times with the *shem Havayah* to introduce new miracles. Sometimes with the *middah* of revenge, and other times with the *middah* of mercy and graciousness. The *Shemos Rabbah*[10] presents this idea as *Hashem* saying to Moshe, "Are you seeking My name? I am called according to My actions." When *Hashem* judges people, He is called *Elokim*; when He makes war against *reshaim*, He is called *Tzevakos*; when He postpones punishment, He is called *Keil Shakai*; and when He has mercy on the world, He is called *Havayah*.

Onkelos translates "*Ekyeh shelachani aleichem*" as, "*Ekyeh* is sending me next to you." The *Ramban* explains that "א-היה" is the *Shem Hashem*, so

8    אמת ליעקב

9    לשכת הסופר כא בשם תש' מאהבה

10    פ' ג, ה-ו

Onkelos does not translate it. Hashem said, "Tell Yisrael that this is the *Shem* with which I am favorable and gracious to people; no one can reach the depth of this name."

May Hashem always be favorable and gracious to us!

## WHO IS THE "CHASSAN DAMIM"?

וַיְהִי בַדֶּרֶךְ בַּמָּלוֹן וַיִּפְגְּשֵׁהוּ ה' וַיְבַקֵּשׁ הֲמִיתוֹ (ה, כד)

וַהֲוָה בְּאוֹרְחָא בְּבֵית מִבָּתָא וְעָרַע בֵּיה מַלְאֲכָא דַיְיָ וּבְעָא לְמִקְטְלֵיה

*And it was on the road at the inn that an angel of*
*Hashem met him and he sought to kill him.*

וַתִּקַּח צִפֹּרָה צֹר וַתִּכְרֹת אֶת עָרְלַת בְּנָהּ וַתַּגַּע
לְרַגְלָיו וַתֹּאמֶר כִּי חֲתַן דָּמִים אַתָּה לִי (ה, כה)

וּנְסִיבַת צִפּוֹרָה טִנָּרָא וּגְזָרַת יָת עָרְלַת בְּרַהּ וְקָרֵיבַת לְקָדָמוֹהִי
וַאֲמַרַת בְּדָמָא דִמְהֻלְתָּא הָדֵין אִתְיְהֵיב חַתְנָא לָנָא

*And Tzipporah took a stone and cut the foreskin of her son,*
*and she brought [Eliezer] close before him [Moshe], and she said,*
*'With the blood of this circumcision, the groom was given to us.'*

וַיִּרֶף מִמֶּנּוּ אָז אָמְרָה חֲתַן דָּמִים לַמּוּלֹת (ה, כו)

וְנָח מִנֵּהּ בְּכֵן אֲמַרַת אִלּוּלֵי דְמָא דִמְהֻלְתָּא הָדֵין אִתְחַיַּב חַתְנָא קְטוֹל

*And he rested from [released] him, then she said, "If not for the blood*
*of this circumcision, the groom had the liability of being killed."*

The *pasuk* states, "ויהי בדרך במלון ויפגשהו ה' ויבקש המיתו." Who wanted to kill whom and why?

*Rashi* explains that the angel wanted to kill Moshe because he was lax for not having circumcised Eliezer. This is as the Gemara writes:[11] Rabbi Yehoshua ben Korchah said, circumcision is so great that all the merits of Moshe did not stand up for him when he was lax with circumcision. Rabbi Yosi says he wasn't lax, rather he was unable to circumcise because it was dangerous to circumcise and then travel. Rather, Moshe was in danger because he was involved with his lodging before performing circumcision. The angel became like a snake and swallowed Moshe up from his head to his hips and then from his feet until the place of circumcision. Tzipporah cut the foreskin of her son, *"va'taga l'raglav,"* which *Rashi* explains to mean that she threw it before Moshe's feet. Then she said, *"*כי חתן דמים אתה לי*."* Tzipporah said to Eliezer about her husband, Moshe, "You [Eliezer] would have caused my groom [Moshe] to be killed." The *Sifsei Chachamim*[12] says that *Rashi* understands *"damim"* to mean "blood, of an occurrence of death-killing." The word *"li"* means *"sheli*—that of mine, my husband."

The following *pasuk* states, *"*וירף ממנו אז אמרה חתן דמים למולות*."* *Rashi* explains that once the angel loosened his grasp, she understood that circumcision had been the cause. The 'ל of *"*למולות*"* means *"al,"* as in *"al devar ha'mulos*—about/because of the circumcision." The *Ibn Ezra* explains that *"la'mulos"* is plural because of *"damim,"* which is plural since it hints to killing and blood. The *Hakesav V'Hakabbalah* quotes from the *Seforno* that it refers to two parts of circumcision: *milah*, cutting off the foreskin, and *periah*, revealing and uncovering the *eiver*.

Hashem spoke to Moshe at length and appointed him to be Hashem's messenger. The *Hakesav V'Hakabbalah* is bothered by the following: why would Hashem now seek to kill Moshe for transgressing a minor sin? True, Hashem is exacting with *tzaddikim* by even as much as a hairsbreadth, but one does not incur the death penalty for failing to circumcise his son. Hashem doesn't desire the death of even a *rasha*, so for sure He didn't desire the death of Moshe, His servant.

Onkelos translates the words *"*ויהי בדרך במלון ויפגשהו ה' ויבקש המיתו*"* as, "And it was on the road at the inn that an angel of Hashem met him and he sought to kill him." The following *pasuk* states, *"*ותקח צפרה צר ותכרת את ערלת בנה ותגע לרגליו ותאמר כי חתן דמים אתה לי*,"* which Onkelos translates as, "And Tzipporah took a stone and cut the foreskin of her son, and she brought [Eliezer] close before him [Moshe], and she said, 'With the blood of this circumcision, the groom was given to us.'" The *Nefesh HaGer* says that Onkelos translates "*li*—to me," which is singular, as "to us [*lana*]" which is plural, referring to Moshe and Tzipporah. This implies that Tzipporah said, "*atah*—you" referring to Eliezer, who was the one that was in danger and was saved. After circumcision, he was given back to his parents alive.[13] This is as the opinion of Rabbi Shimon ben Gamliel in the Gemara who says that the angel wanted to kill their son, Eliezer, and therefore Eliezer became dangerously ill. They understood that this was a punishment for not performing circumcision. Onkelos understands differently then *Rashi*: Hashem did not want to kill Moshe, rather Eliezer.

It states, "כי חתן דמים אתה לי." According to Onkelos, why was Eliezer called a "*chassan*—groom"? The *Ran* says that he is called this because of the circumcision, or as the *Rosh* explains, because this is *mechaten* him with his first mitzvah. Our text in Onkelos reads that the groom "was given [*is'y'heiv*]" in the past tense. The *Lechem V'Simlah* has the text "shall be given" [*yis'y'heiv*], future tense, which meant that Tzipporah was davening: through the merit of circumcision, Eliezer should be given to us and kept alive.

The following *pasuk* states, "וירף ממנו אז אמרה חתן דמים למולת," which Onkelos translates as, "And he rested from him; then she said, 'If not for the blood of this circumcision, the groom had the liability of being killed.'" The *Nesinah LaGer* explains that Onkelos translates "*la'mulos*" as "if not for the blood of this circumcision," as if it read "*lo mulos*." It does not mean "for *mulos*," rather "not *mulos*"—if not for the blood of circumcision. The words "*va'yiref mi'menu*" refer to the angel who stopped causing sickness to the child, Eliezer, and allowed him to return to his original strength.

The *Nefesh HaGer* explains that Onkelos understands that Moshe did not want to circumcise Eliezer because he was afraid that it would be

---

too dangerous for him, so he withheld doing it. And so is the law: if
a child is sick, we wait seven days from when he becomes healthy to perform circumcision. Tzipporah said, "I daven that by being *moser nefesh*
to perform circumcision beyond the law, Hashem will have mercy and
the merit of the circumcision itself will save him," which indeed happened. Similarly, the *Rashbam* explains that the mitzvah helped to save
him, like when one brings a *korban*. Tzipporah brought Eliezer close
to Moshe and said, "*b'damayich chayi*—in the merit of the blood of circumcision, Eliezer shall live." After circumcision, the angel who wanted
to kill Eliezer let go of him and he returned to his original strength.
Tzipporah told Moshe, "You were afraid to perform circumcision lest
he will die; on the contrary, see how great the merit of circumcision is
that by my being *moser nefesh* to perform circumcision beyond the law,
Eliezer has merited to be healed!" This is, as the Midrash brings, that on
the contrary, the circumcision was the curing process for the sickness.

May we be *moser nefesh* to fulfill mitzvos and merit their *zechusim*!

## WHAT DID PHARAOH DENY ABOUT HASHEM?

וְאַחַר בָּאוּ מֹשֶׁה וְאַהֲרֹן וַיֹּאמְרוּ אֶל פַּרְעֹה כֹּה אָמַר ה' ...
שַׁלַּח אֶת עַמִּי וְיָחֹגּוּ לִי בַּמִּדְבָּר (ה, א)

וּבָתָר כֵּן עָאלוּ מֹשֶׁה וְאַהֲרֹן וַאֲמָרוּ לְפַרְעֹה כִּדְנָן אֲמַר יְיָ...
שַׁלַּח יָת עַמִּי וְיֵיחֲגוּן קָדָמַי בְּמַדְבְּרָא

*And after this, Moshe and Aharon entered, and they said to
Pharaoh, "As the following [thus] said Hashem…'Send out My
nation and they shall make a festival before Me in the desert.'"*

וַיֹּאמֶר פַּרְעֹה מִי ה' אֲשֶׁר אֶשְׁמַע בְּקֹלוֹ לְשַׁלַּח אֶת יִשְׂרָאֵל
לֹא יָדַעְתִּי אֶת ה' וְגַם אֶת יִשְׂרָאֵל לֹא אֲשַׁלֵּחַ (ה, ב)

וַאֲמַר פַּרְעֹה שְׁמָא דַּיְיָ לָא אִתְגְּלִי (אִתְקְרִי) לִי דַּאֲקַבֵּיל לְמֵימְרֵיהּ לְשַׁלָּחָא
יָת יִשְׂרָאֵל לָא אִתְגְּלִי (אִתְקְרִי) לִי שְׁמָא דַּיְיָ וְאַף יָת יִשְׂרָאֵל לָא אֲשַׁלַּח

*And Pharaoh said, "The name of Hashem was not revealed
to (chance upon) me that I shall accept His saying [word] to*

*send out Yisrael. The name of Hashem was not revealed to*
*(chance upon) me and also Yisrael I will not send out.*

The *pasuk* states, "ואחר באו משה ואהרן ויאמרו אל פרעה כה אמר ה'...שלח את עמי",
"ויחגו לי במדבר," which Onkelos translates as, "And after this, Moshe and
Aharon entered, and they said to Pharaoh, 'As the following [thus] said
Hashem..."Send out My nation and they shall make a festival before
Me in the desert."'" Onkelos does not translate "*li*" as "to Me," but
as "before Me," as we do *avodah* "before" Him, not actually "to" Him.
Pharaoh responds, "ויאמר פרעה מי ה' אשר אשמע בקלו לשלח את ישראל לא ידעתי
את ה' וגם את ישראל לא אשלח," which Onkelos translates as, "And Pharaoh
said, 'The name of Hashem was not revealed to me that I shall accept
His saying [word] to send out Yisrael. The name of Hashem was not
revealed to me and also Yisrael I will not send out.'" The *Nefesh HaGer*
says that Onkelos does not translate "*mi Hashem*" as a question, "Who
is Hashem?" since this would degrade Hashem. Instead, he explains it
as a statement. Also, it is common for Onkelos to translate a question
as a statement, for the intent. The Midrash says that Pharaoh was
punished for saying "מי" with fifty *makkos*, fifty being the *gematria* of מי.

Onkelos translates "*mi Hashem*" as "The name of Hashem was not
revealed to me [שמא דה' לא אתגלי לי]" and "לא ידעתי את ה'"—the name
of Hashem was not revealed to me [לא אתגלי לי שמא דה']." What does
Pharaoh mean that he does not know the name of Hashem?

The *Nesinah LaGer* teaches from the *Shemos Rabbah*[14] that Pharaoh
said, "I searched for His name in my entire treasury and didn't find it."
Rabbeinu Bachya explains that at that time, Pharaoh took out a scroll
with all the gods, and he started reading: gods of Moav, gods of Edom,
gods of Tzidon. He said, "I read through all of the gods and did not find
the name of your G-d." Pharaoh was very wise and knew about the different types of lands, dwelling places, environments of the world, climates,
and stars. He knew about the seventy nations, with a star and ruler
for each nation. He did not find the name of Hashem in any rulership

14    פ' ה,יד

of the entire world, and therefore he wondered, "What name is this?" He did not know that Hashem is above all powers and all powers are from Him. They have no strength on their own, only through Hashem. Chazal compare this to a Kohen who had a slave that was an imbecile. The Kohen left the city. The slave then went out to search for his master. The slave reached the cemetery and called out to those inside, "Did you see my master in there?" They responded, "Do you not know that your master is a Kohen?" He said, "Yes, I know." They said to him, "Imbecile, is a Kohen ever seen in the cemetery?" So too, Moshe and Aharon said to Pharaoh, "It is common to find dead people among living people, not living people among the dead. These gods which you are mentioning are considered dead, but our G-d is alive and rules forever."

The *Shemos Rabbah* continues that Pharaoh asked them, "Is He young or old? How many cities did He conquer? How many years did He reign?" They responded, "His strength and power fill the world, He existed before the world's existence, and He will be at the end of its existence." Pharaoh asked, "What are His actions?" They responded, "He spreads out the heaven and sets the foundations of the earth; His voice cuts through flames of fire; He dislocates mountains and breaks apart stones; His bow is fire; His arrow is a flame; His spear is a torch; His shield are clouds; His sword is lightening. He creates mountains and valleys, and He brings down rain and dew, and causes grass to blossom." At that time, Pharaoh called all the wise men of Mitzrayim and asked them, "Did you hear about the name of their G-d?" They responded, "We heard that He is '*ben chachamim* and *ben malchei kedem.*'"

The *Nesinah LaGer* explains that Pharaoh refused to recognize the existence of Hashem and said, "I am the master of the world; I created myself and the Nile River." The *Ramban*[15] explains differently: Pharaoh was smart and recognized that G-d exists. This is as he mentioned G-d: "אחרי הודיע אלקים אותך," and, "איש אשר רוח אלקים בו." However, he did not know the *Shem Ha'meyuchad* of י-ה-ו-ה, as he said, "I do not know *the*

---

name of Hashem." The *Ibn Ezra*[16] says this *shem* is used when Hashem does miracles and wonders and makes changes in nature, which show that Hashem can do anything and everything. The *Ramban* says that this *shem* expresses the Shechinah with *middas ha'rachamim*, which is His great name. The following *pasuk* states, "*Va'yomru Elokei ha'Ivrim.*" Moshe and Aharon switched from "*Ko amar Hashem*—As the following [thus] said *Hashem*," to, "*Va'yomru Elokei ha'Ivrim*—And they said, 'the G-d of the Ivrim,'" since Pharaoh knew about G-d.

May we remember that Hashem is the Creator and Master of the world; He exists forever, and all power and strength are from Him!

## WHY DID PHARAOH INTENSIFY THE LABOR?

לָמָּה מֹשֶׁה וְאַהֲרֹן תַּפְרִיעוּ אֶת הָעָם
מִמַּעֲשָׂיו לְכוּ לְסִבְלֹתֵיכֶם (ה, ד)

לְמָא מֹשֶׁה וְאַהֲרֹן תְּבַטְּלוּן יָת עַמָּא מֵעֲבִידַתְהוֹן אִיזִילוּ לְפָלְחָנְכוֹן

*For what reason shall Moshe and Aharon make the
nation idle from [stop] their work? Go to your labor.*

וְהִשְׁבַּתֶּם אֹתָם מִסִּבְלֹתָם (ה, ה)

וּתְבַטְּלוּן יָתְהוֹן מִפָּלְחָנְהוֹן

*And you will annul [stop] them from their labor.*

כִּי נִרְפִּים הֵם (ה, ח)

אֲרֵי בַּטְלָנִין אִנּוּן

*Since they are idle [lazy].*

## תִּכְבַּד הָעֲבֹדָה...וְיַעֲשׂוּ בָהּ וְאַל יִשְׁעוּ בְּדִבְרֵי שָׁקֶר (ה, ט)

יִתְקַף פֻּלְחָנָא...וְיִתְעַסְּקוּן בֵּיהּ וְלָא יִתְעַסְּקוּן בְּפִתְגָמִין בְּטֵילִין

*Make the labor heavier...and they shall be involved with it, and*
*they shall not be involved with things of idleness [laziness].*

The *pesukim* mention that Moshe and Aharon came to Pharaoh and
requested that he send out the nation and let them travel a distance
of three days to bring *korbanos* to Hashem. Pharaoh responded, "למה
משה ואהרן תפריעו את העם ממעשיו לכו לסבלותיכם." *Rashi* explains that "*tafriu*"
means to distance and separate, meaning, Pharaoh said, "Why should
you distance and separate them from their labor; they will listen to you
and think to rest from work! Go back to your labor." Now that Moshe
and Aharon came to take out B'nei Yisrael, Pharaoh said to them, "Stay
out of things; go back to the work that you have in your houses."

Onkelos translates "*tafriu*" differently: as "*tevatlun*—annul or make
idle," as in "*bittul chametz*, to annul *chametz*." Here, it refers to stopping
labor, being idle. Similarly, the following *pasuk* states, "*V'hishbatem
osam mi'sivlosam*," which Onkelos translates as "and you will annul
[stop] them [*u'sevatlun*] from their labor." Pharaoh said, "Why should
you cause them to cease from doing their labor; go to your labor." The
*Ramban* explains that Pharaoh said, "Since you are from the tribe of Levi,
who is free from labor, you are saying, 'Let us go and bring *korbanos*.'
Therefore, you, too, should do the labor as B'nei Yisrael are doing." The
entire tribe of Levi was not included in the slavery of Mitzrayim, as we
see from Moshe and Aharon, who were able to come and go without
permission. The reason is because each nation had a custom that their
scholars and people who would guide and teach them the proper way
would be freed from any subjugation. Therefore, Pharaoh left the tribe
of Levi, which was comprised of the wise and scholarly men of B'nei
Yisrael, to be free from labor.

Onkelos also translates the words "*ki nirpim heim*" as "since they are
idle [lazy] [*batlanin*]." What does Onkelos hint to by translating "תפריעו,"
"והשבתם," and "נרפים" with the word "ביטול—annul and be idle from
labor"?

The *Mesillas Yesharim*[17] explains that Pharaoh intended on keeping B'nei Yisrael so busy that they would not have a second to think about what they were doing. This way, they would not be able to figure out how to change the situation. This is hinted at in the words of Pharaoh, "תכבד העבודה...ויעשו בה ואל ישעו בדברי שקר," which Onkelos translates as, "Make the labor heavier...and they shall be involved with it, and they shall not be involved with things of idleness [laziness] [*b'teilin*]." Make them so busy with the labor that it won't enter their mind to stop what they are doing.

The *Mesillas Yesharim* continues that this is exactly the plot and advice of the *yetzer hara*. The *yetzer hara* keeps a person so busy that he does not take a moment to think about his spiritual wellbeing and check whether he is up to par with his *avodas Hashem* of learning Torah and doing mitzvos. If a person would stop and review his situation, he would be able to detect where to improve. If he doesn't, he will not be able to notice his faults. The *yetzer hara* knows that a person can easily improve by stopping and thinking about his actions and correcting them and does his best to make one busy with less-important things.

May we learn from Pharaoh's wicked advice: take a moment to stop and think about our *avodas Hashem* and bring ourselves to the next level!

# Va'eira

## HOW IS MOSHE AN ELOHIM TO AHARON AND PHARAOH, AND HOW IS AHARON A PEH AND NAVI TO PHARAOH AND YISRAEL?

רְאֵה נְתַתִּיךָ אֱלֹהִים לְפַרְעֹה וְאַהֲרֹן אָחִיךָ יִהְיֶה נְבִיאֶךָ (ז, א)

חֲזִי דְּמַנִּיתָךְ רַב לְפַרְעֹה וְאַהֲרֹן אֲחוּךְ יְהֵי מְתֻרְגְּמָנָךְ

*See that I appointed you a leader for [master over] Pharaoh,*
*and Aharon your brother will be your interpreter.*

The *pasuk* states, "ראה נתתיך אלהים לפרעה ואהרן אחיך יהיה נביא"—See, I gave you for *'elohim'* for Pharaoh, and Aharon your brother will be your *navi*.'" What roles is the *pasuk* saying Moshe and Aharon will play?

*Rashi* explains "*elohim*" as a judge and ruler who enforces with lashes and afflictions. Moshe will be the middleman to cause *makkos* to be brought upon Pharaoh and Mitzrayim. The Brisker Rav[1] explains that the *makkos* were not mainly for the purpose of sending out the nation. Rather, they were to fulfill what Hashem said by the *Bris Bein Habesarim*: "וגם את הגוי אשר יעבדו דן אנכי ואחרי כן יצאו ברכוש גדול"—And also the nation that will enslave you, I will judge, and afterwards, they will go out with great possessions." The order of events needed to be, first *makkos*, and afterwards, sending out. Therefore, Hashem appointed Moshe to be a judge and ruler to judge and afflict with lashes and *yissurim*. Onkelos translates "ראה נתתיך אלהים לפרעה" differently: "See that I appointed you a leader [*rav*] for Pharaoh." Hashem appointed Moshe as a master over Pharaoh to be in charge and in control.

202

*Rashi* notes that Onkelos translates *"nevi'echa"* as *"mesurgemanach."* He explains that *"nevuah"* is when a person lets the nation hear words of rebuke. The root is from "ניב שפתים—speech of the lips," and "ינוב חכמה—speech of wisdom." In *laaz*, a *Navi* is called *prediger*," which the *Targum Halaaz* explains to mean "preacher." So too, the Gemara[2] teaches that *"amoreih,"* which *Rashi* explains as *"metargem,"* is a spokesman who broadcasts the *d'rashah* which a *rav* tells over quietly.

In *Parashas Mikeitz*, it states,[3] *"Ki ha'meilitz beinosam,"* which Onkelos translates as "since the interpreter [*mesurgeman*] was between them." The *Me'at Tzari* says that included in the meaning of *"meturgeman"* is someone who translates from one language to another language and makes the words understood. Similarly, the Gemara uses the word "תרגמא" to mean "an explanation; making something understood." He explains Onkelos like Rabbi Shimon bar Yochai; Moshe said to Aharon in *lashon hakodesh*, and Aharon translated into Egyptian language. Or, as the *Eitz Yosef* says, first Moshe spoke and afterwards Aharon said over his words and clarified them to be understood.

It is interesting to note that Onkelos's translation on Chumash is called *"Targum Onkelos."* Simply, it is a translation of *lashon hakodesh* into Aramaic. Based on the explanations of *"meturgeman,"* the name *"Targum Onkelos"* can be explained as an interpretation of the Torah, as a "spokesman" who expresses the intent of the Chumash, revealing the underlying meaning of the Torah. The *Nefesh HaGer* says that since *Targum Onkelos* was given at Sinai, it is not bound by the literal translation and can translate according to the *pasuk*'s intent.

The *Ibn Ezra* is bothered with *Rashi*'s explanation that the word "נביא" is from the root "ניב." In *Parashas Vayeira*, it states, "השב אשת האיש כי נביא הוא ויתפלל בעדך וחיה—Return the married woman, since he is a *navi* and he will daven on your behalf and you will live." The *Ibn Ezra* asks: If *"navi"* means a talker-preacher, why is this a reason to return the married woman?

2 סוטה מ.
3 בראשית מב, כג

The *Ibn Ezra* explains *"navi"* differently: it means a prophet to whom Hashem reveals His secrets, and he, in turn, tells them over to us. This is as it states that Hashem will not do anything "כי אם גלה סודו אל עבדיו הנביאים—only when He reveals His secrets to His servants, the prophets." Since Avraham prophesized, he knew everything that went on; you were innocent and didn't touch Sarah, therefore, he will daven for you. The א' of נבואה is part of the root, as נביאים and ויתנבאו. The *Ibn Ezra* explains that "אלהים" in this context means an angel, a "G-dly" being. Hashem said to Moshe, see that I made for you a great attribute; I made you to be considered in the eyes of Pharaoh as an angel. You will speak to Aharon the prophet, and he will speak to the people of the generation.

Onkelos answers the *Ibn Ezra*'s question by translating *"navi"* by Avraham as "prophet." *Rashi* explains this to mean that "Avraham knows that you didn't touch Sarah, so he will daven for you." A *navi* means a preacher because of his speech; a prophet who knows inside information, the hidden truth, is included in this title.

The Torah describes Moshe and Aharon's positions in *Parashas Shemos*[4] as, "הוא יהיה לך לפה ואתה תהיה לו לאלהים—He will be a *peh* for you and you will be an *Elohim* for him." What does it mean that Aharon will be a *peh* and Moshe will be an *Elohim*?

Onkelos translates "הוא יהיה לך לפה" as "and he will be for you for a spokesman and interpreter [l'mesurgeman]." Aharon will say over things to the nation, decipher it, and clarify the intent." Both Onkelos and *Rashi* explain "ואתה תהיה לו לאלהים" as "and you will be for him as a leader and ruler [l'rav]." Moshe will take charge over Aharon, he won't lash or afflict him, unlike the *Elohim* for Pharaoh, which *Rashi* explained as a judge and ruler, since he was indeed afflicted.

May Hashem send us leaders and prophets to teach us and express His secrets to us!

# WAS "TENU LACHEM MOFEIS"
## A "WONDROUS THING" OR A "SIGN"?

תְּנוּ לָכֶם מוֹפֵת (ז, ט)

הַבוּ לְכוֹן אָתָא

*Give for yourselves a sign.*

The *pasuk* states that Pharaoh will say, "*Tenu lachem mofeis.*" *Targum Yonasan* translates this as, "Give for yourselves a wonder." *Onkelos* translates "*mofeis*" differently, as an "*os*—a sign." *Rashi* explains that a sign reflects that there is power in the One who sent you. Hashem says, Pharaoh will want to see proof that the One sending Moshe and Aharon has power, so he will ask you to give a sign for yourselves that there is strength behind the one who sent you.

Hashem said to Moshe, "Say to Aharon, 'Take your staff and throw it before Pharaoh and it will become a serpent.'" This reflects that Hashem can make the inanimate staff into a movable serpent. Aharon did this, and Pharaoh called his magicians to do the same. After this, it states, "ויבלע מטה אהרן את מטתם—And Aharon's staff swallowed their staffs." The Gemara[5] explains that a miracle happened within a miracle. What was this unique type of miracle?

*Rashi* explains that it states, "*Va'yivla matei Aharon*—And Aharon's staff swallowed," and not, "*Va'yivla tanin Aharon*—And Aharon's serpent swallowed." This implies that only after the serpent turned back into a staff did it then swallow the others. The *Maharsha* says that the double miracle was: if it would have remained a serpent and swallowed the other serpents, it would have been a miracle. The fact that it only swallowed them after it returned to being a staff was an additional miracle. The *Maharsha* is bothered: this seems to be two separate miracles. In what way is this a miracle within a miracle?

The *Midrash Tanchuma*[6] understands that if the serpent would have swallowed the other serpents while it was still a serpent, it would not have been miraculous, since it is common for a serpent to swallow other serpents. Rather, the first miracle was that it first returned to being a staff and only then swallowed the other serpents. On top of that, if one were to pile up all of the staffs which the magicians threw down that became serpents, there would be ten piles, yet Aharon's staff swallowed them all and did not become any thicker. When Pharaoh saw this, he said, "If Moshe will tell the staff to swallow Pharaoh and his throne, it would do that, too!" The *Maharsha* says that this explanation fits the *lashon* of a "miracle within a miracle."

The *Re'em* explains that it states, "ויבלע מטה אהרן את מטותם—And Aharon's staff swallowed their staffs," which is how Onkelos translates. This reflects that first, all the serpents turned back into staffs and then Aharon's staff swallowed them. Based on the *Re'em*, we could explain the "miracle within a miracle" differently. The first miracle was that Aharon's staff would have swallowed serpents, although staffs can't swallow anything. Second, Aharon's staff swallowing their staffs only after those serpents had all returned to being staffs, was an additional miracle; a double miracle, a staff swallowing staffs!

Onkelos understands that Hashem sent Moshe and Aharon to perform a wondrous act as a sign, to teach Pharaoh that Hashem is in charge of inanimate objects, such as the staff, and living things, such as the serpents. Hashem could change them back and forth to whatever He wants. Therefore, Pharaoh should recognize that Hashem sent Moshe and Aharon and he should follow their request.

May we learn from the sign and the wondrous miracle of the staff that Hashem is the only One with complete power and control over everything!

## DID ONE FROG ASCEND, OR MANY?

# וְשָׁרַץ הַיְאֹר צְפַרְדְּעִים (ז, כח)

וִירַבֵּי נַהְרָא עֻרְדְּעָנַיָּא

*And the river shall raise (make great) [swarm] frogs.*

# וַתַּעַל הַצְּפַרְדֵּעַ (ח, ב)

וּסְלִיקוּ עֻרְדְּעָנַיָּא

*And the frogs ascended.*

The *pasuk* states, "*Va'taal ha'tzefardeia*—And the frog ascended," in sin-gular. *Rashi* first notes that it is common to use a singular language to denote a large group of a single species. *Rashi* quotes another explanation from the Midrash: one frog ascended from the Nile. The Mitzrim began hitting it with sticks; each time it was hit, it opened its mouth and smaller frogs emerged, creating streams and streams of frogs. The obvious thing to do would have been to stop hitting the frog. The Mitzrim, however, did the opposite: since the frog let out more frogs, causing them more aggravation, they needed to "get it back" and hit it as much as they could. Each hit caused more frogs to come out, causing more anger—and so on. The cycle continued until all of Mitzrayim was covered in frogs.

The *Steipler*[7] says that we can learn from here that if someone angers another person, he shouldn't retort, but should rather keep silent and accept it. In this way, the anger will subside and cool off little by little. If, however, he will answer back, the other person will just get angrier, "filling the land with frogs." If the Mitzrim hadn't acted on their anger and continued to hit the frog, more frogs wouldn't have come out.

My cousin Rabbi Roberg suggested a different message from the frogs. Each Mitzri thought that the other Mitzrim weren't capable of stopping the frogs. "His hit wasn't powerful enough; I'll do better." Each Mitzri tried to kill the frog and, of course, didn't succeed. This haughtiness and arrogance led to the land being filled with frogs.

Onkelos translates *"va'taal ha'tzefardeia"* differently: "and the frogs ascended," in plural. This is as it states, *"V'sharatz ha'ye'or tzefarde'im,"* which Onkelos translates as "and the river shall raise [swarm] frogs," in plural. The *Me'at Tzari* explains that there were many frogs nurtured by the river which ascended to participate in the *makkah*. The *Lekach Tov* adds that *"tzefardeia"* refers to the species of frog, as Onkelos translates[8] "ויהי לי שור וחמור"—And there were to me oxen [*torin*] and donkeys [*u'chmarin*], in plural; the ox and donkey species.

May we work on our anger, haughtiness, and arrogance, and be similar to Hashem!

## TO WHAT DOES THE LASHON GEVURAH BY THE MAKKOS HINT?

### וְנָתַתִּי אֶת יָדִי בְּמִצְרָיִם (ז, ד)

וְאֶתֵּין יָת מַחַת גְּבוּרְתִּי בְּמִצְרָיִם

*And I will give the smite [plague] of My might against Mitzrayim.*

### בִּנְטֹתִי אֶת יָדִי עַל מִצְרָיִם (ז, ה)

כַּד אֲרֵים יָת מַחַת גְּבוּרְתִּי עַל מִצְרָיִם

*When I will raise the smite [plague] of My might upon Mitzrayim.*

### הִתְפָּאֵר עָלַי לְמָתַי אַעְתִּיר לְךָ...לְהַכְרִית הַצְפַרְדְעִים מִמְּךָ...רַק בַּיְאֹר תִּשָׁאַרְנָה (ח, ה)

שְׁאַל לָךְ גְּבוּרָא הַב לָךְ (וְהַב לִי) זְמָן לְאֵמָתַי אֲצַלֵי עֲלָךְ...לְשֵׁיצָאָה עֻרְדְּעָנַיָא מִנָּךְ...לְחוֹד בְּנַהֲרָא (דִּבְנַהֲרָא) יִשְׁתְּאַרוּן

*Ask for yourself a show of might, give for yourself (and give for me) a time for when I shall daven for you...to destroy the frogs from you...only (those) in the river will remain.*

## שָׁלַחְתִּי אֶת יָדִי (ט, טו)

דְּשָׁלֵחִית פּוֹן יָת מַחַת גְּבוּרְתִּי

*That it would have been that I sent the smite [plague] of My might.*

## וּלְמַעַן סַפֵּר שְׁמִי בְּכָל הָאָרֶץ (ט, טז)

וּבְדִיל דְּיהוֹן מִשְׁתָּעַן גְּבוּרַת שְׁמִי בְּכָל אַרְעָא

*And in order that they tell over the might
of My name in the entire land.*

Pharaoh requests from Moshe and Aharon to daven to remove the frogs. Moshe responds, "התפאר עלי למתי אעתיר לך." *Rashi* explains that "*hispa'er*" means to "glorify" or "boast," as it states, "היתפאר הגרזן על החוצב בו—Will an ax feel glorified over the one who chops with it?" It is impossible for an ax, which is inanimate, to be better than the person, a live being using the axe to chop. Similarly, Moshe said to Pharaoh, "Be glorified over me." See if you can ask me to do something which is too great for me to do. I will daven that the frogs should be destroyed at the time of your choice. Test me to see whether my prayer will be fulfilled at the time we set.

The *Nefesh HaGer* explains that Moshe said, "I can do anything because I am the messenger of Hashem; I call out in the name of Hashem and He answers me. Although both of us are born to human beings, you cannot raise yourself over me. You are asking me to remove the frogs from within your stomach, which you yourself can't do, so obviously, I am greater than you are. If so, how do you have the audacity to be brazen against Hashem and say, 'Who is Hashem that I shall listen to His voice? I don't know Hashem, and I will not send out B'nei Yisrael'?" Pharaoh requests for the frogs to be removed tomorrow and Moshe responds, "As you requested, למען תדע כי אין כה' אלקינו, in order that you shall know that there is no one like Hashem, our G-d." Hashem will show you there is no one like Him.

Onkelos translates "התפאר עלי למתי אעתיר לך...להכרית הצפרדעים ממך" differently: "Ask for yourself a show of might, give for yourself a time for when I shall daven for you...to destroy the frogs from you." The

*Nefesh HaGer* points out that Onkelos does not translate "*hispa'er*" as "*hisravrav*—become great," but rather, "Ask for yourself a show of might [*she'al lach gevurah*]," and he adds, "give for yourself a time [*hav lach z'man*]" as some are *gores*, or "and give for me a time [*v'hav li z'man*]." It is common for Onkelos to translate the *nimshal*, which is the intent of the *pasuk*. Also, it states about Moshe that he was greater than every person in regards to humility; therefore, it is difficult to say that he was boasting and bragging about his abilities to determine what will be.

Onkelos translates, "Ask for yourself a show of might" with the word "*gevurah*—might," which is how he describes Hashem's actions in Mitzrayim a number of times throughout these *parshiyos*. For example, earlier in the parashah, it states, "ונתתי את ידי במצרים" and "בנטתי את ידי על מצרים," which Onkelos translates as "the smite [plague] of My might [*machas gevur'si*]." Also, it states, "שלחתי את ידי...ולמען ספר שמי בכל הארץ," which he translates as, "That it would have been that I sent the smite [plague] of My might [*machas gevur'si*]...and in order that they shall tell over the might of My name [*gevuras shemi*] in the entire land." So too, in *Parashas Beshalach*, it states, "וירא ישראל את היד הגדלה," which Onkelos translates as "and Yisrael saw the might of the great hand [ית גבורת ידא רבתא]." We mention this *lashon* in *Maariv* as well: "וראו גבורתו שבחו והודו לשמו—And they saw His might by *k'rias Yam Suf*, praise and thank His name." Also, in the haftarah of *Parashas Bechukosai*, it states, "אודיעם את ידי ואת גבורתי וידעו כי שמי ה'—I will let them know about My hand and My might, and they will know that My name is Hashem."

The *Hakesav V'Hakabbalah* explains that the word "*gevurah*" denotes being mightier and stronger than something below it. For example, it states, "והמים גברו מאד מאד על הארץ ויכסו כל ההרים הגבוהים—And the water was extremely mighty upon the land and it covered over all the high mountains." Hashem showed that He is mightier than all people and nature. The *Nefesh HaGer* says that "*gevurah*" hints to the concept brought in the *Baal Haturim*, that when Hashem performs judgment against *reshaim*, His name is elevated. In the same way, here, by punishing the Mitzrim, His name will be elevated, and it will humble everyone. Also, "*gevurah*" reflects "*yeshuah*—savior," as it states, "*B'gevuros yeisha yemino*—with might, the savior of His right hand." We see that Hashem's actions in Mitzrayim reflect His *gevurah*, mightiness and ability to be our savior. Hashem showed His might in order to save us.

The *pasuk* ends, "*Rak ba'ye'or tisha'arnah*—Only in the river will they remain," which Onkelos translates as "only those in the river [*d'v'nahra*] will remain." The *Yekev Eliezer* explains that this hints that the frogs which were in the river during the *makkah* would remain there, not that frogs would gather there. Others have the text, "only in the river [*b'nahra*] will they remain." This indicates that the frogs that were not part of the *makkah*, which did not die, will remain in the river, and they will never enter Mitzrayim. The *Seforno* explains that the frogs in the water will remain in the water and not ascend upon dry land.

May we recognize Hashem's great might and remember that there is no one like Him!

## HOW WAS MAKKAS AROV A COMPLETE DIVISION OF PEOPLE AND LAND?

הִנְנִי מַשְׁלִיחַ בְּךָ ...אֶת הֶעָרֹב (ח, יז)

הָאֲנָא מְשַׁלַּח בָּךְ ...יָת עָרוֹבָא

*Behold I will send against you...the mixture.*

וְהִפְלֵיתִי בַיּוֹם הַהוּא אֶת אֶרֶץ גֹּשֶׁן אֲשֶׁר עַמִּי עֹמֵד עָלֶיהָ ...כִּי אֲנִי ה' בְּקֶרֶב הָאָרֶץ (ח, יח)

וְאַפְרֵישׁ בְּיוֹמָא הַהוּא יָת אַרְעָא דְגֹשֶׁן דְּעַמִּי שָׁרֵי עֲלַהּ ...אֲרֵי אֲנָא יְיָ שַׁלִּיט בְּגוֹ אַרְעָא

*And I will separate on that day the land of Goshen which My nation stands upon it...that I am Hashem who rules within the land.*

וְשַׂמְתִּי פְדֻת בֵּין עַמִּי וּבֵין עַמֶּךָ (ח, יט)

וַאֲשַׁוֵּי פֻרְקָן לְעַמִּי וְעַל עַמָּךְ אַיְתִי מַחָא

*And I will place [make] a redemption for My nation, and upon your nation I will bring smite [plague].*

The *pasuk* states by the *makkah* of *arov*, "If you do not send out My nation, את הערב...הנני משליח בך—behold, I will send against you...the *arov*." *Rashi* explains that all types of wild animals, including snakes and scorpions, came in a mixture and attacked the Mitzrim.

Onkelos translates the word *mashliach* as "will send," and not as "*garei*—contend against by biting or destroying," which is the usual translation of *mashliach* when sending against someone or something. The *Nefesh HaGer* explains in the name of the *Ramban* that Hashem sent animals which generally roam freely to Mitzrayim, and they did not set foot in the land of Goshen. Hashem performed a wondrous miracle by causing the land of Mitzrayim to pull toward it the entire parade of animals, and the land of Goshen to push them away. This ensured a clear division between the neighboring areas of Mitzrayim and Goshen.

It states, "והפליתי ביום ההוא את ארץ גשן אשר עמי עומד עליה," which Onkelos translates as, "And I will separate on that day the land of Goshen upon which My nation stands." The *Hakesav V'Hakabbalah* says that this *lashon* of separation is only used when something is done by way of a *pele*; it can only be done by Hashem, not by any human being. The *Ramban* explains that the Torah uses the *lashon* "*pele*—wondrous" because this *makkah* was an unusual, totally out-of-the-ordinary phenomenon. The nature of animals, especially wild ones, is to roam freely and injure or kill whatever they want. Here, the animals did not step foot into the land of Goshen, only into the land of Mitzrayim. The *Nefesh HaGer* adds that the *pasuk* mentions "land" since Hashem spared the land of Goshen from the *arov* that attacked in the land of Mitzrayim.

The *pasuk* ends, "כי אני ה' בקרב הארץ," which Onkelos translates as "that I am Hashem Who rules within the land." The *Nefesh HaGer* explains that Onkelos adds the word "rules" to his explanation of the *pasuk* to teach that Hashem rules over the land itself. Wonders will be performed with the land by keeping wild animals in control and directed to their target, only entering the land of Mitzrayim, not the land of Goshen.

The *Be'er Yosef* explains that "*arov*" means a mixture; many types of animals came together from all different climates. Although their natural habitat was cold, freezing, warm, boiling, or humid, they all came to Mitzrayim. It is reasonable to suggest that Hashem brought with each animal its own climate in order that it would feel comfortable and be able to do harm. Onkelos, who translates *mashliach* "will send" rather than as "*garei*—to contend against," may hint to the *Be'er Yosef*: the main *makkah* of *arov* was the mixture of different animals coming with their climates which brought sicknesses to the Mitzrim and also ruined the land.[9]

Another *pasuk* states regarding the *makkah* of *arov*, "ושמתי פדות בין עמי ובין עמך—And I will place [make] redemption between My nation and between your nation." What does this add to what was already stated—"*v'hifleisi*"? Onkelos translates as, "And I will place [make] a redemption for My nation, and upon your nation [Mitzrayim] I will bring smite [plague]." The *Nefesh HaGer* explains like the *Ramban*: "*V'hifleisi*" only teaches about the animals not entering into the land of Goshen. However, if a Jew would be in the land of Mitzrayim, maybe he would be attacked. "*V'samti fedus*" adds that even if there was a Jew among the Mitzrim, he was not harmed by the wild animals. The *arov* will only affect the Mitzrim, not the Jew; Hashem will protect him. This is hinted at in this *pasuk*, which does not mention "land," but rather "My nation" and "your nation." Hashem separated the people of each nation, Jews from Mitzrim. In the *makkah* of *arov*, Hashem performed a complete separation, between both the lands and the people.

May we learn from these wondrous miracles to recognize that Hashem is the King and rules over everything!

---

9   ואברבנאל

## WHICH ANIMAL COULDN'T WE SLAUGHTER IN MITZRAYIM? WHAT WAS UNIQUE ABOUT THE LAMB?

לֹא נָכוֹן לַעֲשׂוֹת כֵּן כִּי תּוֹעֲבַת מִצְרַיִם נִזְבַּח לַה' אֱלֹקֵינוּ
הֵן נִזְבַּח אֶת תּוֹעֲבַת מִצְרַיִם לְעֵינֵיהֶם וְלֹא יִסְקְלֻנוּ (ח, כב)

לָא תָקֵין לְמֶעֱבַד כֵּן אֲרֵי בְּעִירָא דְמִצְרָאֵי דָחֲלִין לֵיהּ מִנֵּהּ אֲנַחְנָא נָסְבִין לְדַבָּחָא קֳדָם יְיָ
אֱלָקַנָא הָא נְדַבַּח יָת בְּעִירָא דְמִצְרָאֵי דָחֲלִין לֵיהּ וְאִנּוּן יְהוֹן חָזַן הֲלָא יֵימְרוּן לְמִרְגְּמַנָא

*It is not fixed [correct] to do so, because the animal that the Mitzrim
fear [worship], from it we are taking to slaughter before Hashem,
our G-d. Behold, we will slaughter the animal that the Mitzrim
fear [worship] and they will see, will they not say to stone us?*

The *pasuk* states, "לא נכון לעשות כן כי תועבת מצרים נזבח לה' אלקינו הן נזבח את
תועבת מצרים לעיניהם ולא יסקלנו," which Onkelos translates as, "It is not fixed
[correct] to do so, because the animal that the Mitzrim fear [worship],
from it we are taking to slaughter before Hashem our G-d. Behold we will
slaughter the animal that the Mitzrim fear [worship] and they will see,
will they not say to stone us?" The *Nefesh HaGer* is bothered. First the
*pasuk* mentions, "it is not fixed [correct] to do so," and then it mentions,
"and they will not stone us." Is slaughtering their god something light or
severe? Additionally, the words *"v'lo yiskelunu"* simply mean "and they
won't stone us," a statement. This is difficult to understand, as Moshe
is saying this as a reason to leave Mitzrayim and slaughter elsewhere.
If the Mitzrim won't stone them, why is there a need to leave? Because
of these difficulties, Onkelos translates *"v'lo yiskelunu"* as "will they not
say to stone us [הלא יימרון למרגמנא]?" as a question, and adds "they will
say." It is not advisable to slaughter nearby, where they will see us and
say that they will stone us. The *Ibn Ezra* writes in the name of *Yefes*
that the ה' which represents a question is missing; *"v'lo"* really means
*"v'ha'lo."* The *Ibn Ezra* explains that the word *"hein"* used earlier in the
*pasuk* is like a ה', indicating a question: "Behold, it will be like this, shall
we slaughter before them and they won't stone us?"

Onkelos translates *"to'avas Mitzrayim"* as "the animal that the Mitzrim
fear [worship] [*dachalin*]." The *Nesinah LaGer* explains that this

word means "*yirah*—fear," which refers to their idolatry. They were afraid of the gods that they worshipped. Why does the Torah call it "*to'avas*—abomination," yet Onkelos translates it as "fear"?

The *Hakesav V'Hakabbalah* explains that one word can have opposite meanings. An example is "*kilus*" and "*chessed*," which are each used for both praise and disgrace. "*To'evah*" also has opposite meanings. The Mitzrim called their idolatry "*to'evah*," which in Egyptian means "fear," as a praise, whereas in *lashon hakodesh*, "*to'evah*" means "abominable." The *Nefesh HaGer* explains differently in the name of *Rashi*: the Mitzrim called it their "fear," but Yisrael called it abominable. The *Sifsei Chachamim*[10] explains that Moshe said the words "*to'avas Mitzrayim*" to Yisrael, not to the Mitzrim. The *Ibn Ezra* adds in the name of Rabbi Yeshuah that Moshe wrote "*to'avas Mitzrayim*" in the Torah as a disgrace for idolatry, but he did not say this to Pharaoh; rather, he said, "*elohei Mitzrayim*—gods of Mitzrayim." The *Sifsei Chachamim*[11] and *Nefesh HaGer* bring another explanation in *Rashi*'s name: the Mitzrim call the act of slaughtering their god "*to'evah*."

The Egyptian idolatry was sculpted as a lamb since they worshipped the lamb, thinking it ruled over their land. For this reason, they did not eat meat. The *Ibn Ezra* says they didn't eat any meat of any animal, like the Landiahs from the family of Cham, who comprised more than half the world. Anything which came from a live being, such as blood, milk, fish, and eggs, they stayed away from and were disgusted by those who ate them. Shepherding sheep was also repulsive to them, as it states, "כי תועבת מצרים כל רועה צאן." Until today, the *Ibn Ezra* writes, they do not allow anyone to eat meat in their land. If one of them goes to another country, he will run away from a place which eats meat. They won't even eat anything or use vessels that touch meat.

The *Nefesh HaGer* is bothered that here, it states, "*L'eineihem*," which Onkelos translates as "and they will see [*chazan*]." When Shimon was put in prison, though, it states, "*Va'ye'esor oso l'eineihem*," which Onkelos

10 ר בפרק ח פסוק כב
11 ש שם

translates as "and he tied them in front of their eyes [*l'eineihon*]"—right before them. Similarly, by the *Mei Merivah*, it states, "ודברתם אל הסלע לעיניהם," which he again translates as "and you shall speak to the rock in front of their eyes [*l'eineihon*]." Why the difference? The *Nefesh HaGer* answers that *Rashi* explains that once the brothers left Yosef and Shimon, Yosef took Shimon out. Yosef only locked Shimon up in front of them. Also, by the water of strife, Moshe and Aharon were supposed to speak to the water in front of the B'nei Yisrael. Here, though, Pharaoh said, "Go to your place, Goshen, and slaughter there." Moshe said, "Even if we go to Goshen and we won't be in front of the Mitzrim, they will still see and notice that we are slaughtering the lamb. It won't be enough; we need to leave."

In *Parashas Bo*, it states,[12] "ובכל אלהי מצרים אעשה שפטים" which Onkelos translates as "and with all mistakes [*ta'avas*] of the Mitzrim, I will do judgment [*dinin*]." Onkelos translates "*elohei*" as "*ta'us*," which means "mistakes" or as "*to'eh*—to stray"; this refers to the gods, as they cause people to be mistaken or stray after them. We don't explicitly see in the Torah which gods were punished or how they were punished. What was the judgment which Hashem did with their gods?

The *Menoras Hamaor*[13] answers that the Torah commands us to take a lamb on the tenth of Nissan, slaughter it on the fourteenth, put its blood on the doorposts, roast it whole, and eat it, so that the Mitzrim should recognize it was the lamb of their idolatry and see their god judged in front of their eyes! Also, the Torah commands, "Do not break any bones" of the *korban*, in order for the Mitzrim to recognize even in the morning that B'nei Yisrael slaughtered the lamb. This is as the *Rambam*[14] says that Onkelos understands that the Mitzrim did not eat the lamb because it was their god, as it states, "כי תועבת מצרים כל רועה צאן." Their gods were judged and punished.

---

12   יב, יב
13   נר ג כלל ד ח"ד
14   מ"נ ח"ג פמ"ו

May we learn from the judgment against the lamb god to recognize Hashem's rulership and remember that He is the One and only Master of all!

## WHAT WAS HASHEM'S KINDNESS WITH PHARAOH?

כִּי עַתָּה שָׁלַחְתִּי אֶת יָדִי וָאַךְ אוֹתְךָ וְאֶת
עַמְּךָ בַּדָּבֶר וַתִּכָּחֵד מִן הָאָרֶץ (ט, טו)

אֲרֵי כְּעַן קָרִיב (קְרַב) קֳדָמַי דְּשָׁלַחִית פּוֹן יָת מַחַת גְּבוּרְתִּי וּמְחֵית
יָתָךְ וְיָת עַמָּךְ בְּמוֹתָא וְשֵׁיצִיאַת (וְאִשְׁתֵּיצִיתָא) מִן אַרְעָא

*Since now is close (come close) before Me that I would have sent the smite [plague] of My might, and smite you and your nation with the death plague, and you will be (would have been) destroyed from the land.*

וּלְמַעַן סַפֵּר שְׁמִי בְּכָל הָאָרֶץ (ט, טז)

וּבְדִיל דִּיהוֹן מִשְׁתָּעַן גְּבוּרַת שְׁמִי בְּכָל אַרְעָא

*And in order that they shall tell over the might of My name in the entire land.*

The *pasuk* states, "כי עתה שלחתי את ידי ואך אותך ואת עמך בדבר ותכחד מן הארץ," which Onkelos translates as, "Since now '*kariv*' before Me that I would have sent the smite [plague] of My might, and smite you and your nation with the death plague, and you will be destroyed from the land." What does "*kariv*" mean?

The *Nesinah LaGer* explains that "*kariv*" means "is close," as in "at a time while there is still anger and interest to destroy." Onkelos adds "*pon*," which is conjunctive, as *Rashi* explains, "since now is close before Me that I would have sent the smite [plague] of My might." Hashem is saying, if I would have wanted, I could have destroyed you together with the animals by the death plague—and I was close to destroying you as well."

The *Nefesh HaGer* says that our text reads "*kerav*," which means "come close." This is as Onkelos translates, "*gesh halah*" and "*geshah na*," as "*kerav*" which is a command. Onkelos adds "*pon*," which is conjunctive, and comes when in doubt about something or for a condition. Moshe tells Pharaoh, "Repent and send them out now, because I could've destroyed you by the death plague." This is as the *Shemos Rabbah* notes,[15] that the *pasuk* states, "ויאמר ה' אל משה השכם בבקר..."—And Hashem said to Moshe, wake up early and stand before Pharaoh and say to him, so says Hashem, 'Send out My nation, and if not...'" Hashem is mighty and powerful, who is like Him? Also, who is like Hashem Who shows people the way to repent? Hashem did not want to send another *makkah* before warning Pharaoh and showing him that there was room to repent and return.

The *Nefesh HaGer* says that Onkelos derived this from the word "*atah*" which doesn't flow and seems extra. Therefore, he translates as Chazal say: "*atah*" refers to giving room for repentance. This is as it states by the builders of the Tower of Bavel, "ועתה לא יבצר מהם כל אשר יזמו לעשות"—And now it will not be held back from them all that they plotted to do." Rav Abba bar Kahana said that "*v'atah*" means "to repent," teaching that Hashem provided room for them to repent. Similarly, here, Onkelos translates "*atah*" as "now come close before Me in order to repent and send out My nation."

The *pasuk* continues, "*Shalachti es yadi*—I sent My hand," which Onkelos translates as "that I would have sent the smite [plague] of My might." The *Nefesh HaGer* explains that Onkelos changes in order to distance any reference to physicality regarding Hashem, who has no bodily features. The intent is, "Had I wanted to, I could have punished you together with the animals and people by the death plague and I would have smitten you." However, "בעבור זאת העמדתיך בעבור הראותך את כחי ולמען ספר שמי בכל הארץ—For this reason I kept you existing, in order to show you My power and in order to tell over My name in the entire land."

The *Seforno* explains that Hashem said "בעבור הראתך את כחי—In order to show you My power" to teach Pharaoh to repent. Hashem doesn't desire for people to die; rather, He wants them to return. And he explains "ולמען ספר שמי בכל הארץ—And in order to tell over My name in the entire land" so that many will return from sin. This seems that Hashem wanted Pharaoh and the Mitzrim to recognize and accept the truth: that Hashem is the Creator, Ruler, and in charge of everything.

The Gemara[16] brings that Hashem created two worlds, as it states, "כי בי-ה ה' צור עולמים." *Olam Hazeh* was created with a ה' and *Olam Haba* was created with a י', as it states regarding the creation of this world, "בהבראם," which can be read as "בה' בראם—with a ה', He created the heavens and the earth. The Gemara explains that a ה' is like an open porch, as it is open on the bottom. Whoever wants to leave to sin can leave. It also has an opening on the side to be able to return. It is not enough to return through the place where one leaves. *Rashi* explains that since he needs extra help to escape the *yetzer hara*, he needs a different entrance. The Gemara continues, Hashem helps the person return by making another entrance. *Tosafos*[17] explains that Hashem opens up another entrance to make it easier to enter. This is as Reish Lakish said: "One who comes to purify himself, Hashem helps him." So too, Hashem wanted Pharaoh and the Mitzrim to repent and return.

The following *pasuk* states a second reason to keep Pharaoh alive: "ולמען ספר שמי בכל הארץ," which Onkelos translates as "and in order that they shall tell over [*dihon mishtaan*] the might of My name in the entire land." The *Nefesh HaGer* says that it states, "*saper*—shall say over," not "*tesaper*—you [Pharaoh] shall say over," unlike the beginning of the *pasuk* which states, "*He'emadticha*—I kept you existing," and "*har'oscha*—to show you," which are both *nochach* and refer to Pharaoh. For this reason, Onkelos translates "*saper*" as "that they shall tell over," meaning that Yisrael should talk about the miracles. This is as the *Ibn Ezra* explains: "*u'l'maan saper shemi*" does not refer to Pharaoh telling about Hashem's existence, that he should go around the world and pronounce Hashem's name to honor Him. Rather, Hashem's name shall be pronounced by us, generation after generation, for performing all these miracles.

May we recognize Hashem's kindness such that even for *reshaim*, He provides opportunities for repentance!

---

16  מנחות כט:

17  שבת קד.

# Bo

## DOES "HISALALTI" MEAN "PLAYED," "MOCKED," OR "OCCURRENCES"?

לְמַעַן שְׁתִי אֹתֹתַי אֵלֶּה בְּקִרְבּוֹ (י, א)

בְּדִיל לְשַׁוָּאָה אָתַי אִלֵּין בֵּינֵיהוֹן

*In order to place these [My] signs among them.*

וּלְמַעַן תְּסַפֵּר בְּאָזְנֵי בִנְךָ...אֵת אֲשֶׁר הִתְעַלַּלְתִּי
בְּמִצְרַיִם וְאֶת אֹתֹתַי אֲשֶׁר שַׂמְתִּי בָם (י, ב)

וּבְדִיל דִּתִשְׁתָּעֵי קֳדָם בְּרָךְ...יָת נִסִּין דַּעֲבָדִית בְּמִצְרַיִם וְיָת אָתְוָתַי דְּשַׁוֵּיתִי בְּהוֹן

*And in order that you shall tell over before your
son...the miracles that I did in Mitzrayim and
the signs that I placed against them.*

At the beginning of the parashah, Hashem tells Moshe two reasons why
He brought the *makkos* on Mitzrayim. One reason is "למען שתי אתתי אלה
בקרבו—In order to place My signs among them." The second reason is,
"ולמען תספר באזני בנך...את אשר התעללתי במצרים ואת אתתי אשר שמתי בם וידעתם כי
אני ה'—And in order that you shall tell over to your son and your son's
son that which '*hisalalti b'Mitzrayim*' and My signs that I placed against
them, and you shall know that I am Hashem." What does "*hisalalti
b'Mitzrayim*" mean?

*Rashi* explains that "*hisalalti*" means "that I teased Mitzrayim." Hashem,
so to say, played with, belittled, and disgraced Mitzrayim. The *Ramban*
explains differently: "*hisalalti*" means "that I mocked." Hashem
says, "Tell over to your children that I mocked, put down, and teased
Mitzrayim."

220

Onkelos translates "ולמען תספר באזני בנך...את אשר התעללתי במצרים" as, "And in order that you shall tell over before your son...the miracles that I did in Mitzrayim." He translates "*hisalalti*" differently than *Rashi*: "the miracles that I did in Mitzrayim." The *Nefesh HaGer* says that Onkelos does not translate like *Rashi*, "teased," or as the *Ramban*, "mocked," since it would be degrading for Hashem to say this about Himself to Moshe. Onkelos is extremely careful not to translate in a way that may, *chas v'shalom*, belittle Hashem.

Rabbeinu Bachya explains that Onkelos understands that "*hisalalti*" literally means "occurrences and happenings," as it states, "*Hodi'u va'amim alilosav*—Let the nations know about His occurrences," meaning the actions that Hashem does. The words "התעללתי" and "עלילותיו" come from the *lashon* "עלה—occurrence," which refers to Hashem who is the "עלה—the Cause of all occurrences," as it states, "*V'lo niskenu alilos*—And to Him is calculated occurrences." Anything that happens is able to be done because Hashem enables people's existence and gives them the ability to do things in the world. The *Hakesav V'Hakabbalah* adds that "התעללתי" is also a language of "עליה—raising up and elevation," as Hashem is above everything. The words "את אשר התעללתי במצרים" mean "because of the occurrences in Mitzrayim," which refer to the miracles which Hashem, Who is above everything, performed. Hashem revealed Himself and showed that He is the source of all occurrences. He became known in the world as being the One and Only who is in charge of everything and rewards and punishes. Mitzrayim was the starting point for people throughout the world to know Hashem's name and that He can change nature with miracles and wonders. One of the main purposes of the *makkos* was in order for us to tell over to our descendants that Hashem is the cause of everything.

The *Maharal* says that the ten *makkos* with which Hashem punished the Mitzrim parallel the ten *maamaros* with which Hashem created the world. The purpose of the *makkos* was to express and convey that Hashem created the world and is charge of the entire creation.

It states, "למען שתי אתתי אלה בקרבו," which Onkelos translates as "and in order to place these [My] signs [אתי] among them." The following *pasuk* states, "ולמען תספר...ואת אתתי אשר שמתי בם," which Onkelos translates as "and in order that you shall tell over before your son...and My signs [אתותי] that I placed against them." Why does Onkelos translate אֹתֹתַי in the first *pasuk* as "אתי" and in the second *pasuk* as "אתותי"? The *Ohr Hatargum* answers that the first *pasuk* states "אֹתֹתַי" about *makkas arbeh* and *choshech* that Hashem was going to bring. This is as it states in the beginning of the *pasuk*, "Since I hardened his heart and the heart of his servants in order to place these signs." And by *makkas arbeh* and *choshech* it mentions, "va'yechazek Hashem...—and Hashem strengthened the heart of Pharaoh." Therefore, Onkelos translates as "אתי—My few signs," limiting the amount of signs. However, the second *pasuk* refers to telling over all the signs which Hashem performed, all ten *makkos*, so Onkelos translates it as "אתותי—My many signs."

May we learn from the *makkos* that Hashem is the cause of all actions and He is above everything!

## THE PURPOSE OF THE MAKKOS:
## TO BE HUMBLED AND FEAR HASHEM

### עַד מָתַי מֵאַנְתָּ לֵעָנֹת מִפָּנָי (י, ג)

עַד אִמַּתי מְסָרֵיב אַתְּ לְאִתְכְּנָעָא מִן קֳדָמָי

*Until when will you refuse to humble yourself*
*from before [because of] Me?*

The *pasuk* states, "עד מתי מאנת לענות מפני," which Onkelos translates as, "Until when will you refuse to humble yourself [*l'isk'na'a*] from before [because of] Me?" *Rashi* explains that "לענות" is from the root "עני—poor and low." At the end of *Parashas Vayeira*, Moshe said to Pharaoh,[1] "ידעתי כי טרם תיראון מפני ה' אלקים." *Rashi* explains, "I know that you have not yet been afraid of Hashem, G-d." Onkelos translates "*ti're'un*" differently: "I know that you still have not humbled yourselves [*isk'natun*] from before [because of] Hashem, G-d." The *Nesinah LaGer* explains that "*ti're'un*" indicates *hachnaah*, humbleness, referring to *yiras hachnaah*, humbling oneself out of fear of Hashem. What does Onkelos teach by translating "*lei'anos*" and "*ti're'un*" with "*hachnaah*—to humble"?

Rabbeinu Bachya answers that Hashem seeks from a person to be humble and low. This is as the Navi says, "ואל זה אביט אל עני ונכה רוח וחרד אל דברי—And to this one I will focus, to the humble and the low spirit, and he who is zealous to heed to My word." An *ani*, a poor person, is one who is humbled, as he feels lower than everyone else. King Achav was a *rasha* who worshipped idolatry and was deserving of punishment during his lifetime. However, Hashem saw that Achav humbled himself and therefore did not bring bad in his days, but rather during the days of his son. Nevuchadnetzar, the *rasha*, was haughty and considered himself a god. He did not humble himself and was therefore punished *middah k'neged middah* by Hashem humbling him. For seven years, he was like an animal who ate grass, making him lower than mankind. The punishment for haughtiness and arrogance is to be humbled and lowered down, as it states, "*Lifnei shever, gaon*—Before being broken is haughtiness." In the same way, Pharaoh refused to humble his haughtiness and arrogance, and therefore he was destroyed in the end.

The haftarah of *Parashas Va'eira* states that Pharaoh called himself the "Great Serpent," and he said, "לי יאורי ואני עשיתיני—The *ye'or*, the Nile River, is mine, and I made it." He did not admit that Hashem made the *ye'or*; he denied the truth, claiming that he was the one who made it. He wanted to get rid of Hashem's kingship and become ruler in His place. Rav Wolbe[2] explains that the quality of haughtiness is a contradiction to believing in Hashem. A haughty person claims that he is the reason for his success and does not accredit his success to Hashem; he denies that Hashem is the source of all success. So too, any person who does not accept Hashem as king feels free to do as he wishes, claiming that there is no authority that he needs to heed and no rules that he needs to follow. Pharaoh claimed that he was the head; there was no one above him, and there was no one to whom he had to listen. Onkelos translates with the *lashon "hachnaah"* to reflect that Pharaoh was expected to humble himself because of the *makkos* and miracles that Hashem performed, yet he hardened his heart. He made his soft heart of flesh which feels and is affected into a hardened heart which is not affected or impressed.

The Brisker Rav[3] points out that here, regarding the *makkah* of *arbeh*, Moshe adds the words, "עַד מָתַי מֵאַנְתָּ לֵעָנֹת מִפָּנַי," unlike the earlier *makkos* where he only said, "*Shalach ami v'yaavduni*—Send out My nation and they will serve Me.*" He explains in the name of the *Rambam* that one will not only be punished for sinning, but also for being stubborn and not internalizing the messages from Hashem to repent. Pharaoh should have paid attention to the messages that Hashem was sending him with the *makkos* and humbled himself and repented, yet he did not. Therefore, Moshe warns Pharaoh: you will be punished for continuing to be haughty, stiff, and stubborn instead of paying heed to Hashem's messages.

May we all humble ourselves before Hashem and accept His kingship over us!

## WHEN DID MAKKAS CHOSHECH START AND WHY?

### וִיהִי חֹשֶׁךְ עַל אֶרֶץ מִצְרָיִם וְיָמֵשׁ חֹשֶׁךְ (י, כא)

וִיהֵי חֲשׁוֹכָא עַל אַרְעָא דְמִצְרַיִם בָּתַר דְּיֶעְדֵּי קְבַל לֵילְיָא

*And it will be darkness upon the land of Mitzrayim, after [that] the extreme darkness of the night will be removed.*

### וַיְהִי חֹשֶׁךְ אֲפֵלָה (י, כב)

וַהֲוָה חֲשׁוֹךְ קְבַל

*And it was extreme darkness.*

The *pasuk* states, "וִיהִי חֹשֶׁךְ עַל אֶרֶץ מצרים—And it will be darkness upon the land of Mitzrayim, וְיָמֵשׁ חֹשֶׁךְ." *Rashi* explains that the night will darken more than the standard darkness. The word "ויְמֵשׁ" is from the word "אֶמֶשׁ—yesterday evening,"[4] which refers to the night; it is as though it states "וְיֵאָמֵשׁ—and it will be darkened night," more and more. It is missing the 'א since its pronunciation is not so recognizable.

Onkelos translates the words "וַיְהִי חֹשֶׁךְ...וִיְמֵשׁ חֹשֶׁךְ" as, "And it will be darkness upon the land of Mitzrayim after the extreme darkness of the night will be removed." He translates the first *choshech* as the *makkah* of *choshech*, and the second as extreme darkness of the night, similar to how he translates "*choshech afeilah*—extreme darkness" in the following *pasuk*. *Rashi* explains that Onkelos understands "*v'yameish*" to mean "*hasarah*—to remove." When the day starts and light shines, then the *makkah* of darkness will begin.[5]

Why did the *makkah* of *choshech* start in the morning? The *Nefesh HaGer* explains that this was in order to have complete days for the *makkah*. Also, it meant that the Mitzrim anticipated daylight coming but instead had darkness. Rabbeinu Bachya adds that had the *makkah* started in the evening, the Mitzrim might have thought that the night lasted three days straight and then the miracle would not be as pronounced and noticeable. Therefore, only after the darkness of night left and it was visible by everyone that it was day did the *makkah* of darkness begin.

*Rashi*, however, is bothered by Onkelos's translation because his sequence of events is that first, *v'yameish choshech*—the extreme darkness of night will be removed, and only afterwards, *vi'hi choshech*—the *makkah* of darkness will come. However, the *pasuk* seems to have it the reverse way: it first states, "*Vi'hi choshech*," and only afterwards, "*v'yameish choshech*—and the darkness will be removed."

The *Maharal* explains that Onkelos means that the natural darkness of night will be removed and the miraculous *makkah* of darkness will set in, clearly being noticeable, as it was thick and tangible. The words "*vi'hi choshech*" mean that there was a miraculous *makkah* of darkness, and "*v'yameish choshech*" explains that this thick and tangible darkness had

had no connection to any standard darkness of night. Rabbi Hartman explains that the *Maharal* understands in Onkelos that the miracle set in after the removal of night, but not specifically in the morning. Rather, it was made clear that this was an arrival of a different, miraculous darkness. It does not specify a time, but rather, it defines the *makkah*, a *makkah* of miraculous darkness.

May we learn from Hashem's miracles that He is King and in control of the entire universe!

## WHAT DIDN'T THE DOGS DO, AND WHAT WAS THEIR REWARD?

וּלְכֹל בְּנֵי יִשְׂרָאֵל לֹא יֶחֱרַץ כֶּלֶב לְשֹׁנוֹ לְמֵאִישׁ וְעַד בְּהֵמָה לְמַעַן תֵּדְעוּן אֲשֶׁר יַפְלֶה ה' בֵּין מִצְרַיִם וּבֵין יִשְׂרָאֵל (יא, ז)

וּלְכֹל בְּנֵי יִשְׂרָאֵל לָא יַנְזֵיק כַּלְבָּא בְּלִישָׁנֵיהּ לְמִבַּח לְמֵאֲנָשָׁא וְעַד בְּעִירָא בְּדִיל דְּתִדְּעוּן דְּיַפְרֵישׁ יְיָ בֵּין מִצְרָאֵי וּבֵין יִשְׂרָאֵל

*And no dog will injure all B'nei Yisrael with its tongue by barking, from a person to an animal, in order that you shall know that Hashem separates between the Mitzrim and between Yisrael.*

The *pasuk* states, "וּלְכֹל בני ישראל לא יחרץ כלב לשונו ועד בהמה." *Rashi* explains that "*yecheratz*" means "to sharpen"; "no dog will sharpen its tongue." Onkelos translates "לא יחרץ כלב לשונו" differently: "no dog will injure with its tongue by barking." What does this mean?

The *Nesinah LaGer* quotes from the *Rashbam* that an angel harmed and destroyed the firstborn Mitzrim. However, of the firstborn Yisrael, even the sound of the wild animals barking did not injure them. The *Ibn Ezra* explains that although there will be sent a destroyer from heaven to destroy the firstborns of Mitzrayim, the dogs won't bark or bite, and they won't frighten Yisrael. The *Minchas Shai* teaches that the word "לשונו— his tongue" is written without a ו, as "לשנו," which hints to "his tooth [שן]," indicating that the dogs were prevented from biting.

The *Nefesh HaGer* quotes from the Gemara:[6] Rav Dustai *darshened* that the *pasuk* states, "ובנחה יאמר שובה ה' רבבות אלפי ישראל," which teaches that the Shechinah does not rest on Yisrael if there is one less than 22,000 people. If there were 21,999 people and a dog would bark at a pregnant woman and cause her to miscarry, it would turn out that the Shechinah will be removed from Yisrael as a result. A woman once went to bake in someone else's house. She heard a dog bark when she entered, and her fetus moved out of place; she had a miscarriage. The owner said, "Don't worry, I removed its teeth and claws." She retorted, "Take your good and throw it on the thorns; the fetus already moved," meaning, "Your efforts to resolve danger from the dog did not help whatsoever; I already miscarried." Clearly, dogs are able to cause serious injury by just barking alone, even without using their teeth or claws.

The Gemara[7] teaches that a person who raises a dog holds back kindness. *Rashi* explains that this is because poor people will be afraid to come into his house. The Gemara adds that he also removes from himself *yiras Shamayim*. The *Maharsha* explains that it was common to place a watchdog at the entrance of a house to guard the house. A Yid has a *mezuzah* on the doorpost on which it is written "ש-ד-י," the name of Hashem. The Shechinah is watching over his house, yet he needs a dog? It must be that he does not believe that Hashem guards his house, rather that the dog does.

The *pasuk* ends, "למען תדעון אשר יפלה ה' בין מצרים ובין ישראל," which Onkelos translates as "in order that you shall know that Hashem separates between the Mitzrim and between Yisrael." The *Hakesav V'Hakabbalah* explains that despite the screams of fear of death by the Mitzrim, the dogs won't move their tongues to bark, despite their natural instincts to do so. Yet at the same time, for the Jewish People, the night was pleasant and tranquil, without any worry or nervousness. B'nei Yisrael did not hear any noise from dogs which might frighten and injure them.

---

6   ב"ק פג.

7   שבת סג:-.

By the *makkah* of frogs, the frogs jumped into hot ovens and were *moser nefesh* for Hashem and merited to live. My uncle Mr. Shabsi Rubin asked: shouldn't the frogs receive eternal reward like the dogs, which merited to always have thrown to them carcasses and *tereifos* in return for not barking? He said over that it was easier for the frogs to be *moser nefesh* to jump into hot ovens than for the dogs to remain silent. It is an unusual feat for the dogs to be silent, so they deserved to receive eternal reward.

May Hashem protect us from *mazikim*, and may our *mezuzah* remind us that Hashem's Shechinah protects our house!

## IS THE NAME "PESACH" BECAUSE HASHEM "SKIPPED OVER" OR "HAD MERCY"?

וְרָאִיתִי אֶת הַדָּם וּפָסַחְתִּי עֲלֵכֶם (יב, יג)

וְאֶחֱזֵי יָת דְּמָא וַאֲחוּס עֲלֵיכוֹן

*And I will see the blood and I will have mercy upon you.*

וְעָבַר ה' לִנְגֹּף אֶת מִצְרַיִם וְרָאָה אֶת הַדָּם...וּפָסַח ה'
עַל הַפֶּתַח וְלֹא יִתֵּן הַמַּשְׁחִית לָבֹא אֶל בָּתֵּיכֶם לִנְגֹּף (יב, כג)

וְיִתְגְּלֵי יְיָ לְמִמְחֵי יָת מִצְרָאֵי וְיִחֱזֵי יָת דְּמָא...וְיֵיחוּס יְיָ עַל תַּרְעָא
וְלָא יִשְׁבּוֹק מְחַבְּלָא (לְחַבְּלָא) לְמֵיעַל לְבָתֵּיכוֹן לְמִמְחֵי

*And Hashem will be revealed to smite the Mitzrim and He will see the blood...and Hashem will have mercy over the door and He won't allow (for) the destroyer to enter your houses to smite.*

וַאֲמַרְתֶּם זֶבַח פֶּסַח הוּא לַה' אֲשֶׁר פָּסַח עַל בָּתֵּי בְנֵי יִשְׂרָאֵל
בְּמִצְרַיִם בְּנָגְפּוֹ אֶת מִצְרַיִם וְאֶת בָּתֵּינוּ הִצִּיל (יב, כז)

וְתֵימְרוּן דֵּיבַח חֲיָס הוּא קֳדָם יְיָ דְּחָס עַל בָּתֵּי בְּנֵי יִשְׂרָאֵל
בְּמִצְרַיִם כַּד מְחָא יָת מִצְרָאֵי וְיָת בָּתַּנָא שֵׁיזִיב

*And you shall say, "It is a slaughter of mercy before Hashem that He pitied on the houses of B'nei Yisrael in Mitzrayim when He smote the Mitzrim and saved our houses."*

The *pasuk* states, "And you shall eat it in haste, *pesach hu laHashem*." *Rashi* explains that the offering is called *"pesach"* from the word meaning "to skip and jump over." Hashem skipped over the houses of Yisrael in Mitzrayim, jumping from Mitzri to Mitzri, saving the Yisrael who lived in the middle. Also, it states, "וראיתי את הדם ופסחתי עליכם," which *Rashi* again explains to mean "skip and jump," as it states, "פוסחים על שתי הסעפים—Jumping over the two thoughts/branches." Hashem will see the blood and jump over the houses of Yisrael who lived between them. So too, a lame person is called "פסח" since by limping with one leg, jerking it up and down, it appears as if he is jumping. *Rashi*[8] also explains that Hashem passed over the houses as a king who "passes over" from place to place, at once, with one passing, and smote all the first-borns.

Onkelos translates "וראיתי את הדם ופסחתי עליכם" differently: "And I will see the blood and I will have mercy upon you." *Rashi* explains that this is as it states, "פסוח והמליט," which refers to saving and having mercy by skipping and jumping. So too it states, "ועבר ה' לנגף את מצרים וראה את הדם...ופסח. ה' על הפתח ולא יתן המשחית לבא אל בתיכם לנגף," which Onkelos translates as, "And Hashem will be revealed to smite the Mitzrim and He will see the blood...and Hashem will have mercy over the door and He won't allow the destroyer to enter your houses to smite." Here, too, *Rashi* explains "ופסח" differently: "and He will jump." Another *pasuk* states, "When your children will ask, 'What is this *avodah* for you?' ואמרתם זבח פסח הוא לה' אשר פסח על בתי בני ישראל במצרים בנגפו את מצרים ואת בתינו הציל," which Onkelos translates as, "And you shall say, 'It is a slaughter of mercy before Hashem that He pitied on the houses of B'nei Yisrael in Mitzrayim when He smote the Mitzrim and He saved our houses.'" The *Nefesh HaGer* explains that since Onkelos always distances any physicality from Hashem, he does not translate *"pasach"* as "skip," but as "mercy" or "pity."

The *Mechilta* teaches:[9] "Rabbi Yoshiyah said, do not read it 'ופסחתי,' but as 'ופסעתי,' since Hashem skipped over the houses of Yisrael in Mitzrayim.

8 יב

9 מט

This is as it states, 'קול דודי הנה זה בא מדלג על ההרים מקפץ על הגבעות.' Rabbi Yonasan said, 'ופסחתי' means 'I will have pity over you,' but not over the Mitzrim." The *Nefesh HaGer* says that *Rashi* explains like the opinion of Rabbi Yoshiyah, whereas Onkelos translates like Rabbi Yonasan.

What does Onkelos mean by translating "*pesichah*" as "mercy and pity"? Simply, it means that Hashem had mercy and pity on us and did not smite us together with the firstborns, instead choosing to save us. The *Hakesav V'Hakabbalah* adds that Onkelos means that the word implies "protection" and "salvation." Hashem had mercy and protected us from being killed with the Mitzri firstborns.

The *Me'at Tzari* offers another explanation. *Rashi* records the question:[10]

> *Why was there a special command in Mitzrayim to purchase the Korban Pesach on the tenth of Nissan, which is not necessary for future generations? Rabbi Masya ben Charash explained: Hashem said, "The time has come which I swore to Avraham that I will redeem his sons. However, they are 'unclothed,' without mitzvos, and not deserving. They don't have any mitzvos to do in order to merit being taken out." Therefore, Hashem gave them two mitzvos: blood of the Korban Pesach and blood of circumcision. That evening, they circumcised themselves, slaughtered the Korban Pesach, and sprinkled the blood.*

The *Maharal* explains that circumcision was given to create a sign as a stamp impressed on our body that we are servants of Hashem, as we say in *bentching*, "ועל בריתך שחתמת בבשרנו—And for the circumcision that You impressed in our body." It is not enough for a slave to have a sign that he is a slave without actually serving; therefore, Hashem also gave us the mitzvah of the *Korban Pesach*, which is an act of service, as it states, "ועבדת את העבודה הזאת—And you shall serve this service." Both mitzvos were needed, as it is not enough just to serve Hashem with one act of service, it needed to be impressed in us as well. Rabbi Hartman

---

adds that because we made ourselves into servants, we merited to be taken out of Mitzrayim to serve Hashem. Hashem mercifully gave us the opportunity to accept to be His servants, through which we merited being redeemed.

The *Rambam*[11] teaches that Onkelos understands that the Mitzrim worshipped the lamb, and we were meant to bring the *Korban Pesach* to go to the other extreme and show how unimportant and false their idolatry was. By expressing publicly how worthless it was, we would merit to be saved, atone for our sins, and this would bring us close to *emunah* in Hashem. Therefore, we were commanded to slaughter the lamb, their idolatry, and sprinkle its blood on the outside of our doorways to be seen by all, as is the opinion of Rabbi Yitzchak in the *Mechilta*.[12] The *Hakesav V'Hakabbalah* adds that Hashem commanded B'nei Yisrael to slaughter it with families together and eat it as a group. The intent was for the Mitzrim to see B'nei Yisrael taking their god to slaughter, and their stomachs would churn and bubble. The god which they worshipped and put their faith in was being made worthless, with no power, leaving them with nothing to trust in. Although this would upset the Mitzrim and cause extreme danger for Yisrael, Yisrael did exactly as they were commanded. These actions were meant to enable us to demonstrate complete *teshuvah* and arouse Hashem's mercy to not be smitten by the *makkah*. The blood put on the doorposts served as a sign highlighting their complete *teshuvah* and attachment to Hashem. Hashem mercifully gave us these mitzvos to fulfill to give us the opportunity to express our complete *emunah* in Hashem, through which we merited being redeemed.

The *Seforno* says that we slaughtered the *Korban Pesach* and ate it even before Hashem passed over and had mercy on us. Rav Yerucham[13] explains that Hashem wanted to see our *emunah* in order to give us the

11 מו"נ ח"ג פמ"ו
12 לד
13 דעת חכמה ומוסר ח"ג מאמר א

merit to be redeemed. Hashem had mercy in that He gave us the means to express our *emunah* to merit being redeemed.

Rav Hutner[14] explains that there is *middas ha'chessed* and *middas ha'din*. Hashem exercised His *chozek yad*, His strong hand against Mitzrayim, which was the *middas ha'din*. Hashem's mercy caused the *middas ha'chesed* to assist B'nei Yisrael over the *middas ha'din* against Mitzrayim to save us. Onkelos translates *"pesichah"* as "mercy," since the main purpose of Hashem being merciful was in order to annul the *middas ha'din* and assist us with His *middas ha'chessed*.

May we become dedicated servants of Hashem and merit His mercy!

## WHAT DOES "PATIR" TEACH ABOUT MATZAH?

וּמַצּוֹת (יב, ח)

וּפַטִּיר

*And matzah.*

מַצּוֹת (יב, טו)

פַּטִּירָא

*Matzah.*

מַצּוֹת (יב, לט)

פַּטִּירָן

*Matzos.*

Onkelos translates *"matzah"* as *"patir."* What does it mean, and how does it relate to matzah?

One explanation is that *"patir"* is related to *"cheirus—freedom,"* as it states,[15] "וכתב לה ספר כריתת," which Onkelos translates as "and he will

---

14    ספר הזכרון רשימות עניינים שונים ג

15    דברים כה, א

write for her a document of freedom [*piturin*]," and "*v'shilchah mi'beiso*," which Onkelos translates as "and he will free her [*v'yifterenah*] from his house." Accordingly, when we describe Pesach during davening as "חג המצות זמן חרותינו," that would mean, "The festival of freedom, the time of our being freed." "*Patir*" symbolizes being freed physically from slavery and bondage under the Mitzrim and being freed from the land of Mitzrayim.

"*Matzah*" refers to unleavened bread made from flour and water, without ["freed from"][16] other ingredients, that did not rise. This reflects *anavah*, humility. "*Chametz*" refers to leavened bread that did rise, as the dough was subjected to yeast that causes it to rise. This reflects *gaavah*, haughtiness and arrogance. Matzah hints to being free from the "yeast in the dough," a hint to the *yetzer hara* who causes us to be haughty and sin. If so, "*patir*—freedom" hints to being freed spiritually from the clutches of the *yetzer hara* and from the forty-nine levels of contamination that we fell to in Mitzrayim.

The *Radak* says that "*peter*" means to open up and be sent out, as a first-born child is called "*peter rechem*—opening the womb." This is like the *Yalkut Shimoni*:[17] "What does it mean that Hashem 'took for Himself a nation from within a nation?' It is like a person who pulls out a fetus from within the womb of an animal. We were like a fetus in the womb of our mother in Mitzrayim, and Hashem took us out, which was the birth of our nation." If so, the *lashon* "*patir*" hints to our nation being born and created when we were taken out of Mitzrayim.

The *Radak* says that the word "*patur*—exempt" is often contrasted with "*chayav*—obligated." If so, "*patir*" indicates that we became exempt from the decree of subjugation to be slaves, and we became exempt from the *yetzer hara*'s grasp and from the different levels of contamination that we fell to in Mitzrayim.

---

My good friend Rabbi Elchonon Sosne   16

ואתחנן אות תתכח   17

Thus, Onkelos's translation of *"matzah"* as *"patir"* hints that we were born as a nation at *Yetzias Mitzrayim* and that Hashem exempted us from physical and spiritual subjugation.

May we merit to be freed from the subjugation of the *yetzer hara*, along with the physical and spiritual subjugation of exile!

## IS "BEN NEICHAR" A NON-JEW OR A JEW?

### זֹאת חֻקַּת הַפָּסַח כָּל בֶּן נֵכָר לֹא יֹאכַל בּוֹ (יב, מג)

דָּא גְּזֵירַת פִּסְחָא כָּל בַּר יִשְׂרָאֵל דְּאִשְׁתַּמַּד (דְּיִשְׁתַּמַּד) לָא יֵיכוֹל בֵּיהּ

*This is the decree of the Korban Pesach: any person of Yisrael that became (will become) an apostate shall not eat it.*

The *pasuk* states, *"Zos chukas haPuhsach,"* which Onkelos translates as, "This is the decree [*gezeiras*] of the *Korban Pesach*." Similarly, *Parashas Chukas* starts, *"Zos chukas haTorah,"* which Onkelos translates as, "This is the decree [*gezeiras*] of the Torah." He does not translate as "the statute [*k'yam*]," like he does in most places. The reason is because in both of these places, the Torah starts a new and specific topic with an introduction: this is the "decree." The *pesukim* that follow mention the different statutes and rules about their laws.

The first law stated by the *Korban Pesach* is, "כל בן נכר לא יאכל בו—Any foreigner shall not eat it." *Rashi* explains that this prohibition includes one whose actions became strange to his Father in *shamayim*. The *Ramban* adds that the *pasuk* is only needed for the Jew who is a *meshumad*. The *Re'em* says that the non-Jew is derived from the words *"toshav v'sachir lo yochal bo"*—even a circumcised Arab is prohibited from partaking of the *Korban Pesach*. So too, *Rashi* on the Gemara[18] specifies that this refers to a Jew who did not go away from the entire Torah.

Onkelos translates "כל בן נכר לא יאכל בו" differently: "Any person of Yisrael that became an apostate [*bar Yisrael d'ishtamad*] shall not eat it." Others[19] have the text "*d'yishtamed*—that will be an apostate." The *Me'at Tzari* says that Onkelos, who translates as "any person of Yisrael that will be an apostate," seems to exclude a non-Jew. However, the *Ramban* and *Malbim*[20] explain differently: a non-Jew is certainly included; there is no need to mention him at all, as it is obvious that he is prohibited. Onkelos does not translate "*ben neichar*" as[21] "person of the nations [*bar amemin*]" which is a non-Jew, to explain the intent; this refers to a Jew who became a *meshumad*.

The *Ramban*[22] writes that Onkelos translates "*neichar*" as "*d'ishtamad*—that became an apostate," meaning, this person's actions have become *recognized* as strange and foreign to his brothers and Hashem by doing bad things. He translates with the *lashon* "*meshumad*" mentioned all over. Onkelos translates "*d'ishtamad*" as he translates "ויכר יוסף את אחיו והם לא הכרהו," as, "And Yosef recognized [*v'ishtemoda*] the brothers and they didn't recognize him [*ishtemo'de'uhi*]." "דאשתמד" is like the word "ואשתמודע" with an 'ע, as משמדע; sometimes, the 'ע is shortened and not put in the word.

This seems difficult; "*neichar*" means strange or foreign, and "*minkar*" means recognized. However, the *Ramban* seems to explain "*neichar*" according to Onkelos as "become recognized," yet he says that the person's actions are "strange and foreign" to his brothers and Hashem, which is the exact opposite! The *Hakesav V'Hakabbalah* answers that we find different roots which can mean something and its opposite, such as "שרש," which means both "root" and "uproot." Similarly, the root "נכר" includes both one who you recognize and know, and also one who is strange or foreign. This is as it states, "*Lo sakiru phanim*—Do not *recognize* him" to make him righteous in judgment, even if you love him. Another understanding is, "Do not make him *strange*" if you hate him

---

19  רמב"ם סה"מ מ' ל"ת קכח
20  פח
21  ויקרא כב, כה
22  ורמב"ם סה"מ ל"ת קכ"ח

and make him liable, from the *lashon "pen y'nak'ru tzareimo*—lest your enemies will make strange or foreign." This shows that *"neichar"* can include either meaning, recognized or not recognized.

Rav Yaakov Kamenetsky explains differently:[23] "דאשתמד" means "that became *known*," from "מודע" as in the *pasuk*, "ולנעמי מודע לאישה"—and Naomi became known to a husband," and "בעז מדעתנו—Boaz is known to us; he is a relative." The letters "מד" hint to "become known" and a 'ש is added, just as a 'ש is added to "עבד" to become "שעבוד," and to "חר" to become "שחרור."

The *Sefer Hachinuch*[24] teaches that Onkelos understands that a person who is a *mumar* for idolatry cannot eat the *Korban Pesach*. The purpose of slaughtering the *Korban Pesach* is to remember the miracles in Mitzrayim. Since we are doing this as a remembrance of the time that we entered under the wings of the Shechinah and accepted the covenant of Torah and *emunah*, it is not fitting for a *mumar* to participate. It does not make sense to allow someone who maintains the opposite of our belief to eat from something which is supposed to highlight our belief.

The *Me'at Tzari* teaches that the *Re'em* understands Onkelos differently: even one who is a *mumar* for any type of sin cannot eat the *Korban Pesach*. The *Korban Pesach* is only able to be eaten by a Yisrael who believes in Hashem and fulfills all His mitzvos.

May we constantly serve Hashem, trust in Him, and fulfill His mitzvos!

---

23   אמת ליעקב
24   מצוה יג

# Beshalach

## WHERE WERE YOSEF'S BONES, AND HOW DID MOSHE BRING THEM UP?

וַיִּקַּח מֹשֶׁה אֶת עַצְמוֹת יוֹסֵף עִמּוֹ...וְהַעֲלִיתֶם
אֶת עַצְמֹתַי מִזֶּה אִתְּכֶם (יג, יט)

וְאַסֵּיק מֹשֶׁה יָת גַּרְמֵי יוֹסֵף עִמֵּיהּ...וְתַסְּקוּן יָת גַּרְמַי מִכָּא עִמְּכוֹן

*And Moshe brought up the bones of Yosef with him...and*
*you shall take up my bones from here with you.*

The *pasuk* states, "ויקח משה את עצמות יוסף עמו...והעליתם את עצמתי מזה
אתכם," which Onkelos translates as, "And Moshe brought up the bones
of Yosef with him...and you shall take up my bones from here with
you." Onkelos translates *"Va'yikach Moshe"* as "and Moshe brought up
[v'aseik]," not "and Moshe took [u'ne'seiv]," which is the common translation when taking inanimate objects. The *Nefesh HaGer* explains that
Onkelos changes to translate with the *lashon* *"aliyah"* as it states the
word *"v'ha'alisem*—and you shall take up" at the end of the *pasuk*. The
*Nesinah LaGer* explains Onkelos with the *Mechilta*: Moshe brought up
Yosef's coffin from the Nile River.

How did Moshe find out where Yosef was buried? The Gemara[1] teaches:
they told Moshe that Serach remained from that generation, and that he
should go and ask her. *Tosafos* quotes from *Pirkei D'Rabi Eliezer*: Serach
was given the secret of the redemption, which was a special *nusach* that
reflected redemption. Moshe went and asked her, "Do you know where
Yosef is buried?" She responded, "The Mitzrim made a metal coffin

---

סוטה יג.     1

237

for him and placed it in the Nile River in order for Yosef to bless its waters." *Rashi* explains that the Nile River was the source of water for the entire Mitzrayim, since it did not rain in Mitzrayim. They made irrigation ditches leading from it to all the fields throughout the land. The *Maharsha* quotes from *Rashi* that all of the Shevatim's coffins were actually taken out of Mitzrayim, and B'nei Yisrael knew where their coffins were. However, the Mitzrim hid Yosef's coffin, since they wanted it to remain in Mitzrayim, as it brought them blessing. It caused the Nile River to be plentiful and irrigate the water supply all over Mitzrayim. They specifically made Yosef a metal coffin in order that it should sink down into the water and no one would be able to find it to take it from there. In truth, the water of the Nile River rose and was plentiful in the merit of Yaakov, as well, and they wanted him to be buried there to maintain the blessing. However, since Yosef was the ruler in Mitzrayim, they couldn't stop Yaakov from being taken out from Mitzrayim. Now that Yosef died, there was no one who had control to decide how and where to bury him. Therefore, the Mitzrim buried him somewhere that required his coffin to be found.

Moshe went and stood by the edge of the river and said, "Yosef, Yosef, the time that Hashem promised to redeem us has come, and the time has come which you swore to Yisrael to take you. If you show yourself, good, if not, we are exempt from your promise." Immediately, the coffin floated up.

On the words "ויקח משה את עצמות יוסף," the Gemara teaches: come and see how much Moshe Rabbeinu cherished mitzvos. All of Yisrael were involved in taking booty from Mitzrayim,[2] as it states, "*Va'yenatzelu es Mitzrayim*," which Onkelos translates as "and they emptied out Mitzrayim." The Gemara[3] explains that they emptied out Mitzrayim from all their gold and silver. Yet Moshe was busy with doing mitzvos, as it states, "חכם לב יקח מצות—A smart-hearted person takes mitzvos." The *Maharsha* explains that Moshe calculated the loss of the mitzvah

2   רש"י וב"ח ד שם

3   פסחים קיט.

opposite its gain. He left the pleasures and enjoyments of this world, which are cheap, in order to prepare himself for the next world, which has the real reward.

The *Shemos Rabbah*[4] adds that Yosef was obligated as a son to bury his father, Yaakov. Moshe, however, was not a son or grandson of Yosef, yet he was involved in taking his bones out of Mitzrayim in order to bury him. Hashem said, "Because of what you did, so too I, Myself, Who is not obligated to any being, will be involved with you and I will bury you."

May we learn from Moshe to cherish and grab mitzvos in order to prepare for the next world!

## DO WE DAVEN TO HELP A DIFFICULT SITUATION, OR IS A DIFFICULT SITUATION BROUGHT TO CAUSE US TO DAVEN?

### וַיִּצְעֲקוּ בְנֵי יִשְׂרָאֵל אֶל ה' (יד, י)

וּזְעִיקוּ (וּצְעִיקוּ)[5] בְּנֵי יִשְׂרָאֵל קֳדָם יְיָ

*And B'nei Yisrael screamed (cried out) before Hashem.*

### מַה תִּצְעַק אֵלָי דַּבֵּר אֶל בְּנֵי יִשְׂרָאֵל וְיִסָּעוּ (יד, טו)

קַבֵּילִית צְלוֹתָךְ מַלֵּיל עִם בְּנֵי יִשְׂרָאֵל וְיִטְּלוּן

*Your davening was already answered; speak
with B'nei Yisrael and travel.*

After letting B'nei Yisrael go, Pharaoh and the Mitzrim chased after them. B'nei Yisrael saw the Mitzrim traveling after them and became frightened. The *pasuk* states, "ויצעקו בני ישראל אל ה'—And B'nei Yisrael screamed out to Hashem." *Rashi* comments that "Yisrael took hold of the trade of the Avos, davening as each of the Avos did." The *Ramban* says that Onkelos translates differently: "And B'nei Yisrael cried out [u'tz'iku] or screamed [u'z'iku]," which implies that they complained about their difficult situation, not that they davened. This is as the

פ' כ, יט    4

רמב"ן    5

following *pesukim* mention: they said, "We would have been better off staying in Mitzrayim and laboring there rather than dying in the Midbar." Moshe appeased them by saying, "Do not worry! You will see Hashem's salvation; He will fight for you." Rav Hutner[6] adds that it states, "ואת זעקתם שמעת על ים סוף—And their cries You heard at the Yam Suf," which indicates that we davened. Also, in *Selichos* we say, "מי שענה לאבותינו על ים סוף הוא יעננו—He Who answered our forefathers at Yam Suf, He shall answer us," which implies that we davened. Nevertheless, the acceptance of our davening was not what caused the salvation to come.

The following *pasuk* states, "Hashem said to Moshe, מה תצעק אלי דבר אל בני ישראל ויסעו—For what are you screaming to Me? Speak to B'nei Yisrael and travel.'" The *Ohr Hachaim Hakadosh* explains that Hashem hinted, "It is dependent on you; traveling into the water would be an expression of *emunah*, and with this *zechus* you will be saved."

*Rashi* explains that this teaches us that Moshe was davening and Hashem told him, "Now is not the time for a lengthy davening, since B'nei Yisrael are in a painful situation." The *Maharal* explains that Moshe was answered only after he finished davening. Therefore, Hashem told Moshe it is not the time for a lengthy davening, since he wouldn't be answered until he finished.

Onkelos translates "*Mah titzak eilai*" differently: "Your davening was already answered." Onkelos does not translate "*Mah titzak eilai*" as a question, but as a statement. The *Nesinah LaGer* explains that although Hashem generally desires the davening of *tzaddikim*, here, Hashem did not want Moshe to daven because the davening was already accepted. Moshe started to daven and Hashem said there is no need to continue. The *Nefesh HaGer* teaches from the *Shemos Rabbah*:[7] Rabbi Eliezer said, there is a time to lengthen davening and there is a time to shorten davening. Right now, My children are in pain and the sea is closing them in; why are you lengthening your davening? Speak to B'nei Yisrael and travel, since your davening was already accepted.

The *Shemos Rabbah*[8] asks: Why did Hashem place Yisrael at the sea in this type of situation, stuck without a way to escape? It answers with a parable: there was a king who was traveling, and he heard the daughter of another king screaming, "Save me from the robbers." The king heard her pleas and saved her. After some time, the king wanted to marry her, but she wasn't interested in speaking to him. The king sent robbers to attack her, and she once again cried out to the king. He said to her, "This is exactly what I desired—to hear your voice." In the same way, Hashem desires to hear the davening of B'nei Yisrael.

Rav Hutner[9] explains that we see from here that davening does not only come in response to a difficult situation, but the difficult situation is set up as a trigger to cause us to daven. It follows that while we are in the middle of davening, we won't be answered, because the salvation won't come at a time which will cause our voices to stop being heard. Similarly, at the Yam Suf, Hashem made the situation difficult in order to cause us to daven, as it states in *Shir Hashirim*: "השמיעיני את קולך כי קולך ערב—Let me hear your voice because your voice is sweet." Hashem told Moshe, "Do not lengthen," so that he would complete the davening and allow for Hashem to save Yisrael.

Rabbi Hartman explains that this idea is hinted at in the *pasuk*: "והיה טרם יקראו ואני אענה ואני הם מדברים ואני אשמע—And it will be, before they call out, I have already answered; while they are still speaking, I will listen." Sometimes, Hashem answers a person even before he davens, as it states: "והיה טרם יקראו ואני אענה." However, once a person starts davening, Hashem listens, and He only answers after the person ends his davening, as it states, "עוד הם מדברים ואני אשמע—While they are still speaking, I will hear the davening." Hashem desires to hear a person's voice and will only answer him after he finishes.

May we recognize that Hashem desires to hear our voice and daven with sincerity!

8   שמ ה

9   פחד יצחק פסח מאמר יד אות א

## DID THE MITZRIM FLEE TO THE WATER OR AWAY FROM IT? HOW DID THEY KNOW THAT HASHEM FOUGHT AGAINST THEM IN MITZRAYIM?

וַיֹּאמֶר מִצְרַיִם אָנוּסָה מִפְּנֵי יִשְׂרָאֵל
כִּי ה' נִלְחָם לָהֶם בְּמִצְרָיִם (יד, כה)

וַאֲמַרוּ מִצְרָאֵי נְעְרוֹק מִן קֳדָם יִשְׂרָאֵל אֲרֵי דָא הִיא גְּבוּרְתָּא
דַּיְיָ דַּעֲבֵד (דַּעֲבַד) לְהוֹן קְרָבִין בְּמִצְרָיִם

*And the Mitzrim said, "Let us flee from before
[because of] Yisrael since this is the might of Hashem
that battles (battled) for them in Mitzrayim."*

וּמִצְרַיִם נָסִים לִקְרָאתוֹ (יד, כז)

וּמִצְרָאֵי עָרְקִין לְקַדָמוּתֵיה

*And the Mitzrim were fleeing before [toward] it.*

The *pasuk* states, "ויאמר מצרים אנוסה מפני ישראל כי ה' נלחם להם במצרים." *Rashi* explains: We shall flee from before Yisrael because Hashem is fighting against the Mitzrim, and we had better leave or we will be killed. *Rashi* explains "במצרים—in the land of Mitzrayim" as "במצריים—against the Mitzrim." *Rashi* suggests another explanation: "במצרים" indeed means "in the place of Mitzrayim." The Mitzrim said, "Just as these are being struck by the Yam, so too those who remained in Mitzrayim are getting punished."

Onkelos translates the words "כי ה' נלחם להם במצרים" as, "This is the might of Hashem that battles [*da'aveid*] for them in Mitzrayim." The word "*da'aveid*" is in present tense; Hashem was currently battling against them. The *Nefesh HaGer* infers that Onkelos does not translate "במצרים" as "במצראי," which means "against the Mitzrim," like he translated "מצרים" at the beginning of the *pasuk*, but rather as "במצרים—in the land of Mitzrayim," like *Rashi*'s second explanation. The Mitzrim recognized at the Yam Suf that Hashem, who is striking them there, was the same Hashem who had been fighting against them on behalf of Yisrael the entire time. He was the one who had sent all the *makkos* and performed all the miracles in the land of Mitzrayim, and He was also fighting now in Mitzrayim.

There is a pressing question on both Onkelos's and *Rashi's* second explanation, that "במצרים" is literal. The Mitzrim said that Hashem is smiting the land of Mitzrayim, referring to the Mitzrim who were left in Mitzrayim. How could the Mitzrim by the Yam Suf have possibly known what was happening to those who were in Mitzrayim? The *Nefesh HaGer* answers in the name of the *Mechilta*: "Rabbi Yosi said, Hashem performed a miracle and they were able to see each other." The Mitzrim by the Yam saw the Mitzrim in the land of Mitzrayim getting smitten!

Others have the text "*da'avad*—that battled," past tense, which enables the *pasuk* to be understood simply: The Mitzrim said, "Let us flee from before [because of] Yisrael since this is the might of Hashem that battled for them in Mitzrayim." The Mitzrim understood that it is Hashem who sent the *makkos* and was battling against them the entire time.

It states, "*U'Mitzrayim nasim likraso.*" *Rashi* explains that the Mitzrim were in turmoil and ran toward the water. The *Nefesh HaGer* says that Onkelos translates "*likraso*" as "*l'kadamuseih*—before [toward] it." He explains that Onkelos translates "*l'kadamuseih*" when the word refers to "from before people," and "*la'kavel*" when opposite an inanimate object, as he translates, "ויתן איש בתרו לקראת רעהו—And he placed the half-pieces, a half piece opposite [*la'kavel*] its friend." This implies that Onkelos does not mean that the Mitzrim ran toward the water, which is inanimate, but rather, as the *Mechilta* explains, wherever the Mitzrim fled, the water flowed opposite the Mitzrim to block them from escaping!

The *Ramban* says that Hashem caused the eastern wind to blow and look as though the wind split the sea, so the Mitzrim would continue to chase them. Although winds don't split seas, they did not pay attention to this and entered into the sea because of their great desire to do bad. They did not remember that Hashem fought against them in Mitzrayim, despite saying this themselves a moment before.

The Mitzrim saw that the Yam Suf was split before B'nei Yisrael and they were walking inside the sea on dry land. How could the Mitzrim have the audacity to do bad? This is indeed absurd! The *Ramban* says that there is no greater wonder than this from all of Hashem's wonders! Hashem strengthened their hearts to make them do something foolish in order to punish them for their wickedness.

May we learn from these amazing miracles at the Yam Suf to recognize Hashem and accept Him as King!

## DOES "GA'OH GA'AH" MEAN "LOFTINESS AND GREATNESS" OR "HAUGHTINESS"?

### אָשִׁירָה לַה' כִּי גָאֹה גָּאָה סוּס וְרֹכְבוֹ רָמָה בַיָּם (טו, א)

נְשַׁבַּח וְנוֹדֵי קֳדָם יְיָ אֲרֵי אִתְגָּאֵי עַל גֵּיוָתָנַיָּא וְגֵיאוּתָא
דִּילֵיהּ הִיא סוּסְיָא וְרָכְבֵיהּ רְמָא בְּיַמָּא

*We shall praise and we shall thank before Hashem, since He is haughty [exalted] over the haughty ones and the haughtiness [pride] belongs to Him; the horse and its rider He threw into the sea.*

### שִׁירוּ לַה' כִּי גָאֹה גָּאָה סוּס וְרֹכְבוֹ רָמָה בַיָּם (טו, כא)

שַׁבַּחוּ וְאוֹדוּ קֳדָם יְיָ אֲרֵי אִתְגָּאֵי עַל גֵּיוָתָנַיָּא וְגֵיאוּתָא
דִּילֵיהּ הִיא סוּסְיָא וְרָכְבֵיהּ רְמָא בְּיַמָּא

*Praise and thank before Hashem since He is haughty [exalted] over the haughty ones and the haughtiness [pride] belongs to Him; the horse and its rider He threw into the sea.*

The *pasuk* states, "אשירה לה' כי גאה גאה סוס ורכבו רמה בים." Rav Yerucham[10] asks: Out of all descriptions of praise, why is *"ga'oh ga'ah"* specifically used to describe Hashem? What does this phrase mean? And why are the horse and its rider mentioned together with it?

*Rashi* explains that even if one were to sing all existing songs to thank Hashem and praise Him with all the praises, there is always more to add, as Hashem is unlimited. This is unlike a king of flesh and blood who doesn't even have all the attributes mentioned when he is praised, since he is imperfect. The *Ramban* adds that *Rashi* understands *"ga'oh ga'ah"* means "loftiness and greatness." The *pasuk* continues: "The horse and its rider were thrown into the sea." *Rashi* explains that the horse and rider were tied together and thrown into the sea. The water raised them up to the top of the sea and then tossed them down to the bottom, as if stirring a pot, while keeping them together. Hashem showed His loftiness and greatness by performing this miracle.

Onkelos translates "אשירה לה' כי גאה גאה" differently: "We shall praise and we shall thank before Hashem; He is haughty [exalted] over the haughty ones and the haughtiness [pride] belongs to Him." The *Ramban* explains that Onkelos understands *"ga'oh ga'ah"* literally, as "haughtiness": He is haughty over everyone and over the horse and its rider. The horse is haughty because it goes out to war, and a person is haughty because he rides on top of the horse. My good friend Rabbi Chaim Koehler added from *Rashi*[11] that the Mitzrim were known to be haughty. The *pasuk* emphasizes that Hashem is haughty [exalted] over all people and animals. The *Ramban*[12] says that Hashem considers haughtiness a disgraceful and repulsive *middah* even for a king, for whom it is fitting to raise himself up to greatness, and certainly for anyone else for whom it is not fitting. Greatness and exaltedness are fitting for Hashem alone, and praise is appropriate for Him alone and no one else.

It states, "שירו לה' כי גאה גאה סוס ורכבו רמה בים," which Onkelos translates as, "Praise and thank before Hashem, since He is haughty [exalted] over the haughty ones and the haughtiness [pride] belongs to Him; the horse and its rider He threw into the sea." The Gemara[13] teaches: "Reish Lakish said, sing to the one who is haughty over the haughty. The lion is the king over wild animals, the ox over domestic animals, the eagle over birds, and a person is haughty over all these beings. Hashem is haughty

---

11   בראשית מ, כג
12   דברים יז, כ
13   חגיגה יג:

over all of them and over the entire world." *Rashi* says that these four, the lion, ox, eagle, and person, are the four unique beings who are part of Hashem's chariot, and Hashem is above them. The *Maharsha* explains that a horse has a haughty spirit; it runs freely and can do as it wants. The rider, too, is raised up and feels superior, confident that he will be successful in war. Hashem is above and beyond everyone and everything, including the horse and rider, and He threw them both into the sea.

The *Shemos Rabbah*[14] writes that everyone is haughty over each other and Hashem is haughty over them, as it states, *"Ki ga'oh ga'ah."* The *Nesinah LaGer* explains that this is as we daven,[15] "הגאוה והגדולה לחי עולמים—The haughtiness and the greatness is to Him for eternity." The *Ein Yaakov* says that Hashem is definitely not haughty; He is humble, as He demonstrated when He rested His Shechinah on the *s'neh*. Still, with the crooked He acts crooked, and with the straight, He acts straight. Rav Yerucham explains differently: Hashem acts haughty so that people shouldn't be haughty and arrogant in the world. They should know that there is the kingship of Hashem over them. He is above and beyond all. To Him alone is *gaavah* appropriate. This is the meaning of "ה' מלך גאות לבש": the cloak of *gaavah* is Hashem's, not anyone else's, even in the slightest.

The *Tanya*[16] explains that Hashem keeps everyone alive and existing, since we draw sustenance from Him by nullifying ourselves to Him. A haughty person, however, sees himself as separate from Hashem. This person imagines that he stands independently, as though he has his own source of sustenance, whether it be authority, greatness, or any special attribute. This is incorrect, of course; everything comes from Hashem. Therefore, only Hashem can be truly haughty, since He is complete, and He is the source and essence of everything.

---

14 פ' כג, יג

15 בהקפות ש"ת ובפסוקי דזמרה שבת שחרית נוסח ספרד

16 לקוטי אמרים פכ"ב

May we recognize Hashem's greatness and haughtiness, and may we humble ourselves before Him!

## HOW DID THE WATERS ACT WISELY?

וּבְרוּחַ אַפֶּיךָ נֶעֶרְמוּ מַיִם נִצְּבוּ כְמוֹ נֵד נֹזְלִים (טו, ח)

וּבְמֵימַר פֻּמָּךְ חֲכִימוּ מַיָּא קָמוּ כְּשׁוּר אָזְלַיָּא

*And with the saying [word] of Your mouth, the water became wise; flowing water stood like a wall.*

The *pasuk* states, "וברוח אפיך נערמו מים נצבו כמו נד נוזלים." *Rashi* explains, "With the wind of Your nostrils—as though to say, the water bundled together, flowing water stood up like a wall." The word "נערמו" is from the *lashon* "ערימה—a pile of wheat"; just as wheat is collected together, piled up, and made into a bundle, so too, the water collected together and stood up. The proof is as the *pasuk* continues, "נצבו כמו נד—they stood up like a wall."

Onkelos translates differently: "And with the saying [word] of Your mouth, the water became wise; flowing water stood like a wall." He translates "נערמו" as "חכימו—they became wise," from the *lashon* "ערמימות—sly and cunning." This is difficult: what is the connection between the water becoming smart and the water standing up? The *Vilna Gaon*[17] explains that Hashem blew a *ruach* of *nishmas chaim* into Adam that made him into a *nefesh chayah*, a living being, and gave him wisdom. So too, Hashem blew a *ruach* into the water which gave it wisdom. Rav Yonason David adds that the Gemara[18] teaches that in the fourth hour of Adam's development, Hashem blew into him a *neshamah*, and in the fifth hour, Adam stood up. It took time for the development to materialize so that Adam could use the wisdom. The same happened with the water: first Hashem blew in a *ruach*, and afterwards, it developed to

17   פנינים משלחן הגר"א
18   סנהדרין לח:

use its wisdom to stand up. There is a pressing question: what was the function of the wisdom with which the water was implanted?

The *Maharsha*[19] answers that the wisdom enabled the water to change its nature. It stood up to make space for B'nei Yisrael to pass through and to enable the bottom of the sea to become dry land for B'nei Yisrael to walk on. Also, the water continued to remain standing in its place until the Mitzrim entered, in order to trick the Mitzrim into thinking that there was dry land to walk on. The *Nefesh HaGer* adds that the water provided a very wide area to walk through. Therefore, the Mitzrim would naturally continue chasing after B'nei Yisrael without being aware of any danger. This way, the water would be able to return to itself as a sea with the Mitzrim inside and easily drown them. The Gemara writes that the Mitzrim said, "*Havah nischakmah lo*—Let us use the water to outsmart Him"; since Hashem promised that He wouldn't bring a *mabul*, we will throw the boys into the water and we will be safe. Hashem made the water outsmart the Mitzrim *middah k'neged middah*: the water remained standing until the Mitzrim entered in order to punish them!

The *Chizkuni* explains Onkelos that the water "became wise" by running after the Mitzrim to drown them. This is as it states in *Parashas Eikev*, "אשר הציף את מי ים סוף על פניהם ברדפם אחריכם"—That Hashem floated the water upon them, when they chased after you," in order to drown and destroy them. Similarly, the *Mechilta* teaches, "You gave wisdom to the water, which fought against the Mitzrim by giving them all different types of punishments." The *Nefesh HaGer* explains that the water became wise by chasing after those trying to run away from the Yam Suf. It stood up like a wall and blocked them from escaping, and drowned them. The *Daas Zekeinim MiBaalei HaTosafos* explains that the water became wise to sing *shirah*![20]

May we learn from the wondrous miracles of *k'rias Yam Suf* that Hashem is King over the entire creation!

---

19    מנחות נג.

20    ע"ע במלבי"ם

# WHAT DID HASHEM TEACH MOSHE ABOUT THE WOOD?

וַיִּצְעַק אֶל ה' וַיּוֹרֵהוּ ה' עֵץ וַיַּשְׁלֵךְ אֶל הַמַּיִם וַיִּמְתְּקוּ הַמָּיִם (טו, כה)

וְצַלִּי קֳדָם יְיָ וְאַלְפֵיהּ יְיָ אָעָא וּרְמָא לְמַיָּא וּבְסִימוּ מַיָּא

*And he davened before [to] Hashem, and Hashem taught him about*
*a wood, and he threw it into the water and made the water sweet.*

The *pesukim* mention that the nation came to Marah and they weren't able to drink the water because it was bitter. They complained against Moshe, saying, "What shall we drink?" The following *pasuk* states, "ויצעק אל ה' ויורהו ה' עץ וישלך אל המים וימתקו המים—And he screamed to Hashem and Hashem showed him wood, and he threw it into the water and the water became sweet." Onkelos translates "ויצעק אל ה' ויורהו ה' עץ..." as, "And he davened to Hashem, and Hashem taught him about a wood, and he threw it into the water and made the water sweet." Onkelos does not translate "*va'yoreihu*" as "*v'achz'yeih*—and He showed him the wood," which is the literal translation[21] of "ויראהו" with an א. Rather, he translates as "*v'alfeih*—and He taught him." Onkelos understood "ויורהו" to be from the *lashon* "הוראה—teaching," as it states,[22] "יורך," which Onkelos translates as "ילפנך—will teach you." Similarly, the *Ramban* says that the word "ויורהו" is written when the *pasuk* refers to teaching. What did Hashem teach Moshe about the wood?

The *Ramban* answers that Hashem taught Moshe that this specific wood has a special *segulah* that it was able to make the water sweet naturally. He also teaches in the name of *Rabboseinu* that the stick was bitter, yet it sweetened the water. It was a miracle within a miracle. The bitter stick was able to make bitter water become sweet! This was similar to the miracle that happened at the time of the prophet Elisha. There was bad water that caused illnesses and death. Hashem told Elisha to take salt and put it in the place where the water comes out to cure the water.

21  דברים לה, א
22  שם יז, יא

The *Midrash Tanchuma*[23] writes that Moshe thought Hashem told him to throw honey into the water to sweeten the bitter water. However, it specifically does not state "ויראהו—and He showed him," but "ויורהו—and He taught him." Hashem taught Moshe that His ways are not like that of a person; a person sweetens the bitter with something sweet, whereas Hashem sweetens the bitter with something bitter. He heals with that which He smites. Hashem performed a miracle within a miracle, causing bitter wood to sweeten bitter water.

My grandfather, Rav Yosef Portowicz, offered another explanation: After the stick was thrown in, the water became even more bitter than before. They realized that they could have managed with the previous bitter water, only they decided not to. Hashem taught them that the water was really fine, relatively sweet, and it wasn't so bad before. It could have been worse and tasted more bitter.

The *Mesillas Yesharim*[24] says that a poor person is indebted to Hashem because even in his poverty, he still has *parnassah*; Hashem doesn't leave him to die of hunger. A sick person is also indebted to Hashem because Hashem keeps him alive, even though he is sick. One is always obligated to recognize the good things that Hashem does for him. Indeed, things could be worse; the fact that they are not is because Hashem is being kind to him.

It states in *Tehillim*:[25] "שבענו בבקר חסדך ונרננה ונשמחה בכל ימינו." *Rashi* explains that "*sab'einu va'boker chasdecha*" refers to the day of redemption, which is the "*boker*" to the "nights" of affliction. "ונרננה ונשמחה בכל ימינו" means that "one will recognize that throughout all our days, that which Hashem did was for our good, even the *tzaros*." When we have different types of experiences in life, we can be fooled into thinking that what we see and perceive is the entire picture. However, if we connect the dots, we may actually notice the sequence of events leading toward the outcome that is best for us.

May we merit to notice Hashem's good every day!

---

23  כד
24  פ"ח
25  צ, יד

## THE MIRACULOUS CREATION
## OF THE MAHN AND ITS DETERIORATION

# וּבֹקֶר וּרְאִיתֶם אֶת כְּבוֹד ה' בְּשָׁמְעוֹ אֶת תְּלֻנֹּתֵיכֶם עַל ה' (טז, ז)

וּבְצַפְרָא וְתִחְזוֹן יָת יְקָרָא דַיְיָ בְּדִשְׁמִיעָן קֳדָמוֹהִי תֻּרְעֲמָתְכוֹן עַל יְיָ

*And in the morning, you will see the honor of Hashem, when*
*your complaints against Hashem will be heard before Him.*

# וְלֹא שָׁמְעוּ אֶל מֹשֶׁה וַיּוֹתִרוּ אֲנָשִׁים מִמֶּנּוּ
# עַד בֹּקֶר וַיָּרֻם תּוֹלָעִים וַיִּבְאַשׁ (טז, כ)

וְלָא קַבִּילוּ מִן מֹשֶׁה וְאַשְׁאָרוּ גֻּבְרַיָּא מִנֵּהּ עַד צַפְרָא וּרְחֵישׁ רִחְשָׁא וּסְרִי

*And they did not accept from [listen to] Moshe, and*
*the men retained from it until the morning, and*
*movers moved [it bred worms] and it spoiled.*

# וְחַם הַשֶּׁמֶשׁ וְנָמָס (טז, כא)

וּמָא דְמִשְׁתְּאַר מִנֵּהּ עַל אַפֵּי חַקְלָא כַּד חֲמָא עֲלוֹהִי שִׁמְשָׁא פָּשַׁר

*And what remained from it upon the surface of the*
*field, when the sun warmed upon it, it melted.*

The *pasuk* states, "ובקר וראיתם את כבוד ה' בשמעו את תלונותיכם על ה'." *Rashi* explains, "You asked for bread, which is for a proper purpose; therefore, when it descends in the morning you will see the honor of the shine of His face. He will bring it down in a loving way, with time to prepare it, and with a cover of dew on top and on bottom as if placed in a container." The word "*kavod*—honor" in the *pasuk* means "in an honorable and loving way."

Onkelos translates these words as, "And in the morning, you will see the honor of Hashem, when your complaints against Hashem will be heard before Him." The *Ramban* notes that Onkelos translates "*u'r'isem*" literally: "*v'sichzon*—and you will see" the honor of Hashem, as opposed to "*v'isg'li*—and the honor of Hashem was revealed." The *Nefesh HaGer* says that Onkelos generally changes any mention of something physical about Hashem in order to distance any possible mistake. The *Ramban* says that here Onkelos translates literally, since it is expressing the great wonder of the *mahn*. B'nei Yisrael saw the new phenomenon of *mahn*, which was a manifestation of seeing the honor of Hashem.

It states about the *mahn*, "ולא שמעו אל משה ויותירו אנשים ממנו עד בקר," which Onkelos translates as, "And they did not accept from [listen to] Moshe, and the men retained from it until the morning." Moshe commanded them not to leave over *mahn* until the next day, and they did not listen to his request. What happened to this remaining *mahn*? The *pasuk* continues, "*Va'yarum tola'im va'yiv'ash*." *Rashi* explains that "*va'yarum tola'im*" comes from the word "*rimah*—worms*," as though it states "*v'hisliu tola'im*[26]—and it became infested with worms." Normally, things first spoil and then worms come. Therefore, the order of the *pasuk* needs to be switched to, "*Va'yiv'ash va'yarum tola'im*—And it spoiled, and worms came and made it wormy."

Onkelos translates "*va'yarum tola'im va'yiv'ash*" as "and movers moved [*u'rcheish richsha*], and it spoiled." He does not translate "*tola'im*" with the *lashon* "*tolaas*—worm*," as he translates[27] "התלעת" in *Parashas Ki Savo* as "תולעתא." Rather, he translates like שרץ and רמש by *sheratzim*, with the *lashon* "*richsha*." The *Ramban* explains that "שרץ" is comprised of "רץ-ש—those which run," as they move around. Also, "רמש" refers to *sheratzim* and animals that are "רומש—roam around." Onkelos translates "*sheretz*" as "*richsha*," which means things that move around. The *mahn* became infested with creeping crawlers and it stank. According to Onkelos, who translates as the order of the *pasuk*, why were there insects before it spoiled?

The *Ramban* answers that the existence of the *mahn* was miraculous, and it was not limited to nature's standard rules. The *mahn* didn't spoil at first, only after the worms got to it. It spoiled miraculously. Alternatively, Onkelos can be explained as the *Ramban*, in the name of the *Shemos Rabbah*, who asks: is there such a thing that first has worms

---

26  ש"חג

27  דברים כח, לט

and then spoils? Rather, Hashem wanted to show the actions of Dasan and Aviram to people, so He stopped the *mahn* from smelling in the evening so they wouldn't throw it away and look foolish. The entire night, worms collected together, making rows and rows of worms, and only afterwards did the *mahn* spoil and stink. Clearly, not only the creation of *mahn* was miraculous, but also its spoiling process was miraculous!

It states about the *mahn*, "ונמס וילקטו אתו בבקר בבקר איש כפי אכלו וחם השמש—And they collected it every morning, a person according to its eater, and the sun warmed and melted it." The *Nefesh HaGer* points out that the *pasuk* seems to say that the *mahn* which they collected to eat melted by the sun. This is difficult to understand. Onkelos translates "*v'cham ha'shemesh v'namas,*" as "and what remained from it upon the surface of the field, when the sun warmed upon it, it melted." He adds, "And what remained from it upon the surface of the field" in order to resolve this difficulty. The sun only dissolved the extra *mahn* that had not been collected. The *Hakesav V'Hakabbalah* adds that once they collected the *mahn*, not only did the sun not melt it, but it solidified and became so hard that even fire would not be able to affect it. It was eaten as is and tasted like a honey wafer. The *Nefesh HaGer* explains in *Rashi*'s name that what remained in the field after everyone collected their *mahn* immediately[28] melted and became streams, and the gazelles and deer drank from it. The non-Jewish nations would trap these animals, taste the *mahn*, and they would know the praise of Yisrael. The *mahn* was so special that even the animals and non-Jewish nations tried to taste it!

May we learn from the miracles of the *mahn* that Hashem sustains each and every person!

# Yisro

## HOW DID HASHEM PUNISH THE MITZRIM MIDDAH K'NEGED MIDDAH?

עַתָּה יָדַעְתִּי כִּי גָדוֹל ה' מִכָּל הָאֱלֹקִים כִּי
בַדָּבָר אֲשֶׁר זָדוּ עֲלֵיהֶם (יח, יא)

כְּעַן יָדַעְנָא אֲרֵי רַב יְיָ וְלֵית אֱלָהּ בַּר מִנֵּהּ אֲרֵי בְּפִתְגָמָא
דְּחַשִׁיבוּ מִצְרָאֵי לְמְדָן יָת יִשְׂרָאֵל בֵּיהּ דָּנְנוּן

*Now I know that Hashem is great and that there is no
god besides Him, since with the thing that the Mitzrim
thought to judge Yisrael, with it they were judged.*

The *pasuk* states, "Now I know Hashem is greater than all the other
gods, עליהם זדו אשר בדבר כי." *Rashi* explains that Hashem destroyed the
Mitzrim with the very thing they tried to use to destroy B'nei Yisrael.
The Mitzrim threw the Jewish boys into the water and tried to kill B'nei
Yisrael, and Hashem drowned the Mitzrim in the Yam Suf. *Rashi* quotes
from *Rabboseinu* that the *lashon* of "זדו" is like "נזיד יעקב ויזד—Yaakov
cooked lentils in a pot." In the "pot" that the Mitzrim tried to cook, they
themselves were cooked. Onkelos translates differently: "Since with the
thing that the Mitzrim *thought to judge* Yisrael, with it they were judged."
What does this mean?

The Brisker Rav[1] explains that Onkelos translates "זדו" as "דחשיבו,"
from the *lashon* "מחשבה—thought." In truth, the Mitzrim thought
about doing a lot more bad things, more than they actually did. They
weren't successful in carrying out all their plans. Still, Hashem paid

---

חי' מרן הגרי"ז הלוי החדשות על תנ"ך ואגדה    1

them back not only for the things that they did, but even for the things they thought to do but didn't actually do. *Tosafos* writes that Hashem considers a bad thought of a non-Jew as though he did it. Everyone saw the bad the Mitzrim did to B'nei Yisrael. However, the plans of the Mitzrim were not known to everyone; only those who were part of the planning knew of it. The Gemara says that Pharaoh had three people advising him what to do to B'nei Yisrael: Bilam, Yisro, and Iyov. As one of the advisors, Yisro heard all the different plots and plans of what to do to B'nei Yisrael. The *pesukim* state that Moshe told Yisro all the miracles and wonders that Hashem did for B'nei Yisrael. Afterwards, it states, "עתה ידעתי כי גדול ה' מכל האלקים," which Onkelos translates as, "Now I know that Hashem is great, and there is no god besides Him." The reason is, "כי בדבר אשר זדו עליהם," which Onkelos translates as "since with the thing that the Mitzrim thought to judge Yisrael, with it they were judged." The Brisker Rav says that Hashem punished the Mitzrim *middah k'neged middah* even for the things which they plotted to do to B'nei Yisrael but didn't carry out. Only Yisro, as an adviser to Pharaoh, was able to recognize the *middah k'neged middah* of even the things that the Mitzrim only thought to do.

The Brisker Rav writes that Rav Itzele from Volozhin was asked by a Russian officer: It states "הללו את ה' כל גוים שבחוהו כל האומים כי גבר עלינו חסדו—All the non-Jews sing praise to Hashem, all the nations praise Him because His kindness was overpowering on our behalf." Why should non-Jews need to sing praise to Hashem for performing kindness with B'nei Yisrael? Rav Itzele answered, B'nei Yisrael did not know of the plans, in Petersburg and other places, to do bad to them, which Hashem nullified. Only the non-Jews know of their plans, so only they recognize the kindness Hashem performed for B'nei Yisrael by preventing these plans from actualizing. Therefore, they need to praise Hashem even more than we do!

May we recognize that Hashem is so great that He even punishes for the thoughts against B'nei Yisrael!

## DOES "LI'DROSH" MEAN "TO DAVEN" OR "SEEK TEACHING"? WHAT WAS MOSHE'S ROLE "MUL HA'ELOKIM"?

כִּי יָבֹא אֵלַי הָעָם לִדְרֹשׁ אֱלֹקִים (יח, טו)

אֲרֵי אָתַן לְוָתִי עַמָּא לְמִתְבַּע אֻלְפָן מִן קֳדָם יְיָ

*Since the nation is coming next to me to request teaching from before Hashem.*

כִּי יִהְיֶה לָהֶם דָּבָר בָּא אֵלַי וְשָׁפַטְתִּי בֵּין אִישׁ וּבֵין רֵעֵהוּ (יח, טז)

כַּד הֲוֵי לְהוֹן דִּינָא אָתַן לְוָתִי וְדָאֵינְנָא בֵּין גַּבְרָא וּבֵין חַבְרֵיהּ

*When they would have judgment, they would come next to me, and I would judge between a man and his fellow.*

לֹא טוֹב הַדָּבָר אֲשֶׁר אַתָּה עֹשֶׂה (יח, יז)

לָא תָקֵין פִּתְגָמָא דְּאַתְּ עָבֵיד

*The thing that you are doing is not fixed [proper].*

עַתָּה שְׁמַע בְּקֹלִי אִיעָצְךָ וִיהִי אֱלֹקִים עִמָּךְ הֱיֵה אַתָּה לָעָם מוּל הָאֱלֹקִים וְהֵבֵאתָ אַתָּה אֶת הַדְּבָרִים אֶל הָאֱלֹקִים (יח, יט)

כְּעַן קַבֵּיל מִנִּי אַמְלְכִנָּךְ וִיהֵי מֵימְרָא דַּיְיָ בְּסַעֲדָךְ הֱוֵי אַתְּ לְעַמָּא תָבַע אֻלְפָן מִן קֳדָם יְיָ וּתְהֵי מַיְתֵי אַתְּ יָת פִּתְגָמַיָּא לִקְדָם יְיָ

*Now, accept from me, I will advise you, and the saying [word] of Hashem will assist you. You request teaching from before Hashem for the nation and you shall bring the things before Hashem.*

The *pasuk* states that Yisro asked Moshe, "Why are you sitting and the entire nation is standing from morning until evening?" Moshe responded, "כי יבא אלי העם לדרש אלקים," which Onkelos translates as "since the nation is coming next to me to request teaching from before Hashem." The *Nesinah LaGer* points out that Onkelos translates "*yavo*," which is singular and future tense, as plural, since it refers to the nation.

Also, he translates in present tense, as *Rashi* explains: people would continuously come to Moshe to ask teaching from Hashem.

The *Ramban* explains the *lashon* "*d'rishah*" differently: it refers to davening. The nation would come to Moshe to request from him to daven for someone sick or for a person's success. Similarly, it states by Rivkah, "ותלך לדרש את ה'," which the *Ramban* explains means that she went to the great people to ask them to daven for her difficult pregnancy. There as well, Onkelos and *Rashi* explain that "*li'drosh*" refers to seeking teaching about the difficult pregnancy.

The following *pasuk* states, "כי יהיה להם דבר בא אלי ושפטתי בין איש ובין רעהו," which Onkelos translates as, "When they would have judgment [*dina*], they would come next to me, and I would judge between a man and his fellow." He translates "*ki*" as "*kad*—when," not "*arei*," which the *Chizkuni*[2] explains can mean "if/when," "maybe," "rather," or "because." The *Nefesh HaGer* says that "*kad*" reflects a time; here, it means when the situation arises that people need to request teaching. The *Nefesh HaGer* says that Onkelos translates "דבר" in different ways: "עסק—involvement"; "מדעם—nothing"; "פתגם—thing"; "עצת—advice"; or "פלוגתא—argument," based on the intent. Here, "דבר" refers to the discussion of conflict and strife between people, so Onkelos translates as "judgment." People who had arguments would come to Moshe to clarify who is innocent and who is guilty.

Yisro tells Moshe, "לא טוב הדבר אשר אתה עשה," which Onkelos translates as, "The thing that you are doing is not fixed [proper] [*takein*]." The *Ramban*[3] explains that Onkelos translates "*tov*" as "*takein*," which means the setup is not a good plan of order. Yisro advises Moshe, "עתה שמע בקלי איעצך ויהי אלקים עמך היה אתה לעם מול האלקים והבאת אתה את הדברים אל האלקים," which Onkelos translates as, "Now, accept from me, I will advise you, and the saying [word] of Hashem will assist you. You request teaching from before Hashem for the nation and you shall bring the things before Hashem." Yisro suggests that Moshe have other great people help

---

2   בראשית יח, טו

3   בראשית א, לא

him respond to the people. The *Nefesh HaGer* points out that Onkelos does not translate "מול" literally, as "קבל—opposite" or "קדם—before or opposite," but, rather, "Request teaching from before Hashem." He explains that it is not possible to say "opposite G-d," since Hashem fills the entire world, rather, as *Rashi* explains, it must mean to be a messenger and spokesman between Yisrael and Hashem to ask Him the law. The *Hakesav V'Hakabbalah* adds that Onkelos understands that "מול" is from the *lashon* "מלל—to speak," to be a middleman between Hashem and Yisrael.

*Rashi* explains the rest of the *pasuk* as, "I will advise you, ויהי אלקים עמך—and go ask Hashem whether the advice I give is fitting to be followed." Onkelos translates "עתה שמע בקולי איעצך" as, "Now accept from me, I will advise you, ויהי אלקים עמך—and the saying [word] of Hashem will be at your support." The *Me'at Tzari* explains Onkelos with the *Ibn Ezra*: Yisro says, If you take my advice, then Hashem will assist you. It does not mean to check with Hashem, as *Rashi* explained. He only checks later on, where it states, "If you will do this, וצוך אלקים ויכלת עמוד—and G-d will command you, then you will be able to stand" and be successful.

Just as Moshe was the middleman between Hashem and Yisrael, the Gedolei Hador have the same role. An *avreich* came before Rav Chaim Kanievsky for a berachah for his daughter, whose name was Adinah. He said, "Change her name to something else," as it was Lavan's wife's name. Another *avreich* entered and asked for a berachah for his wife—also named Adinah. To him, Rav Chaim said, "*Berachah v'hatzlachah.*" His grandsons asked him, "Isn't the name no good?" He answered, "Adinah was the mother of Leah and Rachel." One grandson asked, "Why by the other *avreich* did the Rav say to change her name, but this *avreich* not?" He responded, "What Hashem puts into my mouth, I say." We see that Gedolim of the generation bring the word of Hashem to each of us, similar to the *Urim V'Tumim* that relayed Hashem's messages to us.

May we merit to have Gedolim who bring the *d'var Hashem* to the *tzibbur*!

# DID HASHEM TAKE US OUT FROM
# THE "HOUSE OF SLAVES" OR "SLAVERY"?

## מִבֵּית עֲבָדִים (כ, ב)

מִבֵּית עַבְדּוּתָא

*From a place of bondage.*

In both versions of the *Aseres Hadibros*, it states,[4] "אנכי ה' אלקיך אשר
הוצאתיך מארץ מצרים מבית עבדים—I am Hashem, your G-d, who took you
out from Mitzrayim, from a place of slaves." In *Parashas Va'eschanan*, it
states,[5] "השמר לך פן תשכח את ה' אשר הוציאך מארץ מצרים מבית עבדים—Guard
yourself, lest you will forget Hashem who took you out from the
land of Mitzrayim, from a place of slaves." Also, it states,[6] "ויפדך מבית
עבדים—And He redeemed you from a place of slaves." Rabbeinu Bachya
explains that the word "*avadim*" means slaves, in plural. Hashem took
us out from a place of slaves, which implies that we were slaves to the
Mitzrim, who were themselves slaves.

In each of the *pesukim* above, Onkelos translates the words "מבית עבדים"
as "from a place of *bondage* [*avdusa*]," in singular. Why does Onkelos
change from the literal translation, "from a place of slaves," to "from
a place of bondage"?

*Rashi*[7] answers that Onkelos means from the place where you were
slaves. The *Maharal* explains that "מבית עבדים" does not mean "from the
house of slaves," which would mean you were slaves to the Mitzrim who
were the slaves of Pharaoh. This is incorrect; you were not slaves to other
slaves, but rather you were slaves to Pharaoh, the king of Mitzrayim.
Rabbi Hartman adds that this is as *Rashi* explains, מבית עבדים, you were
slaves to Pharaoh, as it states "ויפדך מבית עבדים מיד פרעה מלך מצרים—And

| | |
|---|---|
| דברים ה,ו | 4 |
| שם ו,יב | 5 |
| שם ז,ח | 6 |
| שם ו,יב | 7 |

He redeemed you from the hand of Pharaoh, the king of Mitzrayim." This teaches that you were slaves to a king, not slaves to slaves.

The *Yein Hatov* says that Onkelos translates the words "מבית עבדים" as "from a place of bondage," and does not translate that we were actually slaves, only that we were taken from a place of slavery. This reflects that Mitzrayim was not a place where Yisrael lived, but, rather, where they physically labored. We were slaves in Mitzrayim and became trained to do difficult labor. Hashem took us out for us to become servants to Him. After learning how to work hard, we are meant to serve Hashem with all our strength.

It states, "אשר הוצאתיך מארץ מצרים—That I took you out from the land of Mitzrayim." *Rashi* explains that because I took you out, it is sufficient to make you subservient to Me. The *Sifsei Chachamim*[8] adds that it does not state, "אשר בראתי שמים וארץ—That I created the heavens and the earth." This implies that the main purpose of being taken out of Mitzrayim from slavery was in order to be slaves to Hashem, to serve Him. The *Ramban* says that because Hashem took you out, therefore, you are obligated to be an *eved* and serve Him, and in return, Hashem will be a G-d for you.

In *Parashas Tzav*, it states,[9] "אש תמיד תוקד על המזבח לא תכבה—Burn a fire constantly on the *Mizbeiach*; do not extinguish." The *Sefer Hachinuch*[10] explains that there is a mitzvah to place wood on the *Mizbeiach* in the morning and evening. The Gemara teaches that although there was a fire which descended from Heaven onto the *Mizbeiach*, there is still a mitzvah to provide wood for the fire. The *Sefer Hachinuch* explains that it is known that when Hashem performs great miracles for people, He does so in a hidden fashion. Miracles seem to be a part of nature, or close to it. We find this regarding *k'rias Yam Suf*, where it states, "ויולך ה' את הים ברוח קדים עזה כל הלילה וישם את הים לחרבה ויבקעו המים—And Hashem brought a strong eastern wind the entire night, and He made

---

8   כ

9   ויקרא ו,ו

10   מצוה קלב

the sea into dry land, and the water split." Before Hashem split the sea, the wind blew the entire night. Those who are wise understand that Hashem did this to hide His greatness and also because we are lowly. It is the same with the wood on the *Mizbeiach*: although a fire descends from Heaven, we are commanded to put wood on the *Mizbeiach* in order to hide the miracle.

The *D'rashos HaRan*[11] explains differently: Hashem hides miracles in order to preserve a person's *bechirah chofshis* and the need to choose whether he will serve Hashem. Rav Chaim Shmuelevitz[12] adds that if one would see open miracles, there would not be a choice whether to do good or bad. The truth would be clear as day to choose good without needing to decide. Imagine seeing a sea split without any reason; one would be impressed for quite a while. Hashem hides miracles because He wants us to choose to recognize that they come from Him. We are meant to serve Hashem by working on clarifying the truth.

The Gemara writes that an angel teaches a fetus the entire Torah and then slaps him on his mouth so that he forgets the Torah that he learned. Why teach the fetus so much if he's just going to forget it? Rabbeinu Bachya[13] answers that it's in order to provide him an opportunity to toil and receive reward. Rav Chaim adds that a person is meant to work hard and bring out his own knowledge in Torah. This is why Chazal say, "*Yagata u'matzasa taamin*—If you toil and achieve, believe; *lo yagata u'matzasa, al taamin*—if you did not toil and achieve, do not believe." We are meant to toil to understand Hashem's Torah and to serve Him.

May we work to recognize Hashem's miracles and serve Him with all our strength!

---

11   דרוש יא

12   מאמר קב

13   ויקרא יח, כט

## DOES "אֱלֹהִים אֲחֵרִים עַל פָּנָי" REFER TO "TIME," "PLACE," OR "BEINGS"?

### כִּי גָדוֹל ה' מִכָּל הָאֱלֹהִים (יח, יא)

אֲרֵי רַב יְיָ וְלֵית אֱלָהּ בַּר מִנֵּיהּ

*That Hashem is great, and there is no other god besides Him.*

### לֹא יִהְיֶה לְךָ אֱלֹהִים אֲחֵרִים עַל פָּנָי (כ, ג)

לָא יְהֵוֵי לָךְ אֱלָהּ אָחֳרָן בַּר מִנִּי

*There should not be for you another god besides Me.*

The *pasuk* states, "לא יהיה לך אלהים אחרים על פני." What do the words *"acheirim"* and *"al panai"* mean?

*Rashi* explains that *"acheirim"* means that other people made them into gods, but in truth, they are absolutely not Divine. Alternatively, *"acheirim"* means they seem to be *"acheir,"* like a stranger, for when people cry out to them, they do not answer. This is as we say in Hallel, "They have a mouth, but do not speak; they have eyes, but do not see; they have ears, but do not hear; they have a nose, but do not smell; they have hands, but do not feel; they have feet, but do not walk; and they do not talk with their throats." The *Malbim* explains that these *pesukim* hint that idols do not have the attributes of people who speak, or even the attributes of animals, who see, hear, and smell. The idol has a molded mouth, eyes, ears, and nose, but these have no function.

In *Parashas Haazinu*, it states,[14] "יזבחו לשדים לא אלוה," which Onkelos translates as, "They slaughter to demons who do not have any ability or rulership [דבחו לשדין דלית בהון צרוך]." The *Re'em* explains that if idols would have power, Hashem wouldn't be so upset. But since they don't have any power, yet people worship them, Hashem is doubly angered. The *Ramban*[15] explains there is no need, benefit, or advantage to them,

---

14    דברים לב, יז
15    ויקרא יז, ז

since they don't prevent future damage and they don't notify you to be aware of any hardships that may occur.

*Rashi* explains that "*al panai*" means, "Do not make other gods as long as Hashem exists," which is for eternity. The *Nefesh HaGer* quotes from the *Mechilta*: "Just as I exist forever and ever, so too you and your children, and your children's children until the end of all generations, should never worship idolatry." *Rashi*[16] teaches another explanation: do not have other gods in any place in the world, because Hashem is there. The *dibbur* of "*lo yihiyeh*" comes to forbid the acceptance of another god in any time or in any place.

Onkelos translates "לא יהיה לך אלהים אחרים על פני" as, "There should not be for you another god besides Me." The *Hakesav V'Hakabbalah* says that Onkelos translates "*al*" as "besides for," like it states, "*Al kal le-vonasah*—Besides for all the frankincense." The *Ramban* explains that Onkelos comes to include any angels or celestial beings of the heavens, which are called "*elohim*." One should not believe in any of them, or accept them as a god, or say, "You are my god." This *dibbur* comes to forbid accepting any level of authority over himself besides for Hashem. The *Hakesav V'Hakabbalah* adds in the name of the *Yerei'im* that "*Anochi Hashem Elokecha*" teaches that we must make Hashem king over ourselves. From where do we know not to join anything else with Hashem? As it states, "לא יהיה לך אלהים על פני"—Do not join anything else with Me."

Earlier in the parashah, Yisro said, "כי גדול ה' מכל האלהים—That Hashem is greater than all gods." Onkelos translates as "that Hashem is great, and there is no god besides Him." Similarly, in the *shirah*, it states,[17] "מי כמכה באלים ה' מי כמכה נאדר בקדש," which Onkelos translates as, "There is no one besides for You; You are G-d, Hashem; there is no god, only You, adorned with holiness [לית בר מנך את הוא אלהא ה' לית אלה אלא את אדיר בקדשא]." There is absolutely no other god or power other than Hashem. Hashem is not in competition with any gods, as only He has the true power and authority, no one else. Similarly, we say in *Aleinu*, "There is

---

16    שם ה, ז
17    טו, יא

nothing else at all besides for Hashem, as it states in His Torah, 'וידעת היום והשבות אל לבבך כי ה' הוא האלקים בשמים ממעל ועל הארץ מתחת אין עוד'."[18]

The *Nefesh HaGer* says that both *Rashi's* and Onkelos's explanations are hinted at in a *pasuk* which Hashem says about Himself, and which we mention in *Malchuyos* on Rosh Hashanah. It states in the *Navi*, "כה אמר ה'—So says ה' מלך ישראל וגואלו ה' צבא-ות אני ראשון ואני אחרון ומבלעדי אין אלהים Hashem, King of Yisrael and its redeemer, Hashem of myriads: 'I am first, and I am last, and besides Me, there is no god.'" The words "אני ראשון ואני אחרון" reflect *Rashi's* point: as long as I [Hashem] exist, which is forever. The words "ומבלעדי אין אלהים" reflect Onkelos's point: there is absolutely no authority other than Hashem.

The first two *dibros*, אנכי ה' אלקיך and לא יהיה לך אלהים אחרים על פני, were said together as one *dibbur*. This indicates that they are really one idea: Hashem is in charge of everything, and there is no one else besides Him.

May we constantly remember that Hashem is absolutely in charge forever and in every place, and there is no power besides Him!

## DOES "LO SISA" MEAN "A LIE" OR "FOR NAUGHT"?

לֹא תִשָּׂא אֶת שֵׁם ה' אֱלֹקֶיךָ לַשָּׁוְא כִּי לֹא יְנַקֶּה ה'
אֵת אֲשֶׁר יִשָּׂא אֶת שְׁמוֹ לַשָּׁוְא (כ, ז)

לָא תֵימֵי בִּשְׁמָא דַּיְיָ אֱלָהָךְ לְמַגָּנָא אֲרֵי לָא יְזַכֵּי יְיָ יָת דְּיֵימֵי בִּשְׁמֵיהּ לְשִׁקְרָא

*Do not swear in the name of Hashem, your G-d, for*
*naught, since Hashem will not make innocent [won't*
*forgive] the one who swears in His name falsely.*

The *pasuk* states, "לא תשא את שם ה' אלקיך לשוא כי לא ינקה ה' את אשר ישא את שמו לשוא—Do not swear in the name of Hashem, your G-d, for naught, since Hashem won't forgive the one who will swear in His name for naught." This *pasuk* prohibits swearing in vain with the name

---

of Hashem. Once the Torah warns, "לא תשא את שם ה' אלקיך לשוא—Do not swear in the name of Hashem, your G-d, for naught," why does the Torah need to repeat "את אשר ישא את שמו לשוא—the one who swears in His name for naught"?

Onkelos translates this *pasuk* as, "Do not swear in the name of Hashem, your G-d, for naught [*l'magana*], since Hashem will not make innocent [won't forgive] the one who swears in His name falsely [*l'shikra*]." The *Nefesh HaGer* says that Onkelos translates "*la'shav*" with two different meanings in order to answer this question. The first, he translates "for naught"; for example, do not swear that a tree is a tree or that a stone is a stone. Everyone knows this and there is absolutely no point in swearing about it. In the same way, the *Yerushalmi* teaches that one who swears that figs are figs will receive lashes for swearing for naught. Onkelos translates the second "*la'shav*" as "falsely"; do not swear a false oath. For example, do not swear that a pillar of stone is really gold, and certainly do not swear about something false that no one knows about.

The *Nefesh HaGer* asks: Since Onkelos translates the beginning of the *pasuk* as, "Do not swear...for naught," how does the second part follow, "since Hashem will not make innocent the one who swears in His name falsely"? These are two different types of oaths; what is the connection between them?

The *Chizkuni* answers that the *pasuk* warns a person not to accustom himself to swear for naught in the name of Hashem, because doing so will cause him to also swear falsely in the name of Hashem, which Hashem will not excuse. The *Nefesh HaGer* adds in the name of the *Ibn Ezra* that the issue of not swearing for naught is because people think that one who swears for naught did not transgress a bad *aveirah*. However, in truth, it is worse than all the *lavin* which follow it—do not murder, be immoral, or kidnap. One may be afraid to murder, commit immorality, or kidnap at a time that he desires, limiting his potential for sin. However, one who accustoms himself to swear for naught will come to swear numerous oaths in vain in one day. He will say, "I swear," as part of his regular talk. He will become so accustomed that he won't even realize that he swore in vain and did an *aveirah*. If one will rebuke him for swearing in vain, he will deny it by taking another oath that he didn't swear. A person who constantly swears in vain will end up swearing falsely and profane the name of Hashem. Onkelos understands that the *issur* "*lo sisa*" is to not swear for naught, because by doing so, one will end up swearing falsely and profane Hashem's name.

The *Ramban* teaches in the name of *Rabboseinu*: the Torah states that a person should bring a "*korban laHashem*—an offering for Hashem," which teaches that a person should specifically say, "*olah laHashem*— a burnt-sacrifice for Hashem" or, "*chatas laHashem*—a sin-offering for Hashem," and not, "*laHashem olah*—for Hashem a burnt-sacrifice" or, "*laHashem chatas*—for Hashem a sin-offering." The *Malbim* explains that it is improper to mention Hashem's name at first on nothing. Therefore, the type of offering should be mentioned first and only afterwards should he connect Hashem's name to it. The *Sifri* adds: if when a person sanctifies an animal, the Torah warns not to mention Hashem's name for naught, then surely when one speaks, he should be careful not to say Hashem's name for naught!

May we train ourselves to be careful from saying Hashem's name in vain or by way of a lie!

## WHERE AND HOW DOES HASHEM BLESS YISRAEL?

בְּכָל הַמָּקוֹם אֲשֶׁר אַזְכִּיר אֶת שְׁמִי אָבוֹא אֵלֶיךָ וּבֵרַכְתִּיךָ (כ, כא)

בְּכָל אֲתַר (אַתְרָא) דְּאַשְׁרֵי שְׁכִינְתִי לְתַמָּן אֲשַׁלַּח בִּרְכָתִי לָךְ וַאֲבָרְכִנָּךְ

*In every place that I will rest My Shechinah, there I will send My blessing to you, and I will bless you.*

The *pasuk* states, "בכל המקום אשר אזכיר את שמי אבוא אליך וברכתיך." *Rashi* explains, "In any place that I will give you permission to mention My *Shem Ha'meforash*, there I will rest My Shechinah upon you." From here, we derive that permission is only given to mention the *Shem ha'meforash* in the place where Hashem rests His Shechinah. This refers to the *Beis Habechirah*, where the Kohanim can bless the nation with the *Shem*

*Ha'meforash* during *nesias kapayim*. *Tosafos*[19] adds that when Shimon Hatzaddik died, they weren't *zocheh* to *giluy Shechinah*, so the Kohanim stopped blessing Yisrael with the *Shem Ha'meforash*.

Onkelos translates differently: "In every place that I will rest My Shechinah, there I will send My blessing to you, and I will bless you." He translates "אשר אזכיר את שמי" as "that I will rest My Shechinah [*d'ashrei Shechinsi*]," which the *Yein Hatov* explains refers to the Beis Hamikdash. Others have the text "that they mention the Greatness of My name [דיהון מדכרין גבורן שמי]." Similarly, Onkelos translates "*l'shaken shemo*" and "*la'sum es shemo*" as "to rest His Shechinah."

Onkelos translates "*avo eilecha*" as "there I will send My blessing to you [לתמן אשלח ברכתי לך]," not as the literal "I will come to you." Onkelos changes this since Hashem has absolutely no physicality, and He is all over the world.

The *Nefesh HaGer* says that the *pasuk* does not state, "בכל המקום אשר תזכיר את שמי—In any place that you mention My name," rather, "אזכיר את שמי—I shall cause My name to be mentioned." Therefore, Onkelos translates as "in any place that I will rest My Shechinah," which refers to the Beis Hamikdash, where Hashem rests His Shechinah. From there, Hashem will send His blessing to you. So too, the *Mechilta* writes, "In any place that I will be revealed upon you," which is in the *Beis Habechirah*. The *Ravam* teaches in the name of the *Rasag* that "*azkir*" hints that Hashem will choose the place of the Beis Hamikdash and the *korbanos*. This is because it states "אזכיר" with an א', which means "I," not "תזכיר" with a ת', "you." Hashem will cause His name to be mentioned where He will choose. This is as Dovid said, "כי בחר ה' בציון—Hashem chose in Tzion."

The *Nefesh HaGer* says that "*azkir*—I will mention" instead of "*tazkir*—you shall mention" also hints to Hashem mentioning His name. This is as the Mishnah teaches that the Kohen Gadol would mention the *Shem Ha'meforash* on Yom Kippur, and when those gathered heard it "go out ["*yotzei*"] from the mouth of the Kohen Gadol," they would bow. This formulation ["*yotzei*"] indicates that the *shem* would go out by itself, parallel to "*azkir*" meaning that Hashem Himself also mentioned His name.

Onkelos translates "*avo eilecha u'veirachticha*" as "there I will send My blessing to you, and I will bless you." The *Nesinah LaGer* is bothered by the following question: Why does he translate in a doubled way? If Hashem sends His blessing upon a person, of course he will be blessed. Also, "*avo eilecha*" means "I will come to you," which refers to the resting of the Shechinah. How do these words reflect "sending a blessing"? The *Nesinah LaGer* says that he found another *girsa*: "אשרי שכינתי לך—I will rest My Shechinah for you," which he says is correct. The *Beurei Onkelos* explains our *girsa*: "There I will send My blessing to you" means that Hashem will send the Kohanim to bless us. The seemingly repetitious "and I will bless you" hints that blessing will not depend solely on them, rather, "*va'ani avarcheim*—I will bless Yisrael." The *Me'at Tzari* explains differently: the Beis Hamikdash was a place which received *shefa* from Hashem. It was in between Hashem and Yisrael. First, Hashem sent *shefa* to the Beis Hamikdash, and from there He sent it out to each individual.

In *Parashas Naso*, it states,[20] "ושמו את שמי על בני ישראל ואני אברכם," which Onkelos translates as, "And they will place the blessing of My name upon B'nei Yisrael and I will bless them [וישוון ית ברכת שמי על בני ישראל ואנא אבריכנון]." The *Nesinah LaGer* points out that Onkelos translates "*shemi*" as "blessing of My name," unlike in our parashah, where he translates "*shemi*" as "My Shechinah." *Parashas Naso* states the mitzvah for the Kohanim to bless B'nei Yisrael, so Onkelos specifically translates "the blessing of My name," which is the *Shem Ha'meforash*.

The Gemara[21] teaches: Hillel Hazakein said in the name of Hashem,[22] "If you come to My house, I will come to your house; however, if you do not

---

20  במדבר ו,כז

21  סוכה נג.

22  מהרש"ל

come to My house, I will not come to your house," as it states, "בכל המקום
אשר אזכיר את שמי אבא אליך וברכתיך." The *Maharsha* explains: "My house"
refers to the Beis Hamikdash, which is the place that the *Shem Hashem*
is mentioned.

May Hashem rest His Shechinah and have the Kohanim bless us with
the *Shem Ha'meforash*!

# Mishpatim

## WHAT DOES "V'RAPO YERAPEI" TEACH?

רַק שִׁבְתּוֹ יִתֵּן וְרַפֹּא יְרַפֵּא (כא, יט)

לְחוֹד בָּטְלָנֵיהּ יִתֵּן וַאֲגַר אַסְיָא יְשַׁלֵּם

*Only give [pay] for his idleness,*
*and he shall pay the doctor's wages.*

The *pasuk* states, "רק שבתו יתן ורפא ירפא," which Onkelos translates as, "Only give [pay] for his idleness, and he shall pay the doctor's wages." The *Nefesh HaGer* explains that Onkelos understands "and he shall pay the doctor's wages" as a hint to the Gemara which teaches that even if the damager finds a doctor who is a relative and offers to heal the victim for free, it does not exempt the damager from paying for a doctor. A free doctor is worth nothing. Also, if the damager himself is a doctor and says, "I will heal him," the victim can say, "You are like a lion waiting in ambush to hurt me."

He does not have to go to him to be healed; rather, the one who did the damage has to pay for a different doctor. Or, if the one who is damaged says, "I will heal myself," the one who did the damage can respond, "You will be negligent, and you will cause me to have to pay extra," and provide for a doctor.

The *Nefesh HaGer* says that Onkelos also hints to the *Ramban*'s explanation: if the person wants to take the money for being damaged and use it for other things, he can't claim money from the one who did the damage. The one who did the damage has to pay money for a doctor and the money is specifically meant to be given to the doctor to heal; it may not be used for anything else.

The Gemara derives from *"v'rapo yerapei"* that a doctor has permission to heal. The *Ramban*[1] notes that Chazal do not say, "A patient has permission to become healed," but, rather, "A doctor has permission to heal." This reflects that a person was not given permission to be healed. When a person sins, he should take sickness as a sign of punishment and recognize that only after he repents will Hashem heal him. The Torah obligates payments for damaging one another so as not to rely on miracles. During the time that there was prophecy, the *tzaddikim* would not go to a doctor, but rather to a prophet, as Chizkiyah did when he was sick. This is as it states, "גם בחליו לא דרש את ה' כי ברופאים—Also when he was sick, he did not seek Hashem, rather doctors." Included in the rebuke of Asa not seeking Hashem was also that he went to doctors. When there are prophets around, there is no reason for a person to go to doctors. Hashem prefers that a person should go to the prophet to reveal the sins he did that need atonement, do *teshuvah* and then become healed. Instead, though, people became accustomed to visiting doctors. Once a person who is sick goes to the doctor, the doctor does not need to refrain from checking out the patient; he has permission to heal him. Hashem left people's health to follow natural occurrences with the assistance of doctors.

Chazal say that Hashem gave a doctor permission to heal a patient. Rav Meir Simchah Auerbach infers, however, that if a doctor does not know of a cure, he is not permitted to say that there is no hope, as the doctor is simply unaware of any form of action to help. Hashem, who gave the punishment, can take it away, and the patient should leave it up to Hashem to cure him.

May we repent for our sins and rely only on Hashem to merit being healthy and well!

---

1    ויקרא כו, יא

## WHY SHOULD YOU HELP YOUR ENEMY FIRST?

### וְחָדַלְתָּ מֵעֲזֹב לוֹ עָזֹב תַּעֲזֹב עִמּוֹ (כג, ה)

וְתִתְמְנַע מִלְמִשְׁקַל לֵיהּ מִשְׁבָּק תִּשְׁבּוֹק מָא דִּבְלִבָּךְ עֲלוֹהִי וּתְפָרֵיק עִמֵּיהּ

*And will you (you will) hold back from taking for it?(!) Indeed,*
*leave what is against him in your heart and unload with him.*

The *pasuk* states, "When you will see the donkey of your enemy crouching underneath its package, וחדלת מעזוב לו עזוב תעזוב עמו," which Onkelos translates as, "And will you hold back from taking for it? Indeed, leave what is against him in your heart and unload with him." The *Shaarei Aharon* explains that Onkelos translates "*v'chadalta*" as a question, like *Rashi*: "And will you hold back from taking for it?" Alternatively, it could be explained as a statement: "And you will hold back from taking for it!"

The *Nefesh HaGer* points out that *Rashi* explains "*azivah*" as "helping," literally: "from helping it, indeed help with him," whereas Onkelos translates according to the *d'rashah*: "leave what is against him in your heart," which refers to hatred. Onkelos translates "and unload with him" like *Rashi*: *help* him unload the animal from its burden; one should leave the hatred and remember the love.

The *Shaarei Aharon* explains differently: Onkelos translates "*azivah*" with two "leavings": first, indeed *leave* what is against him in your heart [משבק תשבק מא דבלבך עלוהי], which refers to getting rid of the hatred against the person in your heart; and second, *unload* with him [*u's'fareik imeih*], which refers to *removing* the packages from upon the animal, as the *Ibn Ezra* explains. The *Me'at Tzari* adds that Onkelos understands that the entire *pasuk* refers to the mitzvah of *perikah*—unloading.

What does "leave what is against him in your heart" mean, and to what does it refer?

The Gemara[2] writes that if there is a choice to unload a friend's package or to load an enemy's package, it is a mitzvah for the person to load the enemy's package in order to bend his inclination. Although paining an animal is an *issur d'Oraysa*, still, it is more important for one to resolve the hatred with his enemy. The Gemara[3] says that this refers to a case of a Yisrael that you are permitted to hate—and there is even a mitzvah to hate him. For example, you saw someone doing a sin of immorality. You cannot testify in *beis din*, since you are a single witness and two witnesses are required to testify, but you are permitted to hate him. *Tosafos* is bothered: How is it possible to say that one should help his enemy in order to bend his inclination? *Tosafos* answers that this Gemara is not talking about an enemy who transgressed an *issur d'Oraysa*, but a case where he is upset at him for personal disturbances. The *Nimukei Yosef*[4] explains in the name of the *Ramban* that if the person is an enemy because he transgressed a *mitzvah d'Oraysa*, the friend should certainly precede the enemy, as it is appropriate for the sinner to be hated by Hashem and the Jewish People. Rather, an enemy comes first only where the person hates him for personal reasons. In such a case, helping the enemy will change the person's feeling toward him.

The *Bach*[5] suggests another answer from *Tosafos*:[6] the Gemara is indeed talking about an enemy of the Torah, yet he should be helped first. If you will hate him and not help him, he will hate you back, as it states, "כמים הפנים לפנים כן לב האדם לאדם—Just as one face is to another face, so too is the heart of a person to a person." The way that you look and act toward your enemy is how he will reciprocate toward you. If a person expresses feelings of hatred toward another, this will end up causing the situation to result in one of complete hatred from both sides. Therefore, it is appropriate for one to bend his inclination.

On the words "לא החזיק לעד אפו—He does not hold onto His anger forever," the *Tomer Devorah*[7] explains that even if a person continues to sin, Hashem doesn't express His anger. And if Hashem does, it is not forever;

---

3 פסחים קיג:

4 ב"מ בדפי הרי"ף יז:

5 שם ד

6 פסחים שם

7 פ"א הה'

rather, He annuls His anger, even if a person will not return. We find an example of this at the time of Yeravam ben Yo'ash when the people were worshipping idolatry. Hashem had pity, yet they did not repent. The reason Hashem had pity was because of the *middah* of Hashem being slow to anger. Hashem doesn't express His anger to punish, but rather He lessens His anger while the sin continues to exist. Hashem bears both light and stringent *aveiros*, all for the benefit of Klal Yisrael.

The *Tomer Devorah* writes that each person should learn to do the same with his friend. Even if one is permitted to punish someone because he deserves it, he should not intensely punish him. Rather, if he was angered, he should try to calm down and not hold onto his interest of punishing even if it is permitted, just as Hashem does. This is similar to the *pasuk*, "כִּי תִרְאֶה חֲמוֹר שׂנַאֲךָ רֹבֵץ...," which Onkelos translates as, "Indeed, leave what is against him in your heart." This refers to a person that you alone saw doing an *aveirah*. The Torah commands such a person to leave the hatred in his heart against his enemy and help him unload. Hashem wants a person to bend his inclination in order to help his enemy fix his ways and come close to Him. Come close to your enemy with love, and maybe this will cause him to return to Hashem. *Mori Chami* described this as getting rid of one's "emotional baggage" which is stored inside. He is meant to put it aside in order to arouse his feelings—to care about the other person and help him.

May we care about our friends and even our enemies to help them and bring them close to Hashem!

## WILL HASHEM BLESS "YOUR BREAD AND WATER" OR "FOOD AND DRINK," AND WHY?

וַעֲבַדְתֶּם אֵת ה' אֱלֹקֵיכֶם וּבֵרַךְ אֶת לַחְמְךָ וְאֶת
מֵימֶיךָ וַהֲסִרֹתִי מַחֲלָה מִקִּרְבֶּךָ (כג, כה)

וְתִפְלְחוּן קֳדָם יְיָ אֱלָהֲכוֹן וִיבָרֵיךְ יָת מֵיכְלָךְ
וְיָת מִשְׁתְּיָךְ וְאַעְדֵּי מַרְעִין בִּישִׁין מִבֵּינָךְ

*And you shall labor [serve] before Hashem, your*
*G-d, and He will bless your food and your drink, and*
*I will remove bad sicknesses from among you.*

The Gemara[8] writes that any person who doesn't have wine spill in his house as water is not included in having blessing. The *Maharsha* explains that although it is forbidden to waste food, the Gemara means that the person who is not careful with wine as with water, and sometimes, it will come to spill out, he will be blessed. *Rashi* explains that such a person, who does not have wine spilling in his house, did not attain the complete berachah, even if he is wealthy in other areas. The Gemara derives this point from the *pasuk* that states, "ועבדתם את ה' אלקיכם וברך את לחמך ואת מימיך—And you shall serve Hashem, your G-d, and He will bless your bread and your water." Just as bread can be bought with money of *maaser sheini*, so too water can be bought with money of *maaser sheini*. This inference is challenging, though: the Mishnah teaches that everything can be bought with *maaser sheini* money aside from water and salt. The Gemara explains that "water" in this context refers to wine. Because the Torah terms it "water" in the context of the berachah, we see that if wine spills like water in one's house, there will be blessing, and if not, not.

*Tosafos* says that the simple understanding of the *pasuk* is that "*meimecha*" is literal, "your water," as the *pasuk* ends, "*V'hasirosi machalah mi'kirbecha*—And I will remove sickness from among you." By Hashem blessing the water, it will remove sickness, just like it states by the water of Marah, "כל המחלה אשר שמתי במצרים לא אשים עליך כי אני ה' רפאך—All the sicknesses that I placed in Mitzrayim, I won't put on you, since I am Hashem, your healer." We see that Hashem heals through blessing water. The Gemara adds an additional level of meaning: "*meimecha*" refers to wine which spills like water.

My good friend Rabbi Chaim Koehler added that the Gemara[9] asks: "From where do we know that which people say, 'Sixty runs one will

8   עירובין סה.

9   ב"מ קז:

run and he won't reach the person who ate *pas shacharis*?'" And why do the *Rabbanan* say, "Eat early in the summer because of the heat, and in the winter because of the cold"? As it states, "ועבדתם את ה' אלקיכם וברך את לחמך ואת מימיך." The words "ועבדתם את ה' אלקיכם" refer to *k'rias Shema* and *tefillah*. The *Maharsha* explains that davening is called "*avodah she'b'lev*," as it states, "*b'chal levavchem*." The words "וברך את לחמך ואת מימיך" refer to eating bread with salt and a flask of water. After doing this, "*v'hasirosi machalah mi'kirbecha*—I will remove sickness from your nation." The *Maharsha* adds that the letters of "לחמך—your bread" also spell "מחלך—your sickness." By eating bread and drinking water, it will bring good health to be safe from sickness.

The *Maharsha* says that the Gemara is easy to understand according to the way that Onkelos translates "*lachmecha*" and "*meimecha*." Rather than translating literally, he translates "*lachmecha*" as "your food" and "*meimecha*" as "your drink." The *Maharsha* explains that "*lechem*" refers to a meal, as every meal is called "bread," like it states, "*Avad l'chem rav*," since bread is important enough to require its own special *berachah*. The Gemara compares bread to water. Just as bread means a meal, the comparable "water" must mean something more substantial—wine. Wine also requires its own *berachah*, indicating its status. Thus, the Gemara compares bread which is bought with *maaser sheini* money to "water," meaning wine. The Torah calls wine "water" to teach that if wine spills as water, there will be blessing, and if not, not.

Onkelos translates the words, "וברך את לחמך ואת מימיך והסרתי מחלה מקרבך" as, "and He will bless your food and your drink, and I will remove bad sicknesses from among you." This can be explained as two different points: first Hashem will bless your food and drink, and second, He will remove bad sicknesses. Or, as explained by the *Ramban*, it can be understood as one point: because the food, drink, and air will be blessed, therefore, people's bodies will be healthy and they will function properly. There won't be sicknesses, and people will reproduce. The words "and He will bless your food and drink" are the reason why there will not be sicknesses. Hashem will perform wonders in the heavens and on the earth for people who serve Him and follow His will.

May Hashem bless our food and drink, and remove all sicknesses from among us!

## DID MOSHE ALSO SPRINKLE ON THE NATION?

וַיִּשְׁלַח אֶת נַעֲרֵי בְּנֵי יִשְׂרָאֵל וַיַּעֲלוּ עֹלֹת וַיִּזְבְּחוּ
זְבָחִים שְׁלָמִים לַה' פָּרִים (כה, ה)

וּשְׁלַח יָת בְּכוֹרֵי בְּנֵי יִשְׂרָאֵל וְאַסִּיקוּ עֲלָוָן וְנַכִּיסוּ נִכְסַת קֻדְשִׁין קֳדָם יְיָ תּוֹרִין

*And he sent the firstborn B'nei Yisrael and they*
*brought up burnt-sacrifices, and they slaughtered*
*holy-slaughterings [offerings] before Hashem, oxen.*

וַיִּקַּח מֹשֶׁה חֲצִי הַדָּם וַיָּשֶׂם בָּאַגָּנֹת
וַחֲצִי הַדָּם זָרַק עַל הַמִּזְבֵּחַ (כה, ו)

וּנְסֵיב מֹשֶׁה פַּלְגוּת דְּמָא וְשַׁוִּי בְּמִזְרְקַיָּא וּפַלְגוּת דְּמָא זְרַק עַל מַדְבְּחָא

*And Moshe took half the blood and he placed it in the*
*receptacles, and half the blood he threw on the Mizbeiach.*

וַיִּזְרֹק עַל הָעָם (כה, ח)

וּזְרַק עַל מַדְבְּחָא לְכַפָּרָא עַל עַמָּא

*And he threw it on the Mizbeiach to atone for the nation.*

The *pasuk* states, "וישלח את נערי בני ישראל ויעלו עלת ויזבחו זבחים שלמים לה' פרים," which Onkelos translates as, "And he sent the firstborn B'nei Yisrael and they brought up burnt-sacrifices, and they slaughtered holy-slaughterings [offerings] before Hashem, oxen." The following *pasuk* states, "ויקח משה חצי הדם וישם באגנות וחצי הדם זרק על המזבח," which Onkelos translates as, "And Moshe took half the blood and he placed it in the receptacles, and half the blood he threw on the *Mizbeiach.*" The *Ramban* explains that Onkelos understands that Moshe put both halves in two different receptacles. The *Nesinah LaGer* adds that the receptacles were *klei shareis*—holy vessels.

A bit later, it states, "ויקח משה את הדם ויזרק על העם"—And Moshe took the blood and he threw it on the nation." The *Ibn Ezra* explains that Moshe took the second half of blood and threw it on the elders, who are equivalent to the entire nation; he did not throw it on the entire nation. Rabbeinu Bachya explains differently in *Rashi's* name: Moshe sprinkled on the nation's clothes to make them significant. This sprinkling brought them into a covenant between themselves and Hashem. In *Parashas Ki Sisa*, the Torah calls the stain of blood, "עדי," since it was an ornament and great honor for them. It was a testimony and sign about when they entered the covenant of Hashem. Therefore, when they sinned by the golden calf it was removed. Rabbeinu Bachya writes that others explain that Moshe sprinkled blood in front of the nation, not actually on them. Rabbeinu Chananel explains that the blood hinted that if you fulfill the Torah, good, but if not, I will enable your blood—your soul—to receive the punishment of *kareis* and death.

Onkelos translates "*va'yizrok al ha'am*" differently: "And he threw it on the *Mizbeiach* to atone for the nation." This is similar to what was done to the other half of blood, which states, "And half the blood he threw on the *Mizbeiach*." The *Nesinah LaGer* asks: Why does Onkelos not translate literally, "And he threw on the nation"? Also why does Onkelos not translate "*zarak*" as "and he sprinkled [*v'adi*]," like *Rashi* explains?

The *Nefesh HaGer* answers that Onkelos does not translate literally, "And he threw on the nation," because it was impossible for there to be enough blood to put on the entire nation unless there would be a miracle. Also, Onkelos translates like his *rebbi*, Rabbi Eliezer, who is of the opinion that circumcision alone, without immersing or sprinkling, was enough to convert before the Torah was given, as learned from the Avos.

The *Nefesh HaGer* says that *Rashi*, who explains that the blood was sprinkled on the nation, follows the opinion of Rabbi Yehoshua, who says that immersion was part of conversion even during the time of the Avos. In other words, a convert also needs to immerse; circumcision alone is not enough. The Gemara derives this from "*va'yizrok al ha'am*—and he threw on the nation," which refers to sprinkling. We have a *kabbalah* that there is no sprinkling without immersing. Since there was sprinkling, there must have also been immersing.

Regarding *Matan Torah* it states,[10] "*V'chibsu simlosam*," which Onkelos translates as "and whiten your clothing [*vi'chavrun levusheihon*]." The *Nefesh HaGer* explains this with the Gemara[11] and *Rashi*: this whitening was for cleanliness alone, to be fit to greet the Shechinah. Had "*v'chibsu*" meant "immerse," Onkelos would have translated it as "*v'yitz'ta'be'un*—and immerse," as *Rashi*[12] says this is how he translates by immersions, whereas whitening and cleaning he translates as "*v'yis-chaver*." Onkelos understands that there was no throwing or sprinkling on the nation; rather, the blood was thrown on the *Mizbeiach*, and there was no immersing.

May we remember Hashem's covenant and strengthen our *kesher* by serving Him properly!

## WHAT DOES "וַיֶּחֱזוּ אֶת הָאֱלֹקִים וַיֹּאכְלוּ וַיִּשְׁתּוּ" MEAN?

וְאֶל אֲצִילֵי בְּנֵי יִשְׂרָאֵל לֹא שָׁלַח יָדוֹ וַיֶּחֱזוּ
אֶת הָאֱלֹקִים וַיֹּאכְלוּ וַיִּשְׁתּוּ (כד, יא)

וּלְרַבְרְבֵי בְּנֵי יִשְׂרָאֵל לָא הֲוָה נִזְקָא וַחֲזוֹ יָת יְקָרָא דַיְיָ וַהֲווֹ חָדָן
בְּקֻרְבָּנֵיהוֹן דְּאִתְקַבַּלוּ (בְּרַעֲוָא) כְּאִלּוּ אָכְלִין וְשָׁתַן

*And there was no injury to the leaders of B'nei Yisrael, and they saw
the honor of Hashem, and they rejoiced with their korbanos that
were accepted (with favor) as though they were eating and drinking.*

The *pasuk* states, "ואל אצילי בני ישראל לא שלח ידו ויחזו את האלקים ויאכלו וישתו." *Rashi* explains that "*atzilei*" are "great people," referring to Nadav, Avihu, and the seventy elders, against whom Hashem did not send out His hand to punish. This implies that they were indeed fit to be punished

---

for doing something wrong. *Rashi* explains that they were gazing at the Shechinah while eating and drinking, with lightheadedness, without having the proper awareness of Hashem. Hashem did not want to bring mourning, which would disturb *Matan Torah*, so He held back from sending out His hand to punish them until later on.

Onkelos translates differently: "And there was no injury to the leaders of B'nei Yisrael, and they saw the honor of Hashem, and they rejoiced with their *korbanos* that were accepted with favor, as though they were eating and drinking." The *Nefesh HaGer* explains that Onkelos understands these words as a *mashal*; they reached a high level of perceiving Hashem as though they ate and drank. Similarly, the *Pesikta Zutrasi* writes that they acted as though they ate and drank. Rabbeinu Bachya explains that Onkelos, who translates as "and they saw the honor of Hashem," refers to the great appearance that the Navi Yechezkel saw.

Onkelos translates *"lo shalach yado"* as "there was no injury," rather than literally, "He did not send His hand." The *Nesinah LaGer* explains that Onkelos is careful to distance any physicality from Hashem, as He doesn't have any physical features. Onkelos translates *"va'yochlu va'yishtu"* as "and they rejoiced with their *korbanos* that were accepted with favor, as though they were eating and drinking." Since they did not actually eat or drink, to what does *"lo shalach yado*—He did not injure them"* refer? From what injury were the leaders spared?

This can be answered with the *Ramban*: The *pasuk* states, "And the Kohanim and the nation should not leave their places where they stood to ascend to Hashem, lest there will be a breach with them." The *Ramban* explains that there were dark clouds blocking the nation from having a complete vision, and they only saw Hashem's great fire. The elders, however, were not blocked and were able to see and perceive Hashem with more clarity. Here, the Torah states that they were careful and kept to their boundaries. The leaders, who were great people and were deserving to see the honor of Hashem, did not breach their positions to come close; therefore, there was no injury.

The *Nefesh HaGer* explains differently: *"lo shalach yado"* reflects that there was a claim against them that they enjoyed the radiance of the

Shechinah with a bit of lightheadedness. However, they weren't injured because they rejoiced in bringing *korbanos*, which protected them from being punished immediately. Alternately, Rav Yerucham[13] explains that although they reached an extremely high level, "as though they were eating and drinking" hints that there was something impure. He says that the expectations of these great people are astounding; there must have been something mixed in not for the sake of Hashem. The more *chochmah* one has, the more he needs to have the fear of Hashem instilled in himself in order to reach complete purity.

May we be careful from any lightheadedness, even when we reach extreme heights of happiness or *aliyah*!

# Terumah

## DOES "LI" MEAN "FOR ME" OR "BEFORE ME"?

וְיִקְחוּ לִי תְרוּמָה מֵאֵת כָּל אִישׁ אֲשֶׁר
יִדְּבֶנּוּ לִבּוֹ תִּקְחוּ אֶת תְּרוּמָתִי (כה, ב)

וְיַפְרְשׁוּן קֳדָמַי אַפְרָשׁוּתָא מִן כָּל גְּבַר דְּיִתְרְעֵי לִבֵּיהּ תִּסְבוּן יָת אַפְרָשׁוּתִי

*And they shall separate before Me a separation [portion]; from every*
*man whose heart favors, you shall take My separation [portion].*

וְעָשׂוּ לִי מִקְדָּשׁ (כה, ח)

וְיַעְבְּדוּן קֳדָמַי מַקְדַּשׁ

*And they shall make before Me a Mikdash.*

The *pasuk* states, "*V'yikchu Li terumah.*" *Rashi* explains, "They shall separate from their money for *My sake.*" The *Sifsei Chachamim*[1] adds that because the entire world is Hashem's, one can only separate for His sake. Onkelos translates differently: "And they shall separate *before Me* a separation [portion]." The *pasuk* ends, "מאת כל איש אשר ידבנו לבו תקחו את תרומתי," which Onkelos translates as "from every man whose heart favors, you shall take My separation [portion]." Why does Onkelos translate "*v'yikchu*" as "separate [*v'yafre'shun*]," but "*tikchu*" as "take [*tis-vun*]"? The *Nefesh HaGer* answers that the beginning of the *pasuk* refers to B'nei Yisrael taking to give contributions for Hashem, so he translates in an honorable way: "Separate before Me a separation." The end of the *pasuk* refers to Moshe and Aharon receiving the contributions from B'nei Yisrael, so Onkelos translates with the *lashon* "*sav*," which he uses when taking inanimate objects. The *Ohr Hatargum* explains differently: both *"v'yikchu"* and *"tikchu"* refer to giving contributions. Onkelos translates *"v'yikchu"* at the beginning of the *pasuk* as "separate," since it states *"Li,"* to distance any physicality regarding Hashem. For *"tikchu"* at the end of the *pasuk*, there is no *"Li,"* so there is no need to change from the regular translation of "take."

Later in the parashah, it states, *"V'asu Li Mikdash." Rashi* explains, "And they shall make a holy place for *My sake.*" The *Sifsei Chachamim*[2] adds that before they make a Mikdash, everything which exists also belongs to Hashem, all the material is His; one can only make a holy place for His sake. Onkelos translates differently here, as well: "And they shall make *before Me* a Mikdash." Why does Onkelos translate the word *"Li"* of *"v'yikchu Li terumah"* and *"v'asu Li Mikdash"* as "before Me"?

The *Nefesh HaGer* answers that because Hashem has no physicality whatsoever, it is improper to say, "Take for Me" or "Make for Me"; rather, it means "before Me." Also, Chazal say about the mitzvah of lighting the *Menorah*, "Does Hashem need its light? For forty years in the desert, we traveled with the pillar of fire and the clouds of glory that lit up for us and led the way. Rather, the *ner ha'maaravi* is testimony that the Shechinah rests among Yisrael, as it had the same amount of oil as the others, yet it lasted until the next evening." The same is true regarding the money B'nei Yisrael gave as *terumah*; Hashem doesn't need our money, rather, we need to contribute for our sake, in order to elevate ourselves.

During the *Aseres Yemei Teshuvah*, we say, "אבינו מלכנו חטאנו לפניך—Our Father, our King, we sinned before You." Similarly, on Yom Kippur, we say during the *al cheits*, "She'chatanu le'fanecha—That we sinned before You." Why do we say, "Chatanu le'fanecha—We sinned before You," and not, "Chatanu lecha—We sinned to You," as we say when we ask a person for forgiveness after sinning against them? Rav Chaim Kanievsky answered that *"lecha—to You"* would imply that we affected Hashem with our sin. This, however, is not true; our sins affect us, not, *chas v'shalom*,

Hashem. Therefore, we confess with the *lashon* "*le'fanecha*—before You" by expressing that we have performed improperly "before You," and we want to fix ourselves in order to return to Hashem, who is pure and untainted. Similarly, Onkelos translates in most places throughout the Torah, "*laHashem*—to Hashem," as "*kadam Hashem*—before Hashem," since we do *avodah* before Hashem, not to Him; He is not affected.

A person who sinned to Hashem confesses his *aveiros* by saying, "חטאתי עויתי פשעתי לפניך." The *Rambam*[3] writes that if a person sinned to his friend, he needs to ask forgiveness from that person. If the friend died before he was able to ask forgiveness from him, he is obligated to go to his friend's grave and ask forgiveness, and he says, "חטאתי לה' אלקי ישראל ולפלוני זה—I sinned to Hashem, G-d of Yisrael, and to this person." Why, when a person confesses to Hashem, does he say, "*Le'fanecha*—Before You*," whereas when he confesses to a person, he says, "*LaHashem Elokei Yisrael*—To Hashem, G-d of Yisrael"?

Rav Yosef Dov HaLevi Soloveitchik[4] answers that when one sins to Hashem, he says, "*Le'fanecha*," because one's sins cannot affect Hashem in any way; rather, one sinned before Hashem. Also, wherever a person performed the sin, it is in front of Hashem, Who fills the entire world and sees everything. However, when a person sins to his friend, he says, "*LaHashem Elokei Yisrael*," because we are *banim laHashem* and Hashem is our father. When someone hurts a child, he hurts the father as well. Therefore, one needs to confess that he also sinned to the person's father, Hashem.

May we remember that our *avodah* is before Hashem and He loves us as a father loves his children!

---

3   הל' תשובה סוף פ"ב
4   הררי קדם א בעניני המועדים סי' רלה, ב

## WHAT MIRACLES HAPPENED FOR THE MISHKAN?

# וְעֹרֹת אֵילִם מְאָדָּמִים וְעֹרֹת תְּחָשִׁים (כה, ה)

וּמַשְׁכֵי דְדִכְרֵי מְסַמְּקֵי וּמַשְׁכֵי סַסְגּוֹנָא

*And hides of rams dyed red, and multi-colored hides.*

# לֶחֶם פָּנִים לְפָנַי תָּמִיד (כה, ל)

לְחֵים אַפַּיָא קֳדָמַי תְּדִירָא

*Bread of faces [showbread] before Me, constantly.*

# וְעָשִׂיתָ מְנֹרַת זָהָב טָהוֹר מִקְשָׁה תֵּיעָשֶׂה הַמְּנוֹרָה (כה, לא)

וְתַעֲבֵיד מְנָרְתָּא דִּדְהַב דְּכֵי נְגִיד תִּתְעֲבֵיד מְנָרְתָּא

*And you shall make a Menorah of pure gold; the Menorah*
*shall be made extending (hammered) out.*

# וְעָשִׂיתָ בְרִיחִם (כו, כו)

וְתַעֲבֵיד עָבְרֵי

*And you shall make bolts.*

# וְהַבְּרִיחַ הַתִּיכֹן בְּתוֹךְ הַקְּרָשִׁים מַבְרִחַ
# מִן הַקָּצֶה אֶל הַקָּצֶה (כו, כח)

וְעָבְרָא מְצִיעָאָה בְּגוֹ דַפַּיָא מַעְבַּר מִן סְיָפֵי לִסְיָפֵי

*And the middle bolt within the planks shall*
*pass [bolt] through from end to end.*

The *Mishkan* had many miracles occur with its building and throughout the forty years in the Midbar. Here are a few of them.

## Tachash Skins
One entire covering[5] of the *Mishkan* was made of "*oros eilim me'adamim,*" which Onkelos translates as "and hides of rams dyed red." Another cover

of the *Mishkan* was made of *"oros techashim,"* which Onkelos translates as *"mashkei sasgona."* The Gemara[6] explains that this means it was a multi-colored animal who rejoiced (סס" like "שש") about its splendid color (גונא—color). The *Midrash Tanchuma*[7] writes: Rabbi Yehuda says it was a huge wild animal with one horn on its forehead, and its hide had six different colors. Rabbi Nechemyah says that Hashem miraculously created this gigantic animal, whose hide was thirty cubits long, to be used for the *Mishkan*.

Onkelos translates *"oros eilim"* as "hides of rams [*mashkei d'dichrei*]" by adding a ד׳, whereas *"oros techashim"* he translates as *"mashkei sasgona*—multi-colored hides," without adding a ד׳. The *Nesinah LaGer* explains that the ram's hides were skins of a type of animal, the ram, so Onkelos adds a ד׳, "of." *"Techashim"* was not the name of the type of animal itself, but, rather, a description of the animal's attributes—its hides were multi-colored; therefore, he does not add a ד׳.

## Lechem Hapanim

The Torah describes the *Lechem Hapanim* as "לחם פנים לפני תמיד," which Onkelos translates literally: "bread of the faces [showbread] before Me, constantly." *Rashi* explains that the bread was made like a box with a bottom, was folded upwards as walls, and was open on two sides. It is called *"panim*—faces" because the bread had "faces" seeing two directions from its two sides. The *Ramban* brings this explanation, as the Mishnah teaches: Ben Zoma said, לחם פנים, as it had faces. In *Parashas Bamidbar*, it states,[8] *"v'al Shulchan Hapanim,"* which Onkelos translates as "and upon the table of the bread of faces [showbread] [ועל פתורא דלחם אפיא]." The *Me'at Tzari* says that this follows the opinion that the *Lechem Hapanim* was as an open box. However, the Gemara[9] brings another opinion that it was like a dancing boat, meaning a small boat, which narrows toward its bottom to a point and moves quickly—not

---

6   שבת כח.

7   ו

8   במדבר ד, ז

9   מנחות צד:

faces. This opinion can be explained like the *Ibn Ezra*: "*lechem panim*" means, as it states, that it should be *le'fanai tamid*, it should constantly be before Hashem. The *Targum Yonasan* translates "*panim*" as "inner": the inner bread, excluding outer bread. This bread needed to be placed inside the *Kodesh*. Similarly, the *Hakesav V'Hakabbalah* explains that "*ha'panim*" means "the one inside," which hints to the inside table in the *Kodesh*, excluding the outside table in the *Ulam*.

The *Lechem Hapanim* were baked before Shabbos, since they could not be baked on Shabbos. They stayed on the *Shulchan* from one Shabbos until the next, and then they were removed and eaten. *Tosafos*[10] writes that they were soft as though just baked, while *Rashi* says that they were hot as though just baked! The *Ritva*[11] adds that they were so hot that steam rose up from the breads as though they had just come out of the oven. The Gemara[12] writes that when the Yidden would be *oleh regel*, the Kohanim would pick up the *Shulchan* with the *Lechem Hapanim* and say, "See how beloved you are before Hashem." Hashem performed a miracle to keep the week-old loaves of bread soft and fresh, steaming hot.

## Menorah

The Torah describes the *Menorah* as, "ועשית מנרת זהב טהור מקשה תיעשה המנורה," which Onkelos translates as, "And you shall make a *Menorah* of pure gold; the *Menorah* shall be made extending out." *Rashi* quotes Onkelos, who translates "*mikshah*" as "*n'gid*," and explains that it is from the *lashon* "*hamshachah*—to extend outward." From one mass of gold, you should extend its parts outwards by banging it with a hammer and forming it while attached together. The *Malbim*[13] explains Onkelos differently: "נגיד" means "smite." This is as Chazal say, "Had "נגדוהו—they lashed" Chananya, Mishael, and Azarya, the challenge would have been too hard to withstand. Similarly, *Rashi* explains that "*mikshah*" means "banging," to beat with a hammer. The *Menorah* should

---

10   בחגיגה כו:

11   יומא כא.

12   שם כא:

13   לא

be made from one mass of gold by extending from it branches by hitting with a hammer. For this reason, *Rashi* says[14] that Moshe had difficulty with making the *Menorah*. Hashem said to Moshe, "Throw the *kikar* of gold into the fire and it will be made by itself."

## Mizbechos

The copper *Mizbeiach* and the gold *Mizbeiach* had a thin sheet of metal separating between the fire and its cedarwood. Although the fire was never extinguished, *Rashi*[15] says it did not melt even a bit of the metal! *Tosafos* writes in the name of the *Midrash Tanchuma* that the fire did not burn the cedarwood!

## Berichim

The *pasuk* states, "*V'asisa v'richim,*" which Onkelos translates as "and you shall make עברי." "עברי" means "pass through." *Rashi* explains that these were bolts (עברין) which passed through outside the planks surrounding the *Mishkan*. It states, "והבריח התיכון בתוך הקרשים," which Onkelos translates as "and the middle bolt within the planks." *Rashi* explains that there was a middle bolt between the other bolts, which was placed inside the planks. The *pasuk* ends, "מבריח מן הקצה אל הקצה—Which bolted through from one end to the other end." The Gemara[16] writes that the inner bolt stood with a miracle. *Rashi* explains that after the planks were placed in their sockets in the north, west, and south sides of the *Mishkan*, this inner bolt was put inside. This one bolt went through all three directions by bending and turning at the corners. There is no craftsman who can do this. *Targum Yonasan* adds that when it was put inside, it curved as a snake curls, and when B'nei Yisrael needed to travel, they would dismantle the *Mishkan* and it straightened as a staff of seventy cubits. Others say that each side had its own inner bolt. Onkelos translates "מבריח מן הקצה אל הקצה" as "shall pass [bolt] through from end to end." Although "הקצה" and "קצה" are in singular, Onkelos translates in plural, as "ends." This seems that the middle bolt passed through all the ends,

14   כא
15   חגיגה כו.
16   שבת צח:

in accordance with the opinion that the inner middle bolt miraculously went through all the sides!

May Hashem build the Beis Hamikdash and bring back the Shechinah and His miracles!

## ARE THE AVNEI MILUIM
## STONES "THAT FILL" OR "ARE COMPLETE"?

### אַבְנֵי שֹׁהַם וְאַבְנֵי מִלֻּאִים לָאֵפֹד וְלַחֹשֶׁן (כה, ז)

אַבְנֵי בֻּרְלָא וְאַבְנֵי אַשְׁלָמוּתָא לְשַׁקָּעָא בְּאֵיפוֹדָא וּבְחָשְׁנָא

*Buryl stones and complete [whole] stones to sink
into the Eiphod and into the Choshen.*

The *pasuk* states, "אבני שהם ואבני מלאים לאפד ולחשן." *Rashi* explains that there were two *shoham* stones for the *Eiphod* and twelve *miluim* stones for the *Choshen*. A gold-setting called "*mishbetzos*," in which the stones were placed, was made like a groove. The stones sat on the *mishbetzos* and filled up the entire hole. The word "מלאים" means "מלוי—filling," since the stones filled up the entire hole. In *Parashas Tetzaveh*, it states,[17] "מסבת משבצות זהב תעשה אתם." *Rashi* explains that the stones were completely surrounded with gold settings in the shape of a groove which were the width of the stones.

The *Ramban* is bothered by the following: why should they be called "*Avnei Miluim*" because there will later be a command to fill the hole which will be made for them? Additionally, the *shoham* stones were also surrounded by a gold setting, yet they are not called *miluim*. Why not?

The *Ramban* says that for this reason, Onkelos translates the *pasuk* differently: "Buryl stones and complete [whole] stones to sink into the *Eiphod* and into the *Choshen*." Also, in *Parashas Tetzaveh*, it states about the *Choshen* stones: "ומלאת בו מלאת אבן," which Onkelos translates as "you shall complete it, complete stone [ותשלם ביה אשלמות אבנא]." He does not translate with "*miluy*—filling up," as he translates by filling up a vessel or a hole. For example, Onkelos translates "*va'temalei chadah*" as "and she filled her flask [ומליאה קלתה]." The *Ramban* explains that "*miluim*" means "*shalem*—complete," as the stones weren't hewn with a knife from a big piece of stone and no part of them was cut off at all. Rather, they were created this way and remained unchanged. It is known that the strongest and most precious stones are those found by the streams, untouched and complete. Similarly, Onkelos translates "*malei sh'vua zos*" as "complete [*ashleim*] this week." The *Maharal* adds that anything which is "*malei*—full" is complete.

The Torah states regarding the *Eiphod*, "מעשה חרש אבן פתוחי חותם תפתח את שתי האבנים על שמות בני ישראל." The *Ramban* explains that they made a groove in the stone with the names of B'nei Yisrael; they were not במלואותם, complete stones. However, the *Choshen* stones were complete, as it states, "ומלאת בו מלאת אבן" and "יהיו במלואתם." The Gemara says that "במלואותם" teaches that a knife could not be used on the stones; therefore, Moshe needed the *shamir* worm specifically for the *Choshen* stones. Ink would be put on the stone and the *shamir* worm would go along the ink, causing the stone to crack on its own without chiseling it.

The *pasuk* states, "מסבת משבצות זהב תעשה אתם," which Onkelos translates as "sunken in 'מרמצן' of gold you shall make them [משקען מרמצן דדהב תעבד יתהון]." And it states, "משבצים זהב יהיו במלואותם," which Onkelos translates as "'מרמצן' with gold they shall be in their completeness [מרמצן בדהב יהון באשלמותהון]." What does "מרמצן" mean? The *Ramban* explains that it is a metal instrument with prongs with which things could be picked up. A setting was made underneath the stones to hold them and it had three fork-like teeth which stuck out to hold the stone in order to show its beauty and be able to see it from all sides without it being covered. This type of setting is also found nowadays with rings of all types of precious stones.

The *Ramban* proves this explanation from the description in *Parashas Tetzaveh*: there were two chains stuck onto two rings of the *Choshen*, which were stuck into settings on the shoulder straps of the *Eiphod*. If the *mishbetzos* were receptacles for the stones to sit in, how could they stick chains into them? How did the holes function for them? Rather, they were fork-like metal prongs, and the holes of the chains would enter into them.

The Torah states regarding the *Kesones*,[18] "*U'Kesones tashbetz*" and "*v'shibatzta haKesones sheish*," which Onkelos translates as "and *Kesones* מרמצן'" and "'ותרמיץ' the linen *Kesones*." According to the *Ramban*, "מרמצן" are fork-like prongs. The *Re'em* asks: How does this apply to the *Kesones*? Therefore, he explains "מרמצן" differently: as *Rashi* explains,[19] it means "a nail," like the Gemara[20] writes: "He pierced with 'רמצא,' a long nail of iron." Regarding the stones, "מרמצן" means that pieces of gold were placed around the stones until the stones were sunken into them and nailed down, as though they were in holes of gold as the size of the stones. Regarding the *Kesones*, "מרמצן" means that they took pieces of linen and connected them with nails to the *Kesones*.

Rabbeinu Bachya[21] says that this should arouse us to notice the greatness of Torah. It is more precious than pearls and nothing equals it. Gold and silver are cherished by people, and precious stones even more. Here it states that gold was used for the setting of the precious stones, and the precious stones had letters of the Torah in them. When there is an object and a holder, the holder is of less quality than the precious things which it holds. If so, the letters of the Torah are the most important thing and above everything!

May we learn from the *Avnei Miluim* that the letters of Torah are more precious than anything else!

---

18    כח, ד ולט
19    שבת קג. ונדה סב. במסורת הש"ס
20    שבת שם
21    כח, כ

## WHAT DOES "KERUVIM" MEAN
## AND WHAT DOES IT REFLECT?

וְעָשִׂיתָ שְׁנַיִם כְּרֻבִים זָהָב מִקְשָׁה תַּעֲשֶׂה
אֹתָם מִשְּׁנֵי קְצוֹת הַכַּפֹּרֶת (כה, יח)

וְתַעֲבֵיד תְּרֵין כְּרוּבִין דִּדְהַב נְגִיד תַּעֲבֵיד יָתְהוֹן מִתְּרֵין סִטְרֵי כָפֻּרְתָּא

*And you shall make two Keruvim of gold; you shall make them*
*extend (hammered) out from two sides of the Kapores.*

וּפְנֵיהֶם אִישׁ אֶל אָחִיו (כה, כ)

וְאַפֵּיהוֹן חַד לָקֳבֵיל חַד

*And their faces, one opposite the other.*

The *pasuk* states, "ועשית שנים כרובים זהב—And you shall make two gold *Keruvim*," which Onkelos translates as "and you shall make two *Keruvin* of gold." He translates "זהב" as "דדהב—of gold." The *Ramban*[22] says that in Aramaic it is common that the letter 'ד is used in place of a 'ז. The *Nesinah LaGer* points out that here, Onkelos adds a 'ד, "דדהב," to reflect that it was made of 100 percent gold. So too, throughout the making of the *Mishkan*, when it reflects pure gold, Onkelos translates "דדהב—of gold," and otherwise he translates as "דהב—gold."

The *pasuk* ends, "מקשה תעשה אותם משני קצות הכפרת," which Onkelos translates as, "You shall make them extend out from the two sides of the *Kapores*." *Rashi* quotes Onkelos and explains that "n'gid" is from the *lashon* "hamshachah—to extend outwards," as the *Keruvim* extended out of one mass of gold from the Kapores. The *Malbim*[23] explains that "n'gid" means "smite"; the *Keruvim* were banged and hammered out of one piece of gold.

What were the *Keruvim*, and what did they reflect?

---

22   דברים לג, כה

23   לא

The Gemara[24] quotes Rabbi Avahu, who said that "*keruv*" comes from the word "*ke'ravia*," which means "as a young child," since in Bavel/ Babylonian they called a child a "*ravia*." The *Ibn Ezra* himself explains that the 'כ of "כרובים" is part of the root, and it means "forms" or "pictures." The *Rashbam* explains that "*keruvim*" are birds.

The Gemara[25] is bothered by the following: the Torah describes Moshe's *Keruvim* as "ופניהם איש אל אחיו," which Onkelos translates as "and their faces, one opposite the other," which indicates that they faced each other. However, in *Divrei Hayamim*, it describes Shlomo Hamelech's *Keruvim* as "*u'fneihem laBayis*—and their faces were toward the House," which indicates that they did not face each other. Which way did they face? The Gemara answers that the way the *Keruvim* faced was dependent on B'nei Yisrael. When B'nei Yisrael fulfilled the will of Hashem, the *Keruvim* faced each other, like the expression of affection of a male with a female, showing affection and love. However, if, *chas v'shalom*, B'nei Yisrael did not fulfill the will of Hashem, then the *Keruvim* faced away from each other, toward the entrance of the house. Originally, by Moshe, they were made facing each other in order for the Shechinah to rest with us and so that we should fulfill the will of Hashem. However, once we sinned, they would move apart. The *Rashbam* points out that although the *Keruvim* are inanimate, they miraculously moved to reflect the *hanhagah* between Hashem and Yisrael. The Gemara[26] states: Rav Katina said that when Klal Yisrael went to the Beis Hamikdash for the *Shalosh Regalim*, the Kohanim would open the *Paroches* and show Klal Yisrael the *Keruvim*, which were hugging each other. The Kohanim would say, "See the love which Hashem has for you!"

The Gemara[27] writes that at the time of the *Churban*, the non-Jews entered the *Heichal* of the Beis Hamikdash and saw the *Keruvim* facing each other and hugging. The *Maharsha* asks: Why were the *Keruvim* facing each other and showing affection between Hashem and Yisrael

---

24 סוכה ה:

25 ב"ב צט.

26 יומא נד.

27 שם

at a time when Hashem was clearly very upset with us? The *Maharsha* answers in the name of the *Ritva* that it was a miracle that the *Keruvim* were facing each other by the *Churban*. Why did Hashem make such a miracle at that time?

Rav Chaim Shmuelevitz[28] explains that when Hashem came to destroy the Beis Hamikdash and send Klal Yisrael into *galus*, He first aroused great *ahavah* for Klal Yisrael. Only then did Hashem allow for His *middas ha'din* to rule and destroy. My good friend Rabbi Elchonon Sosne added that this is because when there is love to another, punishment can be properly placed and accepted. Another reason for Hashem arousing great *ahavah* is like a father who doesn't punish his son until he arouses all his feelings of love and mercy and then he punishes. This way, the punishment is exactly what is needed for the good of his son and will be most beneficial.

The Gemara[29] quotes another opinion to answer the contradiction: the *Keruvim* were made facing the house. The statement that they faced each other indicates that they stood tilted. The *Beraisa* writes that this is as Onkelos HaGer explains that the *Keruvim* were "מעשה צעצועים," which the *Rashbam* explains to mean "צאצאים" with an 'א, "children."[30] They were set up to partially face toward the house and partially face toward each other. They tilted their faces as a student departing from his *rebbi*. The *Rashbam* explains that the idea of students hints to children, as the meaning of "*keruv*" is "כרביא—like a child." It was common for young students to depart from their *rebbeim* sideways. The *Maharsha* questions this because adult students also depart from their *rebbi* sideways. He explains that the "צעצועים" were two *Keruvim* made exactly like each other, in shape and size, with equal stature. This way, no heretic might be mistaken to say that one is greater and more important than the other. The Gemara means that just as when any student, whether

---

a child or adult, departs from his *rebbi*, he leaves sideways, so too, the *Keruvim* would partially face each other in an honorable way.

May Hashem rebuild the Beis Hamikdash and merit this miraculous expression of affection!

# Tetzaveh

## WAS THE OHEL MOED A "TENT OF MEETING" OR A "TRANSITORY TENT"?

### בְּאֹהֶל מוֹעֵד (כז, כא)

בְּמַשְׁכַּן זִמְנָא

*In the Tent of Meeting (Transitory Tent).*

The *pesukim* call the *Mishkan* "*Ohel Moed*"; what does this mean?

The *Nefesh HaGer* says that Onkelos translates "*Ohel Moed*" as "*Mashkan Zimna*," which means "a Tent of Meeting." "*Zimna*" means "to meet," as it states, "וְנוֹעַדְתִּי שָׁמָּה לִבְנֵי יִשְׂרָאֵל," which Onkelos translates as "*va'aza-mein—and I will meet.*" This is as *Rashi* explains: Hashem says, "I will become known to B'nei Yisrael by speaking to them, like a king who sets a meeting place to speak with his servants." The *Ohel Moed* was the Tent of Meeting, where Hashem met with Moshe and Yisrael.

The *Hakesav V'Hakabbalah* suggests that Onkelos's translation of "זמנא" is based on the word "מזומן," which means a prepared place that is per-manently ready and available for the *tzibbur*. Whereas *Rashi* explains "*moed*" as a "*beis vaad—meeting place.*" "מזומן" means "*hachanah*," which is a prepared and designated place to meet, whereas a meeting place is where gathering is done.

In *Parashas Terumah*, it states,[1] "וְנוֹעַדְתִּי לְךָ שָׁם וְדִבַּרְתִּי אִתְּךָ מֵעַל הַכַּפֹּרֶת מִבֵּין שְׁנֵי הַכְּרֻבִים...—And I will meet you there, and I will speak with you from above the *Kapores*, from between the two *Keruvim*, all that

---

I will command you about B'nei Yisrael." The Gemara states that when Yisrael would fulfill the will of Hashem, the *Keruvim* faced toward each other, and if not, then they faced toward the entrance of the house. The *Maharsha* explains that when the *Keruvim* faced each other, it symbolized Hashem's love for B'nei Yisrael. However, when they faced the entrance, it symbolized departure, as though there was distance from each other. Throughout all the years in the Midbar, the *Keruvim* faced each other, reflecting Hashem's love, because the Shechinah did not depart from B'nei Yisrael the entire time. However, before the *churban Beis Hamikdash*, the *Keruvim* faced toward the entrance, reflecting the Shechinah's distance in response to the sins of Bnei Yisrael.

The *Hakesav V'Hakabbalah* offers a second explanation in Onkelos: "*Mashkan Zimna*" means "a Transitory Tent." The word "זמנא" means "a time," as it states in *Parashas Bereishis*, "ולמועדים," which Onkelos translates as "לזמנין—and for times." The *Mishkan* was temporary, as it was only built for a short while at a time. When B'nei Yisrael traveled, they took down the entire *Mishkan*, and when they camped, they rebuilt it. Also, it was only built for the time that they camped throughout the forty years in the Midbar. Rabbi Shimon bar Yochai explains that the word "*moed*" hints to a place where the Shechinah rested from *z'man l'z'man*—time to time. However, the Beis Hamikdash that Shlomo Hamelech built is called "*menuchah*—a resting place," as it states, "זאת מנוחתי עדי עד מכון לשבתך עולמים." The Beis Hamikdash was a permanent dwelling place of the Shechinah which stood for hundreds of years. To add, the Torah calls the Beis Hamikdash "*menuchah*," as well as "*nachalah*," as it states,[2] "אל המנוחה ואל הנחלה—To the resting place and to the place of inheritance."

May Hashem rebuild the Beis Hamikdash and permanently return His Shechinah!

---

2   דברים יב, ט

# WHAT WAS THE PURPOSE OF ANOINTING AND THE GARMENTS OF KEHUNAH?

לְכָבוֹד וּלְתִפְאָרֶת (כח, ב)

לִיקָר וּלְתֻשְׁבְּחָא

*For honor and for praise.*

וּמָשַׁחְתָּ אֹתָם (כח, מא)

וּתְרַבֵּי יָתְהוֹן

*And you shall make them great [anoint/sanctify].*

וְלָקַחְתָּ אֶת שֶׁמֶן הַמִּשְׁחָה...וּמָשַׁחְתָּ אֹתוֹ (כט, ז)

וְתִסַּב יָת מִשְׁחָא דִרְבוּתָא...וּתְרַבֵּי יָתֵיה

*And you shall take the oil of greatness [anointing/ sanctification]...and you shall make him great [anoint/sanctify].*

לְמָשְׁחָה בָהֶם (כט, כט)

לְרַבָּאָה בְּהוֹן

*To make them great [anoint/sanctify].*

The *pasuk* states, "And you shall dress Aharon, your brother, with them...and his sons with him, *u'mashachta osam*," which Onkelos translates as "and you shall make them great." Also, Onkelos translates *"v'lakachta es shemen ha'mishchah...u'mashachta oso"* as, "And you shall take the oil of greatness...and you shall make him great." To what does "making great" and "greatness" refer? *Rashi*[3] explains that all the anointing in context of the *Mishkan*, Kohanim, and kings is translated with the *lashon* *"ribuy—great,"* since their anointing was specifically to elevate them and make them great. Other anointings, such as *"u'rekikei matzos meshuchim ba'shamen,"* is translated with the *lashon* of *"meshichah—smearing."*

The Torah describes the garments as *"l'chavod u'l'sifares,"* which Onkelos translates as "for honor and for praise." The *Me'at Tzari* explains that the garments of the Kohanim are unique and special and deserve to be praised. It also states about the garments, "And the sanctified clothes of Aharon shall be for his sons after him *l'mashchah va'hem,"* which Onkelos translates as "to make them great." How do the garments of the Kohanim bring out greatness?

The Gemara[4] asks: Why do the *talmidei chachamim* of Bavel stand out with their clothes? The Gemara[5] answers that when a *talmid chacham* is in Eretz Yisrael, the place where he dwells, he is recognized by his name and that alone brings him honor. However, when a *talmid chacham* leaves Eretz Yisrael and goes into exile, no one knows who he is. Therefore, he should dress with special, honorable clothes to bring attention to his status and be recognized for the sake of his dignity. We see from here that clothing can bring out the dignity of a person.

Rav Yosef Karo, the *Mechaber* of the *Shulchan Aruch*[6] teaches in *Hilchos Yom Tov* that one should wear nicer clothing on Yom Tov than on Shabbos. The *Mishnah Berurah*[7] explains that on Yom Tov, a person is obligated to rejoice, and wearing nice clothes brings a person happiness.

The Gemara[8] brings that if a person sees himself falling into the *yetzer hara*'s trap, he should go to a place where people do not recognize him, dress in black clothes, and do what his heart desires, rather than profane the name of Hashem in public. *Rashi* explains that he should go there, and if need be, transgress the *aveirah* where no one knows him so that he won't profane Hashem's name in public. Rabbeinu Chananel explains differently: he certainly is not permitted to go to another place and sin; rather, this is all to stop his *yetzer hara*. By going to another place, he will weaken himself with the difficult trip; he will humble himself since it is common for a guest to feel uncomfortable; and he

4  שבת קמה:
5  מרש"י
6  או"ח סי' תקכט, א
7  יב
8  חגיגה טז.

won't feel the desire to sin. This is as Chazal say: even a dog won't bark for seven years when it is not in its own city. Also, he should dress in black clothes, like sackcloth, to humble himself by reminding himself about mourning and death. Rav Hai Gaon says that he definitely will break his *yetzer hara* and will not be interested in sinning. We see that the clothes of a person can save him from sin.

Clothing can bring a person dignity and happiness and help him humble himself. Similarly, the special, unique garments of the Kohanim represented rulership and reminded them about their unique responsibility of serving Hashem in the Beis Hamikdash. Their special clothes were a constant reminder of their elevated *avodah*.

May we use our clothing to improve our *avodas Hashem*!

## IS THE WORD "LO" BY THE ARON, CHOSHEN, AND ME'IL AN ISSUR LAV OR A REASON?

וְיִרְכְּסוּ אֶת הַחֹשֶׁן מִטַּבְּעֹתָו אֶל טַבְּעֹת הָאֵפֹד בִּפְתִיל תְּכֵלֶת לִהְיוֹת עַל חֵשֶׁב הָאֵפוֹד וְלֹא יִזַּח הַחֹשֶׁן מֵעַל הָאֵפוֹד (כח, כח)

וְיֶחְדּוּן יָת חֻשְׁנָא מֵעִזְקָתֵיהּ לְעִזְקָת אֵיפוֹדָא בְּחוּטָא דִּתְכֶלְתָּא לְמֶהֱוֵי עַל הֶמְיַן אֵיפוֹדָא וְלָא יִתְפָּרֵק חֻשְׁנָא מֵעִלָּוֵי אֵיפוֹדָא

*And attach the Choshen from its rings to the ring*
*of the Eiphod with a thread of techeiles to be*
*on the belt of the Eiphod, and the Choshen will*
*not dislocate [move] from upon the Eiphod.*

וְהָיָה פִי רֹאשׁוֹ בְּתוֹכוֹ שָׂפָה יִהְיֶה לְפִיו סָבִיב מַעֲשֵׂה אֹרֵג כְּפִי תַחְרָא יִהְיֶה לּוֹ לֹא יִקָּרֵעַ (כח, לב)

וִיהֵי פֻּמֵּיהּ כָּפִיל לְגַוֵּיהּ תּוֹרָא יְהֵי מַקַּף לְפֻמֵּיהּ סְחוֹר סְחוֹר עוֹבַד מָחֵי כְּפֻם שִׁרְיָן יְהֵי לֵיהּ דְּלָא יִתְבְּזַע

*And its opening shall be folded inward; a row shall go*
*around its opening all around; the work of a weaver, as*
*the opening of armor shall be for it that doesn't tear.*

The *pasuk* states, "וירכסו את החשן מטבעתיו אל טבעת האפוד בפתיל תכלת להיות על חשב האפוד," which Onkelos translates as, "And attach the *Choshen* from its rings to the ring of the *Eiphod* with a thread of *techeiles* to be on the belt of the *Eiphod*." The *Nefesh HaGer* explains that Onkelos translates "וירכסו" as "ויחדון" from the *lashon* "סגר," which Onkelos translates as "אחד—closed," or from the *lashon* "נאחז," which Onkelos translates as "אחיד—held." This is as *Rashi* explains: "וירכסו is a language of "*chibbur*—connecting"; connect and hold the *Choshen* to the rings of the *Eiphod* to be attached to the *Eiphod's* belt.

The *pasuk* ends, "ולא יזח החשן מעל האפוד." *Rashi* says that "יזח" is an Arabic word, which Dunash ben Labrat explains is a *lashon* of "*nituk*—detaching"; the *Choshen* will not be detached from upon the *Eiphod*. Onkelos translates these words as, "And the *Choshen* will not dislocate [move] from upon the *Eiphod*." The *Sefer Hachinuch*[9] quotes Onkelos and explains that if the *Choshen* wouldn't be tied, then it would move back and forth and separate from the *Eiphod* and bang against the Kohen's heart. One who dislocates the *Choshen* from the *Eiphod* transgresses an *issur*. Hashem wanted the vessels and garments to be in their proper size and place, to be complete and nice. When the *Choshen* is fastened to the belt of the *Eiphod* and doesn't move, it is like a nice ornament.

Regarding the *Me'il*, it states, "והיה פי ראשו בתוכו שפה יהיה...לא יקרע"—And its opening shall be inwards, it shall have a rim...*lo yikarei'a*." What does "*lo yikarei'a*" mean? *Rashi* explains, "Make a hem in order that it won't tear, and one who rips it transgresses a *lav*." The Brisker Rav[10] explains that there are two things derived from here: first, a reason—weave a hem around its opening so that it shall not tear. Second, a prohibition: one who rips it transgresses an *issur lav*. The *Sifsei Chachamim*[11] adds that although "*lo yikarei'a*" seems to be a reason for making a hem, since it does not state, "*She'lo yikarei'a*—so that it shall not rip," it indicates that it is also a *lav*. The *Sefer Hachinuch*[12] explains that ripping is a disgraceful

9   מצוה ק
10  חי' מרן הגרי"ז הלוי החדשות על תנ"ך ואגדה
11  א
12  מצוה קא

thing and ruins the garment. Although it is not a vessel, only a garment, there is a *lav* in order for the one who wears it to have fear and proper honor to be afraid not to rip and destroy it. The *Rambam*[13] says this *lav* applies to any of the garments of the *kehunah*. *Rashi* adds that the same applies to the *Choshen*, about which it states, "*V'lo yizach*," and with the poles of the *Aron*, about which it states, "*Lo yasuru mi'menu*."

Onkelos translates "והיה פי ראשו בתוכו שפה יהיה לפיו סביב מעשה ארג כפי תחרא יהיה לו לא יקרע" as, "And its opening shall be folded inward; a row shall go around its opening all around; work of a weaver, as the opening of armor shall be for it that doesn't tear." He translates "*lo yikarei'a*" as "that does not tear." The Brisker Rav explains that Onkelos translates like the first explanation of *Rashi*, that "*lo yikarei'a*" is a reason for why the hem is there; you need to make the *Me'il* in this way, folded, so that it doesn't tear. The Gemara teaches that since the *pasuk* does not state, "*she'lo yikarei'a*," it implies that it is an *issur lav*. The *Nesinah LaGer* suggests that Onkelos can mean like *Rashi*, that "*lo yikarei'a*" reflects two points: first, a reason for doing so—so that it doesn't tear, and second, an *issur lav*. The Brisker Rav asks: what is the proof to explain "*lo yikarei'a*" as a reason, "so that it doesn't tear"? Maybe it is just an *issur lav*! He answers that in *Parashas Pekudei*, after they made the *Me'il*, it states, "ויעש את מעיל...ופי המעיל...שפה לפיו סביב לא יקרע—And he made the *Me'il*...and the opening of the *Me'il*...a hem for its opening, *lo yikarei'a*." Since it also states, "*Lo yikarei'a*" about the actual making of the *Me'il*, it doesn't fit to be saying that it is an *issur lav*. Rather, it implies that the hem needed to have been made in a way so that it wouldn't tear.[14]

In *Parashas Terumah*, it states[15] about the poles of the *Aron*, "בטבעות הארון יהיו הבדים לא יסרו ממנו," which Onkelos translates as, "In the rings of the *Aron* shall be the poles; do not remove them from it [*lo yi'don mineih*]." The *Sefer Hachinuch*[16] explains that since the *Aron* is the place where the Torah dwells, we are obligated to act in the most honorable and proper

13   הל' כלי המקדש ט, ג
14   ע"ש שהקשה לפי גרסתו "לא יתבזע" אבל לפי גרסתינו "דלא יתבזע" מובן וע"ע בת"א בפס' כ"א על "ולא יזח"
15   כה, טו
16   מצוה צו

way possible with it. Therefore, we can't remove the poles, since we might have to quickly move the *Aron* to another place and the Kohanim won't check that the poles were inserted properly, causing it to fall from their hands. Also, each of the vessels of the Mikdash represent and hint to lofty ideas, in order for a person to be positively affected by thinking about them. Therefore, Hashem wanted that no part of the shape or form should be missing, even temporarily.

May Hashem return the *keilim* and the *bigdei kehunah bi'meheirah bi'ya-meinu, Amen!*

## DOES "KETORES" MEAN TO "SMOKE" OR "BRING UP"?

### וְלָקַחְתָּ אֶת כָּל הַחֵלֶב...וְהִקְטַרְתָּ הַמִּזְבֵּחָה (כט, יג)

וְתִסַּב יָת כָּל תַּרְבָּא...וְתַסֵּיק לְמַדְבְּחָא

*And you shall take all the fat...and you shall bring [it] up to the Mizbeiach.*

### וְהִקְטַרְתָּ אֶת כָּל הָאַיִל הַמִּזְבֵּחָה (כט, יח)

וְתַסֵּיק יָת כָּל דִּכְרָא לְמַדְבְּחָא

*And you shall bring up the entire ram to the Mizbeiach.*

### וְהִקְטִיר עָלָיו אַהֲרֹן קְטֹרֶת סַמִּים...יַקְטִירֶנָּה (ל, ז)

וְיַקְטַר עֲלוֹהִי אַהֲרֹן קְטֹרֶת בֻּסְמִין...יַקְטְרִנַּהּ

*And Aharon shall smoke on it Ketores-incenses...he shall smoke it.*

The *pasuk* states about the bull, "וְלָקַחְתָּ אֶת כָּל הַחֵלֶב...וְהִקְטַרְתָּ הַמִּזְבֵּחָה—And you shall take all the fat...and you shall smoke it on the *Mizbeiach*." Onkelos translates "*v'hiktarta haMizbeichah*" as, "And you shall bring [it] up to the *Mizbeiach* [*v'sa'seik*]." It also states about the ram, "וְהִקְטַרְתָּ אֶת כָּל הָאַיִל הַמִּזְבֵּחָה—And you shall burn the entire ram on the *Mizbeiach*." Here again, Onkelos translates "*v'hiktarta...haMizbeichah*" as "and you shall bring up...to the *Mizbeiach* [*v'sa'seik*]." Similarly, he translates "*va'yikach*" regarding the bones of Yosef[17] as "and he brought up [*va'a'seik*]." Onkelos does not translate "והקטרת" with the *lashon* "הקטרה—smoke" or "בער" or "תוקד," which mean "burn." At the end of the parashah, it states, "והקטיר עליו אהרן קטרת סמים...יקטירנה," which Onkelos translates as "and Aharon shall smoke [*v'yaktar*] upon it *Ketores*-incenses...he shall smoke it [*yakterinah*]." Why does Onkelos translate the *lashon* "הקטרה" by *korbanos* as "bring up," not literally "smoke," as he does for the *Ketores*? And what does "bring up" mean?

The *Me'at Tzari* explains that "bringing up" refers to the Kohen who brings up pieces of limbs from the *Azarah* onto the *Mizbeiach*. The *Lechem V'Simlah* adds that this is the *lashon* of the *pasuk* that states, "ואל המזבח לא יעלו—And to the *Mizbeiach* it shall not be brought up." The *Me'at Tzari* suggests that Onkelos is of the same opinion as Rav Chaim from Brisk[18] that the mitzvah of "*haktarah*—incinerating" starts from when the Kohen brings up the limbs onto the *Mizbeiach*, so there is no *p'sul* for the limbs to remain on the *Mizbeiach* overnight without being burnt. Although this is not the actual burning, it is included in the process of burning, as he is bringing it up to the *Mizbeiach* to be burnt and smoked. Regarding the *Ketores*, he translates as "*Ketores busmin—Ketores*-incenses," since this refers to smoking the spices of the *Ketores*.

Onkelos translates "המזבחה" as "למדבחא—to the *Mizbeiach*," as if the Torah had written "להמזבח." The *Me'at Tzari* explains that the 'ה at the end of the word is in place of a 'ל at the beginning. The words "והקטרת המזבחה" literally mean "and you shall burn to the *Mizbeiach*," which is hard to understand. The *Mizbeiach* is not burned, rather the parts are burned and smoked on the *Mizbeiach*. There seems to be something missing. For Onkelos, who translates "הקטרת" as "and you shall bring up," it fits well to translate "המזבחה" literally, as "to the *Mizbeiach*": "and you shall bring [it] up to the *Mizbeiach*."

17   יג, יט

18   חידושי הגרי"ז זבחים פז.

May Hashem rebuild the Beis Hamikdash and restore the *avodah* of *korbanos bi'meheirah bi'yameinu, Amen!*

## WHERE WERE THE BLOOD AND OIL PLACED ON THE "TENUCH" AND "BOHEN"?

וְלָקַחְתָּ מִדָּמוֹ וְנָתַתָּה עַל תְּנוּךְ אֹזֶן אַהֲרֹן וְעַל תְּנוּךְ אֹזֶן בָּנָיו
הַיְמָנִית וְעַל בֹּהֶן יָדָם הַיְמָנִית וְעַל בֹּהֶן רַגְלָם הַיְמָנִית (כט כ)

וְתִסַּב מִדְּמֵיהּ וְתִתֵּין עַל רוּם אָדְנָא דְּאַהֲרֹן וְעַל רוּם אָדְנָא דִּבְנוֹהִי
דְּיַמִּינָא וְעַל אִלְיוֹן יַדְהוֹן דְּיַמִּינָא וְעַל אִלְיוֹן רַגְלְהוֹן דְּיַמִּינָא

*And you shall take from its blood, and you shall put upon the tip of Aharon's ear and upon the tip of his sons' ear, the right, and upon the top [thumb] of their right hand, and upon the top [big toe] of their right foot.*

The *pasuk* states, "And you shall slaughter the ram, ולקחת מדמו ונתתה על תנוך אזן אהרן ועל תנוך אזן בניו הימנית ועל בהן ידם הימנית ועל בהן רגלם הימנית—and you shall take from its blood, and you shall put it upon the *tenuch* of Aharon's ear, and upon the *tenuch* of his sons' ear, the right, and upon the *bohen* of their right hand, and on the *bohen* of their right foot." What is the *tenuch* and the *bohen*, and where is the blood supposed to be placed?

The *Radak* says that the *tenuch* is the soft part at the end of the ear. *Rashi* explains differently: the *tenuch* is the cartilage of the middle-inner wall inside the ear, which is where the blood should be placed. So too, the *Radak* quotes from the *Sifra* that it is the inner wall of the ear. *Rashi* explains that the *bohen yadam* is the middle joint of the thumb, which is where the blood should be placed. The *Sifsei Chachamim*[19] adds that this is similar to *Rashi*'s *tenuch*, where the blood was placed on the inner part of the ear. So too, the *bohen raglam* follows that the blood was placed on the middle joint of the big toe.

Onkelos translates "ונתת על תנוך אזן אהרן ועל תנוך אזן בניו הימנית" differently: "And you shall put upon the tip of Aharon's ear and upon the tip of his sons' ear, the right." He translates "*tenuch*" as "*rum*—tip," which refers to a high place on the ear. The *Nesinah LaGer* quotes from the *Toras Kohanim* that "*nuch*" is a *lashon "govah."* The *Nefesh HaGer* teaches from the Gemara: Rabbi Elazar says that Yudin B'Ribi *darshened*, that when they would do *retziah*, the piercing of the ear of the *eved Ivri*, they only did it in the place of "*milsa.*" *Rashi* explains that this is in the tail of the ear, in the fleshy part on the earlobe, not in the cartilage. The *Chachamim* say that an *eved Ivri* who is a Kohen does not have *retziah* because it will make a blemish on him. The Gemara says that this indicates that *retziah* is in the *govah* of the ear. The translation of "*govah*" is "*rum*," which is exactly how Onkelos translates. It refers to the cartilage of the ear which is high up and hard, not the fleshy part on the earlobe.

Onkelos translates "ועל בהן ידם הימנית ועל בהן רגלם הימנית" differently: "And upon the top [thumb] of their right hand, and upon the top [big toe] of their right foot." Onkelos translates the word "*bohen*" by their hand and feet as "אליון." The *Me'at Tzari* explains that "אליון" with an א is like "עליון" with an ע, which means "the top." This refers to a high place by the thumb and the big toe. Onkelos translates both the *tenuch* and the *bohen* as a high place, the tip and top, both being a high point where the blood was placed: on the tip of the ear and on the top of the thumb and big toe.

Or, Onkelos translates "*bohen*" as the thumb, which is above the other four fingers. It does not imply where the blood should be placed on the thumb. This is as the *Midrash Tanchuma*[20] teaches on the words, "ונתנך ה' אלקיך עליון—and Hashem, your G-d, will make you above:" Rabbi Levi said, "What is עליון? As this אליון. If you will merit, you will be above all the other four fingers; if not, you will be below the four fingers." The *Eitz Yosef* explains that the comparison is, just as the thumb is above the rest of the fingers of the hand, so too Yisrael is separated and above the other four kingdoms.

May Hashem help us be separated from and elevated above the other kingdoms!

## IS "MILUY YAD" "FILLING UP A HAND," "COMPLETING A HAND," OR "OFFERING KORBANOS"? HOW IS THIS RELEVANT FOR THE INAUGURATION?

וּמִלֵּאתָ אֶת יָדָם וְקִדַּשְׁתָּ אֹתָם וְכִהֲנוּ לִי (כה, מא)

וּתְקָרֵיב יָת קֻרְבָּנְהוֹן וּתְקַדֵּישׁ יָתְהוֹן וִישַׁמְּשׁוּן קֳדָמָי

*And you shall offer their korbanos, and you shall sanctify them, and they will serve before Me.*

וְהָיְתָה לָהֶם כְּהֻנָּה לְחֻקַּת עוֹלָם וּמִלֵּאתָ יַד אַהֲרֹן וְיַד בָּנָיו (כט, ט)

וּתְהֵי לְהוֹן כְּהֻנְּתָא לִקְיָם עָלַם וּתְקָרֵיב קֻרְבָּנָא דְּאַהֲרֹן וְקֻרְבָּנָא דִבְנוֹהִי

*And it shall be for them kehunah for a statute forever, and you shall offer the korban of Aharon and the korban of his sons.*

כִּי אֵיל מִלֻּאִים הוּא (כט, כב)

אֲרֵי דְּכַר קֻרְבָּנַיָּא הוּא

*Since it is the ram of the korbanos.*

וּלְמַלֵּא בָם אֶת יָדָם (כט, כט)

וּלְקָרָבָא בְּהוֹן יָת קֻרְבָּנְהוֹן

*And to offer with them their korban.*

שִׁבְעַת יָמִים תְּמַלֵּא יָדָם (כט, לה)

שִׁבְעָא יוֹמִין תְּקָרֵיב קֻרְבָּנְהוֹן

*Seven days you shall offer their korbanos.*

The *pesukim* state by dressing Aharon and his sons with the garments of *kehunah,* "וְהָיְתָה לָהֶם כְּהֻנָּה לְחֻקַּת," and, "וּמִלֵּאתָ אֶת יָדָם וְקִדַּשְׁתָּ אֹתָם וְכִהֲנוּ לִי," and, "עוֹלָם וּמִלֵּאתָ יַד אַהֲרֹן וְיַד בָּנָיו," and, "וּלְמַלֵּא בָם אֶת יָדָם." And it states by the inauguration, "כי איל מלאים הוא," and, "שבעת ימים תמלא ידם." What does the *lashon* "*miluy*" mean and what does it accomplish?

*Rashi* explains that every "*miluy yad*—filling up of the hand" reflects "*chinuch*—inauguration," when one enters into something to be established in it from that day on. It is common that when a person is appointed to fulfill a responsibility, the one in charge gives a glove of leather into his hand which fills his hand, with which he becomes established over the thing to have authority. The *Sifsei Chachamim*[21] adds that this is a sign that he has strength and ownership over the job, just as the leather fills up his hand. The *Ramban* is bothered: how does "*miluy yad*" fit for the inauguration of all different things, such as with being dressed with clothing? The *Hakesav V'Hakabbalah* answers that just as a cloth is given over into another person's hand to become appointed, so too, the clothing was what gave Aharon and his sons authority over their responsibility of *kehunah*.

The *Ramban* explains the *lashon* "*miluy yad*" differently: it means *sheleimus*, completeness, as it states, "*Ki mal'u yamai*—Since my days are completed," and, "*B'chesef malei*—With the complete amount of silver." So too, here, a foreigner who will never achieve purity to bring a *korban* or serve the king is lacking and incomplete for that *avodah*. When one becomes fitting, his hand becomes completed and suitable for all *avodos* and the different types of work.

The *Nesinah LaGer* says that Onkelos translates the *lashon* "*miluy yad*" differently, as "offering *korbanos*." For example, he translates "*u'mileisa es yadam*" as "and you shall offer their *korbanos*." The *Ramban* explains that the *lashon* "*miluy yad*" literally means "and you shall complete their hands," while Onkelos translates according to the intent. Through these *korbanos*, their hands will become full with any service. The *Nefesh HaGer* says that since Onkelos translates with the *lashon* "offering *korbanos*" also by the dressing by the inauguration, this reflects that the main inauguration happened through Moshe bringing *korbanos* during the seven days. The *Yein Hatov* explains that this was part of the *chinuch*, training process, for Aharon and his sons. This will teach them the way to do the *avodah* of *korbanos*. Similarly, the Gemara[22] teaches that a minor who does not need his mother is obligated *mi'd'Rabbanan* to sit in a sukkah. *Rashi* explains that this is in order to make him accustomed and familiar with mitzvos so he should become *mechunach*, trained, to fulfill them.

The *pasuk* mentions to take the fats of the second ram, "כִּי אֵיל מִלְאִים הוּא." *Rashi* explains that "מִלְאִים" is a *lashon* of *sheleimus*—it was complete with everything. The *Sifsei Chachamim*[23] adds that the word "מִלְאִים—full" is in place of the word "שְׁלָמִים—a *Korban Shelamim*." It is complete since some parts are burnt on the *Mizbeiach*, some go to the Kohen who did the *avodah*, and some go to the owner. Here, since Moshe served as the Kohen during the seven days of inauguration, therefore, the chest needed to be given to him for a portion. The rest of the ram was eaten by Aharon and his sons, aside from what was burned, since they were the owners. The *Nefesh HaGer* says that Onkelos translates "כִּי אֵיל הַמִּלְאִים הוּא" differently: he does not translate as "since it is the holy-slaughterings [*nichsas kudshaya*]" which is how he generally translates "*Korban Shelamim*," but as "since it is the ram of the *korbanos*." This hints that the *korbanos* are what completed the hands of the Kohanim to be fitting for their *avodas kehunah*.

May we merit to have the inauguration of the Third Beis Hamikdash *b'karov*!

## WHY IS A "ZAR" DESCRIBED AS "CHILONI"?

### וְזָר לֹא יֹאכַל כִּי קֹדֶשׁ הֵם (כט, לג)

וְחִילּוֹנִי לָא יֵיכוֹל אֲרֵי קַדְשָׁא אִנּוּן

*And a foreigner [outsider] shall not eat since they are holy.*

---

22  סוכה ב:

23  נ

# לֹא תַעֲלוּ עָלָיו קְטֹרֶת זָרָה (ל, ט)

## לָא תַסְקוּן עֲלוֹהִי קְטֹרֶת בֻּסְמִין נֻכְרָאִין

*Do not bring up upon it strange ketores incenses.*

The *pasuk* states, "לא תעלו עליו קטרת זרה—Do not bring up upon it 'ketores zarah.'" What is a *ketores zarah*? *Rashi* explains, "Do not bring a personal free-will offering of the same amount of Aharon's *Ketores*, as all of them are foreign aside from the obligatory *Ketores*." Other types of incense or different amounts than the proscribed amount is not included in this *issur*.[24] Onkelos translates "*ketores zarah*" as "strange *ketores* incenses [*ketores busmin nuchra'in*]." The *Ramban* says that Onkelos does not translate "*zarah*" as "*nuchreisa*—the strange one," in singular, which would refer to a different *ketores* than Aharon's of the same amount, but rather as "*nuchra'in*," in plural, which refers to the incense spices; do not bring other strange incenses.[25] This hints that it is *assur* to make *Ketores* from other incense or to add other incense to the proscribed amount.

Earlier in the parashah, it states, "וזר לא יאכל כי קדש הם—And a foreigner shall not eat, since they are holy." *Rashi* explains that the Torah forbids a foreigner from eating *kodshei kodashim* because they are holy. The *Sifsei Chachamim*[26] adds that any type of *kodshei kodashim* are *assur* for a foreigner to eat. Onkelos translates "*v'zar*" as "and a *chiloni* [*chilonai*] shall not eat." What does "*chiloni*" mean?

The *Vayikra Rabbah*[27] teaches: Rabbi Shmuel bar Nachman gave a *mashal* involving a Kohen Gadol to explain "*kedoshim tihiyu*—be holy." A Kohen Gadol was traveling and met a *chiloni*, who said, "I will go with you." He responded, "I am a Kohen, and I need to go on the pure path; I can't go through the cemetery. If you come with me, good, and if not, I will leave you and I will go on my own." So too, Moshe said to Yisrael, "כי ה' אלקיך מתהלך בקרב מחניך להצילך—Since Hashem, your G-d, goes within

---

24   פני ירושלם ברמב"ן טוב ירושלם

25   מעט צרי

26   ל

27   פ' כה, ז

your camp to save you." The *Eshed Hanechalim* explains that everyone was commanded "*kedoshim tihiyu*—be holy," and the reason is because Hashem goes among you. Since Hashem goes among you, you will need to attach yourselves to Hashem's *middos* for Him to continue to go together with you.

The Midrash describes the person the Kohen Gadol met as "*chiloni*." The *Matnas Kehunah* and *Eitz Yosef* explain that the *lashon* "*chiloni*" is like the way Onkelos translates "*zar*"—"*chiloni*." This can be explained, like the *Radak*, as coming from the *lashon* "*chol/chullin*—mundane" or "*chillel*—profane," meaning held bad from *kedushah*. Onkelos translates "*v'zar*" as "and *chiloni*," since only a Kohen who is holy can eat *kodshei kodashim*, the most sanctified food, whereas a *chiloni*, who is mundane/profane and removed from this lofty level of *kedushah*, cannot eat it; he can only eat *kodashim kalim*.

In Eretz Yisrael, there are a number of groups of Yidden who have different standards. One group is called "*chareidim*" and another group is called "*chilonim*." The name *chilonim* refers to people who are not as meticulous with fulfilling mitzvos, whereas *chareidim* refers to those who are more careful. The Gemara[28] teaches that Yidden who are worried to fulfill *mitzvos* cause themselves to heat up. *Rashi* explains that they are "*chareidim*" to make sure to keep the mitzvos. In the haftarah of Shabbos Rosh Chodesh, it states,[29] "ואל זה אביט אל עני ונכה רוח וחרד על דברי—And to this one I will focus, to the humble and the low spirit, and he who is *chareid* to My word." A bit further, it states,[30] "שמעו דבר ה' החרדים אל דברו—Heed the word of Hashem, those who are *chareidim* to His word." The *Radak* explains "*chareid*" as "fear which causes trembling," as it states, "*Va'yecherad Yitzchak*—And Yitzchak trembled." The *pasuk* describes those who have fear and tremble to heed His word. The *Metzudas Tzion* explains differently: "*chareid*" means "quick, to be zealous." The *Malbim* adds that Hashem is telling us that the purpose of the Beis Hamikdash and its *korbanos* are to bring a pleasant feeling

---

28   נדה לד:
29   ישעיה סו, ב
30   שם ה

before Him, that He commanded and His will was fulfilled. The *korban* itself is not the most wanted thing, rather the fulfillment of His will, and by humbling oneself before Him to heed His word. "*Chareid*" means fear that causes trembling or quickness-zealousness to heed to Hashem, whereas "*chiloni*" is the opposite—one who does not fear Hashem and is removed from *kedushah*.

*Avi Mori* said that a *rebbi* once asked his student where he was learning. The student answered that he was learning in Ohr Somayach, but he was not *a baal teshuvah*. The *rebbi* responded, "Why not?!" Whatever level we are at, we have to hope to grow in our *avodas Hashem*.

It is interesting to note that Onkelos translates "*zarah*" regarding the *Ketores* as "strange [*nuchra'in*]," whereas regarding not eating *kodesh* he translates "*v'zar*" as "*chilonai*." The reason is because "*zarah*" refers to forbidden *Ketores*, so he translates as "strange." "*V'zar*" refers to a *person* who is not fitting to eat, so he translates as "*chiloni*—mundane, profane, and removed from *kedushah*."

May Hashem help us inculcate *kedushah* into our beings and heed His word with fear and zealousness!

## DOES "B'HEITIVO" MEAN "LIGHTING" OR "FIXING"? WHY IS AHARON SPECIFICALLY MENTIONED BY THE MENORAH AND KETORES?

לְהַעֲלֹת נֵר תָּמִיד (כז, כ)

לְאַדְלָקָא בּוֹצִינַיָּא תְּדִירָא

*To light lamps continually.*

וְהִקְטִיר עָלָיו אַהֲרֹן קְטֹרֶת סַמִּים בַּבֹּקֶר בַּבֹּקֶר
בְּהֵיטִיבוֹ אֶת הַנֵּרֹת יַקְטִירֶנָּה (ל, ז)

וְיַקְטַר עֲלוֹהִי אַהֲרֹן קְטֹרֶת בּוּסְמִין בִּצְפַר בִּצְפַר בְּאַתְקָנוּתֵיהּ יָת בּוֹצִינַיָּא יַקְטְרִנַּהּ

*And Aharon shall smoke [burn] on it Ketores incenses each and every morning, when he fixes [cleans] the lamps, he shall smoke [burn] it.*

## וּבְהַעֲלֹת אַהֲרֹן אֶת הַנֵּרֹת בֵּין הָעַרְבַּיִם יַקְטִירֶנָּה (ל, ח)

### וּבְאַדְלָקוּת אַהֲרֹן יָת בּוֹצִינַיָּא בֵּין שִׁמְשַׁיָּא יַקְטְרִנַּהּ

*And when Aharon lights the lamps between the*
*suns [at twilight], he shall smoke [burn] it.*

The *pasuk* states, "והקטיר עליו אהרן קטרת סמים בבקר בבקר בהיטיבו את הנרת
יקטירנה—And Aharon shall burn upon it the *Ketores* incenses each
and every morning, '*b'heitivo es ha'neiros*' he shall burn it." What does
"*b'heitivo es ha'neiros*" mean? *Rashi* explains that "*b'heitivo*" is a *lashon*
of cleaning. Each and every morning, they would clean out the receptacles of the *Menorah* from ash and wicks that burned during the
night. The *Kesef Mishneh*[31] writes that *Rashi* explains that if a lamp was
extinguished halfway through the night or before the morning, they
would replace the wick and oil with a new wick and oil and light it. Also,
the *Rashba* explains that "*hatavah*" means fixing the wicks, not lighting,
as it states, "ובהעלות אהרן את הנרת בין הערבים יקטירנה—And when Aharon
would light the lamps in the evening, he would burn the *Ketores*." We
see that the mitzvah to light the *Menorah* was specifically in the evening, not in the morning. The *Kesef Mishneh* writes that Onkelos, who
translates "*b'heitivo*" as "when he fixes [*b'askanuseih*] the lamps," is also
of the opinion that "*hatavah*" means fixing. So too, the *Biur Onkelos*
writes in the name of the *Ibn Ezra* that at the time when Aharon fixed
the wick and oil, he also burned the *Ketores*. Lighting, though, was only
in the evening, not in the morning.

The *Rambam* writes that "*dishun haMenorah*" is when a lamp became
extinguished, a Kohen would remove the wick and all its oil and throw
it into the place of the ash next to the *Mizbeiach*. He would clean out
the lamp completely, put in another wick and half a *lug* of oil, and light
it, which is called "*hatavah*." If a lamp was found burning, he did not
extinguish it; rather, he would fix it. The *Kesef Mishneh* says that the
*Rambam* is of the opinion that he would also light the *Menorah* in the

---

31    על רמב״ם הל׳ תמידין ומוספין ג, יב

morning, as it states, "והקטיר עליו אהרן קטרת סמים בבקר בבקר בהיטיבו את הנרות," understanding that "*hatavah*" means "lighting the lamps."

It states, "ובהעלות אהרן את הנרות בין הערבים יקטירנה," using the *lashon* "*aliyah*." Also, in the beginning of the parashah it states, "*L'haalos ner tamid*," again with the *lashon* "*aliyah*." *Rashi* explains that this *lashon* indicates how you should light: light the lamps until they are able to go up on their own. Onkelos translates "*u'v'haalos*" and "*l'haalos*" differently: "And when Aharon lights the lamps," and "To light lamps," which describes the general mitzvah of *hadlakas neiros*.

The *pesukim* above mention Aharon regarding the *Menorah* and *Ketores*. The *Ramban* asks: Since the mitzvah of lighting the *Menorah* and burning the *Ketores* can be performed by any Kohen, why does the Torah specifically mention Aharon?

Later on, the *pasuk* states, "וכפר אהרן על קרנתיו אחת בשנה מדם חטאת הכפרים אחת בשנה יכפר עליו לדרתיכם—And Aharon shall atone on its corners, once a year, from the blood of the sin-offering of atonements; once a year, he shall atone upon it for your generations." The *Ramban* suggests that since it speaks about Aharon doing the *avodah* of Yom Kippur, it also mentions Aharon by the other *avodos* as well. Alternatively, the *pasuk* is hinting that Aharon should be the first one to start the *avodos*.

The *Seforno*[32] answers that each day in the Midbar was like Yom Kippur. The cloud rested over the *Mishkan* throughout the forty years in the Midbar, as it states, "כי ענן ה' על המשכן יומם ואש תהיה לילה בו," just as it states about Yom Kippur, "כי בענן אראה על הכפרת." The *Shemos Rabbah*[33] teaches that Aharon went into the *Kodesh Hakodashim* whenever he wanted to while in the Midbar. Similarly, the *Meshech Chochmah*[34] quotes from the *Vayikra Rabbah*: Hashem said to Moshe, "It is not as you thought, that Aharon can only enter into the *Kodesh Hakodashim* sometimes; rather, he can enter whenever he wants in order to do the *avodah* like the *seder* of Yom Kippur." The *Meshech Chochmah* quotes from the *Vilna Gaon*

---

that on Yom Kippur, Aharon was obligated to do the *avodah*, whereas the rest of the year, it was optional for him. Aharon's sons and Kohanim Gedolim of later generations were not allowed to enter whenever they wanted, only on Yom Kippur. The *Seforno* says that since on Yom Kippur, the *avodah* of the *Menorah* and *Ketores* was done by the Kohen Gadol, so too, it was fitting for Aharon to do these *avodos* each day in the Midbar as well.

The *Seforno*[35] says that the Shechinah rested so permanently over the *Mishkan* that for forty years it never left, other than when B'nei Yisrael would travel. This did not occur in Shiloh, nor by the first or second Batei Mikdash. However, the third Beis Hamikdash will be even greater, as it states, "וֹאני אהיה לה נאם ה' חומת אש סביב ולכבוד אהיה בתוכה."

May Hashem bring back the Shechinah with the third Beis Hamikdash *bi'meheirah bi'yameinu, Amen!*

---

# Ki Sisa

## HOW IS WASHING HANDS AND FEET "SANCTIFYING"?

לְרָחְצָה (ל, יח)

לְקַדּוּשׁ

*For sanctifying.*

וְרָחֲצוּ אַהֲרֹן וּבָנָיו (ל, יט)

וִיקַדְּשׁוּן אַהֲרֹן וּבְנוֹהִי

*And Aharon and his sons shall sanctify.*

יִרְחֲצוּ מַיִם (ל, כ)

יְקַדְּשׁוּן מַיָּא

*They shall sanctify with water.*

וְרָחֲצוּ יְדֵיהֶם וְרַגְלֵיהֶם (ל, כא)

וִיקַדְּשׁוּן יְדֵיהוֹן וְרַגְלֵיהוֹן

*And they shall sanctify their hands and their feet.*

The *pasuk* states, "You shall make a copper *Kiyor* and its base of copper, '*l'rachtzah*—to wash.'" The following *pesukim* state, "When they enter the *Ohel Moed*, '*yirchatzu mayim*—they shall wash with water," and, "*V'rachatzu yedeihem v'ragleihem*—And they shall wash their hands and feet." Here, the Torah introduces the making of the *Kiyor* for the *Mishkan*. Earlier, in *Parashas Terumah*, the *pesukim* discuss the different vessels of the *Mishkan* and does not mention the *Kiyor*. Why is the *Kiyor* mentioned independently after all the vessels of the *Mishkan*? And what was the *Kiyor*'s function?

The *Seforno* explains that the vessels discussed in *Parashas Terumah* were used for the *avodah* that brings the Shechinah. This included the *Shulchan, Menorah,* and the *Mizbeiach* on which the Kohanim used to serve in the *Mishkan.* However, the *Kiyor* was not used for an actual *avodah*; it was needed to prepare the Kohanim to serve in the *Mishkan.* The *Ramban* says that we derive from the *Kiyor* the requirement of a *"kli shareis*—a holy vessel"* to wash one's hands and feet before entering the *Mishkan* to do *avodah.* However, washing from the *Kiyor* itself is not a mitzvah and is not *me'akev.* For this reason, the Kohen Gadol on Yom Kippur was allowed to sanctify his hands and feet with a flask of gold, which they made for his honor. Since the *Kiyor* itself is not *me'akev,* it is not so essential, so it is not mentioned earlier.

The *Ramban* explains that the reason for the *Kiyor* is because it is fitting for anyone who comes close to the King's table to touch food and drink to clean his hands, as the hands are constantly moving and touching dirty things. The Kohanim should also clean their feet because they would serve barefoot, and people often have dirt and filth on their feet. This washing was done for the honor of Hashem.

The *Ramban* teaches that Onkelos translates *"rechitzah"* by the *Kiyor* as *"kiddush*—sanctification,"* not literally "wash." The *Me'at Tzari* adds that Onkelos translates the lashon *"rechitzah"* as "sanctification," just like Chazal call sanctifying the hands and feet *"kiddush yadayim v'raglayim."* The *Ramban* explains that the hands and feet of a person are the two ends of a person's body; the feet are at the bottom, and the hands are at the top, since when one raises his hands, they ascend above the head. By washing the hands and feet, the entire body is encompassed, sanctifying the entire Kohen to enter the *Ohel Moed* and serve before Hashem. The point of this washing was not done to clean the Kohanim, but to sanctify them, as they are the ones who serve Hashem.

The *Rashba*[1] says that one needs to wash his hands in the morning with a vessel before davening, but in the evening, one does not need to do so. Why is this? He explains that when one wakes up in the morning,

---

he becomes a new being, as it states, "חדשים לבקרים רבה אמונתך—Anew in the mornings, great is Your trust to believe in." By washing our hands with a vessel, we are meant to sanctify ourselves with holiness like a Kohen who sanctifies his hands from the *Kiyor* before his service in the *Mishkan* or Beis Hamikdash. So too, each person is meant to serve Hashem with his own personal *avodah*. By washing our hands, we sanctify ourselves and prepare ourselves for the *avodah* we are meant to accomplish for the day.

May we elevate ourselves by washing our hands in the morning and prepare ourselves for each day's *avodas Hashem*!

## WERE "BIGDEI SERAD" "SERVICE GARMENTS" OR "HOLY GARMENTS"?

### וְאֵת בִּגְדֵי הַשְּׂרָד וְאֶת בִּגְדֵי הַקֹּדֶשׁ לְאַהֲרֹן הַכֹּהֵן וְאֶת בִּגְדֵי בָנָיו לְכַהֵן (לא, י)

וְיָת לְבוּשֵׁי שִׁמּוּשָׁא וְיָת לְבוּשֵׁי קֻדְשָׁא לְאַהֲרֹן כַּהֲנָא וְיָת לְבוּשֵׁי בְּנוֹהִי לְשַׁמָּשָׁא

*And the service garments, and the holy garments for Aharon the Kohen, and the garments of his sons, to serve.*

The *pasuk* states, "ואת בגדי השרד ואת בגדי הקדש לאהרן הכהן ואת בגדי בניו לכהן." What are the *bigdei ha'serad*?

*Rashi* explains that the *bigdei ha'serad* cannot be *bigdei kehunah* since the Torah states, "And the *bigdei ha'serad* and the *bigdei ha'kodesh*." Rather, *bigdei ha'serad* are the garments of blue-green, crimson, and bright color mentioned in *Parashas Bamidbar* that were used to cover the vessels when B'nei Yisrael traveled in the Midbar. *Rashi* proves this point, as the Torah does not mention "*sheish*—linen" together with the *bigdei ha'serad*. Every garment of the *bigdei kehunah* incorporates linen. *Rashi* explains that "*serad*" is an Aramaic word that means fabric woven with a needle and has holes, like netting in the shape of a sieve, just as Onkelos translates "*kela'im*" as "*seradei*" and "*michbar*" as "*serada*." These garments were made as a netting.

The *Ramban* is bothered: it doesn't make sense to say that the garments that covered the vessels for protection had holes, like a sieve. Rather, he explains that "שרד" is from the *lashon* "שריד," like the *Ibn Ezra* says; each was made from the remnants of that type of material.

Onkelos translates "*bigdei ha'serad*" differently: as "service [*shimusha*] garments." Rabbeinu Bachya explains that they were garments which served to cover the vessels of the *Mishkan* when they traveled, like *Rashi*. There was greenish-blue to cover the *Aron*, crimson to cover the *Mizbeiach*, and a bright reddish color to cover the *Shulchan*. The *Nesinah LaGer* adds that the covering would protect them from rain and dust.

The *Ramban* asks: Why doesn't the Torah mention how many *bigdei serad* to make and what they were for? Also, the *bigdei serad* are always mentioned before *bigdei kodesh*. Why should the Torah mention the covering of the vessels first, before the *bigdei kehunah* themselves? Also, in *Parashas Vayakhel*, it states, "את בגדי השרד לשרת בקדש;" the words "*l'shares ba'kodesh*" are used throughout the Torah for *avodah* in the *Mishkan*. This implies that the *bigdei ha'serad* were used for *avodah* of *korbanos*.

For these reasons, the *Ramban* explains "*bigdei serad*" differently: they were the *bigdei kehunah* themselves. This is as the Gemara brings on the words "את בגדי השרד לשרת בקדש": Rabbi Chama Bar Chanina said, if not for the *bigdei kehunah*, there would not have been in Yisrael "שריד ופליט—anyone remaining." *Rashi* explains that this is because with the *bigdei kehunah*, they were able to bring *korbanos*, which would atone for Yisrael. The *Maharsha* adds that "*serad*" hints that the garments would cause Yisrael to remain, as the garments themselves atoned for the sins of Yisrael. The Gemara teaches: Rabbi Shmuel bar Nachmani said, these are garments that they would cut with their weaving equipment as the Kohen's size and shape, and they left over a little bit that was not woven with them. This refers to the sleeve, which was woven by itself and sewn on with a needle. *Rashi* explains that it was woven in such a way that it would be in a cylindrical form when removed from the loom and was able to be worn as is, without cutting or sewing. The bit remaining is from the *lashon* "*serad—remnant*." The *Maharsha* says that this Gemara does not follow *Rashi*'s opinion that "*serad*" means as "*kela'im*," but the *Ramban*'s understanding of *bigdei kehunah*.

In the *Selichos* for *Taanis Esther*, we say, "נתעטף בבגדי שרד כטעה במנין קצב סדר להשתמש בשונים כלי המחצב ויבא גם השטן בתוכם להיתיצב." Achashveirosh dressed in *bigdei serad*, as he was mistaken in the count of finishing the exile, thinking that the Jews had not been redeemed. He arranged the hewn vessels to use, and the Satan also came among them to set them upright. This refers to the Gemara[2] which teaches that Achashveirosh took out garments of the Beis Hamikdash and used them. Also, in the *seder avodah* of Yom Kippur,[3] it is written, "*Pei'arto b'vigdei serad*." We see that the *bigdei serad* refer to the garments of the Kohanim.

The *Ramban* says that they are called "*serad*" because they hint to unique garments worn by the person who is above everyone, being Aharon or the Kohen Gadol anointed after him. "*Serad*" hints to garments of a king, as it states, "ובשרידים אשר ה' קרא—And with the unique people whom Hashem calls." The *pasuk* mentions two special qualities: first, they are *bigdei ha'serad*, only for the Kohen Gadol, and second, they are *bigdei ha'kodesh*, holy garments. The *pasuk* does not mention *sheish*—linen by the *bigdei serad* because it is not honorable.

*Rashi* quotes Onkelos, who translates "*bigdei serad*" as "service [*shimusha*] garments," and explains that the word "*serad*" is a *lashon* of *avodah* and *sheirus*—service. The *Me'at Tzari* says that this implies, like the *Ramban*, that they were *bigdei kehunah*, unlike the Rabbeinu Bachya above. Onkelos translates with the *lashon* "*shimush*—service," as the Gemara[4] teaches that the garments of the *kehunah* are called *klei shareis*.

May Hashem return the Kohanim to their *avodah* with the *bigdei kehunah*!

---

2   מגילה יא:

3   ב"אתה כוננת"

4   יומא כד: ורש"י

## DID MOSHE DAVEN ON HIS OWN
## AFTER THE CHEIT HA'EIGEL?

# וְעַתָּה הַנִּיחָה לִּי וְיִחַר אַפִּי בָהֶם וַאֲכַלֵם (לב, י)

וּכְעַן אֲנַח בָּעוּתָךְ מִן קֳדָמַי וְיִתְקַף רֻגְזִי בְּהוֹן וַאֲשֵׁיצִינוּן

*And now, rest [stop] (put down) your request [davening] from before*
*Me, and My anger will ignite against them, and I will destroy them.*

The *pasuk* states: Hashem said to Moshe, "ועתה הניחה לי ויחר אפי בהם
ואכלם—And now, let go of Me, and My anger will fire up against them,
and I will consume them." The Gemara[5] writes that Rabbi Avahu
said, since it states, "*Hanichah Li*," this reflects that Moshe took hold
of Hashem like a person who grabs his friend's garment. Moshe said,
"I will not let go of You until You forgive them." Moshe started to daven
to Hashem on his own on behalf of B'nei Yisrael to overturn the decree
of destroying all of Yisrael.

The Gemara writes that Rabbi Eliezer taught, "Hashem said to Moshe,
'*lech reid*—descend from your greatness.' I only gave you greatness because of Yisrael; now that they sinned, what greatness do you need?"
Immediately, Moshe's strength weakened and he did not have energy
to speak. Once Hashem said,[6] "*Heref mi'meni v'ashmideim*—loosen up
from Me and I will destroy them," Moshe understood and said, "It is
dependent upon me." Immediately, he stood up and strengthened
himself with davening and asked for Hashem's mercy. This is similar
to a king who got angry at his son and hit him hard. The king's good
friend was sitting there and was afraid to say anything. The king said,
"If not for my good friend sitting before me, I would kill him." Once the
friend recognized that it was dependent on him, he immediately stood
up and saved the king's son. So too with Moshe: once he realized it was
dependent on him, he davened for Yisrael and saved them.

5   ברכות לב.

6   דברים ט, יד

The *Maharsha* says that it seems from these two Gemaros that there are two opinions as to whether Moshe started to daven on his own or only started to daven after Hashem showed him that it was dependent on him. However, since the Gemara does not mention that they argue, it seems that all the opinions coincide. The *Nefesh HaGer* explains that these opinions are inferred from the change of words, from *"hanichah Li"* to *"heref mi'meni."* Since Hashem set the words for *Sefer Shemos*, therefore it states *"hanichah Li,"* which implies an unbelievable thing—that Moshe "grabbed" Hashem. In *Sefer Devarim*, where Moshe repeated the Torah, Moshe did not say the *lashon "hanichah Li"* because he did not want to say about himself that he took hold of Hashem.

The *Maharsha* explains that originally, Moshe did not think to daven to Hashem, as he assumed that there was no hope. Hashem said, *"Heref mi'meni"* and showed Moshe that there was room to daven and it indeed depended on him. Moshe then immediately started to daven to Hashem. Afterwards, Hashem said, *"Hanichah Li*—let go of Me," stop davening so that I can destroy B'nei Yisrael. Even so, Moshe continued to daven, until Hashem accepted his davening and forgave them.

We see that although Hashem decreed to destroy Yisrael, Moshe's davening helped cause Hashem to forgive them. Moshe did not let go; he was persistent, and was able to change Hashem's decision. This teaches the tremendous power of davening; no matter what, one should never give up hope, and daven to Hashem for His salvation!

Onkelos translates both *"hanichah Li"* and *"heref mi'meni"* as "rest [stop] your request [*anach ba'usach*] from before Me." The *Me'at Tzari* explains that the *lashon "anach"* is similar to the way Onkelos translates *"va'yanach"*—as *"v'nach*—and He rested," hinting to *menuchah*—resting. The *Nefesh HaGer* explains that Onkelos does not translate *"hanichah Li"* as "let go" since it is improper to say that Moshe grabbed onto Hashem, which is, *chas v'shalom*, degrading to the honor of Hashem. He understands like *Rashi*: Moshe did not start davening on behalf of B'nei Yisrael. Hashem said, *"V'atah hanichah Li,"* to indicate an opening and let him know that it is dependent on him. If he will daven on behalf of B'nei Yisrael, Hashem won't destroy them. Hashem told Moshe to leave the request in order to hint that davening could help. A proof to this is from the *Shemos Rabbah*:[7] "It states, 'ועתה הניחה לי ויחר אפי בהם ואכלם.' Was Moshe holding onto Hashem that He said, 'Let go'? Rather, it is comparable to a king who got angry at his son and brought him into an inner room to hit him. The king screamed from inside, '*Hanichah li*—Leave me alone; allow me to hit him.' The one who nurtured the child was outside and heard. He understood that the king was saying '*hanichah li*' because he wanted him to appease him about his son. So too it was with Hashem and Moshe. Hashem hinted to Moshe to appease Him on behalf of B'nei Yisrael. Hashem said, "Don't daven for them, since I would forgive them through their request"; immediately, he started to daven. The *Nefesh HaGer* says that because it is improper to say that Moshe held onto Hashem, *Rashi* too left the Gemara's explanation and chose to follow *Targum* and the *Midrash*.

May we always daven and know there is hope, no matter how bad the situation may seem to be!

## WHO CAME CLOSE TO MOSHE WHEN HE CALLED OUT, "MI LAHASHEM EILAI," AND WHY? WHAT DID THEY MERIT?

וַיֹּאמֶר מִי לַה' אֵלָי וַיֵּאָסְפוּ אֵלָיו כָּל בְּנֵי לֵוִי (לב, כו)

מַאן דָּחֲלַיָּא דַּיְיָ יֵיתוּן לְוָתִי וְאִתְכְּנִישׁוּ לְוָתֵיהּ כָּל בְּנֵי לֵוִי

*He who fears Hashem shall come next to me, and all the B'nei Levi gathered next to him.*

Hashem sanctified the firstborn of B'nei Yisrael in Mitzrayim when He smote the firstborn Mitzrim and saved the firstborn Yisraelim. After B'nei Yisrael sinned by the golden calf, Hashem separated the Leviim from B'nei Yisrael, elevated them, and sanctified them in exchange for the firstborn Yisraelim. *Rashi*[8] explains that the Leviim were chosen out

7  פ' מב, ט

8  במדבר ג, יב

of all B'nei Yisrael since they did not worship the golden calf. When Moshe descended from the mountain, he saw that B'nei Yisrael were doing improper things and said, "*Mi laHashem eilai*," which literally means, "Whoever is to Hashem, to me." This is difficult to understand; what does this mean? Onkelos answers this by translating as, "He who fears Hashem shall come next to me." The *Nefesh HaGer* explains that Onkelos adds "shall come" to explain the intent of the shortened *pasuk*. "*Mi laHashem*—Whoever fears Hashem," which are those who didn't sin, "*eilai*—shall come next to me." The *Nesinah LaGer* adds that Onkelos translates as "*yirei Hashem*—those who fear Hashem" in plural, referring to all those who didn't sin.

The *pasuk* ends, "ויאספו אליו כל בני לוי," which Onkelos translates as "and all the B'nei Levi gathered next to him." Throughout all the tribes, there were people who strayed after the golden calf. Some actually worshipped it, and others honored it. However, all the Leviim stayed firm with dedication to Hashem. *Rashi* explains that every single person in the tribe of Levi was loyal to Hashem and did not worship the golden calf. Therefore, the tribe of Levi was chosen to serve Hashem instead of the firstborn Yisraelim.

There is a famous story about the time Rav Shimon Schwab visited the Chafetz Chaim on his way back from yeshiva. The Chafetz Chaim asked Rav Schwab, "Are you a Kohen?" He responded, "No." He asked, "Why not?" He responded, "Because my father was not a Kohen." "And why was your grandfather not a Kohen? Because his father was not a Kohen." Rav Schwab understood that the Chafetz Chaim was hinting at something here, so he waited for him to explain. The Chafetz Chaim said, "When Moshe called out, '*Mi laHashem eilai*,' my great-grandfather came, but your great-grandfather did not. So I am a Kohen and you are not." Rav Schwab responded to this message and decided he would always be one to respond to the call of "*Mi laHashem eilai*." Rav Schwab's grandson added that Rav Schwab said, "Hashem constantly calls out, '*Mi laHashem Eilai*,' and we should heed the call."[9]

---

The entire tribe of Levi came together to Moshe; not one was drawn after the rest of the Klal Yisrael. Therefore, Hashem selected the Leviim to be His people who perform the *avodah*. Now, Klal Yisrael is spread out among the nations with numerous challenges surrounding us both physically and spiritually. We are so minute that we can easily be persuaded and affected by the non-Jewish nations. The *Yaavetz* says that the biggest miracle is that Klal Yisrael still exists and was not eradicated, as were the many other nations that were killed off or simply ceased to be. We are like one sheep among seventy wolves, constantly in danger. Hashem loves us and protects us in all situations and wherever we are, to keep us alive and help us continuously exist.

Rav Yonasan Ibishitz[10] was asked by a wise non-Jew, "The Torah states, '*Acharei rabbim l'hatos*—Follow the majority.' Since you are the minority from all the nations, why don't you follow the majority and accept our beliefs?" He answered that the concept of following the majority is only where there is a doubt and a need for clarification. It is not said where something is clear and definite. For example, if a piece of meat clearly came from a non-kosher store, we do not say follow the majority, as there is no doubt; we know it is *treif*. The same goes for our belief; we have no doubt in the truth of our belief that Hashem is *emes*, and the majority of non-Jews won't make us budge from our faith.

May we heed Hashem's daily call of "*mi laHashem eilai*" and stay loyal to Him despite the challenges around us!

## DOES "ISH" MEAN "A MAN" OR "A PERSON"?

וְהִרְגוּ אִישׁ אֶת אָחִיו וְאִישׁ אֶת רֵעֵהוּ וְאִישׁ אֶת קְרֹבוֹ (לב, כז)

וּקְטוֹלוּ גְּבַר יָת אֲחוּהִי וּגְבַר יָת חַבְרֵיהּ וַאֱנָשׁ יָת קָרִיבֵיהּ

*And kill, a man, his brother, and a man, his
fellow, and a person, his relative.*

10   הובא בקובץ מאמרים מאמר על אמונה ס"ק ח

The *pasuk* states, "והרגו איש את אחיו ואיש את רעהו ואיש את קרבו"—And kill, a man, his brother, and a man, his friend, and a man, his relative." Since the entire tribe of Levi feared Hashem and didn't sin, why does Moshe command them to kill their brothers and relatives? *Rashi* explains that this refers to the brother of his mother, who is a Yisrael, not to the brother of his father, who is a Levi.

In *Parashas V'zos Haberachah*, it states,[11] "האומר לאביו ולאמו לא ראיתיו ואת אחיו לא הכיר ואת בניו לא ידע כי שמרו אמרתך ובריתך ינצרו"—That who said, to his father and to his mother he did not see, and his bother he did not recognize, and his sons he did not know, because they guarded Your words and Your covenant they watched." Onkelos translates "*lo re'isiv*" as "did not implement love [*lo re'cheim*] for his father and mother when they had iniquity from the judgment." He translates "*lo hikir*" and "*lo yada*" together: "he did not take appeasement for the face of his brother or son." He translates "כי שמרו אמרתך ובריתך ינצרו" as "since they guarded Your saying and Your covenant they did not change." *Rashi* explains that when B'nei Yisrael sinned with the golden calf, the entire B'nei Levi were instructed to kill anyone who worshipped the golden calf, whether the person was the father of his mother, or brother of his mother, or son of his daughter, all of whom could have been Yisraelim, and so they did. Levi's tribe stood firm by not worshipping the golden calf, and also by executing punishment to anyone who did worship without taking pity or having mercy on their own family members.

It states, "והרגו איש את אחיו ואיש את רעהו ואיש את קרבו," mentioning the word "*ish*" three times. Onkelos translates the first and second as "man [*gevar*]"—and kill, a man, his brother, and a man, his fellow. However, the third "*ish*" he translates as "person [*anash*]"—and a person, his relative. The *Nefesh HaGer* asks: Why does Onkelos change the translation of "*ish*" from "man" to "person"?

The *Nefesh HaGer* answers that the Torah states, "Kill his brother," who is a relative. Then it adds, "Kill his fellow," although a friend is sometimes more beloved than a brother, as it states, "טוב שכן קרוב מאח רחוק—A close neighbor is better than a faraway brother." A Levi might have loved his friend and would have had mercy on him and break boundaries to not kill him. Therefore, he needs a specific mention: "And kill his fellow." However, once the Torah commands, "Kill a brother and fellow," what is the need to add "and kill his relative," which is certainly included in the other commands? Says the *Nefesh HaGer* that the Torah adds, not only a man who saw a Yisrael sin needs to eradicate bad, but even any *anash*, person, including a woman, who saw a Yisrael sin, whether a relative or not. She, too, is included in the command to kill him or to give over this information to *beis din* to take care of. She cannot cover up for and pity him. Onkelos does not translate "*ish*" as "*gevar*—a man," but rather as "*anash*—a person," to include women.

May Hashem help us remain firm in our belief and serve Him with dedication!

## WHAT IS THE MEANING OF "EDYO" AND WHAT WAS ITS FUNCTION?

### וְלֹא שָׁתוּ אִישׁ עֶדְיוֹ עָלָיו (לג, ד)

וְלָא שַׁוּוּ גְּבַר תִּקּוּן זֵינֵיהּ עֲלֹוֹהִי

*And no man placed the fixing of his weaponry upon himself.*

### וְעַתָּה הוֹרֵד עֶדְיְךָ מֵעָלֶיךָ וְאֵדְעָה מָה אֶעֱשֶׂה לָּךְ (לג, ה)

וּכְעַן אַעֵד (אַעְדִּי) תִּקּוּן זֵינָךְ מִנָּךְ וּגְלֵי קֳדָמַי מָא אַעֲבֵּיד לָךְ

*And now remove the fixing of your weaponry from you; it is revealed before Me what I will do to you.*

### וַיִּתְנַצְּלוּ בְנֵי יִשְׂרָאֵל אֶת עֶדְיָם מֵהַר חוֹרֵב (לג, ו)

וְאַעְדִּיוּ (וְאַעֲדִּיאוּ) בְּנֵי יִשְׂרָאֵל יָת תִּקּוּן זֵינְהוֹן מְטוּרָא דְחוֹרֵב

*And B'nei Yisrael removed the fixing of their weaponry from the mountain of Chorev.*

The *pasuk* states, "*V'shalachti le'fanecha Malach*—And I will send before you an angel." The nation heard this bad statement and they mourned, "ולא שתו איש עדיו עליו"—and no person put on *edyo*." What does "*edyo*" mean? *Rashi* explains that these were crowns which were given to B'nei Yisrael at Har Sinai when they said, "*Naaseh v'nishma*." The *Ramban* explains differently: they were ornaments. Rabbeinu Bachya adds that when Yisrael accepted the Torah, they had great happiness. Now that they heard that the Shechinah would not go with them, they had great anguish, *middah k'neged middah*, and they mourned.

Onkelos translates "ולא שתו איש עדיו עליו" differently: "And no man placed the fixing of his weaponry upon himself." The following *pasuk* states, "And Hashem said to Moshe, say to B'nei Yisrael, 'You are a stiff-necked nation…and I will finish you off, ועתה הורד עדיך מעליך ואדעה מה אעשה לך,'" which Onkelos translates as, "And now, remove the fixing of your weaponry from you; it is revealed before Me what I will do to you." Immediately, "ויתנצלו בני ישראל את עדים מהר חורב," which Onkelos translates as, "And B'nei Yisrael removed the fixing of their weaponry from the mountain of Chorev." Onkelos translates the *lashon* "עדי" as "the fixing of weaponry." What fixing of weaponry did B'nei Yisrael have from Har Sinai, and what was its purpose?

The *Midrash Tanchuma*[12] teaches: Rabbi Abba bar Kahana said that when B'nei Yisrael said, "*Naaseh v'nishma*," Hashem immediately cherished them and sent two angels to each of them. One girded each person with weaponry, and the other gave a crown. The *Beis Halevi*[13] explains that these two presents parallel the two acceptances that each person made, which is hinted in the word "*naaseh—we* shall do," as opposed to "*e'eseh—I* shall do." Each person accepted on himself to fulfill the Torah and each accepted *arvus*, responsibility to another Yid so that he, too, should fulfill the Torah. Each person received a crown for his personal commitment to fulfill the Torah, and he received weaponry, a sword, for the acceptance to help his friend, since he'll need strength and might to

---

12 תצוה י"א

13 פ' משפטים

do so. The *Midrash Tanchuma* teaches that when B'nei Yisrael stood by Har Sinai, they were all united, of one heart to accept Hashem's kingship with happiness, and they also took responsibility for each other. By the golden calf, they didn't say, "*Eileh eloheinu Yisrael*—These are *our* gods, Yisrael," which would include them too in idolatry. Rather, they said, "*Eileh elohecha Yisrael*—These are your gods, Yisrael," as though talking to others who worshipped idolatry, not referring to themselves. Although they may have bowed down, the main sin of idolatry is in one's mind and thoughts, not with his action, as the Gemara teaches that if one bows down to something but does not accept it as a god, he is not liable. By saying, "These are your gods, Yisrael," they hinted that they themselves did not accept idolatry, only the others did. This is as the *Yalkut Shimoni* writes: B'nei Yisrael were saved from that action of idolatry, as they did not say, "*Eileh eloheinu Yisrael*"; rather, it was the *eirev rav* who ascended with them from Mitzrayim. If so, the sin which B'nei Yisrael did was that they did not oppose those who thought to practice idolatry. So too, the *Shemos Rabbah* teaches: it was good that Yisrael said, "*Naaseh*," since they included responsibility for other Yidden, but it was not good that they said, "*Eileh elohecha Yisrael*," because they didn't stop others. The *Beis Halevi* says that Onkelos translates the *lashon* "עדי" as the fixing of weaponry, which hints that they were granted weaponry for accepting responsibility on another Yid. However, once they transgressed fulfilling *arvus*, they lost it.

The *Ramban* explains Onkelos differently: at *Matan Torah*, Hashem dressed B'nei Yisrael with spiritual weaponry, the *sheimos* of Hashem, for protection against the angel of death. So too, Chazal *darshen* that "*charus al haLuchos*" means "*cheirus*—freed from the angel of death." Rabbeinu Bachya says this was the *Shem Ha'meforash*. They had the *sheimos* of Hashem with them; therefore, death was not fitting to rule over them. The *pasuk* uses a *lashon* of "*horeid mei'alecha*—remove from upon you," not "*hafsheit*—take off clothes," since "*aliyah*" and "*yeridah*" reflect elevation and lowering. Similarly, the *Shemos Rabbah*[14] quotes

14   פ' מה, ב ונא, ח ומדרש תנחומא תצוה יא

from Rabbi Shimon bar Yochai: "עדי" refers to the weaponry Hashem gave B'nei Yisrael with the *Shem Ha'meforash* engraved on it. As long as they had it, the angel of death could not overcome them. The *Eitz Yosef* says that this is inferred from the following words: "ואדעה מה אעשה לך—And I will know what I will do to you," meaning which punishment to implement. As long as this special weaponry was on, they were protected from any possible danger. The *Nefesh Hachaim*[15] says that this unique weaponry was an expression of an elevated grip of the *neshamah* and the ability to tap into hidden secrets of the Torah.

The *Ramban* explains that after the sin of the golden calf, they heard that Hashem would send an angel to lead them, which was bad news, so they did not put on the special fixing of weaponry. Then Hashem said, "Remove this special weaponry," and B'nei Yisrael listened. The *Seforno* says that once Hashem gives a present to a person, He won't take it back from the one who received it without his acceptance to give it up. The *Ramban* explains that they accepted upon themselves to be deserving of punishment for the purpose of atonement for the sin of the golden calf. This was a great repenting and confessing of sin. Rabbeinu Bachya adds that the elevation and radiance that each person received, similar to *Malachei Hashareis*, were taken away from them, and they lost their elevation and protection, and Moshe merited it.

The *Nefesh HaGer* points out that both Onkelos's and *Rashi*'s explanation are brought in the Midrash.[16] Rabbi Shimon bar Yochai says that "edyo" was weaponry that Hashem gave them with the *Shem Ha'meforash* engraved upon it, as Onkelos translates. Rav Chanin[17] says it was a crown, as *Rashi* explains.

May we once again merit spiritual protection from the angel of death and the *yetzer hara*!

15    שער א, טז
16    שם
17    אור ר' יוחנן

# DID HASHEM SPEAK WITH MOSHE, OR DID MOSHE OVERHEAR HASHEM SPEAKING? WAS IT "SPEECH WITH SPEECH" OR "FACES WITH FACES"?

## וְדִבֶּר עִם מֹשֶׁה (לג, ט)

וּמִתְמַלַּל עִם מֹשֶׁה

*And He would be speaking with Moshe.*

## וְדִבֶּר ה' אֶל מֹשֶׁה פָּנִים אֶל פָּנִים (לג, יא)

וּמְמַלֵּיל יְיָ עִם מֹשֶׁה מַמְלַל עִם מַמְלָל

*And Hashem would be speaking with Moshe, speech with speech.*

The *pasuk* states that "the pillar of cloud would descend, '*v'diber im Moshe*—and He would speak with Moshe.'" Onkelos translates differently: "and He would be speaking [*u'mismallal*] with Moshe." *Rashi* says that Onkelos translates "ודבר" as "ומדבר," in present tense.[18] A bit further, it states, "ודבר ה' אל משה פנים אל פנים—And Hashem would speak with Moshe face to face." The *Hakesav V'Hakabbalah* adds, "As a friend speaks to one whom he loves, with a happy, thoughtful expression." Onkelos translates here as well, "And Hashem would be speaking [*u'mimalleil*][19] with Moshe, speech with speech," in present tense. The *Nesinah LaGer* adds that this is the verb form "אתפעל." Why does Onkelos translate "*v'diber*" as "and He would be speaking," and not literally as "and He would speak" or "and He spoke [*u'malleil*]"?

*Rashi* answers that Onkelos changes for the honor of the Shechinah, as it states, "וישמע את הקול מִדַּבֵּר אליו...וידבר אליו." It states, "מִדַּבֵּר," the 'מ with a *chirik*, which means "מִתְדַּבֵּר," as though one talks to himself and someone hears. Onkelos translates "מדבר" as "דְּמִתְמַלַּל," and "וידבר" as "וּמִתְמַלַּל—He would be speaking." Whereas when the 'מ of "מדבר" is with a *sh'va*, it means someone speaks directly to the other person. So too here, Hashem spoke, in a manner of speaking, to Himself, and Moshe

---

18  ש"ח ס

19  לרש"י צ"ל ומתמלל וע' גור אריה למהר"ל שמיישב

overheard what was being said. It does not state that the King spoke to the person, which would imply that Hashem spoke directly to Moshe.

The *Rambam*[20] writes that regarding *Matan Torah*, Onkelos differentiates between Hashem speaking to Moshe and speaking to B'nei Yisrael. It states, "וידבר אלקים את כל הדברים האלה," which he translates as, "And Hashem spoke all these things [ומליל ה' ית כל פתגמיא האלין]." However, B'nei Yisrael said to Moshe, "You speak with us and we will hear, ואל ידבר עמנו אלקים," which he translates as "and it shall not be spoken with us from *before* Hashem [ולא יתמלל עמנא מן קדם ה']." The *Rambam* explains that Hashem spoke directly to Moshe, as Onkelos translates throughout the Torah, "וידבר ה' אל משה לאמר—ומליל ה' עם משה למימר—And Hashem spoke with Moshe to say." Moshe[21] did not see like the other prophets; it was not a *mashal*; he saw completely. Whereas B'nei Yisrael only heard Hashem's "voice" and Moshe said the *dibros*, aside from the first two, *Anochi* and *Lo yihiyeh lecha*.

Onkelos translates "ודבר ה' אל משה פנים אל פנים" as "and Hashem would be speaking with Moshe, speech with speech." Similarly, in *Parashas Behaalosecha*, he translates[22] "פה אל פה אדבר בו" as "*speech with speech* I spoke with him [ממלל עם ממלל מלילנא עמיה]." Also, in *Parashas Eikev*, he translates[23] "פנים בפנים דבר ה' עמכם" as "*speech with speech* Hashem spoke with you [ממלל עם ממלל מליל ה' עמכון]." The *Hakesav V'Hakabbalah* says that Onkelos does not translate literally "mouth to mouth" to distance any physicality from Hashem, as is common for him to do. In *Parashas V'zos Haberachah*, it states,[24] "אשר ידעו ה' פנים אל פנים." *Rashi* explains that Moshe's heart was open and friendly with Hashem and he felt comfortable to speak whenever he wanted to with Hashem. This is as it states, "ועתה אעלה אל ה'—And now, I will ascend to Hashem," and "עמדו ואשמעה מה יצוה ה' לכם—Stand up and listen to what Hashem will command for you." Onkelos translates differently: "that Hashem was revealed to him

20  מו"נ ח"ב פל"ג וע' רמב"ן שמות כ, טו
21  הל' יסודי התורה ז, ו
22  במדבר יב, ח
23  דברים ה, ד
24  דברים לד, י

*faces to faces* [דִּי אִתְגְּלִי לֵיהּ ה' אַפִּין בְּאַפִּין]." Also, in *Parashas Vayishlach*, it states,[25] "כִּי רָאִיתִי אֱלֹקִים פָּנִים אֶל פָּנִים," which Onkelos translates as "since I saw the angel of Hashem, *faces with faces* [אֲרֵי חֲזֵיתִי מַלְאֲכָא דַה' אַפִּין בְּאַפִּין]." The *Nefesh HaGer* asks: Why does Onkelos sometimes translate the double *lashon* of "*panim*" and "*peh*" as "speech with speech" and other times "faces with faces"?

The *Nefesh HaGer* answers that when the *pasuk* refers to "speaking" and "hearing," as in our parashah, and by "פֶּה אֶל פֶּה אֲדַבֶּר בּוֹ" and "פָּנִים בְּפָנִים דִּבֶּר ה' עִמָּכֶם," Onkelos translates as "speech with speech," which is appropriate. However, when the *pasuk* refers to "seeing" or "being revealed," as "כִּי רָאִיתִי אֱלֹקִים פָּנִים אֶל פָּנִים" and "אֲשֶׁר יְדָעוֹ ה' פָּנִים אֶל פָּנִים," he translates as "faces to faces," which is appropriate.

The *Nefesh Hachaim*[26] writes that Moshe Rabbeinu reached a higher level of closeness to Hashem than the Avos. The *Devarim Rabbah*[27] states that Yitzchak Avinu said to Moshe Rabbeinu, "I became elevated over you since I spread out my neck to be slaughtered and I saw the Shechinah." Moshe responded, "You saw the Shechinah and your eyes dimmed; I spoke with the Shechinah face to face and my eyes didn't dim." Rav Chaim Vital says this is hinted at in the words "*Moshe Moshe*" without a *p'sik*, a *trup* that separates, unlike "*Avraham, Avraham*" which has a *p'sik*. This hints that Avraham was a bit separated from the Shechinah, whereas Moshe did not have that separation from the Shechinah. The Gemara teaches: greater is that which was said by Moshe, "*V'nachnu mah*—What are we?" than what was said by Avraham, "*V'anochi afar va'eifer*—And I am dirt and ash;" dirt can produce, and ash comes from something. Avraham described himself as dirt and ash, which is something minute, whereas Moshe described himself as having absolutely no self.

The *Nefesh Hachaim* explains that the reason Moshe was above the Avos is because he considered himself as "*v'nachnu mah*"—not deserving

---

25 בְּרֵאשִׁית לב, לא

26 שַׁעַר ג, יג

27 פ' יא, ג

at all, whereas Avraham said he was something. Since Moshe made himself so small, he merited extreme greatness. This is as it states, "לא מרבכם מכל העמים חשק ה' בכם ויבחר בכם כי אתם המעט מכל העמים—Not because you are many over all the nations did Hashem desire you and choose you, rather you are smaller [*ha'me'at*] than all the nations." The Gemara writes: Hashem said to Yisrael, "I desire you the most, because even when I make you great, you lower [*me'ma'et*] yourselves. You don't feel that you are deserving of the greatness, and you are completely aware that it is a present." *Rashi* explains, "You don't have arrogance, rather you have humility."

The Gemara[28] writes that a person who is shown gourds in a dream is a complete *yerei Shamayim*. Why is *yiras Shamayim* compared to gourds? Rav Chaim Brim quoted Rav Nissim Gaon, who explains that gourds are the biggest of all vegetables that grow from the ground. Although they are huge, they do not raise themselves above the ground; on the contrary, as they grow bigger and bigger, they lower themselves. The same is true with a *yerei Shamayim*. There is no one who is as great as him, and still, the more greatness, honor, and authority which is added to him, the more he makes himself small and adds humility to himself. The more humility one has, the bigger his receptacle is opened to be filled with more and more greatness. The *Nefesh Hachaim* explains that Moshe's humility superseded everyone else's. Moshe said, "What are we?" reflecting that he felt he was nothing. This is as the Torah states about Moshe, "עניו מאד מכל האדם—He had the greatest humility of any person in the world." Even with all the greatness that Hashem gave him, he lowered himself, feeling undeserving, and remained completely aware that everything he had was a present from Hashem.

Rav Aharon David said in the name of Rav Chaim Brim that if one doesn't make himself small, he is in great danger of losing Hashem's berachah. This is hinted at in our daily davening: "משפיל גאים ומגביה שפלים—He lowers the haughty and He lifts up those who lower themselves." One who receives greatness from Hashem and feels haughty and brags will be lowered by Hashem, while one who lowers himself and feels undeserving, will be lifted up and showered with more and more greatness.

May we humble ourselves before Hashem and become bigger receptacles for more greatness!

## HOW AND WHY IS HASHEM SLOW TO ANGER?

### אֶרֶךְ אַפַּיִם (לה, ו)

מַרְחִיק רְגַז

*Distances anger.*

The *pasuk* states, "Hashem is *erech apayim*." The Gemara[29] comments that "*apayim*" is plural, which hints to lengthening *apayim* for both *tzaddikim* and *reshaim*. *Rashi* explains that "*apayim*" hints to a happy, smiling face and to a distraught, disturbed face. Hashem is happy for the *tzaddikim* to postpone their reward *l'asid lavo*, and Hashem is upset at the *reshaim*, yet is slow to anger, and He postpones being angry in order to punish them in *Olam Haba*. *Tosafos*[30] says that this implies that Hashem gives time for the *reshaim* to exist in order to punish them in *Olam Haba*.

Another Gemara[31] writes that when Moshe ascended to the Heavens, he found Hashem sitting and writing "*erech apayim*." Moshe said, "Hashem, lengthen Your anger [be slow to anger] for the *tzaddik* alone." Hashem responded, "Also for the *reshaim*." Moshe said, "Let them be destroyed!" Hashem said, "You will see that you will need it." When B'nei Yisrael sinned by the golden calf, Hashem said, "Did you not say lengthen Your anger [be slow to anger] for the *tzaddik* alone?" Moshe responded, "Did You not tell me also for the *reshaim*?" *Rashi* explains that Moshe

29    עירובין כב.
30    ב"ק נ:
31    סנהדרין קיא.-:

was happy when he saw that there was good feeling even toward the *reshaim*. *Tosafos* points out a seeming contradiction: this implies that Hashem is slow to anger for the *reshaim* for their own good, whereas in the previous Gemara, it seems that Hashem is slow to anger to their detriment. *Tosafos* answers that it depends on whether the *reshaim* will end up repenting.[32] If they will repent, Hashem will lengthen [be slow to anger] for their good, as it will be good for them that they repented. If they do not repent, then Hashem will lengthen [be slow to anger] for bad, as He will severely punish them later on. *Tosafos*[33] also answers that it is good that Hashem extends Himself for the *reshaim* so that they will have time to repent. Similarly, *Rashi* explains in this parashah that Hashem lengthens His anger [is slow to anger] and doesn't hurry to punish so a person will have an opportunity to repent.

Onkelos translates "*erech apayim*" differently: "distances anger [*marcheik regaz*]." The *Nesinah LaGer* explains that Onkelos does not translate literally, "lengthens anger [is slow to anger]," since that would imply that Hashem has anger like a human being. Onkelos changes to distance any physicality with Hashem. What does "distances anger" mean?

Rabbeinu Bachya quotes from the *Yerushalmi* on the words "*marcheik regaz*": Rabbi Levi gives a *mashal* to a king who had two strict officers who dwelled near him in the metropolis. The king said, "If these two strict officers will dwell near me, then when someone angers me, they will be immediately judged, and the punishment will be executed, and the offender will be destroyed. Therefore, I am going to send these two officers far away. If anyone will upset me, there will be time for the person to appease me until I send for the officers to come and judge." So too, Hashem says, "*Af*, anger, and *cheimah*, wrath, are My two strict angels of destruction. If they will dwell near Me, when Yisrael will upset Me by sinning, these two angels of destruction will immediately destroy them. Therefore, I am going to send the two angels of destruction far away. This way, in case Yisrael will upset Me, there will be time for them

---

32  ב"ק שם
33  עירובין שם

to repent before *af* and *cheimah* return and execute punishment, and I will accept them."

Furthermore, in the *Selichos*[34] during *Aseres Yemei Teshuvah*, we say, "We are afraid and worried from two servants who prosecute: *af* and *cheimah*, when we check into our actions and realize that they are improper and not worthy." In *Tehillim* it states,[35] "הרף מאף ועזב חמה—Loosen from anger and leave wrath." The *Malbim* explains that *"cheimah"* is wrath which is in the heart, inside the person, and *"af"* is anger expressed on the outside. Also, on the 'ה of ב"ה we say in the *Selichos*, "זועכים אף בלחשם חמה עוצרים בשועם—They scream in their silent davening against *af*, and with their davening, they hold back *cheimah*." This *selichah* mentions that we are missing special people who had the merit to stop bad decrees and protect us. They were able to daven to prevent *af* and *cheimah* from destroying.

The *Yerushalmi* continues that this is as it states, "באים מארץ מרחק מקצה השמים ה' וכלי זעמו—Coming from a faraway land, from the end of the Heavens, Hashem, and the vessels of His anger." The *pasuk* uses the *lashon "merchak—far* away" to reflect this point; they are far away, which gives time for repentance. Rabbi Yitzchak adds that Hashem even seals the door before them, as it states, "פתח ה' את אוצרו ויוצא את כלי זעמו—Hashem opens His storehouse and takes out the weaponry of His wrath." Hashem merely opens the storehouse of weaponry, and during that time, He has mercy and seals the door. A *Beraisa* taught in the name of Rabbi Meir that Hashem is *yotzei*, He goes out of His place; He leaves the *middas ha'din* and comes to *middas ha'rachamim*.

Onkelos, who translates "distances anger," refers to sending away the two angels of destruction from within the partition of Hashem. Hashem provides us with the opportunity for repentance by giving us time to rethink our actions and change ourselves. He even locks away the *middas ha'din* and brings *middas ha'rachamim* to help us.

34   סט
35   לו, ח וע' דברים ט, יט וכט, כו

The *Tomer Devorah*[36] says that a person is supposed to be similar to his Creator by following in His ways. If not, one will falsify his being. We can deduce that just as Hashem distances anger and gives us time to repent, so too, we should give people a chance to correct themselves and change their ways.

May we merit Hashem's kindness of distancing anger and allow others the opportunity to correct themselves!

# Vayakhel

---

כֹּל נְדִיב לִבּוֹ (לה, ה)

כֹּל דְּיִתְרְעֵי לִבֵּיהּ

*Everyone whose heart favors.*

וַיָּבֹאוּ כָּל אִישׁ אֲשֶׁר נְשָׂאוֹ לִבּוֹ וְכֹל אֲשֶׁר נָדְבָה
רוּחוֹ אֹתוֹ הֵבִיאוּ אֶת תְּרוּמַת ה' (לה, כא)

וַאֲתוֹ כָּל גְּבַר דְּאִתְרְעִי לִבֵּיהּ וְכֹל דְּאַשְׁלֵימַת רוּחֵיהּ עִמֵּיהּ אַיְתִיאוּ יָת אַפְרָשׁוּתָא קֳדָם יְיָ

*And every man whose heart favored came, and all who
completed [perfected] with himself his spirit, brought
the separation [portion] before Hashem.*

רְאוּ קָרָא ה' בְּשֵׁם בְּצַלְאֵל (לה, ל)

חֲזוֹ דְּרַבִּי יְיָ בְּשׁוּם (בִּשּׁוּם) בְּצַלְאֵל

*See that Hashem made great [elevated] by name, Betzalel.*

וַיְמַלֵּא אֹתוֹ רוּחַ אֱלֹקִים בְּחָכְמָה בִּתְבוּנָה
וּבְדַעַת וּבְכָל מְלָאכָה (לה, לא)

וְאַשְׁלֵים עִמֵּיהּ רוּחַ נְבוּאָה (קֻדְשָׁא) מִן קֳדָם יְיָ בְּחָכְמָא בְּסֻכְלְתָנוּ וּבְמַדַּע וּבְכָל עֲבִידָא

*And He completed [perfected] him with a spirit of prophecy
(ruach hakodesh) from before [because of] Hashem, with wisdom,
with understanding, and with knowledge, and in every work.*

## מְלֵא אֹתָם חָכְמַת לֵב (לה, לה)

### אַשְׁלֵים עִמְּהוֹן חַכִּימוּת לִבָּא

*He completed [perfected] them with wisdom of the heart.*

The *pasuk* states, "Moshe said to B'nei Yisrael, 'ראו קרא ה' בשם בצלאל,'" which Onkelos translates as "see that Hashem made great [elevated] [*d'rabi*] by name, Betzalel." The following *pasuk* states, "וימלא אתו רוח אלקים בחכמה בתבונה ובדעת ובכל מלאכה," which Onkelos translates as, "And He completed [perfected] [*v'ashleim*] him with a spirit of prophecy from before [because of] Hashem, with wisdom, with understanding, and with knowledge, and in every work." Similarly, in *Parashas Ki Sisa*, Hashem said to Moshe,[1] "ראה קראתי בשם בצלאל," which Onkelos translates as "see that I made great [elevated] [*d'rabisi*] by name, Betzalel." And the following *pasuk* states, "ואמלא אתו רוח אלקים בחכמה ובתבונה ובדעת ובכל מלאכה," which Onkelos translates as, "And I completed [perfected] [*v'ashleimis*] him with a spirit of prophecy[2] from before [because of] Hashem with wisdom, and with understanding, and with knowledge, and in every work." So too, in this parashah it states "מלא אותם חכמת לב," which Onkelos translates as "He completed [perfected] [*ashleim*] them with wisdom of the heart." What does it mean that Hashem "made great" and "completed"?

The *Nesinah LaGer* explains that "making great" reflects anointing and greatness.[3] Hashem made Betzalel great by completing him with the wisdom, understanding, and knowledge needed to build the *Mishkan*. The *Nefesh HaGer* adds that Hashem also prepared Betzalel at that time with prophecy or *ruach hakodesh* to have in mind holy thoughts of putting together *sheimos* of Hashem. The *Nesinah LaGer* says that this is as the Gemara teaches: "בצלאל" is comprised of "בצל—in the shade," and "א-ל—*Keil*." Betzalel knew to put together the letters from which the heaven and earth were made, which the *Mishkan* parallels. He was

---

1   לא, ב

2   יש שלא גורסים נבואה

3   ע' רש"י ל, כט

unique and was able to figure out how to build all the vessels of the *Mishkan* and have proper intentions and thoughts while making them. Hashem completed Betzalel with great *ruchniyus* abilities as well.

The *Nefesh HaGer* explains that Onkelos often translates "מלא" as "שלם—complete," which reflects complete attributes of perfection and excellence. The *lashon* "וימלא," "ואמלא," and "מלא" hint to all the people who did the work of building the *Mishkan* and its vessels; they were fully equipped to do their work.

The *Shemos Rabbah*[4] comments that it does not state, "*Karasi b'shem Betzalel*—I called by name, Betzalel," but "*re'eh karasi*—see that I called." When Moshe ascended to the Heavens, Hashem showed him all the vessels of the *Mishkan* and said, "This is how you shall make the *Mishkan* and all its vessels." When it was time for Moshe to descend, he thought he would be the one to build everything. Hashem called to him and said, "Moshe, I made you king, and it is not fitting for a king to do this. Rather, you decree, and others will do it." The *Nefesh HaGer* explains that Moshe thought that he was complete and he would be the one to build the *Mishkan* and its vessels. Hashem said, "You are incomplete alone; rather, decree for others to come build it. Betzalel will complete it with you. Don't think that he is a simpleton and he will simply follow your commands. Rather, I have completed him with wisdom, understanding, and knowledge with the ability to build, and I have granted him prophecy to have in mind holy thoughts of putting together *sheimos* of Hashem." Moshe, Betzalel, Oholiav, and all the wise-hearted people complemented and completed each other to build the *Mishkan* and its vessels. The *Nefesh HaGer* says that Onkelos, who translates with the *lashon "ashleim,"* expresses this idea as well; they were complete [*shleimim*] and they *complemented* each other's positions and responsibilities, as the related word, *"hashlamah."*

It states, "ויבאו כל איש אשר נשאו לבו וכל אשר נדבה רוחו הביאו אתו את תרומת ה׳." Who are the people about whom it says *"nesa'o libo"* and *"nadvah rucho,"* and what did they do? Onkelos translates *"nesa'o libo"* as "whose heart

---

favored [*d'isr'i libei*]," meaning he had interest and desire. The *Nefesh HaGer* says that he translates "*nesa'o libo*" with the same *lashon* as he translates "*nediv libo*—whose heart favors [*d'isr'i libei*]" which *Rashi* explains to mean "one whose heart pledges to contribute." The people who were "*nesa'o libo*" are those who pledged and brought their contributions for the *Mishkan*.

Onkelos translates "*nadvah rucho*" as "who completed [perfected] with himself his spirit [*d'ashleimas ruchei*]," which are those who helped build the *Mishkan*. The *Nefesh HaGer* says the words "*nadvah rucho*—who completed [perfected] with himself his spirit" continue with the words "*heivi'u…*—they brought contributions for the work of the *Mishkan*." This teaches that those who labored with building the *Mishkan* also contributed for its building.

The *Ramban*[5] explains "*nesa'o libo*" and "*nadvah rucho*" differently: "*nadvah rucho*" refers to those who donated contributions for the *Mishkan*. "*Nesa'o libo*" refers to people who stepped forward to do the labor for building the *Mishkan*. In Mitzrayim, B'nei Yisrael did backbreaking labor with lime and stones. They did not study or practice to work with gold, silver, precious stones, or woodwork. It was a wondrous thing that there were people who were able to work with all types of stone, wood, and metal, do embroidery and weave, and could envision in their minds what to do. Even people who study from a wise and talented person won't become experts in all the different fields of work. Also, people who dealt with mud and cement are not normally able to do fine, meticulous work. Although they did not learn any of these crafts from anyone, they naturally found in themselves the knowledge and ability to do it. They raised up their hearts in the ways of Hashem to come forward to Moshe, saying, "I will do all that my master commands." This wondrous thing is hinted at in the *lashon* "*re'u*": Moshe told Yisrael, "*re'u*—see" and pay attention to this wondrous thing and know that Hashem did this in order to build the *Mishkan*. Rav Chaim Shmuelevitz[6] adds that the same

---

5   לה, כא; לא, ב

6   מאמר כח וסד

is true for any person who desires and commits to do something in *avodas Hashem* and trusts in Hashem; Hashem will help him accomplish that goal. Rav Chaim[7] adds that this concept is certainly true regarding *ruchniyus*. If one decides to achieve higher levels, Hashem will help him be successful.

May we raise up our hearts to strive for new levels, and may Hashem help us succeed in reaching them!

## WHAT WAS THE WISDOM OF THE SMART WOMEN?

וְכָל הַנָּשִׁים אֲשֶׁר נָשָׂא לִבָּן אֹתָנָה בְּחָכְמָה טָווּ אֶת הָעִזִּים (לה, כו)

וְכָל נְשַׁיָּא דְּאִתְרְעִי לִבְּהוֹן עִמְּהוֹן בְּחָכְמָא עֲזָלָן יָת מַעֲזַיָּא

*And all the women whose heart favored with themselves*
*with wisdom [wise-hearted] spun the hair of the goats.*

The *pesukim* state that a few coverings were made to place over the *Mishkan*. One was called "*yerios haMishkan*," which were sheets covering the *Mishkan* and were visible inside. They were made from wool dyed three different colors as well as with linen. Another covering was called "*yerios izim*," which were sheetlike drapes sewn from goat hair that were placed over the bottom sheets. *Rashi*[8] says that the top covering was called "*ohel*—a roof-covering," whereas the bottom covering was called the *Mishkan* itself, as they were made for beauty with their nice colors: greenish-blue, crimson, and a bright reddish color.

The Gemara[9] writes that the wisdom needed to create the top sheets was greater than that of the bottom sheets. The Torah states regarding the bottom sheets, "וכל אשה חכמת לב בידיה טוו"—And every woman who was smart sewed with her hands." Regarding the top sheets, it states, "וכל הנשים אשר נשא לבן אתנה בחכמה טוו את העזים"—And all women that raised

---

7   מאמר סז
8   שבת צח:
9   שם צט.

up their hearts with wisdom sewed the goats." It states by the sheets of goat hair "*nasa liban*," which implies greater wisdom than the bottom sheets.[10] What is this greater wisdom? The Gemara explains that they washed and spun the hair of the goats while it was still attached to the goats. This was unusual and needed an especially advanced wisdom.

Onkelos translates the *lashon* "*izim*" by the contributions and building of the *Mishkan* differently from the rest of the Torah. He generally translates "*izim*" as "*izin*—goats" or "*izaya*—the goats," or "*b'nei i'zaya*," when referring to the species of goats,[11] whereas here, he translates "*ma'zay*" or "*ma'azya*." *Rashi*[12] explains that this means "the hair from the goats"; they did not bring actual goats for contributions, rather goat hair. The *Nesinah LaGer* adds that the מ' of Onkelos's translation of "*ma'azya*—from the goats" is a source for the Gemara's statement: they spun the hair while it was still attached to the goats.

Why did these women specifically sew the hair from upon the goats? The *Seforno* explains that when something is detached from its source, it weakens and diminishes. The wise women wanted to spin the hair right off the back of the goats while still fresh and completely intact in order for it to have the brightest shine. *Avi Mori* explained differently in the name of the *Maharsha*:[13] When something is detached from the ground or from a live animal, it is able to become *tamei*, whereas when something is attached, it cannot become *tamei*. The wise women spun the goat hair from upon the animals to make the threads in a completely *tahor* way. The bottom cover, though, was made with detached material that could have become *tamei*. The *Meshech Chochmah* points out that one *pasuk* states, "וכל אשה...בידיה טוו—And every woman...sewed with her hands"; "*ishah*—woman" is singular. The following *pasuk* states, "וכל הנשים...טוו את העזים—And all women...sewed from upon the goats"; "*ha'nashim*—women" is plural. This reflects that all types of the extra-smart women, even those who were *tamei*, were able to spin the goat

10   רש"י שם

11   רמב"ן ויקרא ג, יב

12   כה, ד

13   שבת צח:

hair since it was still attached to the animal and not able to become *tamei*, unlike the bottom cover which could only have been made by *tahor* women.

The Torah uses the *lashon* "*nesius lev*" by the making of the *Mishkan*, as it states, "*Nasa liban*." Onkelos translates "*nasa*" as "*ratzon*," meaning desire and interest. Whoever desired to offer contributions and help build the *Mishkan* came close to dedicate his special talents: the men with their talents of building, and the woman with their talents of sewing.

After we had our first girl, my Rosh Yeshiva gave me a berachah which Rav Chaim Brim gave him as well: "You should be *zocheh* to bring her up *tzu kachin un tzu baken*—to cook and bake." The Gemara[14] writes a similar idea: A wise woman asked Rabbi Eliezer, "Why were there different punishments by the golden calf, if seemingly all their actions were identical?" He answered, "Wisdom for a woman is with her needlepoint, her sewing. And so it states, ‏'וכל אשה חכמת לב בידיה טוו‎'!"

May we learn from the builders of the *Mishkan* to direct our personal talents for *avodas Hashem*!

## WHICH WOMEN CONTRIBUTED TO MAKING THE KIYOR, AND WHAT CONTRIBUTIONS DID THEY GIVE? TO WHAT DOES THE LASHON "TZAVA" HINT?

בְּמַרְאֹת הַצֹּבְאֹת אֲשֶׁר צָבְאוּ פֶּתַח אֹהֶל מוֹעֵד (לח, ח)

בְּמֶחְזְיָת נְשַׁיָּא דְּאָתְיָן לְצַלָּאָה בִּתְרַע מַשְׁכַּן זִמְנָא

*With the mirrors of women who would come to daven at the entrance of the Tent of Meeting (Transitory Tent).*

It states that the *Kiyor*—water basin—and its base were built "*b'mar'os ha'tzov'os*." What does this mean and to what does it refer?

*Rashi* quotes from Rabbi Tanchuma: in Mitzrayim, the Jewish women had mirrors which they used to decorate themselves for their husbands. The women contributed them for the *Mishkan* and did not keep them for themselves. Moshe was repulsed by them because they are made for the *yetzer hara*. The *Ramban* adds that Moshe was not disgusted with other contributions which were even more inappropriate, because those contributions were either brought with other contributions or the intended vessel would be made together with other metals and materials. The *Kiyor*, however, was to be made solely from these mirrors. Hashem said to Moshe, "Accept them, because these are more cherished than everything, since with them, they stood up myriads of children in Mitzrayim." When the men would return from labor, weary and weak, their wives would prepare food and drink to revive them. They would take a mirror, look at themselves together with their husbands, and say, "I am prettier than you," and help bring out children. The *Kiyor* was made from the mirrors of all the women who helped strengthen their husbands in Mitzrayim. The *Sifsei Chachamim*[15] adds that "הצובאת" is from the same root as "צבאות—myriads," referencing the mirrors that facilitated myriads in Mitzrayim. The *Kiyor* was made to take water for the *sotah* to drink in order to make peace between a man and his wife, just as the mirrors brought together couples in Mitzrayim. *Rashi* explains that the following words, "*asher tzav'u*," mean "that gathered together to bring their contributions."

Onkelos translates the words "במראות הצבאת אשר צבאו פתח אהל מועד" differently: "with the mirrors of women who would come to daven at the entrance of the Tent of Meeting." The *Ramban* explains in the name of the *Ibn Ezra* that this refers to women who served Hashem exceptionally. They contributed their mirrors for the *Mishkan* to remove themselves from all desires of this world in order to serve Hashem. They would come to daven by the *Mishkan* daily and listen to the mitzvos being taught. The *Shaarei Aharon* adds that because these mirrors were sanctified through breaking their desires, therefore Hashem said to use them for the *Kiyor*, with which the Kohanim were going to wash to sanctify themselves. Or, because these mirrors were brought with zealousness and pure-hearted dedication to the service of Hashem, therefore Hashem said to use them for the *Kiyor*, with which the Kohanim will wash to become pure to serve Hashem. The *Nefesh HaGer* says that although *Rashi* writes that Onkelos also translates "*b'mar'os ha'tzov'os*" as "mirrors of women," *Rashi* does not bring the *d'rash* at the end of Onkelos. Onkelos understands that the *Kiyor* was made from the mirrors of those women who gathered to grow in *ruchniyus*.

It seems from the *pasuk* that these women brought their mirrors to the *Ohel Moed*. The *Ramban* asks: The *Mishkan* was not yet built, so to where did these women bring their mirrors? The *Ramban* answers that they brought their mirrors to the *Ohel Moed* of Moshe, as it states in *Parashas Ki Sisa*,[16] "ומשה יקח את האהל...וקרא לו אהל מועד—And Moshe would take the tent...and he called it '*Ohel Moed*.'" The *Shaarei Aharon* asks: Onkelos generally translates the words "*Ohel Moed*" when referring to the *Mishkan* as "*Mashkan Zimna*—the Tent of Meeting or Transitory Tent." However, he translates Moshe's *ohel moed* as "*mashkan beis ulfana*—the tent of a place of learning," which was where Moshe taught B'nei Yisrael Hashem's teaching. Here, though, Onkelos translates as he does for the *Mishkan*, which seemingly didn't exist at that point, as the *Ramban* asked!

The *Nesinah LaGer* explains that Onkelos translates "*ha'tzov'os*" as "of women," which is not the literal translation, but rather, a description for the women. The *Nefesh HaGer* says that Onkelos translates "*asher tzav'u*" as "who would come to daven." Based on this, the *Me'at Tzari* answers that Onkelos does not translate "*asher tzav'u*" as "who came," in past tense, since there was no *Ohel Moed* yet. Rather, he translates as "who would come," in present tense, hinting to the women who would gather to come daven. The *lashon* "צבאו" is from "צבא—myriads," which refers to these many women who gathered to come daven.

---

The *Shaarei Aharon* answers differently: for this reason, Onkelos does not translate "*asher tzav'u*" at all, since there was no *Ohel Moed* yet. First these women gave their contributions, and after the *Mishkan* was built, they came to daven and listen to the mitzvos. "*B'mar'os ha'tzov'os*" means "with the mirrors of women who would come to daven"—after the *Ohel Moed* was set up. The *Me'at Tzari* adds that "*ha'tzov'os*" is translated as "who would come," and the translation "of women" is added.

The Gemara[17] teaches that in the merit of *nashim tzidkaniyos*, we experienced miracles to be taken out of Mitzrayim. May Hashem help that in the merit of the *nashim tzidkaniyos* of our generation, we should be taken out of *galus* and bring Mashiach *bi'meheirah bi'yameinu*, Amen!

# Pekudei

## WERE THE BELLS "BETWEEN THE POMEGRANATES" OR "INSIDE THEM," AND WHAT WAS THEIR FUNCTION?

וַיִּתְּנוּ אֶת הַפַּעֲמֹנִים בְּתוֹךְ הָרִמֹּנִים עַל שׁוּלֵי
הַמְּעִיל סָבִיב בְּתוֹךְ הָרִמֹּנִים (לט, כה)

וִיהַבוּ יָת זַגַּיָא בְּגוֹ רִמּוֹנַיָּא עַל שִׁפּוֹלֵי מְעִילָא סְחוֹר סְחוֹר בְּגוֹ רִמּוֹנַיָּא

*And they put the bells inside the pomegranates on the bottom
of the Me'il, all around, within the pomegranates.*

In *Parashas Tetzaveh*, it states,[1] "עַל שׁוּלָיו רִמֹּנֵי...עַל שׁוּלָיו סָבִיב וּפַעֲמֹנֵי זָהָב
בְּתוֹכָם סָבִיב—And you shall make on its bottom, pomegranates...on its
bottom around, and gold bells *b'socham* around." What does the Torah
mean, to make gold bells *b'socham*?

Onkelos translates *"b'socham"* as "between them [*beineihon*]." The
*Nesinah LaGer* says that this is like *Rashi* and the *Rambam*[2] explain that
the bells were placed between the pomegranates around the *Me'il*. The
pomegranates were round and hollow in the shape of pomegranates.
On the bottom of the *Me'il* one bell was hung between every two
pomegranates.

The *Ramban*[3] is bothered by the following: According to *Rashi*, the
pomegranates and bells were between each other; the pomegranates
served no purpose. If they were for beauty and niceness, why were they
made in the shape of hollow pomegranates? They should have made

---

כח, לג    1
הל' כלי המקדש ט, ד בכ"מ    2
כח, לא    3

them as golden apples. Also, the Torah should have mentioned with what to hang the bells, and if there was a need to make rings to hang them. Therefore, the *Ramban* explains differently: the bells were actually placed inside the pomegranates, before they were put on the *Me'il*. They were in the shape of small, hollowed-out closed pomegranates, and the bells were placed inside of them.

In our parashah, it states, "ויתנו את הפעמנים בתוך הרמנים על שולי המעיל סביב בתוך הרמנים," which Onkelos translates as, "And they put the bells inside the pomegranates on the bottom of the *Me'il*, all around, within the pomegranates." He translates *"b'soch"* as "inside [*b'go*]." The *Nesinah LaGer* says that this seems to be in accordance with the *Ramban*, that the bells were placed inside the pomegranates. However, in *Parashas Tetzaveh*, he translated *"b'socham"* as "between them [*beineihon*]," which seems to be in accordance with *Rashi* and the *Rambam*. The *Nesinah LaGer* wonders, Which one was it—inside or among?

The *Nesinah LaGer* answers that *"b'go"* can mean "being inside" something else, but it can also mean "being within" other things or beings. This is as Onkelos translates *"b'soch ha'ba'im"* as "within [*b'go*] those entering." The brothers entered Mitzrayim among other people, not inside anyone. Also, he translates *"b'soch matosam"* as "within [*b'go*] their staffs." Aharon's staff was among the other staffs, not inside them. The *Hakesav V'Hakabbalah* gives an example: Onkelos translates "ויצא בן אשה ישראלית...בתוך בני ישראל" as "and the son of a Jewish woman...went out within [*b'go*] B'nei Yisrael." The man went out from within the B'nei Yisrael, not inside them. We see that *"b'go"* can mean literally inside something, or within other things or beings. The *Me'at Tzari* explains that the root "גו" means when something goes into something else, as it states, "וכל אשר יפול אל תוכו," which Onkelos translates as "לגויה—inside." "גו" is also used when something is among other things. The *Nesinah LaGer* says that in *Parashas Tetzaveh*, Onkelos translates *"b'socham"* as *"beineihon,"* not *"b'go,"* because *"b'socham"* comes with a *kinuy*.

It states, "והיה על אהרן לשרת ונשמע קולו בבאו אל הקדש לפני ה' ובצאתו ולא ימות—And it [the *Me'il*] shall be on Aharon to serve, and its noise shall be heard when he enters the *Kodesh* before Hashem and when he exits, and he won't die." What noise shall be heard, and what was the purpose of this noise? Also, why is this necessary when he enters and when he leaves? What message can we take from the *Me'il*?

The *Hakesav V'Hakabbalah* explains that the purpose of the bells was so that they should make noise when moved to remind the Kohen Gadol about his *avodah*, similar to the mitzvah of tzitzis. By hearing its noise, he is supposed to remember his uniqueness that he is holy and has many more mitzvos than other Kohanim and Yisraelim. When he enters and leaves, throughout his entire *avodah* and wherever he goes, he is meant to remember that he is serving before Hashem. He shouldn't take his mind off of his elevated *kedushah* for even a moment. Similarly, we can learn from the *Me'il* to remember that we, too, as servants of Hashem, should keep in mind our responsibility to accomplish our mission throughout the day.

The *Ramban* and Rabbeinu Bachya explain differently: the sound of the bells is because it is proper conduct to knock before entering before the King, and not to come in suddenly, as it states by King Achashveirosh: one who enters without permission will be killed. The bells functioned as knocking before entering the *Mishkan*, as though asking permission to enter. Also, the noise was in order to let it be known that the Kohen Gadol wants to enter. Although Hashem knows everything, and also the angels before Him know such things, it was a warning for the angels to leave and clear away "space" for the beloved one of the King to enter and serve Hashem. So too, when the Kohen Gadol left, although it was not part of the *avodah* such that he would be liable at that point for any missing garments of *kehunah*, he needed to wear the *Me'il* in order to make noise, as though notifying the angels that he was finished with his service and they were now able to return to serve before Him.

The Gemara[4] teaches that Rabbi Akiva commanded his sons, "Do not suddenly enter your house." The *Vayikra Rabbah*[5] explains that the reason is because it might scare or shock someone. The *Rashbam* quotes

---

4   פסחים קיב.

5   פ' כא, ח

from the *Vayikra Rabbah* that a person should make noise before entering his house, as maybe someone inside is doing something private. When Rabbi Yochanan would enter his house, he would make noise, which he learned from the *pasuk* about the Kohen Gadol that states, "ונשמע קולו בבאו אל הקדש." Rav Chaim Shmuelevitz[6] adds that if the Kohen Gadol does not wear the *Me'il*, he is lacking *derech eretz* and he will be punished severely with death from *Shamayim*. So too, we should take this lesson to be careful to have *derech eretz* with other people.

May we learn from the *Me'il* to remember our *avodah* and have proper *derech eretz* with others!

## WHAT FIRE AND CLOUD WERE ABOVE THE MISHKAN?

### כִּי עֲנַן ה' עַל הַמִּשְׁכָּן יוֹמָם וְאֵשׁ תִּהְיֶה לַיְלָה בּוֹ (מ, לח)

אֲרֵי עֲנַן יְקָרָא דַיְיָ עַל מַשְׁכְּנָא בִּימָמָא וְחֵיזוּ אִישָׁתָא הֲוֵי בְּלֵילְיָא בֵּיהּ

*Since the cloud of the honor of Hashem was on the Mishkan during the day, and an appearance of fire would be on it during the night.*

The *pasuk* states, "ובהעלות הענן מעל המשכן יסעו בני ישראל"—When the cloud would ascend from upon the *Mishkan*, B'nei Yisrael would travel." The following *pesukim* state, "And if the cloud did not leave, they would not travel until it departed, because "ענן ה' על המשכן יומם, Hashem's cloud was over the *Mishkan* during the day." Onkelos translates ענן ה' על המשכן יומם as, "The cloud of the honor of Hashem was on the *Mishkan* during the day." The *Nesinah LaGer* says that Onkelos adds "the honor" of Hashem, for the honor of the Shechinah.

The *pasuk* ends, "ואש תהיה לילה בו לעיני כל בית ישראל בכל מסעיהם." *Targum Yonasan* translates as, "And a pillar of fire would shine during the night, and all of B'nei Yisrael were able to see for all their travels." He understands that the *eish* mentioned in this *pasuk* is the pillar of fire. This as it states in *Parashas Beshalach*:[7] "וה׳ הולך לפניהם יומם בעמוד ענן לנחותם הדרך וְלַיְלָה בעמוד אש להאיר להם ללכת יומם ולילה—And Hashem would lead before them during the day in a pillar of cloud to lead them on the road, and during the night in a pillar of fire to shine for them, to go during the day and during the night." There were two pillars: the pillar of cloud and the pillar of fire. Here too, "*v'eish*—and fire" refers to the pillar of fire that shone for them during the night.

Onkelos translates "ואש תהיה לילה בו" differently: "and an appearance of fire would be on it during the night." The *Nesinah LaGer* says that Onkelos adds "an appearance" for the honor of the Shechinah, as he added in his translation "honor" at the beginning of the *pasuk*. This was not the regular pillar of fire which we had at Yam Suf. Onkelos translates as it states in *Parashas Behaalosecha*, "*U'mar'ei eish laylah*—and an appearance of fire during the night." To what does "an appearance of fire" refer?

The *Malbim*[8] explains that when B'nei Yisrael went out of Mitzrayim, there were two separate, independent clouds, the pillar of cloud and the pillar of fire. The pillar of cloud served during the day and the pillar of fire served at night. Also, both these pillars only went before them when they traveled, not when they camped. However, by the *Mishkan*, there was a different arrangement: one pillar of cloud was over the *Mishkan* and served during the day and also at night. During the day, the *Mishkan* was covered with a pillar of cloud, and at night the cloud transformed into having an appearance of fire within it. This pillar of cloud constantly stayed over the *Mishkan*. The *Nefesh HaGer* says that Onkelos, who translates "and an appearance of fire would be on it during the night," understands that it wasn't another pillar of fire, but an appearance of fire which was within the pillar of cloud.

The *Nefesh HaGer* explains Onkelos with the *Chizkuni*. There was a special cloud over the *Mishkan* which was elevated more than the other

---

7    יג, כא

8    במדבר ט, טו-טז

clouds. This is as the *Midrash Tanchuma* teaches:[9] during the traveling, the cloud of the Shechinah that was over the *Mishkan* would leave and go over the camp of the Leviim, in the middle of the other camps. A different cloud, called the "pillar of cloud," was like a beam, and it would travel before the camps to direct them where to go and when to stop. The special cloud stayed in the center area throughout their travels.

The *Nefesh HaGer* says that aside for the appearance of fire, there was also a pillar of fire during the forty years in the Midbar. This is as it states in *Parashas Shelach*:[10] "וענך עומד עלהם ובעמוד ענן אתה הולך לפניהם יומם ובעמוד אש לילה—And Your cloud stood over them, and in a pillar of cloud You would lead before them during the day and in a pillar of fire at night." The *Shemos Rabbah*[11] teaches in the name of Rabbeinu Hagadol that since Hashem wanted to place the fear of Yisrael upon the seven nations, He held back B'nei Yisrael in the Midbar for forty years and provided light for them with a pillar of cloud during the day and a pillar of fire at night. When the nations heard about this, awe and trepidation fell upon them.

May Hashem return His Shechinah *bi'meheirah bi'yameinu, Amen!*

---

9   במדבר יב

10   במדבר יה, יד

11   פ' כ, טז